D1356628

RUSSIA'S ENTANGLED EMBRACE

RUSSIA'S ENTANGLED EMBRACE

THE TSARIST EMPIRE AND THE ARMENIANS, 1801–1914

STEPHEN BADALYAN RIEGG

CORNELL UNIVERSITY PRESS

Ithaca and London

First published 2020 by Cornell University Press

Library of Congress Cataloging-in-Publication Data

Names: Riegg, Stephen Badalyan, 1986– author.
Title: Russia's entangled embrace : the tsarist empire and the Armenians, 1801–1914 / Stephen Badalyan Riegg.
Description: Ithaca [New York] : Cornell University Press, 2020. | Includes bibliographical references and index.
Identifiers: LCCN 2019038970 (print) | LCCN 2019038971 (ebook) | ISBN 9781501750113 (hardcover) | ISBN 9781501750137 (pdf) | ISBN 9781501750120 (ebook)
Subjects: LCSH: Armenians—Russia. | Russia—Relations—Armenia. | Armenia—Relations—Russia. | Russia—History—1801–1917. | Armenia—History—1801–1900. | Russia—Politics and government—1801–1917. | Russia—Territorial expansion.
Classification: LCC DK34.A75 R54 2020 (print) | LCC DK34.A75 (ebook) | DDC 947/.00491992009/034—dc23
LC record available at https://lccn.loc.gov/2019038970
LC ebook record available at https://lccn.loc.gov/2019038971

This publication was made possible by a generous grant from the
Dolores Zohrab Liebmann Fund

To my parents, my first professors

Contents

ILLUSTRATIONS

Maps

Figures

ACKNOWLEDGMENTS

Good luck has played a crucial role in whatever professional success I have enjoyed. A big part of that fortune has been the number of wonderful people and institutions that supported this project. I had the privilege of studying history at the University of North Carolina at Chapel Hill (UNC), where Louise McReynolds and Donald J. Raleigh trained me. Truly caring mentors, Louise and Don invested much time in my intellectual growth, but most important, they have taught me how good scholars can also be good people. Louise's lasting dedication to my work and special talent for finding solutions to problems, big and small, are a key reason for this book's existence. Years ago, I took a moment from cheering on the University of Kansas (KU) Jayhawks inside Allen Fieldhouse to read Don's e-mailed prediction that I would have no regrets about attending graduate school at Carolina. As is usual, he was right.

Before I arrived at UNC, Eve Levin and Gerald Mikkelson at KU stoked my interest in Russian history. In Chapel Hill, my experience would have been poorer were it not for the camaraderie of my graduate comrades, especially Emily Baran, Amanda Bellows, Liz Ellis, Peter Gengler, Dan Giblin, Gary Guadagnolo, Aaron Hale-Dorrell, Dakota Irvin, Max Lazar, Mike Paulauskas, Andrew Ringlee, Alex Ruble, Michael Skalski, and Lars Stiglich. Trevor Erlacher was, and is, the type of close friend with whom one can go into battle and into a bar with equal pleasure. In Moscow, I am grateful to the Evoyan and Sahakyan families for their hospitality.

During the writing process, I benefited from the generosity of several colleagues and friends who endured various drafts. Paul Werth took interest in this project from its inception, provided me with archival tips, invited me to workshops, and wrote incisive feedback on the full book manuscript. Ronald Suny graciously shared his encyclopedic knowledge of the Caucasus with me when he commented on the complete text. Erik Scott carefully read an early version of the full draft. Several scholars read individual chapters, improving key parts of the manuscript and saving me from embarrassing mistakes: Houri

Berberian, Trevor Erlacher, Jo Laycock, Eve Levin, Ivan Sablin, and Jeff Sahadeo. Of course, I alone am responsible for the final product, but to all of them I am very grateful. I thank also the following people for helping me in various ways along the way: Cemil Aydin, Chad Bryant, Chester Dunning, Ilya Gerasimov, Sam Hirst, Zach Hoffman, Kathleen Kearns, Eric Lohr, Anatoly Pinsky, and Alexander Semyonov.

I will always remain indebted to Texas A&M University's Department of History for taking a chance on me. Led by David Vaught and Carlos Blanton, my colleagues—too many to list here—have encouraged and supported me. Aggieland would be less enjoyable were it not for outings with Olga Dror, Felipe Hinojosa, Trent MacNamara, Brian Rouleau, Dan Schwartz, Kate Unterman, and others. Jason Parker's band, Ride the Panda, has brought out the best in all of us and the worst singers in some of us. Generous start-up funding from the Department of History and the College of Liberal Arts sponsored supplemental archival fieldwork and other book-related work. My enthusiastic students are a daily reminder of our work's importance.

Several institutions made this project possible. The American Councils Title VIII Research Scholar Program and a Fulbright-Hays fellowship allowed me to mine the archives of St. Petersburg, Moscow, and Yerevan. A short-term grant from the Kennan Institute of the Woodrow Wilson International Center for Scholars sponsored my preliminary work at the Library of Congress. The timely, expert assistance of the staffs at Russian and Armenian archives and libraries was indispensable. I am particularly grateful to Irina Nikolaevna Volnukhina and the rest of the employees of the Russian State Historical Archive (RGIA) for their help over the years.

It has been a pleasure to work with the team at Cornell University Press. Roger Haydon's support and cogent advice were instrumental in completing the project. The expertise of Karen Laun, Erin Davis, Jane Lichty, Sarah Noell, and other publishing professionals made this a smooth experience. Armine Harutyunyan made the beautiful maps with much care and patience.

Portions of this book first appeared in print elsewhere, and I am thankful to Wiley and *Ab Imperio* for permission to publish this material here in revised form: "Imperial Challengers: Tsarist Responses to Armenian Raids into Anatolia, 1875–90," *Russian Review* 76, no. 2 (2017): 253–71, and "Neotraditionalist Rule to the Rescue of the Empire? Viceroy I. Vorontsov-Dashkov amid Crises in the Caucasus, 1905–1915," *Ab Imperio*, no. 3 (2018): 115–39.

My family made the greatest contribution to the gestation of this book. Sarah McNamara's love and companionship are a source of strength for me. She has trudged through more of my writing than anyone, braved northern

Russia's climate and the backroads of the Caucasus, and stood by me at every step. My sister, Diana Nicole Riegg, is simply wonderful. My parents—Natalya Tovmasyan Riegg, Ruben Badalyan, and Nicholas Riegg—have taught me more than has anyone else. They modeled for me the trait of diligence, inculcated in me a passion for learning, and loved me unconditionally. I dedicate this book to them.

A Note to the Reader

To avoid confusion, I use the modern "Yerevan" for the capital of Eastern Armenia, rather than the "Erivan'" of pre-1936 Russian sources. I opt for the neutral "South Caucasus" rather than the Russian-inspired "Transcaucasus" (Zakavkaz'e). Russian sources referred to the leader of the Armenian Church at Ejmiatsin as both patriarch and catholicos, but I use only catholicos for him and patriarch for the leaders of the other Armenian religious centers, such as the patriarchates of Constantinople and Jerusalem. For much of the nineteenth century, Russians, Armenians, and Europeans called Azeris "Tatars." This confusing nomenclature conflated the native Muslims of the South Caucasus with the Tatars of the Kazan, Volga, and Crimea regions, who shared little more than religion and Turkic dialects. I use "Azeri" for the residents of the South Caucasus and "Tatar" for the groups outside of the Caucasus that today continue to self-identify as Tatar. All dates follow the Julian calendar that imperial Russia used. In the nineteenth century, the Julian calendar was twelve days behind the Gregorian calendar used in the West; in the twentieth century, it lagged by thirteen days. Russian and Armenian words are transliterated per the modified Library of Congress system. Unless otherwise noted, all translations are my own.

Introduction

In 1841, an Armenian pupil at the prestigious Lazarev Institute of Oriental Languages in Moscow smothered his hated Latin teacher's chair with enough glue that the instructor, after sitting down, required a rescue from his colleagues. The institute's administration not only expelled the troublemaker but also tried to banish him to his parents in the Caucasus. The future looked bleak for young Mikhail, and probably few could have imagined then that within four decades, the mischievous Armenian teenager would become the second-most powerful man in the Russian Empire: interior minister and chief of the gendarmes Count Mikhail Loris-Melikov.

The Armenian prankster's career was a unique case, but the success afforded by the cooperation of the Russian government and the Armenian social elite was not. The history of the Lazarev Institute is one element in a narrative that helps us understand how the Romanovs relied on non-Russians to rule over the world's largest state, as well as millions of non-Russian, non-Slavic groups. Conceived by the aristocratic family of Russified Armenians, the Lazarevs, and encouraged by the imperial government, the Lazarev Institute for ambitious Russian and non-Russian youths opened in 1815 and for generations stood as an intermediary between the autocracy and its minority subjects. The academy not only brought Russians and Armenians closer but also served as an extension of the government's integration efforts that focused on the political, social, and cultural incorporation of non-Russians. With the authorities' full blessing, the academy sought to turn natives of the Caucasus into well-rooted residents of the empire,[1] allowing the students to maintain their cultural identities while giving them the tools for social mobility in their adoptive homeland. An uncommonly enduring creation of a diasporic community in the center of Russian life, the Lazarev Institute softened the experience of empire building for imperial agents and subjects.

Loris-Melikov and the Lazarevs are small reminders of how closely the leaders of Russia in its multiple iterations—from the Romanov Empire to the Soviet Union to the Russian Federation—have engaged politically with various layers of the diverse Armenian nation. The examples are as varied as they are colorful. In 1659, a wealthy Armenian merchant from Persia gifted Tsar Aleksei Mikhailovich with a diamond-studded golden throne.[2] Decades later, Peter the Great recruited Armenian peasants from Turkey to become Russia's frontiersmen.[3] In the twentieth century, the venerable Old Bolshevik Anastas Mikoyan formulated Soviet policy under the watchful eye of his Georgian boss, Joseph Stalin.[4] Today, Vladimir Putin's half-Armenian, half-Russian foreign minister, Sergei Lavrov, is the face of the Kremlin's diplomacy. Indubitably, "Russians" and "Armenians" were, and remain, deeply entangled, their collective and individual identities fluid, and their interactions complex and resistant to static categorizations.

This book explores Russia's political encounter with Armenians from its expansion into the South Caucasus in 1801 to its fateful entrance into the First World War in 1914. I argue that Russia tried to harness the stateless and dispersed Armenian diaspora to build its empire in the Caucasus and beyond.[5] The tsars relied on the stature of the two most influential institutions of that diaspora, the merchantry and the clergy, to accomplish several goals: to project diplomatic power from Constantinople to the Caspian Sea; to benefit economically from the transimperial trade networks of Armenian merchants in Russia, Persia, and the Ottoman Empire; and to draw political advantage from the Armenian Church's extensive authority within far-flung Armenian communities. This imperial arrangement remained largely symbiotic until the clash of nationalism and empire-wide social instability jolted Russia's traditional nationalities policies. In the late nineteenth and early twentieth centuries, after decades of regional tranquility and economic vitality, tsarist authorities implemented aggressive policies toward Armenian priests and activists as a desperate, and ultimately unsuccessful, reaction to real and imagined dangers from within and without.

Yet this summary of Russia's political approach to Armenians belies the reality that dramatic vicissitudes of policy and perception characterized Russo-Armenian ties throughout this era. Entwined Armenophilia and Armenophobia on the part of tsarist agents marked practically every encounter of Russian officials with Armenian subjects. Ethnonationally and linguistically different while culturally familiar, Armenians were alternatively, and often simultaneously, derided as uncivilized, subversive "Asiatics" or hailed as Russia's most loyal subjects. If some imperial administrators resented Armenians as a liability, many others promoted them as essential allies. Given such diverse attitudes, how do we assess the evolution of tsarist policies toward Armenians? What goals did the Russian government pursue through the conduits of the Armenian diaspora and religion? How did Armenians contribute to, or hinder, Russian expansionism?

Armenians make a compelling vehicle for investigating Russian strategies of imperialism for several reasons. First, unlike other territories in the Caucasus, Armenia initially embraced tsarist patronage. While some Christian and Muslim groups resisted St. Petersburg's expansion for decades, Armenians welcomed it out of fear of Persian and Ottoman threats. Second, owing to their diaspora's distribution not only along social and economic lines but also across regional and imperial borders, Armenians could be found in numerous milieus. This story takes us to the Persian and Ottoman Empires, to universities and printing presses from Yerevan and Tiflis to Moscow and St. Petersburg, and from Caucasian battlefields to Russian provincial capitals. Third, Armenians— as an artificially homogenized category in the formulations of many tsarist statesmen—experienced a wide spectrum of group identities in the minds of imperial officials. In the early nineteenth century, Romanov agents recognized Armenians as distant Persian vassals lauded for their economic prowess; at midcentury, tsarist officials elevated them into loyal Russian allies who were crucial for the administration of the South Caucasus; yet, by the turn of the 1900s, Armenians found themselves labeled seditious nationalists. The period explored in this book follows the evolution of "Russian" perceptions of "Armenians" alongside the dual processes of tsarist empire-building and Armenian nation-building.

Identity and Diaspora

Several interwoven themes shaped the Russo-Armenian encounter. Neither ethnically Slavic nor Russian-speaking, Armenians were nevertheless culturally familiar to Russians. The foundation of this acquaintance was laid when Armenian merchants ventured from the Byzantine bazaars on the shores of the Black Sea to the trading posts on the banks of the Dnieper River in Kievan Rus.[6] Thus, Russo-Armenian interactions predated the formation of the first centralized Russian state. After centuries of migration and mingling across the medieval and early modern Muscovite spaces, Armenian communities in Russia were almost as common as they were in its neighboring multiethnic empires.

Devoid of a state of their own since 1375, Armenians were dispersed across Eurasia. Until the tsar defeated the shah in 1828, the core of the Armenian diaspora remained divided between the Ottoman (Western Armenians) and Persian (Eastern Armenians) Empires. Given their historic distribution, Armenians assumed, or were ascribed, multiple labels that distinguished their political affiliations. Tsarist officials referred, and many historians continue to refer, to the Armenian subjects of the Russian emperor alternatively as "tsarist Armenians," "Russian Armenians," or "Eastern Armenians." Romanov representatives usually identified Armenians abroad according to their imperial overlord, such as "Ottoman Armenians" or "Western Armenians" and "Persian Armenians."

Like territoriality, religion is central to the Russo-Armenian encounter. Ecumenical kinship between Oriental Orthodox (also known as Apostolic) Armenians and Eastern Orthodox Russians was an enduring "thread of empire" that maintained the intimate bond between these imperial actors even when ecclesiastical disputes threatened to undo the Russo-Armenian political symbiosis.[7] Driven by a sense of religious familiarity and promises of physical security, Armenians embraced Russian patronage in the early nineteenth century to escape social and political marginalization in the Persian and Ottoman Empires. Tsarist officials resettled Armenian peasants from northern Persia and eastern Anatolia into newly conquered territories in the South Caucasus, collaborated with Armenian clerics against Western missionaries, and institutionalized exclusive tax breaks for the Armenian communities of Astrakhan and other southern Russian cities. After St. Petersburg captured the headquarters of the Armenian Church from Persia in 1828, it maneuvered to ensure the election of a prelate most open to Russia's geopolitical objective of spreading influence over the Armenian diaspora.

Imperial Inconstancies and Inconsistencies

While scores of Baltic German and other non-Russian elements stood at the apex of tsarist politics, ethnic Russians dominated the empire's power structure. This study, however, joins research that shows that non-Slavic, non-elites were indispensable to the state's imperial project. Armenians and many other minority groups facilitated the expansion and stability of the Romanov Empire.

Successive tsars and viceroys turned to Armenians for temporary and long-term help in administering the South Caucasus and to promote Russian interests beyond the empire's perpetually fluctuating borders. A full spectrum of success, failure, and outright disaster marked these efforts. Some Armenians in the tsarist empire suffered dramatically, while many led comfortable lives, and others thrived even more than Russians.

The point is that the Armenian case allows us to glimpse the "nuts and bolts" of the complex processes by which imperial Russia mobilized certain groups into loyal minorities.[8] This evidence reinforces Nancy Shields Kollmann's assertion about the early modern tsarist empire, which I posit also applies to Russia's long nineteenth century: "Assertive central control established empire; what kept it together were flexible policies of governance, policies that ran along a continuum from coercion to co-optation to ideology, with a large middle embracing many forms of mobilization by rulers and accommodation by subjects."[9] The pages that follow chart this continuum by seeking to penetrate conceptual abstractions about empire building in order to illuminate the details of the empire's practical functionality.

This book demonstrates how Russia depended on foreign-subject Armenian peasants and elites to colonize the South Caucasus, thereby rendering Armenians both agents and recipients of what the Romanovs portrayed as "European" imperialism. Some of the key protagonists were ethnic Armenian officers in the tsarist service who worked in the state bureaucracy and commanded Russian troops, often against their own compatriots. Before and after the Russian annexation of the South Caucasus in 1828, Armenians served as tsarist spies, settlers, and soldiers. Many of them joined Georgians and other Christian and Muslim natives of the Caucasus in collaborating with St. Petersburg's imperial project in the South Caucasus, together pulling the region closer to Russia. Armenians enjoyed exclusive privileges—from reduced taxation to relative religious and cultural freedom—and many communities from Tiflis to St. Petersburg prospered.

Yet, much as in other cases of European imperialism and in other corners of the Romanov Empire, the nineteenth-century encounter between Armenians and the Russian state yielded a complex interplay of national and imperial identities.[10] Russians lauded Armenian traders' contributions to the economic development of the imperial periphery, but distrusted their affiliations with British and French merchants in Asia Minor. The government supported an Armenian family's establishment of the Lazarev Institute of Oriental Languages in Moscow, but prohibited the formation of smaller Armenian academies elsewhere. Tsarist diplomats amplified the clout of the Armenian

Church in European capitals, but the authorities shuttered Armenian parish schools and imprisoned clergy when they detected links between the church and a nebulous nationalist movement. By the late nineteenth century, a multifaceted Armenian nationalism infused students, aristocrats, and clerics. In the early 1900s, the meticulously constructed partnership of the nineteenth century foundered in the storm of Russification, nationalism, revolution, and imperial turmoil, sparking the greatest crisis of Russo-Armenian ties in the modern era. Indeed, one of the core questions of this study is whether, why, and how Russia succeeded in orienting the majority of the Armenian diaspora toward its orbit.

In the broadest sense, the Russo-Armenian relationship was symbiotic but hierarchically ordered, even when Armenian-heritage officials outranked Russian bureaucrats. The Russian Empire resembled an ecosystem, where positive reciprocal relationships between vastly different species occur often, in a situation known as mutualism. For example, the Russian government and its Armenian subjects, like a pine tree and a band of jaybirds, performed separate roles, yet they generally worked together, despite occasional maladies. Just as the pine shelters and feeds the jays, the state provided protection and promotion to Armenians in exchange for their performance of specific tasks. Analyzing the complexities of this imperial relationship—beyond the reductive question of whether Russia was a friend or foe to Armenians—allows us to study the methods of tsarist imperialism in the context of diasporic distribution, interimperial conflict and alliance, nationalism, and religious and economic identity.

Spurred by postcolonial studies, the "new imperial history" paradigm has moved beyond static power dynamics to accentuate "different kinds of imperial mediators and agents, zones of contact and interaction, gender, race, and other regimes of difference, and multiple social experiences."[11] Embracing many of these innovations, historians of the Romanov Empire have highlighted the situational partnerships between tsarist officials and non-Russian intellectuals, religious elites, and even nationalists who periodically sought parallel political aims.[12] Indeed, Alexander Morrison is right to insist that "nowadays it would be hard to find any historian of any empire who did not acknowledge that violence and co-option, resistance and accommodation, differentiation, assimilation and mingling all existed simultaneously in imperial statecraft and imperial societies."[13] A mountain of scholarship written since the opening of the Russian archives in the 1990s tells us that empire and nation-building involved interwoven scenarios of acculturation and assimilation—partial or full acceptance of new identities—that allowed certain ethnonational minorities to regulate, or parry outright, the degree of Russification they were willing to tolerate.[14] Russia's successful and failed attempts to absorb Armenians demonstrate that the full spectrum of nationalities policies could be, and in this case was, applied to individual minority groups.[15] For Armenians, and some other subjects, imperial rule represented not hypothetical, clear-cut alternatives but simultaneous, messy realities.

The methods of Romanov expansionism appear contradictory at first blush, but reflect an observation made by Ann Laura Stoler and Carole McGranahan about empires, or what they term "imperial formations." Neither politically static nor socially rigid, "imperial formations are polities of dislocation, processes of dispersion, appropriation, and displacement. They are dependent both on moving categories and populations."[16] Such polities "are not, as we once imagined them, based on fixed forms and secure relations of inequity: they produce unstable relationships of colonizer and colonized, of citizen to subject, and unequal struggles over the forms of inclusion and the principles of differentiation."[17] In Russia's case, Valerie A. Kivelson and Ronald G. Suny stress that "what might look to some as inconsistencies might be better appreciated as examples of flexible and pragmatic approaches that contributed to the empire's longevity."[18]

Armenians are not a unique exemplar of these circumstances. Since the collapse of the Soviet Union, scholars have increasingly studied not only the separate "national" experiences of Romanov minorities but also the basis of the imperial cohesion that kept more than 130 individual nationalities living in a single state.[19] To administer and control the vast empire, the government co-opted national elites and buttressed the social and cultural standing of various groups.[20] This tactic blurred the ostensibly fixed lines not only between imperial agents and subjects but also between the ostensibly dominant (i.e., Russian) and dominated nations. Charles Steinwedel shows in his study of Russian imperialism in Bashkiria, for example, that "officials sought to give people, or at least their elites, sufficient stake in the empire to ensure loyalty while maintaining the hierarchy necessary to preserve privileges and to provide the sense of 'imperial destiny' and grandeur that connected the emperor and his elite servitors."[21] More broadly, in promoting the Russian "imperium as a creative space," Nicholas Breyfogle underscores that the state "offered important opportunities and possibilities—not to mention resources—that could be used to push local agendas."[22] Applying these insights to Armenians gives us a better understanding of how the Old Regime identified, incentivized, and regulated loyal service minorities while confronting their unique self-interests and ambitions.

Historians of, and from, Empires

This book emerges from the ground cultivated by other historians' decades of research on imperial Russia, the Caucasus, and Armenians. The rich contributions of Armenian, Russophone, and Anglophone scholars have sharpened our understandings of many aspects of tsarist imperialism in the long nineteenth century. Few writers, however, armed with archival documents and unencumbered by ideologies, have tackled the question of tsarist policies toward Armenians directly.[23]

Soviet-era scholarship on Russo-Armenian ties, while rich in detail and scope, left room for asking new questions. Many studies portrayed Persian and Ottoman suzerainty over Armenians as wholly oppressive. Twentieth-century historians—mainly Armenians—presented the Russian conquest of Eastern Armenia in 1828 as the timely deliverance of a fellow Christian people, echoing the Stalinist trope of "friendship of peoples."[24] In the post-Stalinist era, researchers continued to underscore the Marxist vision of a supranational proletarian movement that pushed beyond bourgeois nationalisms on the path toward communism.[25] Even when glasnost and perestroika helped Soviet scholarship move away from ideologically driven histories of Russo-Armenian relations, Soviet historians continued to bypass the contradictions of imperial policy and to outline a ubiquitous "Armenian Question."[26] Post-Soviet Armenian and Russian writers have produced incisive analyses of diverse sources, yet the tendency to present Russians and Armenians either as allies *or* as adversaries has been slow to fade.[27]

Anglophone historians of the Caucasus, working before and after the opening of Soviet archives in the early 1990s, have proved particularly influential for my own approach because of their tendency to contextualize individual case studies in broader discussions of "European" statecraft and to dissect imperial mechanisms. Ronald G. Suny studied the responses of myriad Caucasian social layers to Russian imperialism, highlighting the topics of intelligentsia, populism, and socialism, with a special accent on the Soviet era.[28] Other researchers have strengthened our understanding of the state's categorization of indigenous peoples, the evolution of Russian "colonial" policies, and the ambiguities of conquest and governance.[29]

Scholars of Armenian history, too, have shaped my approach.[30] The many painful chapters of the Armenian past, culminating in the genocide of 1915, have tilted studies of the relationship between Armenians and the state more toward the experiences of Western Armenians than Eastern Armenians.[31] English-language writers have spotlighted Western Armenians' tragedies and triumphs, providing penetrating explanations of their search for national liberation and security.[32] Suny has been one of the few Anglophone scholars of Eastern Armenians in the Russian political orbit. In *Looking toward Ararat*, he asked, "What is Armenianness?" and focused on the internal divisions of Armenian national, cultural, and class identities more thoroughly than on the fluidity of tsarist engagements with Armenians.[33] These works have taught us much and have paved the road for this exploration of the long-term methods, aims, and results of the Russian political elite's encounter with Armenians.

Methods, Sources, and Chapters

Two methodological and analytical schemes, in particular, guide this book. First, it seeks to zoom in on the evolution of Russia's Armenian policies to glimpse the inner gears of tsarist imperialism, with its ostensible contradictions and inconsistencies. For example, how did strategic disagreements, and even professional feuds, among tsarist agents affect their dialogues with Armenian clerics and traders? Second, to achieve the first goal, the narrative presents an intimate portrayal of the protagonists' actions and ambitions, allowing the reader to appreciate the subjective, and at times even emotional, investments of the historical actors.

This is a story of tsarist governance, and most of the sources here are Russian.[34] The topic of Armenian responses to Russian imperialism deserves its own study, and future research must continue the work of Richard Hovannisian, V. G. Tunian, Suny, and others to elucidate Armenian reactions to Russian political strategies and give voice to the tsars' Armenian subjects. This book's focus rests on the paradoxical goals and results of the Russian imperial project. To assess the official machinery of tsarist imperialism, I use state and regional correspondence, bureaucratic and ethnographic reports, military records, royal decrees, travelogues, petitions, popular newspapers, and other materials.

State-produced sources present both limitations and advantages. Diverse government records offer an intimate glimpse of the evolution of imperial methods of rule throughout the nineteenth and early twentieth centuries. To understand the inner mechanisms of the imperial administration is to uncover the political motivations of the Russian Empire. Yet state-produced documents must be approached with caution, given the fact that all empires exaggerated both threats and successes, seeking to glorify achievements while minimizing failures. State sources may not fully reveal the realities of tsarist politics, but they do unveil the pivotal aspirations and assumptions of the Old Regime.

Beginning in 1801 and ending in 1914, the chapters trace the progression of Russian engagements with cornerstones of Armenian life, such as religion, territoriality, education, commerce, and nationalism. Because foreign conflicts often dictated the course of Russia's encounter with Armenians, the approximate dates of major clashes serve as the checkpoints between the chapters. Charting how, and why, the officialdom's attitudes and actions vis-à-vis Armenians changed—and did not change—over time enables us to appreciate the consistency of the partnership that marked this complex, and often contentious, relationship.

Chapter 1 elucidates the forging of the Russo-Armenian political partnership in the fires of the First Russo-Persian War, during which the shah's Armenians systematically assisted the tsar's military and political agents. That chapter also examines Russo-Georgian and Armeno-Georgian tensions and Russia's rivalries with its Western and Eastern counterparts. Chapter 2 traces the political and economic factors that rendered Armenians key to tsarist imperialism. That chapter focuses particularly on Russia's conquest of Eastern Armenia during the Second Russo-Persian War, on the Lazarev family of entrepreneurs, and on the inconsistent economic policies that governed the commerce of Armenians in several southern Russian regions.

Chapter 3 explores senior statesmen's competing visions for the social and economic roles that Armenians should play in the tsarist empire at midcentury. That chapter uses the first viceroy of the Caucasus, Mikhail Vorontsov,

MAP 1. The Caucasus at the end of the eighteenth century, on the eve of Russia's expansion into the region.

and other officials to examine the evolution of Russian perceptions of Armenian political loyalty and also inspects the codification of the state's cooperation with the Armenian Church. Chapter 4 relies on the cleric and intellectual Gavril Aivazovskii to chart how the tsarist authorities navigated internal Armenian tensions surrounding visions of national identity based on religious and secular principles. It also uncovers the government's alliance with the Armenian Church against U.S. and European proselytizers. However, if St. Petersburg continued to promote itself as the defender of Western Armenians, cheered on by the liberal newspaper *Golos* (The Voice) during the Russo-Ottoman War of 1877–78, then the first cracks in the political symbiosis had already appeared in the mid-1870s.

Chapter 5 highlights the rise of a diverse Armenian nationalist sentiment in the last decades of the nineteenth century. The manifestations of what Russian officials lumped under the label "Armenian nationalism" took on multiple forms that were not always distinct to Romanov imperial agents, who struggled to discern and disarm the various Armenian political agendas. Chapter 6 examines the nadir in modern Russo-Armenian ties—the temporary abrogation of Armenian ecclesiastical independence in 1903—and the subsequent restoration of the familiar political mutualism on the eve of the conflagration of World War I. With a brief comparative glance, the book's conclusion points to the unique and representative aspects of the Armenian experience amid the evolution of Russian nationalities policies in this era.

It is a testament both to the range of tsarist methods of imperialism and to the Armenian perceptions of it that Khachatur Abovyan, the father of modern Armenian literature, celebrated Russia's liberation of Armenians from Persia and also condemned tsarist assimilationist tendencies in the same work. The great author wrote in 1841, "Blessed be the hour when the blessed Russian foot stepped upon the holy Armenian land," in reference to the tsar's conquest of Eastern Armenia from the shah in 1828.[35] However, he also insisted: "If you are Russian, speak Russian: if you are Turkish, speak Turkish. . . . The Armenian language has its own words. . . . And if you know your language, if you speak your language, the Russians will snatch the very bread from your hands. They will send you to Siberia."[36] Periodic storms—nationalisms, wars, and rivalries—strained, fortified, and molded the Russo-Armenian symbiosis.

CHAPTER 1

The Embrace of an Empire, 1801–1813

This chapter explores how, and why, Armenians emerged as imperial Russia's primary partners in the early nineteenth century. Although their political symbiosis blossomed in that era, Russians and Armenians were familiar to each other well before the onset of tsarist imperialism in the Caucasus. To be sure, the Russo-Armenian encounter antedates by centuries the Romanov incorporation of Eastern Armenia in 1828.[1] We must begin with a glance at pre-nineteenth-century developments.

While Russo-Armenian interactions dated to Kievan Rus,[2] their links solidified in the early modern era. Since the mid-seventeenth century, Russo-Armenian relations developed around two axes: economic and ecumenical ties. Having become frequent visitors to Russian bazaars and trade posts, Armenians earned special status by that period based on their real and mythologized economic prowess, as well as the value of the rare goods they carried from the Orient.[3] In 1667, Tsar Aleksei Mikhailovich (1645–76), eager to take advantage of Persian Armenians' silk imports, included Armenians among the ethnic groups permitted to trade at advantageous rates in major Russian commercial centers, such as Astrakhan and Moscow.[4]

Under Peter the Great (1682–1725), Russia absorbed Armenians from abroad and sympathized with the first manifestations of an Armenian liberation movement. In 1701, the Russian emperor received Israel Ori, an envoy whom Persian Armenians dispatched in hopes of securing a tsarist alliance against the shah. Peter granted the Armenian emissary the symbolic rank of colonel in the Russian army and promised to "extend his hand of assistance" toward the Armenians of Persia.[5] Although Ori failed to deliver Eastern Armenians from the grasp of the shah, he inspired other young Armenians to look to the Russian Empire for liberation.

Russia codified its recruitment of Armenians from abroad in 1711, when the Governing Senate recommended that the state "increase Persian trade and court [*prilaskat'*] Armenians as much as possible and ease their lot, in order to encourage them to arrive [in Russia] in large numbers."[6] In 1724, Peter issued economic privileges for Armenians settled throughout his realm, granting them exemptions from military service and other exclusive rights.[7] In 1746, Armenian merchants in Astrakhan, a strategically important commercial center in southern Russia, gained the right to trade tax-free and to establish their own court; in 1769, Astrakhan Armenians received the exclusive right to build seagoing vessels for trade in the Caspian Sea.[8] Catherine the Great (1762–96) continued these policies, absorbing new Armenian subjects in 1779 by resettling Ottoman Armenians from Crimea to Nor Nakhichevan, a town on the Don River.[9]

Religious solidarity drove Russo-Armenian relations in the eighteenth and nineteenth centuries. From the adoption of Christianity by the two nations, in 301 by Armenians and 988 by Eastern Slavs, the links between the Armenian Apostolic and the Russian Orthodox Churches remained strong. These autocephalous national churches are members of Orthodox Christianity, with Russia part of the Eastern Orthodox branch and Armenia part of the Oriental Orthodox wing. Although close liturgical cousins, the two churches never entered into full communion, and they developed independently after members of Oriental Orthodoxy rejected the dogma of the Council of Chalcedon in 451. Shared religion, then, played at once a unifying and a divisive role between Russians and Armenians.

While the distinction between Eastern and Oriental Orthodox Christianity could be schismatic for Russians and Armenians, it paled in comparison to the abyss between Russia and the predominantly Muslim Ottoman and Persian Empires. Michael Khodarkovsky has shown that, in the eighteenth-century North Caucasus, "the imperial Russian frontier was conceived as a Christian one," where St. Petersburg urged Armenians, Georgians, and even Catholics to settle.[10]

The politicization of religion grew once the tsarist empire portrayed itself as the patron of Orthodox Christians in the Ottoman Empire. When Russia forced Turkey to sign the Treaty of Küçük Kaynarca in 1774, it stipulated that "the Sublime Porte pledges to give the Christian faith and its churches firm

FIGURE 1. St. Catherine's Armenian Church in the heart of St. Petersburg, Nevskii Prospekt. One of the earliest Armenian stone churches in Russia, it was sponsored by Ivan Lazarevich Lazarev and built in 1771–76. Author's collection.

protection and it grants the Ministers of the Russian Imperial Court [the right] to protect all interests" of Christians.[11] As one of the largest Ottoman Christian subject groups, Armenians became not just an aspect of the Eastern Question but also a key part of Russia's answer to it. Before he was elected catholicos—head of the Armenian Church—in 1800, Archbishop Iosif Argutinskii-Dolgorukov (Hovsep Arghutian) of Astrakhan advised Catherine the Great and statesman Grigorii Potemkin on Caucasian affairs. He also advocated for Russia's annexation of the South Caucasus from Persia and published with royal approval a history of Russo-Armenian relations.[12] Thus, religious kinship and the allure of guaranteed security drove even commercially successful Armenians to abandon their homes in Ottoman and Persian territory in search of a better life in Russia.

A New Imperial Venture

In the early nineteenth century, Russians needed Armenians almost as much as Armenians needed Russians. In its foray into the Caucasus, the expanding

Romanov Empire searched for non-Russian allies. Within a few short years, Tsar Alexander I (1801–25) annexed the Georgian kingdom of Kartli-Kakheti, defeated the shah in the First Russo-Persian War (1804–13), and incorporated new Armenian subjects into his realm. But while mutual distrust hindered early Russo-Georgian and Armeno-Georgian ties, Armenians cooperated systematically with Russian imperial goals during and after the Russo-Persian war. They served not only as tsarist moles, messengers, translators, and negotiators but also as the frontiersmen of Russian expansion into the region, settling newly conquered territories. The tsarist state sought to align its political interests with Armenian desires, prioritizing the election of a pro-Russian catholicos, the ecclesiastical and often political leader of the stateless Armenians. Driven by the pursuit of physical and cultural security, commercial prosperity, and ecumenical solidarity, Armenian peasants, clergymen, and nobles defected from the shah's khanates to the tsar's provinces.

Tsarist authorities chose Armenians as their key diplomatic and military allies because of their diasporic distribution across imperial borders. While Georgians possessed a large aristocracy with sizable resources at its disposal, Russian statesmen sought to capitalize on Armenian commercial and religious networks that penetrated countries and societies inaccessible to Russian agents. Indeed, Russia's borders with Persia and Turkey, effectively impenetrable to Russian and even Georgian elements, remained porous to Armenian merchants and priests. Beyond the Caucasus, too, the potential political advantages of the Armenian diaspora informed Russian foreign policy. Moreover, Armenians as an ethnonational group were familiar to Russians. Since the mid-seventeenth century, members of the two nations interacted in markets, border towns, and imperial capitals. By 1800, Russian-born and Russian-educated Armenian-heritage officers in the Romanov service were few but not an anomaly. These agents of tsarism shared more in common with their ethnic Russian colleagues than with the Armenians of Persia and the Ottoman Empire, but their recognizability was important for the Russian engineers of empire.

Russia's methods in annexing the South Caucasus blended the settler colonialism of an external intruder with the indirect rule of an indigenously administered dependent. Armenians blurred the traditional colonizer/colonized binary by becoming both the agents and the subjects of imperial expansion, at once colonizing and being colonized in the South Caucasus during the first two decades of the tsarist absorption of the region. They joined the Russian bureaucracy and army, attended elite institutions in St. Petersburg, and commanded (Russian) troops in the Caucasus. At the same time, scores of new Armenian refugees and immigrants from Persian khanates, such as Yerevan, gravitated toward life in the tsar's empire, settling recently annexed territories, fighting alongside tsarist forces, and supplying them with intelligence.

In their initial forays into the politics of the South Caucasus, tsarist imperial representatives defined Armenians as ethnically distinct "Asiatics." Armenians' brand of Christianity may have been a close dogmatic cousin of their new overlords' religion, but that did not keep it from being lumped together with Islam and Judaism as a "foreign confession."[13] Rooted in theological grounds, latent Orthodox antagonism toward Armenian Apostolicism was based on the proposition that it was "heretical" for rejecting certain teachings of the later ecumenical councils.[14] Tsarist statesmen affirmed cultural distinctions between the Great Russian nation and Armenians, but considered them more reliable than Georgians and other regional natives.

Armenians challenged Russian officials to redefine and maintain their otherness. While arriving Russian agents in the South Caucasus perceived indigenous Armenians as foreign and exotic, in other corners of the empire Armenian officers served seamlessly alongside their Russian colleagues during Napoleon's invasion. To be sure, St. Petersburg's incorporation of the South Caucasus in the early nineteenth century created a space of increasingly unclear divisions. Many prominent tsarist officials tasked with expanding and securing new frontiers were non-Russians, reflecting both Alexander I's cosmopolitanism and the realities of empire building. Such generals and administrators as the Baltic German Karl Heinrich Knorring, the Italian Philip Paulucci, the Georgian Pavel Tsitsianov (Tsitsishvili), and the Armenian Ivan Petrovich Lazarev (Lazarian) are but the most famous examples. Their superiors in the imperial metropole, too, included powerful non-Russian officials, such as Foreign Minister Karl Nesselrode, a Baltic German. Thus, to speak of "Russian imperialism" in "Eastern Armenia" in the early nineteenth century, then, is to speak of a complex dialogue that involved non-Russian tsarist officials as well as imperial agents and subjects drawn from the same nationality.

Early Armeno-Georgian and Russo-Georgian Strife

Georgian numerical and political importance in the region demands an examination of Armeno-Georgian and Russo-Georgian relations during and after St. Petersburg's annexation of the Georgian kingdom of Kartli-Kakheti in 1801. While it is tempting to see Georgia as a precursor to the Armenian case, significant contrasts marked their respective encounters with the tsarist state. Both Christian nations sought Russian refuge from imminent Persian and Ottoman threats; however, Georgian elites objected to the methods of tsarist annexation and hesitated to accept their new imperial overlord. Moreover, Armeno-Georgian social and cultural strife not only estranged these neighbors but also informed Russian perceptions of the two nations. Armenians and Georgians, the two largest and most prominent representatives of Christianity in the Caucasus, had shared deep cultural ties since the premodern era, yet tensions between the two nations defined the nineteenth century and continue to influence contemporary regional politics. "One of the mysteries of the Caucasus," Thomas de Waal has observed, "is why the relationship between the Armenians and the Georgians . . . is frequently fraught and suspicious."[15]

The roots of this discord reach into antiquity. Georgian king Mirian III adopted Christianity around 330, just a few decades after his Armenian counterpart's conversion in 301. Their faith became a sacrosanct cornerstone of Georgian and Armenian national identities, linked by their perennial friction with neighboring Muslims. But, as early as the fifth century, the two national churches chose separate paths. The Georgian Orthodox Church looked toward Byzantium and Eastern Orthodoxy, while the Armenian Apostolic Church aligned itself with the Oriental Orthodox branch of Christianity. Consequently, as de Waal notes, "the Armenian and Georgian churches traded anathemas, and the Armenian catholicos forbade Armenians to communicate with, eat with, pray with, or marry Georgians."[16]

In the modern era, social and economic factors divided Armenians and Georgians more than theology. From the late Middle Ages and well into the nineteenth century, Armenians, Muslims, and other foreigners outnumbered Georgians in Georgian towns.[17] Fleeing Seljuk advances and Byzantine conquests in 1045, Armenian nobles and their peasants found asylum in Georgian towns, especially Tiflis. Georgian kings ascribed to them the role of urban traders, a vocation in which Armenians soon excelled, engaging in regional and long-distance trade. By the turn of the nineteenth century, outsiders and locals alike concurred that among the Georgian capital's population, "the group that truly stood out in the economic and administrative life of the city was the Armenians."[18] This reputation of Armenians as the merchants of the Caucasus endured for the rest of the century. By contrast, as Ronald G. Suny has written, Georgians relied on an agrarian economy in the countryside that sought to satisfy local needs without producing surplus for resale and trade.[19]

Lopsided national proportions of the Tiflis population contributed to Armeno-Georgian tensions. By some estimates, the Armenian domination of Tiflis amounted to three-fourths of the city's roughly 20,000-resident population in 1801.[20] Armenians reigned over the city's bazaars and moneylending sector, accruing not only financial gain but also the attendant social and political leverage. As some of the first tsarist officials to arrive in Tiflis reported,

"The Armenians control most of the trade here."[21] A decade later, one of the tsarist commanders of the Caucasus remarked that in Tiflis the merchantry comprised "almost exclusively Armenians."[22] Georgian nobles and peasants, more at ease with the seigniorial economy of the early modern era than the mercantile practices of urban retailers, disdained the Armenians who dominated the Georgian capital and other towns. One indignant Georgian noble, Prince Iese Baratashvili, derided Armenians for their lack of aristocratic pedigree and for their scattered diaspora: "Where do Armenians possess nobility? They have been dispersed by God! Is it in Man's power to reunite them?"[23]

Visitors to Georgia from Russia and the West often noted the ostensibly "indolent" work ethic of Georgians, although such observations often tell us more about the authors than their subjects. To be sure, as Suny has stressed, "consistently distressed by the Georgians' attitude toward work, economy, and self-improvement, noble officers from the north or travelers from the West found their own explanations in racial, climatic, or educational factors."[24] Scottish writer and diplomat Robert Ker Porter, on visiting Tiflis in 1817, remarked that "the Armenians set a stimulating example of the ways and means of industry, and show many persuasive advantages, resulting from their extensive exercise," a trend that he hoped would "inspire" Georgians.[25] Arriving Russians expressed surprise at the degree to which Georgian elites had retreated from the economic and social life of Tiflis, Gori, and other cities, apparently contented with age-old arrangements of enserfed labor and wanting little to do with trade and industry. Thus, the image of Georgians as economically backward and socially isolated began to solidify in the political imagination of early Russian imperial agents.

Yet aristocratic Russian officers often found more in common with the Georgian gentry of the countryside than with the Armenian businessmen of the towns. Based on "shared values of military bravery, chivalry, and a love of grace and largess," tsarist elites welcomed the few Georgian nobles who joined the Russian service.[26] But at the same time as Russian administrators faulted Armenians for what they perceived as avarice, their eagerness to animate regional commerce necessitated the Russian reliance on the Armenian bourgeoisie and its commercial networks. Armenians, therefore, gradually earned the reputation of "diligent" natives, juxtaposed by Russian observers against their supposedly less ambitious Georgian neighbors. Despite residual distrust of Armenian entrepreneurship, tsarist officials looked to Armenians as their more capable indigenous ally in the Caucasus.

Economic competition and social strife defined Armeno-Georgian relations at the turn of the nineteenth century. Georgians not only were in the minority in Tiflis but also felt increasingly marginalized in the city's commercial sector.

The combination of theological, national, economic, and social differences between Armenians and Georgians fueled a simmering antagonism between the two groups and also precipitated distinct Russian understandings of those two nations and their roles in the tsarist expansion into the South Caucasus. Russia's seizure of Tiflis in 1801 exacerbated old tensions and created new ones.

The tsarist annexation of the Georgian kingdom of Kartli-Kakheti, while negotiated and bloodless, generated Russo-Georgian discord, mainly driven by the manner of the Russian incorporation of Georgia.[27] In 1783, Catherine the Great pledged to King Erekle II that Russia would defend the tiny Georgian kingdom against "foreign" invasion, but Romanov promises soon evaporated, and in 1795 the Persian army destroyed Tiflis and carried off thousands of Georgians into slavery. Although between 1795 and 1801 Persia redoubled its efforts to bring Kartli-Kakheti to heel and to establish a vassal state relationship, no more attacks occurred after 1795, and King Erekle II remained on the throne until his death in 1798. In 1795, during the Persian assault of Tiflis, the 1783 agreement with the Russian Empire had proved tragically ineffective against Persian aggression, but Georgian elites had no choice but to seek deeper ties to their northern neighbor. In September 1799, Erekle's successor, Giorgii XII (1798–1800), personally petitioned Tsar Paul I (1796–1801) for the Kartli-Kakheti kingdom to become part of the tsarist empire "on the same footing as the other provinces of Russia."[28] Giorgii understood this as legal protection of his territory's status within Russia concurrent with the continuation of his reign over Georgia. In return for fusing his nation to Russia, Giorgii asked that the Bagrationi family remain on the Georgian throne and that the Georgian nobility be absorbed into the Russian system of ranks.

Even before Giorgii's petition, Paul looked to project his empire's authority into Kartli-Kakheti. In April 1799, a special tsarist representative to Georgia was chosen, State Councilor Petr Kovalenskii. Citing the 1783 treaty as legal precedent, Paul dispatched this envoy to the Georgian court to represent Russia's interests, protect economic links, and gather intelligence.[29] A less publicized objective, however, constituted a core mission for the diplomat.

In what soon became state policy, the tsarist government tasked Kovalenskii with recruiting Armenians from abroad to the South Caucasus. The Foreign Ministry instructed him to facilitate the resettlement of several Armenian communities, per their wishes, from such nearby Persian khanates as Karabakh into Kartli-Kakheti.[30] Kovalenskii was to secure favorable land grants from King Giorgii for the use of these hereditary Armenian nobles, or *meliks*, and their communities. Tsar Paul, who wished to see "this new Christian community in Georgia prosper as much as possible," insisted that the influx of

Persian Armenians would only benefit the Georgian kingdom. He impressed on Kovalenskii the importance of obtaining from Giorgii land allotments for Armenians "on as favorable terms as possible" and emphasized that these new Armenian communities should "not be a kind of vassal" of the Georgian king, although they were expected to pay "moderate" tribute and do their share to protect the region from external attack. "You will have no trouble," the Foreign Ministry assured Kovalenskii, "in making the Georgian tsar understand how beneficial for him can be the settlement of various Christian communities in those areas, where [they can] counteract the activity of Muslims, so harmful and ruinous to Christian peoples."[31]

Tsar Paul drove home the point himself by asking the Georgian king in June 1799 to "grant the requested land for them, give them the freedom and privileges proper for guests, and maintain all of the rights and advantages over their Armenian subjects [i.e., peasants] that they enjoyed in their former homelands, never depriving them of this rightful authority, as long as they stay loyal and diligent."[32] Eager to expedite the recruitment of Armenians into the South Caucasus, the tsar also decreed large annual payments to individual Armenian *meliks* from the imperial treasury.[33] Giorgii acquiesced to Paul's pressure, presenting to one of the *meliks*, Dzhimshid Shakhnazarov, the stately Lori fortress and the territory surrounding it, with control over the area's non-Armenian peasants. Another *melik* received from the Georgian king the right to settle in the Borchali District and to collect a toll from passing merchant caravans.[34]

King Giorgii had every reason to accept Kovalenskii's arrival in hopes that St. Petersburg's new attention toward his kingdom would thwart Persian aggression. Giorgii initially embraced the Russian envoy's appointment to Tiflis. Kovalenskii sent a gushing report a few months after his arrival, also boasting of his influence over the Georgian monarch: "He has come to love me as a son and a friend, accepting all my suggestions as holy."[35] But the tsarist diplomat's presence alone was an insufficient guarantee of security for Giorgii, who continued to lobby for Russian troops to be stationed in his kingdom as a redoubt against Persian invasion. Anticipation of an attack grew in 1800, as repeated reports of gathering Persian forces inundated Georgian and Russian officials.[36] Yet the tsarist empire's newfound dedication to Georgia's security vis-à-vis Persia had to be balanced with a desire to expand economic ties between the two empires, again blunting Russia's aid to the besieged kingdom.

In late 1799, Tsar Paul consented to Giorgii's requests for military protection, dispatching two small forces. General Karl Heinrich Knorring, a Baltic German, led the first group, while Major General Ivan Petrovich Lazarev, an ethnic Armenian born in Russia, marched another contingent of soldiers into Tiflis. But the Georgian king grew frustrated by what he saw as Russia's inadequate military assistance, imploring Knorring to double the size of the Russian contingent from three thousand to six thousand men.[37] Indeed, the Persian threat to Kartli-Kakheti rose to new levels in 1800. In July, Crown Prince Abbas Mirza, son of Fath-Ali Shah, encamped his army at Yerevan, a short distance from the Georgian capital. As the first year of the nineteenth century drew to a close, these Russo-Georgian tensions swelled.

Giorgii was not alone in his growing frustration with the kingdom's geopolitical situation. Questions of royal succession swirled as it became clear that Giorgii intended to fuse Kartli-Kakheti to Russia. Giorgii's half brother, Alexander, evinced this anxiety by fleeing the kingdom. Alexander had long opposed Giorgii's orientation toward Russia's orbit and found an eager welcome from neighboring khans. He represented a simmering Georgian elite that disapproved of Giorgii's policies, fearing the loss of its authority and wealth. His protracted anti-Russian rebellion, stretching over a decade and backed not only by some Persian khans but also by various North Caucasian tribes, disrupted the Russo-Georgian ties of the early nineteenth century. Alexander's first strike came in November 1800, when he and Omar Khan, the ruler of Dagestani Avars, launched a unified attack. A joint Russian-Georgian army that enjoyed the advantage of artillery repelled the assault, but officials remained wary of Georgian allegiances.[38]

Alexander's abortive attempt to expel Russians from Kartli-Kakheti directly precipitated the final act of the tsarist empire's annexation of Georgia. Just eight days after the battle, on 15 November 1800, Tsar Paul informed General Knorring: "[King Giorgii,] seeing his kingdom threatened by external foes as much as, and perhaps more, by the growing internecine war within his own family over succession to the throne, has ordered his embassy to declare to me his wish to see Georgian lands in our direct subjecthood [*poddanstvo*]."[39] Paul was not exaggerating. Under Giorgii's orders, the Georgian legation in St. Petersburg had announced to the Russian court: "King Giorgii of Georgia, . . . dignitaries, the clergy, and the people, unanimously wish to enter forever into the subjecthood of the Russian Empire, solemnly pledging to carry out all that which Russian subjects carry out, without avoiding any laws or commands."[40] In January 1801, a month after the Georgian monarch's death, and just two months before his own murder at the hands of palace conspirators, the tsar decreed Georgia a part of the Romanov Empire.

Paul's successor, Alexander I, confirmed his father's decision, but chose to dethrone the Georgian royal family, breaking the agreement his predecessor had reached with the Bagrationis. Despite the outcry of Georgian nobles,

Alexander claimed the decision was not calculated to "increase my powers, secure profit, or enlarge the boundaries of an already vast empire," but rather was intended to "establish in Georgia a government that can maintain justice, ensure the security of persons and of property, and give to everyone the protection of law."[41] Suny has argued that Alexander "decided that Russia's interests and Georgia's future could best be guaranteed by outright incorporation into the empire."[42] The motivations behind Alexander's reversal of his father's agreement remain unclear, but imperial events in a different corner of the world may shed light here.

St. Petersburg closely watched Napoleon's invasion of Ottoman-administered Egypt in 1798, hostile to both Paris's and Constantinople's expansionist ambitions.[43] With the tide of war having turned decidedly to the Ottoman side by early 1801, Russia saw a renewed threat from the sultan's empire. It is fair to interpret Alexander's decision regarding Georgia, made almost concurrently with the French defeat in Egypt, as calculated to secure Russia's borders with the Sublime Porte. The weakened Bagrationi dynasty was likely to become a liability in the event of a new Russo-Ottoman showdown. With the Georgian royal family forcefully removed to Russia, the political authority of the ancient Bagrationi clan, for centuries the steadfast leader of the Georgian nation, dissolved.

Capitalizing on his gains and emboldened by Persian inaction, the young tsar set his sights on further expansion, instructing his ministers in March 1802 that all territory north of the Kura and Arax Rivers must be conquered.[44] Responding to complaints about Knorring and unsatisfied with the general's "weak" command of the Georgian situation, Alexander removed him from command in the fall of 1802.[45] Perhaps seeking to smooth the tumultuous relationship with Georgian elites who continued to resist the unilateral annexation of their kingdom, Alexander appointed General Pavel Tsitsianov as high commissioner (*glavnoupravliaiushchii*) of Georgia. A Russian-educated Georgian with an impressive military record, the general took up the tsar's task with alacrity. Although his tenure at the helm of the Caucasus administration lasted less than three and a half years—cut short by his death at the siege of Baku in 1806—Tsitsianov's influence on Russo-Caucasian narratives cannot be underestimated. Tsitsianov was Russia's first Caucasus commander to be granted both military and civilian jurisdiction, eventually taking over the responsibilities previously carried out by Knorring and Kovalenskii, respectively. The reasons for such a promotion are important.

The practically unknown story of Kovalenskii's demotion deserves attention for the insight it provides into the gestation of early Russian perceptions of the South Caucasus and its inhabitants.[46] While the problem stemmed from the envoy's personal arrogance toward his Russian colleagues and Georgian counterparts, the wider tensions he caused in Russo-Georgian ties reverberated deeply. Kovalenskii ignored the de rigueur observances of diplomatic protocol, seemingly trivial actions that in practice inflamed animosity between the Russian administration and the Georgian elite. From the beginning, he displayed insufficient deference toward the Georgian king, failing to report to him on arrival in Tiflis and repeatedly declining the king's dinner invitations, citing ill health, but sending in his stead low-ranking representatives. He also demanded custom-built armchairs for his audience with the Georgian monarch, moving his seat so close to the king during their meeting that their feet touched, a gross breach of etiquette.[47] In putting an end to Kovalenskii's debauchery, Tsitsianov scolded the bureaucrat: "[Your downfall was] a consequence of your insensitivity toward local nobles, whom you offended by your behavior and thereby compelled to come to hate [our] administration to such a degree, that I have found a terrible wavering of minds against the Russian administration."[48]

If the Kovalenskii affair was grounded in individual haughtiness, more consequential factors obstructed early Russo-Georgian ties. In one of the most salient manifestations of their friction, General Lazarev was murdered in April 1803, not by a disgruntled Georgian prince or an obscure sympathizer, but by Queen Mariam, the widow of Georgia's last king.[49] Tsitsianov ordered Lazarev to detain the queen and her children to prevent their imminent flight from Tiflis, and when Lazarev approached her, Mariam thrust a dagger into his chest. Before his demise, Lazarev had characterized the entire Georgian court and nobility as "filled with intrigues and internecine conflicts [mezhdusobiia]."[50] He found that not only external threats but also internal "secret conspiracies of various prominent people" compromised Georgia's security.

Beyond the family politics of the Georgian court, tsarist officials elucidated the rift between their administration and the locals. Although Tsitsianov initiated several measures to soothe relations with the Georgian nobility, notions of Russian cultural superiority informed his efforts. True, in his first year in command he opened doors to Georgian elites for daily meetings, issued orders to local officials about the primacy of egalitarian "justice" in all aspects of law enforcement, and even declared a two-month amnesty for all nobles who had fled Tiflis with Prince Alexander and other rebellious Bagratids. Tsitsianov also supported the spread of schools and education throughout the Caucasus, the expansion of trade, and the official recognition of Islam.[51] At the same time,

Tsitsianov remained convinced: "Nature, which delegated Asiatic peoples to unlimited autocratic authority, has left an indelible mark here. Against wildness and intransigence strong and determined measures are necessary."[52] Georgian nobles, for whom "the word 'law' has no meaning," grumbled the tsarist general, sought every opportunity to evade new laws and regulations and treated Russian officials with contempt if their familial background did not match Georgian notions of eminence and status. Tsitsianov highlighted the early gulf between Russian imperial officials and the Georgian elite when he quipped, "For them everything is new; for us everything is strange."[53]

Georgian nobles had tangible reasons for their discontent. New Russian laws let peasants file complaints against their hereditary overlords. Many landowners were incensed when provincial police and newly established courts demanded that nobles account for their mistreatment of their serfs and respond to accusations of physical abuse.[54] Moreover, argued Knorring, the removal from political office of several aristocrats who had achieved their positions through hereditary prestige rather than merit "has given [another] reason for discontent to those who place their individual well-being ahead of that of the community."[55] Despite his engagement with Georgian elites, Tsitsianov's actions unnerved them as much as Knorring's policies had, especially after Tsitsianov confiscated all estates and properties belonging to nobles who had fled Kartli-Kakheti after the annexation.[56]

Ordinary Georgians voiced their own grievances. "Many" Georgians protested to General Lazarev that locally stationed Russian troops "interfere[d] in the internal affairs of the locals, willfully taking supplies and horses—less out of necessity than whim" and refused to compensate the peasants. Rank-and-file Russian soldiers also "inflicted personal harm on the residents"; "stole their cattle, fowl, produce, [and] wine"; and filled emptied wine jugs with sand out of "reckless mischief" (*bezrasudnaia shalost'*).[57]

The discontent of the dethroned Bagratids and other Georgian nobles boiled over into open rebellion periodically throughout the first half of the nineteenth century. In 1810–11, Prince Levan, a grandson of King Giorgii, mobilized Ossetians into an anti-Russian insurrection.[58] More Georgian uprisings followed in Kakheti in 1812–13 and in Imereti in 1819–20. A pan-Georgian rebellion exploded in 1832, followed by large peasant disturbances in Guria in 1841 and in Mingrelia in 1857.[59] Although tsarist authorities easily quelled such resistance, the image of Georgians as unreliable at best and rebellious at worst took hold in the imagination of early Russian administrators of the South Caucasus. With few trustworthy subjects, Russia searched the South Caucasus for new, dependable allies.

Imperial Ambitions

In the first decade and a half of the nineteenth century, Russia maintained its grip on Georgia despite actively feuding or battling with Persians, Ottomans, the French, Georgian rebels, North Caucasian highlanders, and the British. Against the efforts of these parties, the tsarist state fortified its position as a regional power and prepared for further expansion into the shah's domain. St. Petersburg's goals and incentives for conquest in the South Caucasus, and their implications for Russo-Armenian ties, cannot be divorced from the context of the Napoleonic Wars and broader Russian imperial strategy. Rapidly shifting European alliances informed Russia's engagement with Armenians at least as much as Caucasian developments. Romanov imperial ambitions in northern Persia and eastern Anatolia were often defined vis-à-vis its European rivals' actions: competition among Russia, France, Britain, Austria, and Prussia in the early nineteenth century affected the tsar's relations with the shah and the sultan.

Although Russian elites often distrusted their British counterparts, at the turn of the nineteenth century St. Petersburg sided with London against Paris, wary of French overtures toward Russia's traditional adversaries: Swedes, Poles, and Ottomans.[60] By 1807, Napoleon had routed Europe's largest armies and forced Britain into a defensive war. In July 1807, Tsar Alexander had few options but to sign the Treaty of Tilsit with Napoleon, which stipulated Russian assistance to France against its British and Swedish enemies. The new accord required Russia to support Napoleon's Continental System, which sought to suffocate London's economy by restricting its commerce on the continent.[61]

In the years leading up to the French invasion of Russia in 1812, the Russian elite grumbled against Alexander's treaty with Napoleon. Admiral Nikolai Mordvinov, the Anglophile minister and economist, was not alone in arguing that Russia's economic and political interests aligned with Britain's, and he emphasized that Britain was Russia's most prized commodities market.[62] Foreign Minister Nikolai Rumiantsev maintained that the Continental System effectively punished Britain's major trading partners, including Russia, more than it punished London. Russian foreign policy could hardly benefit from a French victory over Britain. Furthermore, numerous statesmen and cultural leaders, such as Nikolai Karamzin, feared Napoleon's ability to establish an independent Polish state, anathema to tsarist imperial policy. These and other eminent individuals privately advocated Russia's withdrawal from European rivalries. Some officials proposed instead that the state return to its eighteenth-century foreign policy of expansion at the expense of the Ottoman and Persian Empires.[63]

Napoleon's campaign against Austria in 1809 and a flood of reports about French overtures toward Russia's antagonists, including the Ottomans, Poles, and Swedes, gave Alexander another reason to suspect French imperial ambitions.[64] This political climate directly influenced the tsar's calculations regarding his ties with the shah and the sultan, both of whom waged war against Russia, in 1804–13 and 1806–12, respectively. When Ottoman forces attacked Russian troops in 1806 but were quickly overwhelmed in Moldavia and Wallachia, for example, the sultan dragged out negotiations in anticipation of an imminent Russo-French break. General Mikhail Kutuzov forced the Ottomans to sign a treaty only in June 1812, just days before the French invasion of Russia.

The rivalry with European powers hardly constrained Russia's goals in the Caucasus. To the contrary, facing threats from the west, St. Petersburg looked for resources and allies in the south. Within a couple of years of securing Kartli-Kakheti and establishing Tiflis as the regional seat of the Russian administration, the tsarist empire continued to expand into the Caucasus. The incentives for this growth were primarily political and secondarily economic. First, several formidable fortress cities remained between Persia proper (to the south of the Arax River) and the newly annexed Russian territories. The tsar and his officials saw these citadels at Yerevan, Shusha (in Karabakh), and Baku as potential bases for Persian incursions into Georgia and the rest of the Russian Caucasus domain.

As early as April 1802, Tsar Alexander supported Knorring's aspirations for Yerevan as "a measure of utmost necessity."[65] When Russians learned that the city's *sardar* (prince-governor) refused to accept the authority of Fath-Ali Shah and was in open rebellion, they saw an opportunity. The *sardar* had expressed vague interest in coming under the tsar's aegis, yet during protracted negotiations he hesitated to accept the main demand of the tsarist side—that the Yerevan fortress be garrisoned by Russian forces. Alexander was certain that rebellious Persian khans south of Georgia would realize the necessity of his protection against the shah's army. "These reasons are so self-evident, that he must recognize them himself and agree to our demands," confidently declared Alexander about Yerevan's overlord. Alexander remained convinced that by occupying the fortress cities between Georgia and the Arax River, Russia would ensure the safety of Tiflis and also display its resolve to the local lords (*vladel'tsy*).

Political considerations beyond the South Caucasus also drove Russia's pursuit of the Yerevan Khanate. Just twenty kilometers from the Yerevan fortress stood the Ejmiatsin monastery complex, the headquarters of the Armenian

Apostolic Church, to whose authority submitted much of the dispersed Armenian diaspora. While control of Yerevan, the region's second city after Tiflis, promised Russia full dominion over the South Caucasus, control of Ejmiatsin promised extensive political and economic sway in those countries, such as the Ottoman Empire, Persia, and even India, where Russian diplomats struggled for influence while local Armenian bishops enjoyed social prominence. Enticed by the strategic advantage of the Yerevan fortress and the ecumenical-political clout of the Ejmiatsin monastery, St. Petersburg viewed those historic Armenian centers as vital elements of its broader foreign policy in the East.

Political incentives for expansion into Persian-held territory overshadowed economic goals, but the latter also attracted St. Petersburg. Trade between Georgia and Persian khanates, such as Yerevan, had the potential to render Georgia one of Russia's most profitable imperial territories, and even during the height of the First Russo-Persian War, cross-border commerce continued almost uninterrupted. By mid-1809, approximately 1,080,000 pounds of cotton, valued at about 250,000 rubles, reached Tiflis from Yerevan, usually delivered by Armenians.[66] Moreover, the famously lucrative vineyards and other agricultural industry of the Yerevan Khanate, coupled with the metal ores of the eastern South Caucasus (today's Azerbaijan), promised to reimburse the tsarist treasury for the costs of the Georgian annexation and maintenance. Alexander made this clear to Knorring's successor, General Tsitsianov, to whom he complained in September 1802 that despite Knorring's assurances that Georgia would be financially self-sufficient, it continued to drain the state treasury.[67] "There is still nothing from [Knorring] about the profits derived [from Georgia]," carped the tsar. "Meanwhile the costs of various issues, multiplying from day to day, have risen to a very deliberate [narochitaia] sum, and while the welfare of this people has become the government's general concern, I would not want the weight of its administration to fall solely on Russia."[68]

Tsitsianov interpreted this signal as an expansionist mandate. Through a deft combination of negotiation and coercion, in 1803 and 1804 he brought several Persian-held khanates and principalities, including Georgian Mingrelia and Imereti, into the tsar's realm. However, in January 1804, Tsitsianov entered Ganje Khanate, ostensibly part of Georgia, and the First Russo-Persian War (1804–13) erupted.[69] At the onset of the war, the Russian army's first and most formidable objective was Yerevan and its strategically positioned fortress.

The invitations and pleas that tsarist agents received from local Armenians made Yerevan's capture even more appealing. As early as April 1803, Tsitsianov reported to the emperor: "Armenians who populate [northern Persian provinces], owing to a single Christianity and to their confidence in commerce under the protection of Russian rule, for their own well-being exhibit toward us devotion and a desire to see the speedy and successful establishment in these lands of Russian overlordship [*vladychestvo*], [and] call to me every day to hasten [our] expedition on Yerevan."[70] The citation of the two nations' ecumenical bond, well entrenched in Russian society and culture by this stage, provided the type of guarantee that tsarist agents sought in their imperial mission in the Caucasus. In November 1803, Tsitsianov invited the Armenians of Ganje to resettle in any part of Georgia, vowed to defend them, and pledged to grant them the status of state peasants rather than serfs.[71] It is not clear whether Armenians heeded these enticements before the war started in early 1804, but by mid-1804 Persian Armenian refugees seeped into Russian territory. Even if, as George Bournoutian has argued, Armenians and other minorities in Persian domains were not as oppressed as Russian officials imagined, their marginalization in local communities provided them with incentives to seek Russian security.[72] The stream of Armenian refugees escaping from Persian to Russian territory confirmed this circumstance for the tsar and his agents.

In anticipation of the approaching Russian army, in the summer of 1804 several Armenian *meliks* fled from Yerevan to Russian territory.[73] These hereditary Armenian nobles brought with them "over 200 families" of their peasants, likely numbering between eight hundred and one thousand individuals. They immediately urged Tsitsianov to rescue over five hundred other Armenian families from Yerevan, who had been left, under guard, "in the hands of the unreliable Persians."[74] These Armenians also provided tactical information about the size and strength of the Persian contingent—a staple of Russo-Armenian engagement in the South Caucasus for the next several years. Warning that the *sardar* had already executed several Armenians, seized the property of others, and threatened to expel the rest of the khanate's Christians to Persia proper, the newly resettled Armenians implored Tsitsianov: "With tears we beg you, be the savior of the Armenians left behind, who are in an extreme situation, have no help from anywhere, and suffer various offenses and persecutions."[75]

In May 1804, Tsitsianov issued to Yerevan's *sardar* several peremptory demands, which he likely knew would be unacceptable. The *sardar* had to recognize the tsar as his supreme ruler, yield the fortress to Russian forces, and agree to pay a large annual tribute.[76] In return, Yerevan's overlord would be permitted to maintain his rights and powers, except the ability to decree the death penalty, and would be guaranteed safety and protection. When the khan dawdled, Tsitsianov thundered, "I do not frighten with words but act with bayonets and prove with deeds."[77] By June, the brusque general wrote: "According to European custom, before launching an assault on the city, I must offer it to surrender, but if I do not receive by tonight a satisfactory and definitive answer, then God and bayonets will deliver it for me, despite a hundred Baba Khans or his son, who rides around in the distance like a hare avoiding a pack of lions."[78]

Memorable as they were, Tsitsianov's threats soon proved futile, and the city's Persian garrison repelled a Russian attack. Despite this setback, or perhaps due to it, the Russian general continued to look toward Armenians to advance tsarist borders in the South Caucasus. When, in 1805, Persian reinforcements arrived in the region, replaced the rebellious Yerevan *sardar*, and once again threatened to remove local Armenians beyond the Arax, Tsitsianov expressed his hope that "if the developments of this war do not interfere and God helps us drive Baba Khan from Karabakh, then I will try to resettle [Armenians] in Georgia, which is what they want."[79] At the same time, the Russian commander expected the Armenians' active participation in their "liberation" and the expansion of Romanov domains.

In June 1805, a year after his abortive assault on Yerevan, Tsitsianov sought to recruit Armenians from Karabakh to fight against the shah's army. His declaration to them lauded their onetime "famous bravery" and asked rhetorically whether they had lost it, becoming "womanly [*zhenopodobnymi*], like those Armenians who engage only in commerce."[80] "No," he replied to his own question, "I am aware of your past bravery, which is why I call on you . . . with the glorious and invincible Russian army . . . to help the strong and unsurpassable Russian troops against the Persian forces, which are encroaching to ruin Karabakh and to steal each one of your properties."[81] Specifically, Tsitsianov urged Karabakh Armenians to attack retreating Persian forces after the main Russian assault. By the second half of 1805, the tsarist army firmly controlled Karabakh,[82] no doubt in part thanks to the participation of local Armenians. Indeed, the Russian satisfaction with Karabakh Armenians' efforts suggests that Tsitsianov's petition was heeded.[83]

At the same time as he enlisted these regional natives in the tsarist imperial project, Tsitsianov promoted ethnic hierarchies and tightened his state's control over newly annexed societies and spaces. The general represented Russia's idea of itself as an empire, one that welcomed non-Russian participation in the state's imperial project provided that the metropole initiated such participation. For example, when in January 1806 Tsitsianov learned that up to ten thousand Armenian families from the Western Armenian town of Bayazet in Anatolia had expressed a desire to resettle in Yerevan on its capture by the tsar's army, he feared that the immigrants would eschew "proper obedience" and would maintain ties to elements in Anatolia and Persia without tsarist approval.[84] Moreover, Tsitsianov accused Armenian merchants of the South

Caucasus of raising prices during wartime and consequently prohibited them from trading in mountainous villages (*auly*).[85] In April 1804, he ordered regional police to monitor local commerce: "[Seek out] resellers who greedily raise prices on necessities, a practice in which, after the Yids, the Armenians are the most capable, to the general detriment of the population."[86]

These sentiments were in line with Tsitsianov's broader perception of the region's residents and Russia's new role in the South Caucasus. A committed imperialist who took pride not only in military glory but also in administrative efficiency, Tsitsianov set the contours of the tsarist imperial policy for decades to come. Such successors as General Ivan Paskevich later echoed many of the views Tsitsianov expressed in the early 1800s. The sine qua non of successful imperial administration, Tsitsianov believed, lay in "sternness" (*strogost'*) coupled with "fairness" (*spravedlivost'*) and "selflessness" (*bezkorystie*).[87]

"Asiatic" intransigence, argued the Russian general, could not be eradicated through annual tribute payments or extended sojourns in St. Petersburg. To combat the locals' supposedly egocentric and corrupting tendencies, tsarist authorities had to demonstrate both the benefits of egalitarian justice and the consequences of straying from prescribed norms. "In an Asiatic," insisted Tsitsianov, "nothing is as effective as fear, as a natural consequence of force. Thus, in my opinion, while expecting, with God's help, a change in Asiatic mores and customs over the course of several generations, for at least thirty years fear, sternness, fairness, justice, and selflessness must be the characteristics or rules of the local administration."[88] Russia's imperial ideology gradually absorbed such orientalist sentiments, expressed, celebrated, and condemned as often on the pages of literary masterpieces as in bureaucratic memorandums.[89]

Tsitsianov's bravado caught up to him on 8 February 1806, when he rode up to the walls of besieged Baku to demand its surrender. The Persian forces inside the city shot the Russian general, decapitated his corpse, and sent his head to the shah in Tehran. Tsitsianov's body was held hostage for five years, and its release to Russian officials once again confirmed tsarist agents' reliance on the region's Armenians. In November 1811, Baku's Armenians, who had kept the slain Russian commander's body in the city's main Armenian church, played the intermediary in the ceremonial handoff of the general's casket to Russian officials.[90]

After Tsitsianov's death, St. Petersburg had to reorient its military, economic, and political resources away from the Caucasus. Facing Napoleon's forces in 1804–7 and the sultan's army in the Balkans in 1806 required a focus on the European theater. Nevertheless, Tsitsianov's successor, General Ivan Vasil'evich Gudovich, continued the Russian war effort against Persia in the

South Caucasus. A less ostentatious and more experienced commander than his predecessor, Gudovich was as eager to conquer Yerevan. Soon after his arrival in Tiflis, the general beseeched the tsar to send him additional troops in order "not only to maintain the integrity of Your Majesty's borders, but also to make incursions into enemy territory."[91]

Making the most of his available resources, Gudovich by October 1808 besieged Yerevan.[92] The general promised to spare life and property if the city surrendered voluntarily and guaranteed safe passage for the Persian garrison back to Persia proper. Should they refuse, however, he vowed to take the city by force and to slaughter the Persian soldiers. With Tsitsianov's failed assault fresh in the minds of the attackers and defenders alike, Gudovich warned the inhabitants of Yerevan to ignore the Russian attempt of 1804, when the young Tsitsianov, "not yet experienced in the military art," failed to take the city.[93] Now, armed with decades of experience and a seasoned army, Gudovich thundered that he had come with enough soldiers "not only to annihilate the fortress, but also to march through all of Persia."[94] Unmoved by the threats, the commander of the Persian garrison sardonically offered to let Gudovich join the shah's army, promising in return overlordship of the Yerevan and Tabriz Khanates.[95]

A two-month siege ensued, during which Gudovich bombarded the fortress with as many ultimatums as artillery shells.[96] But even as small groups of residents, mainly Armenians, voluntarily crossed into tsarist territory during this time,[97] the tsar's army failed—for the second time in four years—to capture Yerevan. An assault on 17 November was repelled at a high cost to the Russian side, and by 28 November Gudovich ordered a retreat.[98] In his report to the tsar, the general blamed the failure on European interference: French engineers, not Persian riflemen, had created the greatest obstacle to Russian victory at Yerevan. Gudovich conceded that the citadel had been buttressed according to "all European military standards" and that the work of French advisers was evident not only in the design of the fortifications and the sophisticated weaponry but also in the previously unseen tactics the Persians employed.[99] Indeed, French military specialists had trained up to four thousand Persian infantrymen and artillerymen.[100]

Tsarist officials saw French interference in Russia's conquest of Persian lands manifested in more than the supply of weapons and engineers. Gudovich complained during the siege, "The French mission to Persia, despite the friendly relations with us, harms my affairs with Persia now more than they did during the war with France. For they have empowered Baba Khan and convinced the Persian government that it can do whatever it wishes."[101] Evidence of European collusion included intercepted letters from the French representative in Tehran, diplomat and general Claude Gardane, to the *sardar* of Yerevan.[102] Despite the Treaty of Tilsit between Napoleon and Alexander, a steady stream of reports reached Gudovich and other Russian officials about the strengthening Franco-Persian alliance, in which Napoleon had assured the shah of his support against the tsar, promising various rewards and territorial gains.[103] Gudovich also received personal letters from various French officials, including from Gardane in Tehran, urging the Russian general to withdraw from Yerevan Khanate and other Persian territories.[104]

Although St. Petersburg's main military objective failed in 1808 and Persian forces remained stationed to the north of the Arax River, other developments heralded success for Russia's imperial ambitions. First, Gudovich's army easily overwhelmed Persian opposition in Nakhichevan and Karabakh, confirming for tsarist officials that only such city-fortresses as Yerevan helped the shah to maintain his grip on the South Caucasus. Second, several local communities welcomed Gudovich's advancing army. He reported that retreating Persian forces had razed Armenian villages and seized their harvests, giving new incentive for the Armenians to turn to Russian protection.[105] When, during his march to Yerevan, Gudovich stopped at the Ejmiatsin monastery, the senior Armenian clergy "joyfully welcomed" him.[106] The Russian general's growing rapport with ecclesiastical and lay Armenians boded well for imperial policy, a fact that Prince Aleksandr Saltykov, a senior aide to the foreign minister, reinforced to the general after the abortive assault on Yerevan. Saltykov emphasized that the tsar "is particularly pleased to see the care with which you protect residents from the effects of war, which roots in them trust and attachment toward the Russian government, to which end the patronage that you demonstrate to the Armenian Ejmiatsin monastery can be especially helpful."[107] With an embryonic alliance forming, tsarist agents soon capitalized on this merger of interests between the Russian state and the Armenians of the South Caucasus.

Soon after the Russian army's withdrawal from Yerevan Khanate, Aleksandr Tormasov succeeded Gudovich, and the First Russo-Persian War turned into a tense standoff. Between 1808 and 1813, occasional skirmishes and many failed negotiations yielded no progress and the dynamic remained influenced as much by European as by Caucasian developments.[108] Citing ill health but perhaps also frustrated by the lack of progress, Tormasov retired and in September 1811 was replaced by the joint command of Generals Philip Paulucci and Nikolai Rtishchev. The former headed the administration of the South Caucasus, while the latter commanded the Caucasus Line and the nearby

Astrakhan Province. Within half a year, however, Paulucci was recalled to St. Petersburg and the region's supreme power fell to Rtishchev, who remained in charge until the arrival in 1816 of one of Russia's most famous Caucasus field marshals, General Aleksei Ermolov.

While the core of the tsarist army struggled against the onslaught of the Grande Armée in Russia proper, in the Caucasus Russian forces confronted an unprecedented array of formidable threats. In the spring of 1812, local Russian troops not only vied for control of Dagestan in the North Caucasus but also fought on three fronts in the South Caucasus: against an Ottoman assault on the Akhalkalaki fortress (which threatened to open an unimpeded corridor to Tiflis), against Persians in Karabakh, and against a new Georgian uprising in Kakheti. This third threat particularly unnerved tsarist authorities not only because of its epicenter in the heart of the regional Russian administration but also because of the furtive manner in which the conspirators had launched their attack by slaughtering Russian soldiers sleeping in their quarters. In his report to the tsar, Paulucci wrote that the rebels had "carried out horrifying atrocities, examples of which the French Revolution presents to us."[109] In no small part thanks to the cooperation of local Armenians, who not only provided information but also fought alongside Russian troops, by early spring Paulucci and Rtishchev had quelled the Georgian uprising and captured its leader, Prince Giorgii, a grandson of the late King Giorgii.[110]

Despite these conflicts, and unfazed by the two abortive attempts to capture Yerevan, Paulucci and Rtishchev made several incursions into Yerevan Khanate to force a peace treaty.[111] By September 1812, reflecting the turn of the tide in the Russo-French and Russo-Ottoman wars, and also the signing of an anti-French Russo-British pact, Rtishchev succeeded in forcing Abbas Mirza to the negotiating table. Although Persians invited British officers to mediate, the shah had few options in the wake of Russian advances in Karabakh and the capture of the British-fortified Lenkoran fortress.[112] On 12 October 1813, the signing of the Treaty of Giulistan in Karabakh ended the First Russo-Persian War.[113] The terms of the accord proved generous to the victor. Persia relinquished control of the khanates of Karabakh, Baku, Ganje, Shakki, Kuba, Shirvan, and parts of Talysh.[114] However, the Yerevan Khanate, with its eponymous capital city and the Ejmiatsin monastery, remained under the shah's control. By 1814, thousands of new Armenian subjects had joined the expanding tsarist empire. The turmoil of the preceding decade had pitted St. Petersburg against an array of enemies in the Caucasus. To fortify itself in the conquered territories, Russia moved to cement an alliance with indigenous communities.

Spies and Settlers: Armenians in the Russian Service

Armenians served in the Romanov military and bureaucracy starting in the era of Peter the Great. From 1722 to 1917, more than 150 Armenians attained the rank of general in the Russian army.[115] Benefiting from religious kinship with the ruling nation and educated in Russia or abroad, these individuals reached professional success that remained out of reach for other tsarist national minorities. For example, the government did not draft Jews until 1827 and even then prevented them from advancing to the officer corps unless they converted to Christianity.[116] Jews also saw such positions as "clerks, artisans, draftsmen, escorts, orderlies, [and] munition factory workers" barred to them by official regulation and de facto practice.[117] Historians have highlighted the participation of integrated Armenians—those long settled and trained in Russia—in the tsarist military, but the story of indigenous Armenian collaboration with Romanov imperialism in the Caucasus in the early 1800s remains less explored.[118]

Russia looked to Armenian cooperation to facilitate its expansion as soon as it entered the interimperial politics of the South Caucasus with the annexation of Kartli-Kakheti. From 1801, the aims of tsarist agents and the hopes of the region's Armenians coincided. Russia relied on Armenians—with their eager participation—to advance into Persian territory and to settle newly conquered lands in the first fourteen years of the nineteenth century.

Just weeks before his assassination, Tsar Paul tasked General Knorring with expanding the Romanov realm in the South Caucasus through diplomacy. The tsar cautioned the general: "Do not seek new [territorial] acquisitions, aside from those that voluntarily search for my patronage; it is better to have allies interested in an alliance than unreliable subjects."[119] Paul made clear which of the indigenous national groups he had in mind. "Look to attract Armenia[ns]," he wrote, "into a rapprochement [*sblizhenie*] for, and through, trade, in order to establish avenues through them, and maintain [their] privileges, but institute our order." More explicitly, the tsar identified Armenians as the key to expanding Russian borders and influence in the region: "Engage now not in conquest but in acquisition through the voluntary consent of Armenia."[120] The tsar had good reason to expect Armenians' cooperation. In February 1801, Armenians from Constantinople petitioned tsarist officials to permit their immigration to Crimea, where they wished to become tsarist subjects.[121] The Armenians pledged to advance regional commerce by establishing silk and paper mills on the peninsula, and they asked for no additional privileges in return beyond those granted to Armenians already living in

Crimea. Apparently sympathetic to this request, Tsar Paul forwarded it to the Senate not long before his death.[122]

Paul's successor, Alexander, shared his father's commitment to an alliance with Armenians. Persian and Ottoman Armenians, as well as other regional Christian groups, were to be recruited to settle the newly annexed Georgian territories. In September 1801, Alexander emphasized to Knorring that his "particular attention must be given to the attraction into Georgia of settlers from abroad, especially Christians."[123] These colonizers were to be granted fertile land, as well as various "assistance," "benefits," and "privileges." Russia specifically targeted Armenians from among the Christian communities living in Ottoman and Persian territories adjacent to Georgia. Alexander's instructions to Knorring in this regard were unequivocal: "I place under your particular attention the attraction of the Armenian nation through various kindnesses [oblaskaniia]. This method, owing to the large population of this people in regions adjacent to Georgia, is one of the most reliable ways for increasing the [regional] population's strength and also for ensuring the dominance of Christians. To this end, I decree that you demonstrate whatever possible patronage of the Ejmiatsin patriarchal monastery and maintain friendly relations with its head."[124]

Foreign-subject Armenians had been enticed by economic privileges in Russia proper since the seventeenth century, but with the turn of the nineteenth century their economic role assumed a broader dimension. Armenians became the frontiersmen of Russian expansion. Several closely intertwined factors coalesced to grant Armenians this status in the Russian political imagination. First, Russians saw their real and mythologized economic prowess under difficult political and social conditions as a sign of Christian resilience in hostile environments, a characteristic that made them capable of settling new domains. Second, the religious bond between Orthodox Russians and Apostolic Armenians, most of whom remained under the hegemony of the shah and the sultan, provided the kind of guarantee of loyalty that the tsar sought in recruiting colonizers. Third, Russians often exaggerated and took advantage of Persian and Ottoman Armenians' minority status in Muslim empires to advocate for their resettlement into ostensibly more welcoming and egalitarian tsarist territories. The tsar summarized some of these perceptions to Tsitsianov in 1802: "Armenians, as an industrious people that holds in its hands the entire trade of this part of the Orient, deserve your particular attention and protection, for, given their persecution in Persia, there can be no doubt that the majority of that people will settle in Georgia as soon as they feel themselves provided with an orderly government."[125] This was a gamble, to be sure, but it paid off.

Armenians heeded the Russian calls. During the First Russo-Persian War, in particular, significant numbers of Persian Armenians became Russian subjects. Most frequently, Armenian *meliks* defected from Persia to Russia with their Armenian peasants. For example, in November 1807, two Armenian *meliks* from Yerevan crossed into Georgia with their peasants and requested noble status in Russian society.[126] General Gudovich reviewed their credentials and granted their request, admitting them into the Russian Table of Ranks with all its rights and privileges. The Russian commander demonstrated similar flexibility and openness to Armenian migrants in another case, where an Armenian *melik* refused to settle on land picked for him by tsarist officials. After the Armenian's protest, Gudovich acquiesced to his demands and granted him and his peasants "however much they need" of state-owned land in the exact locale that the *melik* had specified.[127] Moreover, in March 1809, during heightened tensions with the Yerevan *sardar* in the wake of the abortive Russian assault, incoming Armenians refused to settle in districts adjacent to Persia's borders, fearing incursions from the shah's forces. Once again, Gudovich agreed to their requests and facilitated their relocation to territory farther north, away from Yerevan.[128] In the last stages of the war, with the Persian army on the retreat, tsarist troops freed imprisoned Armenians and resettled them into Russian territory. In one such case from December 1812, Russian soldiers "liberated" three thousand Armenian families that had been "captured" by Persians near Lenkoran and brought them to Russian-held Karabakh.[129]

Tsarist officials also took advantage of Armenian participation in the military conquest of Persian lands. Before his fall from grace, Petr Kovalenskii argued that Georgian kings' ancient control over Yerevan and surrounding lands justified claiming those Persian domains along with the rest of Georgia.[130] To achieve these goals, Kovalenskii emphasized that local Armenians, seeing Ejmiatsin come under tsarist protection, were sure to support Russian expansion. It is hardly surprising, then, that Tsitsianov and other tsarist generals recruited Armenians in Karabakh, Yerevan, and elsewhere to fight alongside the Russian army.

The military participation of non-Slavic subjects of the tsar in various engagements was a staple of Russian strategy since the Muscovite era.[131] Mounted units often included nomadic horsemen, and Tatars, Bashkirs, and Mordvians were regular members of early modern Russian armies.[132] Kalmyk cavalry fought alongside Russians in the Seven Years' War, defended their emperor from Napoleon's invasion, and marched into Paris in 1814.[133]

Indigenous Armenian involvement in the Russian war effort in 1804–13 manifested itself primarily in the form of intelligence gathering. These activities fell into two categories: Persian Armenians sneaking out of Yerevan and other Persian territories into Russian camps with information and Russian officials dispatching Armenians on specific espionage missions. Armenians also served as intermediaries between Russian and Persian negotiators, often ferrying messages between the two sides. Successive tsarist commanders relied on the reports and information provided by Armenians to formulate strategy, ascertain Persian and Ottoman actions, and communicate with entities where the Russian presence was impossible.

Romanov officials capitalized on the Armenian diaspora's transimperial links. As early as 1802, Russian authorities dispatched Armenians from Tiflis into the neighboring states to determine the activities of hostile forces. In one example from June 1802, a Tiflis Armenian returned from Ottoman Akhaltsykh to report to Russian commanders that the Georgian rebel Prince Alexander had joined forces with Lezgin highlanders from Dagestan to mount an anti-Russian campaign.[134] Tsarist agents tracked Alexander's movements in no small part thanks to the work of such Armenian sympathizers. Armenian merchants from the Persian city of Ganje, on arriving in Tiflis to conduct trade, reported to local Russian officials about Alexander's entrance into that city with a small army and eagerly answered all Russian queries.[135] When Prince Alexander set his sights on an outpost with a small Russian garrison in November 1802, several local Armenians snuck into the Russian camps to alert tsarist officials to the imminent danger.[136] A month later, another Armenian merchant of Tiflis who had traveled to Ganje for commerce returned to report to Russian commanders about where Prince Alexander and his allies were and the composition of their troops.[137] Russian commanders dispatched Armenians to Yerevan not only to spy but also to deliver messages to Persian forces.[138] During the Russo-Ottoman conflict, too, Armenians from Kars made unsolicited reports to Russian officers about the movement and composition of local Ottoman forces.[139] Gudovich and his commanders also employed trusted Armenians to gather intelligence in eastern Anatolia, often sending them to Armenian monasteries and churches to speak with the clergy and to determine local conditions.[140] Despite individual instances of Armenian collusion with anti-Russian forces,[141] Armenians cooperated with tsarist authorities by taking advantage of their relatively unhindered cross-border traffic.

Of the diverse intelligence that Armenians provided to Russians before and during the First Russo-Persian War, perhaps none of it was as sensational as the information that Armenian escapees from Yerevan brought to tsarist officers in July 1806.[142] The men told General Petr Nesvetaev that two French envoys, Pierre Amédée Jaubert and Alexandre Romier, had recently arrived at the Persian court.[143] The emissaries had conveyed to the shah Napoleon's request to allow the French navy access to Persian shores and to use the shah's territory to strike the Russian Empire through the South Caucasus. To assuage the shah's fears, various promises and assurances accompanied this audacious scheme. Nevertheless, the Armenians reported—and Nesvetaev verified through other sources—that the shah had declined Napoleon's request, because this daring plot, no matter the result, would only further complicate the shah's relations with the tsar. Disappointed, the Frenchmen returned to France through Ottoman lands. Learning of these developments, Generals Nesvetaev and Gudovich entreated local Ottoman pashas to detain and hand over the French emissaries, promising lucrative rewards.[144] Napoleon and Fath-Ali Shah did sign an accord in May 1807, the Treaty of Finkenstein, but it fell far short of the French emperor's dreams of a strategic alliance.[145]

The autocracy also prized Armenians' ability to reach distant elements beyond the Caucasus. In 1810, Foreign Minister Rumiantsev proposed to Caucasus commander General Rtishchev that an anti-Persian partnership with Afghans could be arranged "through the help of Armenians."[146] Although little came of this initiative, its deliberation among senior tsarist statesmen reveals the Russian confidence in transregional Armenian networks. In this case, officials saw Armenians as a means to secure new military alliances. Coupled with Armenians' active participation in the Russian war effort in the South Caucasus, the view of Armenians as St. Petersburg's key regional ally set the stage for a partnership that remained intact for several decades.

This alliance strengthened in late 1812, when an uprising by elite Georgian subjects of the tsar provided a new opportunity for Armenians to demonstrate their loyalty to Russia. During this rebellion, members of the dethroned Bagrationi family and their allies sought to regain control of Kartli-Kakheti by expelling the Russian administration. Rtishchev's report to the tsar emphasized that nearly "all Kakhetinian nobles and princes" had taken part in the rebellion.[147] Although thousands of ordinary Georgians remained devoted to the Russian state, the protracted resistance of Georgian aristocrats to tsarist rule eroded the foundations of the Russo-Georgian partnership and promoted the increasingly exclusive standing of the South Caucasian Armenians within the regional and imperial hierarchies.

In May 1813, Rtishchev, the supreme commander of the Caucasus, submitted to Tsar Alexander an effusive report on the Armenian role in recent developments. The document's implications cannot be ignored, for, indeed, it set a precedent for Russo-Armenian symbiosis for several decades. "The Armenian people [*narod*]," wrote the tsarist general, "composing a notable portion of Georgia's population, continues to demonstrate exemplary zeal and unwavering loyalty to the Russian Empire. From the establishment of the Russian administration here, the Armenian society has always distinguished itself by its devotion to it, and during all of the often-rising malicious Georgian parties . . . our administration always found in Armenians faithfulness, unmovable by any deceits, and zealous service that they contributed to Your Majesty's advantage."[148]

This juxtaposition of Armenians with Georgians is particularly important not only because the Georgian faith represented a closer dogmatic cousin of Russian Orthodoxy than the Armenian Apostolic creed but also because Georgians possessed a large aristocracy with sizable resources at its disposal. Yet tsarist statesmen identified Armenians as their indigenous allies, eager to capitalize on their commercial and religious networks, which penetrated countries and societies inaccessible to Russian agents.

To be sure, Rtishchev singled out Armenians as an example of a loyal national group. During the recent Georgian uprising in Kartli-Kakheti, stressed the general, when "almost all" locals took up arms or in other ways resisted the Russian presence, Armenians "sacrificed their property and, indeed, their lives, in solidarity with Russian troops, arming themselves in Kakheti against the rebels . . . [and] demonstrated through action against the conspirators the most excellent example of courage and their sincere loyalty to Your Imperial Majesty."[149]

Armenian volunteers provided intelligence to local Russian authorities during their struggle to quell the Georgian insurrection. These Armenian collaborators "readily accepted" Russian tasks and "repeatedly paid with their lives" for the benefit of the regional administration. Armenian merchants of Tiflis, additionally, sold supplies to Russian officials at discounted rates during a poor harvest, when food supplies to Tiflis nearly dried up. Finally, Rtishchev, having summarized the "great diligence, allegiance, and devotion to Your Majesty of the loyal Armenians" of the South Caucasus, expressed confidence that "any encouragement [*poshchrenie*] of them will deliver additional, highly significant benefits for the administration and the local region, increasing their diligence and sparking among Georgians competition with [Armenians]."[150] Thus, the engineers of Russian imperialism continued to hold up Armenians to other regional natives, including Georgians, as an example of proper conduct and devotion.

The autocrat gratefully responded to this Armenian assistance. A month after the signing of the Treaty of Giulistan, he expressed to the Armenians of Georgia his "appreciation to this people for its exemplary loyalty to the Russian Empire and for its many confirmations of its most zealous diligence toward the benefits of" the Russian state.[151] Alexander's proclamation was read, in both Russian and Armenian, to a large Armenian crowd in Tiflis's main square on 22 November 1813. A jubilant ceremony in the city's main Armenian church, led by Archbishop Astvatsatur, celebrated the community's acceptance of this honor. Rtishchev's sentimental summary of this fete to Foreign Minister Rumiantsev emphasized that the "sincere awe and tears of emotional tenderness, . . . visible on the faces of members of every Armenian estate at the event, are the most genuine signs of their true feelings of gratitude and diligence toward His Imperial Majesty." During a citywide Armenian celebration of the emperor's goodwill, wealthy Tiflis Armenians hosted a lavish feast, inviting Russian officials and several Georgian princes. Over two hundred people, from the city's Armenian, Russian, and Georgian communities, attended the banquet. Around the city, Armenians celebrated by decorating their neighborhoods and vending stalls. Rtishchev declared that the Armenians displayed "unfeigned joy that accompanied sincere gratitude" to Russia.

Other manifestations of the Armenian embrace of the tsarist empire fortified the early Russo-Armenian bond. When a new port opened in Baku in August 1809, local Armenian traders were at the forefront of celebrating what they saw as the state's "patronage" and "benevolence" toward the Armenian nation. During the opening ceremony, one Armenian merchant, no doubt eager to secure personal approbation from local Russian officials, summarized the attitudes of the region's Armenians: "From ancient times the Armenian nation has awaited liberation from the yoke of its merciless former rulers. . . . Now behind the shield of His Imperial Majesty's power, we feel complete tranquility while freely exercising our faith and [also feel] the strong sign of the emperor's favor, which protects commerce with egalitarian laws and [allows us to] enjoy new happiness chiefly ahead of others."[152]

Two aspects of this saccharine praise deserve examination. First, the explicit contrast between the socioeconomic life of Armenians under the tsar and under the shah underscored the Armenian preference for Russian patronage. The majority of Eastern Armenians at this time continued to live under the rule of the shah, and the essential Armenian centers of Yerevan and Ejmiatsin remained within the Persian Empire. This exaltation of the ostensible benefits of Russian governance not only served to reinforce the feelings of Armenians already settled in Georgia and other Russian territories but also was intended to attract Armenians still living outside tsarist borders. The speech celebrated the economic freedom of local Armenians while praising the religious liberty they enjoyed under the aegis of the Christian tsar in order to juxtapose these rights with the life of Muslim-ruled Armenians in the neighboring states. Indeed, these not-so-subtle messages signaled not only Armenian gratitude toward Russians but also an effort to recruit Armenians from the neighboring empires.

Second, the reference to the exclusive "happiness" (commercial and, by extension, social rights) enjoyed by Armenians within Russian society cannot be overlooked. Living alongside the tsar's Muslim subjects and also such Christians as Georgians, this reference almost certainly was intended to highlight the perception of Armenians as the Romanov emperor's most "reliable" community in the South Caucasus. Addressing the tsar directly, Baku Armenians drove home these points by praising the "abundance and total happiness" that they enjoyed under the direction of tsarist commerce officials, as well as the "complete tranquility and safety from our former abusers and hostile neighbors" afforded by the command of General Tormasov.[153] With the strengthening political and economic links between Russian authorities and foreign-subject Armenians, the partnership between the Armenian Church and St. Petersburg became the last major element of the rising Russo-Armenian alliance.

Patriarchal Patronage

The head of the Armenian Apostolic Church, the catholicos, doubled as the political leader of the stateless Armenians. From his see in Ejmiatsin, within Persian territory until 1828, the catholicos presided over Armenian ecclesiastical affairs in Russia, Turkey, western Europe, and wherever else large Armenian communities established local eparchies. The combination of ecumenical and political influence over the Armenian diaspora granted the catholicos unique leverage, rendering control over Ejmiatsin essential for any neighboring empire that counted Armenians among its population. As early as 1800, a senior tsarist official in Tiflis emphasized that the catholicos exercised authority over Armenians "spread across the entire face of the earth." The Russian representative wrote: "[His] commitment to the faith and his flock's devotion to him, which he can skillfully utilize, grant [him] a strong influence in his nation."[154]

The Ejmiatsin catholicos, representing a religious minority in Persia, had to negotiate a delicate balance between supporting the growth of Russia's Armenian community and protecting the interests of the shah's own Armenian subjects. Any perceived support of Russian goals, such as encouraging the emigration of Persian Armenians into tsarist territory, was certain to elicit opprobrium or worse from Persian authorities. Tsarist officials understood this. When Catholicos Luka died in 1799 after two decades of leading Ejmiatsin, Russian representatives reported to St. Petersburg: "The position of this monastery and of the politics of the entire Armenian nation demand from its church's leader quite delicate politics, which the [previous catholicoi] always employed, maintaining both their authority and their lifestyle despite all of the tyrannies and cruelties that surrounded them."[155] When Iosif Argutinskii-Dolgorukov, the well-known advocate of Russia's liberation of Armenians, was elected to succeed Luka, one tsarist agent from Tiflis warned St. Petersburg: "The Persians quite dislike Patriarch Iosif, owing to his famous devotion and diligence toward Russia, and this case could be a point of contention in their relations with Russia for a long time."[156] Both concerns and hopes were allayed in March 1801, when Argutinskii-Dolgorukov died while en route to take up his post and before he was consecrated as catholicos.

To be sure, the Armenian Church played an important role in Russian diplomatic calculations as soon as Romanov representatives arrived in the South Caucasus. Knorring and Lazarev entered into close relations with Armenian ecclesiastical officials and kept a watchful eye over their treatment by Persian officials, beginning to present their government as the patron of the Armenians in Persia. When reports reached Knorring that Persians had raided an Armenian monastery and "inflicted many dishonors, abuses, and thefts," the general rushed to notify the tsar.[157]

Yet relations between the Armenian Church and Russian officials were often tense. Knorring assigned Armenian-heritage General Lazarev to facilitate ties between the newly formed Russian administration and the local Armenian ecclesiastical authorities. The young commander worked with Archbishop Efrem, the head of the Armenian eparchy in Georgia, to compile detailed information about the composition, legal and financial procedures, and other matters of the Armenian Church's activities in Georgia.[158] However, in April 1801, Efrem complained to Knorring that Lazarev had interfered in the patriarchal election.

Before the selection of a new catholicos after Argutinskii-Dolgorukov's sudden death, four senior Armenian archbishops from Persia had arrived in Tiflis to pay their respects to the late church leader. According to them and Efrem, Lazarev inexplicably detained in Tiflis these four Armenian clergymen, preventing them from returning to Ejmiatsin, where the election of a new catholicos was set to take place soon.[159] While Lazarev denied these accusations, this incident pushed Lazarev's superior, General Knorring, to emphasize that Russia intended to facilitate an unhindered election of the Armenian religious leader. As Knorring made clear to Lazarev, "The selection of the patriarch depends on the will of the Armenian people and its clergy, and [you] from here on must not engage in even the smallest interference; I prohibit this to you, for such an event can precipitate unpleasant consequences."[160] A crisis, however, was not to be avoided.

Argutinskii-Dolgorukov's death, while alleviating potential conflict with Persia over his devotion to Russia, created a new difficulty. During the year he headed the Armenian Church and before his arrival in Ejmiatsin, Argutinskii-Dolgorukov had named a successor, Archbishop David, the curator of the Ejmiatsin monastery. Although the entire Armenian diaspora of the Russian, Persian, and Ottoman Empires, as well as a few representatives from other states, confirmed a new catholicos, Argutinskii-Dolgorukov's endorsement of David gave his candidacy considerable cachet. The ensuing drama over the new catholicos's selection pressed Russia into defining its relationship with the Ejmiatsin leader and helped solidify an official policy that remained intact for half a century.

In the spring of 1801, candidates for the Ejmiatsin patriarchy were selected. Of the three archbishops, only two were serious contenders: David, the Persian-subject curator of the Ejmiatsin monastery, and Daniil, an Ottoman-subject archbishop from Constantinople.[161] With the death of Argutinskii-Dolgorukov, the Russian Empire reluctantly conceded that the next catholicos would not be a tsarist subject. However, owing to the death of Tsar Paul in March and the wresting away of Kartli-Kakheti, along with its sizable Armenian community, the 1801 election of the Ejmiatsin leader acquired new significance for Russian imperial officials.

This affair was exacerbated when, on 28 April 1801, David, the late church leader's chosen candidate, was secretly "confirmed" as the new head of Ejmiatsin.[162] This unilateral decision of Persian Armenians, supported by the Persian khan of Yerevan but taken without the participation of Armenian delegates from the Ottoman Empire or Russia, caused a tri-imperial crisis. Knorring immediately alerted the freshly crowned Tsar Alexander I to the news. Ottoman Armenians and their government, in a rare display of parallel aims, protested. The Russian envoy in Constantinople, Vasilii Tomara, informed Knorring that "the Armenians around here, or, more specifically, local Armenian bankers, are attached to Daniil" and wished to see no one but him confirmed catholicos.[163] Tomara was adamant that Daniil's potential replacement of David boded poorly for tsarist interests, cryptically labeling the Ottoman Armenian archbishop "devious" (khitryi).[164] The Russian diplomat emphasized that David's election, while unpopular in Constantinople, was legitimate because it not only obeyed Argutinskii-Dolgorukov's endorsement but also corresponded to the wishes of non-Ottoman Armenians. Tomara urged Knorring to help him ensure the confirmation of David and to prevent Constantinople Armenians and the Sublime Porte from replacing him with Daniil. Lazarev, too, backed David, portraying him as "the one who has always been loyal to Russia."[165] The Armenian faith emerged as a key arena for imperial rivalries.

When, in June 1801, Ottoman Armenians dropped their opposition to David's election, and the Porte signaled its consent, the matter appeared resolved. However, within months, Tsar Alexander wrote to his ambassador in Constantinople, Tomara, expressing concern at the number of petitions he had received from various Armenian communities that wanted Daniil, not David, to be catholicos.[166] Convinced that these petitions represented the wishes of the majority of Armenians, the tsar made clear that he supported Daniil.[167] By April 1802, Knorring pressed the khan of Yerevan to allow the replacement of David with Daniil, a decision that he emphasized corresponded to the desires of "all" Russian and Ottoman Armenians and was affirmed by the respective monarchs. Knorring underscored that "according to ancient customs and privileges of the Armenian nation, the choice must be left to the complete and precise decision of this people, without the slightest external interference."[168] The Yerevan khan, embroiled in tensions with the new shah and interested in Russian protection, had little incentive to oppose this turn of events. On 19 May 1802, Constantinople archbishop Daniil received the tsar's formal recognition as catholicos and permission to travel through Russia.[169]

The active involvement—and even interference—of Russian agents in the selection of the catholicos signaled their acknowledgment of his geopolitical leverage. The tsar and his officials vacillated between supporting David and Daniil, ostensibly until they ascertained the desire of the "majority" of Armenians, suggesting that the individual's subjecthood was not as important to St. Petersburg as his popularity with Armenians. The David-Daniil saga also demonstrated the delicate balance that the Russian government maintained between pursuing its interests, such as ensuring the confirmation of a catholicos sympathetic to Russian ambitions, and the wishes of the vast Armenian diaspora, within and outside of the tsar's realm. Russian officials knew little about Daniil's political leanings, but despite the objections of such tsarist agents as Ambassador Tomara and General Lazarev, the affirmation of the candidate who appeared most appealing to Eastern Armenians (in Russia and Persia) dictated the resolution of this affair. Finally, Lazarev's warning to the Yerevan khan about the need to demonstrate "due deference" and proper treatment toward the Ejmiatsin monastery and its clergy evinced Russia's growing position as a patron of Armenians living under Muslim rule.[170] For the rest of the nineteenth century, this element of Russo-Armenian ties not only influenced the politics of the Caucasus but also informed the Eastern Question.

With Daniil's appointment, St. Petersburg continued to promote itself as the protector of Christians in neighboring Muslim empires. Since the Treaty of Küçük Kaynarca in 1774, Russia's emperors pressed successive sultans to abide by their commitment to safeguard the material and spiritual cultures of their minority Christians.[171] By the early nineteenth century, this notion of Russian protection for foreign-subject Christians had spread to include Persia. Indeed, Tsitsianov intimated this ideology to Daniil in February 1803, pledging to use to Daniil's "benefit" all the "resources and methods" that he had at his disposal.[172]

Russian authorities confirmed their commitment to Daniil when, in April 1803, Tsitsianov learned that Daniil endured "harassment and offenses, inflicted on him by the hate of various evil people, who are driven solely by greed."[173] The offending villains were not Persian khans or bandits, but rather the shah's Armenian subjects. A sizable group of Armenians in Yerevan, coalescing around a few wealthy patrons, mounted a vociferous campaign in support of David. Responding to the apparent harassment of Daniil by Persian Armenians, Tsitsianov vowed to uphold the tsar's decision at all costs, if need be with the use of the "invincible and mighty" Russian army. The general threatened that if any more "offenses and disrespect" or "animal-like" abuses befell Daniil, the tsar's "terrifying ire" would be unleashed on the tormentors of the legitimate Armenian catholicos. Tsitsianov cleverly appealed to the shared Christian faith of the Armenian and Russian peoples and juxtaposed it to the Muslim rule of the shah and the Yerevan khan. "Come to your senses!" pleaded the general. "Compare the meekness [*krotost'*] of Christian rule with the ferocity [*liutost'*] of Muslim rule; measure the tyranny of the latter against the tolerance of the former—you will see that ours reflects Christian laws inscribed in the Holy Gospel, while theirs [reflects] contrary laws. Think again and fear!"[174]

Tsarist patronage of the Armenian Church leadership soon bore geopolitical fruit. After Tsitsianov's failed assault on Yerevan in 1804, Armenian clergy at great risk organized the relocation of Persian Armenians into Georgia, where they were granted generous tracts of land. In one case, Archbishop Hovannes oversaw the migration of some 11,100 Armenian families from Yerevan to Georgia, an act for which Tsitsianov praised him to the tsar.[175] Soon thereafter, suggesting his approval of this emigration, Catholicos Daniil nominated Hovannes to oversee the Armenian eparchy of Georgia. In his support of this decision, Tsitsianov wrote to Tsar Alexander that Hovannes demonstrated "unlimited diligence toward Russian benefits and his devotion to [the tsarist empire]."[176] The emperor responded by confirming Hovannes in his new role. The tsar also, as attestation of the Armenian priest's "excellent diligence toward Russian benefits," presented Hovannes with a "paean" to commemorate his contributions to Russia's efforts in the resettlement of Persian Armenians.[177]

At the onset of the First Russo-Persian War in 1804, the shah's authorities removed Catholicos Daniil from Ejmiatsin, suspecting him of covert partnership with Russian authorities after the tsar's insistence on his promotion over David. Persian-subject David temporarily took the reins of the Armenian

Church. In a sign that Persian officials understood the degree to which many senior Armenian clergymen, and Daniil in particular, sympathized with Russian political aims, the Persian government imprisoned the catholicos for more than three years. In September 1807, after Gudovich made Daniil's release and reinstatement a core demand of negotiations with Persian crown prince Abbas Mirza, the senior prelate returned to Ejmiatsin.[178]

Despite, or perhaps owing to, this experience, Daniil continued to correspond with tsarist statesmen, not only in the Caucasus but also in St. Petersburg. In 1808, not long before Gudovich's renewed assault, Daniil wrote to the minister of education, Count Petr Zavadovskii, thanking him for Russia's patronage of Armenians and asking Zavadovskii to continue cooperating with Russia's Armenian elites, including the Lazarev family.[179] Persian authorities did not overlook the Armenian religious leader's close rapport with the shah's foe. When the tsar's army reentered Yerevan Khanate in October 1808, Persian officials again removed Daniil from Ejmiatsin to Yerevan, where the catholicos died—apparently of natural causes—not long after the siege. With a new Ejmiatsin election looming, the Russian Empire solidified its policy toward this important event.

As Argutinskii-Dolgorukov had done in 1799, Daniil before his death in February 1809 endorsed a candidate to succeed him. The chosen priest, Archbishop Efrem, was a Russian subject who was reputed to sympathize with St. Petersburg's political goals, especially with regard to relocating Persian Armenians into Russian territory. The tsar and his ministers did not object to Efrem's confirmation, and they ensured that the frail catholicos's wishes were widely publicized throughout Russia proper and the Caucasus.[180] When Assistant Foreign Minister Saltykov asked General Gudovich to provide his assessment of Efrem's candidacy, the state's geopolitical imperatives were on full display. "It goes without saying," emphasized Saltykov, "that the Russian court must give its backing to that candidate, who, invited by the voice of the people, is well known for his commitment and diligence toward the benefits of the Russian Empire." So crucial was the placement of a Russian-backed candidate, such as Efrem, at the apex of the Armenian Church, that Saltykov ordered Gudovich to do everything in his power to prevent the Persian government from installing its own candidate—David, for instance. The potential implications of this decision compelled Saltykov to grant Gudovich the authority to confirm, without waiting for the tsar's consent, any Armenian-chosen candidate whom Gudovich deemed to be "a person loyal to Russia and pleasing to the Armenian people."[181]

The tsar's court pursued a goal of ensuring the election of a catholicos who was first and foremost sympathetic to Russian politics. Yet at the same time the Russian government sought to merge its interests with Armenian desires. True, so paramount were state interests in this matter that Saltykov conceded that even in the unlikely event of Persian-backed David's election—which Russia opposed—the tsarist court could still affirm this selection as long as David could be used to pursue Russian goals, such as securing a peace treaty with Persia.[182] But these issues were left to Gudovich's discretion, with Saltykov emphasizing, "The most important wish of the tsar emperor is that the selection of the patriarch combine the benefits for the Russian court with the desires of the Armenian people, leaving everything else to your discretion."[183]

After Daniil's death in February 1809, several senior Armenian clergymen from Ejmiatsin endorsed Efrem, as did many lay Armenians in Georgia and the rest of the South Caucasus. Despite the opposition of some Persian Armenians, the Armenians of the Ottoman and Russian Empires elected Efrem as the next catholicos. Gudovich rushed to affirm this selection in the name of his government, expressing to St. Petersburg confidence in the new catholicos's political reliability. Efrem's "long-term residence in Russia and the immense generosities displayed to him by His Imperial Majesty," stressed the general, "can be firm guarantees that he, of course, will remain forever loyal and diligent to Russia, [which is why] I consider that his royal confirmation as the Armenian patriarch could be as compatible with Russia's interests as [it could be] pleasing to the local Armenian people and clergy."[184] Tsar Alexander's confirmation of Efrem's election in September 1809 praised the new catholicos for his "sincere diligence and loyalty to my imperial throne, as demonstrated through many exploits."[185]

Despite frequent conflict, Persian authorities at times courted Ejmiatsin as actively as their Russian rivals. Whereas as recently as 1807 the then pro-Russian catholicos, Daniil, was arrested and forcefully removed from Ejmiatsin to Yerevan, the reception that the new, openly pro-Russian catholicos Efrem received in 1809 illustrated important developments. Persian crown prince Abbas Mirza personally greeted the prelate on his arrival in the Persian realm. The crown prince insisted that Efrem and his retinue take an oath of allegiance to the shah and also demanded that Efrem wear the awards that Abbas Mirza had presented to him in addition to the medals given by the tsar.[186] At the same time, Abbas Mirza—to the Russians' surprise—decreed an annual payment to Efrem equivalent to 4,000 rubles, a sum that exceeded the salaries of any preceding Armenian catholicos. These Persian overtures toward the Ejmiatsin leader appeared at least partially successful, because soon after his arrival in Ejmiatsin Efrem requested the venerable Armenian monastery's treasures, which Tsitsianov had removed in 1804 "for safekeeping" in Tiflis, to be returned to the monastery in Persian territory. Despite Tormasov's resistance, the autocrat approved this request in late October 1810. For the next several decades, this Russo-Persian competition for influence over the Ejmiatsin leader, entwined with the role of Ottoman Armenians and their government's interests, defined the dynamics of the tri-imperial rivalry in which Russian policies toward Armenians evolved.

The Russo-Armenian encounter of the early nineteenth century represented a two-way dynamic. Armenians invited tsarist patronage and made tangible contributions to the fortification of Romanov rule in the South Caucasus. During these formative years of the Russo-Armenian partnership, Armenians entered the tsarist service and began to achieve prominence within Russia's social and bureaucratic hierarchy.[187] To cite one example from this era, the son of Armenian-heritage tsarist general Iosif Bebutov, Vasilii, who had been raised in Tiflis during his father's posting in the South Caucasus, returned to the region in 1810 to serve under the command of General Tormasov after becoming the first Armenian to graduate from the elite Cadet Corps in St. Petersburg.[188] Individual Armenians complemented the hundreds of non-Russian officials in the tsarist service, in which aristocratic Baltic Germans, Finns, and even Poles often reached senior positions at the turn of the nineteenth century.[189] In contrast, other groups, most notably Jews and some Muslims, were barred from the Russian bureaucracy and military until decades later. In the first fourteen years of the nineteenth century, in the shadow of the restlessness of North Caucasian highlanders and the passive resistance of Georgian elites, among the native peoples of the Caucasus Russia had no closer ally than the Armenian nation.

The estate-based Russian social system of the early nineteenth century granted not the individual rights characteristic of modern citizenship but collective rights and obligations that allowed it to respond to the growth of the empire.[190] To be sure, some ethnic or national communities received preferential status based on their immediate or projected contributions to the vitality of the empire. Alexander Morrison has argued that in the 1860s, Russia "saw the creation of legal and administrative differences that offer some parallels to the division between metropole and colony seen in the British and French empires."[191] But such differences existed in the early decades of the nineteenth century, as St. Petersburg privileged Armenians and other groups in a manner that challenged narratives of European hegemony over non-Europeans. While the Russo-Armenian bond was grounded in religious kinship, Armeno-Georgian and Russo-Georgian ties show that the autocracy considered factors other than religious affiliation when picking its allies.

Russia annexed the South Caucasus mainly for political reasons, including a desire to maintain parity with the expanding French and British Empires, but it also remained eager to take advantage of the economic opportunities interstate and international trade provided in the Near East. With all of Georgia and several Persian khanates annexed and thousands of new subjects absorbed into the tsar's realm, the Romanov state between 1801 and 1813 made key advancements on its way to claiming the Caucasus. However, with such formidable Persian citadels as Yerevan—the capture of which had eluded two tsarist generals—still maintaining the shah's grip on parts of the region, Emperors Alexander I and Nicholas I (1825–55) set their sights on consolidating their imperial possessions by completing the Russian conquest of Eastern Armenia. New challenges and opportunities between 1814 and 1829, when St. Petersburg finally seized Yerevan and Ejmiatsin, shaped and reshaped the evolving Russo-Armenian partnership.

CHAPTER 2

Armenians in the Russian Political Imagination, 1814–1829

In 1816, Admiral Count Nikolai Mordvinov envisioned his empire's future engagement with, and domination of, the Orient. Russia's first naval minister and one of its most eminent political thinkers, Mordvinov suggested that adroit diplomacy and economic incentives would do more than artillery and bayonets to ensure Russia a peaceful and profitable future in the Caucasus and beyond. "Europe is antiquated and requires little of our surplus," he argued. "Asia is young, immature, [and] can connect with Russia more closely, and all [our] superiority in enlightenment and labor will serve to increase Russia's might over this vast and most important part of the world."[1] Buoyed by recent triumphs over the French emperor, the Persian shah, and the Ottoman sultan, the tsarist elite set its sights on claiming the still-unconquered parts of the Caucasus. To do so, as Mordvinov and other influential liberals proposed, required flexible strategies that drew Caucasus natives into participation in Russian imperialism.

In the first half of the nineteenth century, St. Petersburg relied on the Armenian diaspora within and outside the Russian Empire to help it absorb the Caucasus. This chapter explores the contingent objectives of an imperial project aimed toward distinct communities of the Armenian diaspora: impoverished immigrants from the Ottoman and Persian Empires, established merchants in southern Russia, and elite families aspiring to social and political prominence in St. Petersburg and Moscow. Because they were all tsarist subjects, the government needed tailored responses to their needs. Through shifting but complementary Russian perceptions of Armenians in the 1820s, the autocracy both recruited and distrusted Armenians from abroad, and it concurrently promoted and restrained the commerce of Armenians already settled in southern Russian cities.

These circumstances illustrate the evolution of a multifaceted project that resists traditional labels of "colonial expansion" or "economic exploitation." Russia's encounter with Armenians in the 1810s and 1820s, when thousands of Armenians from Persia and the Ottoman Empire became tsarist subjects, shows that Ann Laura Stoler and Carole McGranahan's concept of "imperial formations" is a more appropriate description of the tsarist nationalities policy under Alexander I (1801–25) and the early reign of Nicholas I (1825–55). Unlike the powers of Victorian western Europe, imperial formations "are not, as we once imagined them, based on fixed forms and secure relations of inequity: they produce unstable relationships of colonizer and colonized, of citizen to subject, and unequal struggles over the forms of inclusion and the principles of differentiation."[2]

Russians tried to reconcile their often-divergent perceptions as Armenians resettled into Russia and the newcomers' improving economic position gave rise to acrimony. During this era, the state's nationalities policies were less contradictory than conditional. Moreover, in their dialogue with tsarist officials, lay and ecclesiastical Armenian community leaders emphasized sociopolitical ambitions, demonstrating the leverage the tsars' non-Russian subjects in the Caucasus exercised. The Russo-Armenian relationship in this era can shed light on how Russian imperial rule was established, organized, and maintained. This chapter uncovers the processes through which statesmen essentialized Armenians into broad categories: hardworking frontiersmen, greedy minorities, political allies, faithful comrades, and privileged brokers.

Studying several groups within the Armenian diaspora, and the role Armenians played in the discourse of such statesmen as Mordvinov, shows the complexity of the Russo-Armenian encounter. From starving refugees on the outskirts of Tiflis to powerful philanthropists in central St. Petersburg, Armenians experienced different—usually complementary, but sometimes incongruous—policies. Social and economic status, geography, acculturation, and other factors shaped the autocracy's perceptions of its Armenian subjects. While the Lazarev family of Russified Armenian magnates attained the standing of mediators between the tsarist government and the external Armenian diaspora, long-settled Armenians in southern Russian cities experienced a waning of economic privileges, as senior officials debated and disagreed over the socioeconomic role that Armenians were playing, and should play, in Russia.

To be sure, Romanov politics evolved as rapidly as Romanov policies. The rule of Tsar Nicholas I marked a departure from his brother's more progressive nationalities laws, when the state granted incentives to foreigners to attract them to the Russian Empire.

The Lazarev Dynasty

Assessing how, and why, the Russian state came to support the Lazarev Institute of Oriental Languages reveals the internal mechanisms of imperial rule. An elite Armenian family long settled in Moscow, the Lazarevs established a private academy for Armenian, Russian, and other children to study Eastern languages and cultures in preparation for careers in private commerce and state service. Rather than an Orientalist scholarly center on the Kazan model, the Lazarev Institute became an important school for youths of several nationalities whose career aspirations accounted for Russia's expansion into the Caucasus.[3] Staffed less by professional scholars than by young teachers, the Lazarev Institute in the first years of its existence sought to integrate distinct experiences of empire: those of state agents and newly incorporated natives of the Orient, and also those of intellectuals and the lay masses.

The Russian government in the early nineteenth century confronted not just the geopolitical and economic demands of its expansionist agenda but also its epistemological requirements, resulting in the state's gradual support of the Lazarev family's vision of social and political integration. To achieve imperial cohesion among Russia's polyethnic communities, St. Petersburg pursued what one historian has termed "civic Russification" by relying on the Lazarev Institute of Oriental Languages to educate both new Armenian immigrants and future Russian clerks.[4] Unlike the aggressive "cultural," haphazard "administrative," or passive "unplanned" variations of Russification that another scholar has identified, "civic Russification" constituted a "rather modest and tolerant program" that "would have recognized bilingualism and respected non-Russian cultures."[5] Often fruitless, this effort was more notable in the late imperial era, but the Lazarev Institute shows its early iterations in the first half of the nineteenth century.

More than a proverbial imperial middle ground, the Lazarev Institute of Oriental Languages institutionalized Armenian collaboration with Russian politics in the first half of the nineteenth century. A privately conceived but state-backed organization, the Lazarev Institute provided a dual service to its Russian patrons and mostly non-Russian students. It helped disseminate cultural knowledge and created avenues for social mobility by helping the children

FIGURE 2.   The original building of the Lazarev Institute of Oriental Languages in Moscow. Today it houses the Armenian Embassy to Russia. Author's collection.

of poor Armenian families to attain successful careers, while staffing the imperial Foreign Ministry and other organs with skilled civil servants. The institute's immigrant graduates became socially, culturally, and economically rooted in their adopted homeland, and many of them later added to the government's expertise on the Orient. In acknowledging the institute's contributions to Russia's imperial aims, Tsars Alexander I and Nicholas I assigned prominent statesmen to oversee its growth. Well before St. Petersburg's conquest of Eastern Armenia from Persia in 1828, the Lazarevs facilitated the Old Regime's "civic Russification" of Armenians and other natives of the Caucasus. Given the intermediary position of the Lazarev Institute in the political discourse of empire, the academy's history reveals the integrating mechanisms of tsarist rule in an era of rapid territorial expansion and population absorption.

The Lazarevs were entrepreneurs, bureaucrats, philanthropists, generals, and educators. In addition to establishing a renowned academy, they allied with the Armenian Church, oversaw the resettlement of Persian and Ottoman Armenians into Russia, and acted as intermediaries between the tsarist state and the Armenian nation and church. The history of their family is one of acculturation, resistance, co-optation, and interethnic discourse between Russian

and non-Russian elites under the Romanovs. By establishing the Lazarev Institute of Oriental Languages, they responded directly to the demands of the
Russian state as it absorbed foreign-subject Armenians and other Near East-
erners into the empire. The institute represented Russia's broader objective
of understanding its new imperial possessions, their inhabitants, and their
cultures in pursuit of their civic integration.

The Lazarev genealogy in Russia began in 1747, when Eleasar Nazar'ian
Lazariants, the scion of a wealthy Armenian family from New Julfa, emigrated
from Persia. The young man Russified his name to Lazar Nazarovich Lazarev
and, in 1758, purchased a silk mill on the outskirts of Moscow, paving the way
for his growing family's financial future. Lazar and his wife, Anna, had three
sons: Ivan, Minas, and Ekim (Ioakim). Reflecting the family's economic position, in 1774 the Lazarevs were admitted into the noble estate, receiving the
right to own serfs and fortifying the economic foundation on which their social and political clout would be based in the following century. In Moscow,
where the Lazarevs financed the construction of the city's second Armenian
church in 1779, they were part of a small but vibrant Armenian community
that traced its presence in the city to the late fourteenth century.[6]

The death of Ivan Lazarev, the eldest son of the clan's patriarch, precipitated the rise of what later became the Lazarev Institute of Oriental Languages.
As one of Catherinian Russia's wealthiest tycoons, Ivan not only benefited
from his father's wealth but also amassed his own fortune. He engaged in the
tsarist capital's jewelry trade and accumulated land, factories, and mines from
other prominent industrialists and aristocrats.[7] Cognizant of the advantages
his family enjoyed in Russia, Ivan Lazarev set out to improve the lives of Armenian youths in Russia and, indirectly, to strengthen Russo-Armenian ties.
At his death in October 1801, he left 200,000 rubles for the establishment of
"an academic institution for Armenians" in Moscow.[8] His younger brother
Ekim, agent and custodian of this will, shared his late brother's vision and
would contribute 300,000 rubles to it by 1823.[9] But without a home for the
school or permission from authorities, more than a decade passed before the
Lazarev dream was realized.

From the moment the school opened in 1815, the Lazarevs fashioned it as
a vehicle for Armenian upward mobility. Its original name was the Armenian
Lazarev Academy, reflecting the institution's focus on the education of the Armenian diaspora's youth. By 1819, the first year for which statistical data is
available, the academy enrolled thirty-one pupils.[10] Yet the academy attracted
fewer pupils, wealthy or poor, than the Lazarevs had hoped, and the family
petitioned local education officials as well as Tsar Alexander I to grant the academy more advanced accreditation, often invoking the ecumenical bond be-

tween Russians and Armenians to help make their case.[11] That theme found a receptive audience among some layers of the educated Russian public. The newspaper *Moskovskie vedomosti* (Moscow Herald), in hailing the new institution as an affirmation of the "Christian brotherhood" between Russians and Armenians, predicted that "an alliance forged on this solid foundation with a nation that is distinguished by its exemplary internal connection, a broad trade in a large part of the Orient, and especially [one that] maintains the closest and most direct relations with India and Persia, provides . . . a vast field of flattering [*lestnye*] benefits for Russia."[12] Invigorated by such support, Ekim Lazarev sought to have the academy be designated a *gimnaziia*, or secondary school, akin to similar privately funded lyceums, the graduates of which automatically entered the lowest rung of the Table of Ranks. The early debate over the mission of the new institution allowed the Lazarev family to engage with officials at a time when important changes to Russian secondary education were transforming the social, economic, and political ties of the Russian aristocracy.

The government, keen to standardize the education of nobles by nudging them away from private tutors and into universities, supported the formation of several lyceums in the early nineteenth century. These privately conceived but state-backed institutions became intermediate points for elites who aspired to continue their education at universities or to join the civil service. After the formation of the preparatory academy (*pansion*) alongside Moscow University in 1779, several more lyceums appeared between 1803 and 1820. These academies recruited both Russians and non-Russians, and all but the Imperial Tsarskoe Selo Lycée admitted limited numbers of nonnobles.[13] Although regulations fluctuated throughout the first quarter of the century, the graduates of some of these elite institutions were often admitted into higher rungs of the Table of Ranks than university graduates. The Lazarev family wished to create an analogous institution for Armenians and non-Armenians in Moscow, distinguishing their academy by a broad curriculum that included Oriental studies.

The Lazarevs imagined that their lyceum would fill an important niche in the Russian educational system. It would become only the second preparatory academy in Moscow and only the eighth such institution in the empire, and it would also reflect a growing interest in and demand for Oriental studies in Russia. Orientology in this era attracted Russian elites not only because of its potential political benefits but also because Russians, "conscious of their own Asian heritage," sought to explore their hybrid East-West identity through the study of the Near East and Asia.[14] Although Emperors Peter and Catherine had promoted the study of the Orient in the eighteenth century, the first serious steps toward the professionalization of this endeavor occurred with the formation of chairs of Eastern languages and literatures at three Russian universities in 1804.[15] In 1810, Sergei Uvarov, who would later become minister of education and president of the Academy of Sciences, urged the government to establish a scholarly Asian academy in St. Petersburg, where diplomats, teachers, translators, and administrators could be trained in thirty-one languages, including Chinese, Arabic, Persian, Turkic, Hebrew, and, in the future, Armenian and Georgian.[16] Distinct motives drove Uvarov and Lazarev, but they were part of a growing Russian elite that stressed the sociopolitical value and urgency of Orientology in view of the empire's expansion.

The government had its own ideas for the Lazarev institution. In June 1819, the Chief Administration of Schools (Glavnoe pravlenie uchilishch) discouraged Ekim Lazarev from turning the fledgling academy into a general-purpose lyceum, warning him of the stiff competition for students and faculty that it was likely to face from its more established and prestigious counterparts. Instead, the Chief Administration of Schools proposed a narrow curriculum focused on the vocational training of future businessmen, "since they [Armenians] mostly engage in trading, and various industry."[17] It argued that such an institution would "have its own purposeful goal, distinct from others, making it quite commendable and useful in this regard."[18] To attain this vision, the administration urged the academy to convert into an exclusively Armenian institution with only Armenian-heritage pupils.

An incensed Ekim Lazarev insisted that his family's academy must admit non-Armenian students alongside Armenians in order to increase its "general benefit" to the Russian state as well as the Armenian nation and thereby attain the prestige enjoyed by comparable institutions.[19] Lazarev also rejected the Chief Administration of Schools' recommendation for a vocational curriculum based on commercial training. He envisioned the graduates of his academy advancing not only to bazaars and trade posts but also to universities and bureaucratic offices. For these goals to succeed, Armenian pupils had to be trained in a diverse environment that fostered Armenian and non-Armenian interaction. In his appeal, Lazarev also cited the government's interests and emphasized the state benefits of agents versed in Armenian and other Oriental languages, cadres "in whom, it is known, the Department of Foreign Affairs has a need."[20] Thus, the Lazarevs sought to facilitate the integration of Armenians into the Russian Empire as both agents and subjects.

Although Ekim Lazarev declined the Chief Administration of Schools' recommendations and state officials rejected Lazarev's petitions for granting his institution the status of a *gimnaziia*, the two sides compromised and the academy grew rapidly. By late 1821, its seventy students enjoyed a wide range of classes: Armenian Apostolic and Russian Orthodox doctrines; Armenian, Russian, Persian, Latin, French, and German grammar and literature; rhetoric and ethics; physics and natural history; macroeconomics; "general commercial science"; "general and particularly Russian history"; law; geography and statistics; and calligraphy, drawing, and dancing.[21]

This curriculum mirrored the "encyclopedic" programs of other prestigious lyceums,[22] but only the Lazarev academy offered training in Armenian, Persian, and other Eastern cultures. Yet at least one other analogous institution in the Russian Empire—the Volynskii lyceum in Kremenets—emphasized the national education of a non-Russian group. The Volynskii lyceum, in modern Ukraine, catered to the Polish nobility, used Polish as the language of instruction, employed almost exclusively Polish faculty, and had just one Russian teacher, responsible for language, literature, and history courses.[23] The Lazarev academy differed from this model not only because Russian was its primary language of instruction but also because the institution was located not in the imperial periphery but in Moscow. The Lazarevs sought social and political integration, not the fortification of an insular national identity.

By the early 1820s, the academy's status began to stabilize. Students benefited from a 3,000-volume library, an expanded curriculum, larger enrollment, and an improved financial situation, all of which added punch to Ekim Lazarev's continuing appeals for elevating the status of his institution. The petitions succeeded. In May 1823, Tsar Alexander I approved the first charter of the rebranded Armenian Lazarev Gymnasium of Advanced Studies and Oriental Languages.[24] The charter emphasized that the *gimnaziia* catered to all Armenians and non-Armenians, irrespective of subjecthood or financial status. Merit, not social status, determined admission. In theory, "anyone" demonstrating academic promise and interest in Oriental languages and cultures could seek admission. Into the ranks of subsidized students, the *gimnaziia* admitted "preferably children of the poorest families and orphans of the Armenian confession, not excluding children of other nations [as long as funds permit]."[25] Thus, five years before Russia wrested Eastern Armenia from Persia, the tsar affirmed the Lazarev vision for the civic integration of Armenians before their geopolitical incorporation. The Lazarevs grew increasingly confident in their promotion of this strategy, emphasizing to officials the political and economic benefits to the tsarist state of their institution—the first lyceum with a focus on Oriental studies. "The importance of these goals in terms of Russia's commercial as well as political relations is so obvious, that it requires no explanation," they declared boldly.[26] The first institution of its kind in Russia, the Lazarev academy preceded the introduction of Arabic, Persian, and Turko-Tatar courses at the famed First Kazan Gymnasium in 1836.[27]

The Lazarev *gimnaziia* focused on producing graduates for state (mainly civil) service and commerce. It sought not only to provide "much-needed" teachers, translators, and bureaucrats versed in Armenian, Turkish, Persian, and Arabic but also to educate the public about the culture and history of these peoples.[28] With Russia's southern borders creeping outward, the Lazarevs argued that their institution would fill an important void in the empire's professional and academic spheres by producing dedicated cadres of well-educated and ambitious young men. On graduation, foreign-subject Armenians were promised "complete freedom" to become Russian subjects or to return to their original state of residence.[29]

The confirmed charter delivered prestige but fell short of granting the rights and privileges Ekim Lazarev had sought. The Armenian magnate hoped that his institution would receive the same economic exemptions the empire's elite lyceums did, and he also wanted an assigned benefactor (*pokrovitel'*), who would formally represent the monarch and thus remove the need for the Education Ministry's oversight. The Lazarevs showed their political sagacity in pursuing eminent statesmen, members of the tsar's inner circle, for this post. When former war minister Count Aleksei Arakcheev visited the school in November 1823, Lazarev seized his chance.[30] A vicious martinet whom colleagues and subordinates despised for his sternness and, later, for his draconian enforcement of the ill-fated military colonies project, Arakcheev enjoyed the tsar's trust, making him attractive to the Lazarevs.

Although less than a year had passed since the original charter's confirmation, Ekim Lazarev and his assistants drew up a revised charter that revealed their institution's increasingly explicit focus on Oriental studies rather than general education and commercial training. Education Minister Aleksandr Golitsyn told his colleagues: "Without any violation of the general rules [the Lazarev *gimnaziia*] can be freed from the oversight of the Education Ministry and, as a special kind of institution, which educates mainly Armenian children, be placed under a special supreme leadership."[31] The Council of Ministers agreed with this opinion in November 1824, a decision that the tsar soon confirmed.[32] Count Arakcheev became the school's principal (*nachal'nik*), making him the official representative of the government in all matters pertaining to the institution. After nearly a decade as a small private academy, the Lazarev Gymnasium of Oriental Languages gained the formal backing of the Russian state, providing St. Petersburg with a new tool for integrating non-Russians into the empire's social, political, and cultural spheres.

Several privileges accompanied this support. First, the *gimnaziia* was allowed to establish its own printing press and to use the state seal. Second, the school's main building on Armenian Lane in central Moscow, as well as all other structures owned by the Lazarev family for the explicit benefit of the *gimnaziia*, was "freed forever from all billeting and all rural and city duties."[33] Moreover, the *gimnaziia*'s professors and teachers were classified as "serving in active state service, enjoying all rights and privileges in the promotion of rank and eligibility for the receipt of [royal] graces for excellence in service."[34] Finally, Lazarev *gimnaziia* faculty members were permitted to wear the state-issued uniforms of the Moscow Educational District.

Radical transformations in the Lazarev *gimnaziia*'s mission and identity continued in the 1820s. The tsar's unexpected death in late 1825, the subsequent Decembrist uprising, the Second Russo-Persian War (1826–28), and the death of the institution's founder, Ekim Lazarev, in 1826, contributed to the school's reorientation. By 1827, Arakcheev had left his role as *popechitel'* (trustee) of the institution, a position that during his tenure had amounted to little more than a sinecure, according to one historian.[35] Before another eminent statesman replaced Arakcheev in 1828, the tsarist state refocused its attention on this useful instrument of imperialism. The education authorities tasked distinguished Orientologist Christian Martin Frähn, economist G. F. Shtrokh, and linguist F. Adelung with composing a new charter for the institution. As a result of these scholars' proposals and the petitions of a Lazarev descendent, Ivan Ekimovich, on 26 December 1827 the committee sanctioned the newly reimagined Lazarev Institute of Oriental Languages.

The state's elevation of the Lazarev institution from a *"gimnaziia"* to an "institute" represented another step toward "civic Russification" and integrating Near Eastern natives into the empire. It also reflected two important developments. First, tsarist agents recognized the school's success in producing cadres of professional clerks versed in Oriental languages and cultures. By the later 1820s, little doubt existed that the lyceum "opened up broad prospects for staffing the Russian diplomatic agency."[36] As the Lazarev Institute's reputation expanded beyond Russia's Armenian diaspora, growing numbers of the institution's early graduates joined the ranks of state translators, junior bureaucrats, and language teachers. Second, this promotion acknowledged the state's need for such bureaucrats and diplomats, validating the Lazarevs' proclamations and coinciding with the empire's expansion into Persian domains in the South Caucasus. Thanks to the Lazarev vision, by 1828 Russia was well positioned to incorporate the population as well as the territory of the South Caucasus. When, in the Treaty of Turkmenchai, the shah ceded to the tsar Yerevan and Nakhichevan, the tsarist bureaucracy had moved closer to recognizing that the need for an institution like the Lazarev Institute had never been more acute. The selection of a new patron confirmed these priorities.

With Arakcheev's departure, the Lazarevs and their allies in the Armenian Church launched a campaign for a new patron. The target of their efforts became diplomat and general Konstantin von Benkendorf.[37] Another member of the tsar's inner circle and a former envoy in Baden and Stuttgart, Benkendorf had recently earned Armenians' respect for his military prowess during the Second Russo-Persian War, where his forces captured Ejmiatsin and routed Persian troops near Yerevan. By March 1828, just weeks after that conflict ended, Ivan Lazarev and Archbishop Hovannes successfully appealed to Nicholas I for Benkendorf to become the institute's *pokrovitel'*. This symbolic act implicitly recognized the general's role in the political annexation of Eastern Armenia and his new role in the civic integration of Armenians.

Yet the post-Decembrist political climate produced obstacles for Benkendorf. Per the monarch's decree of 19 August 1827, reflecting the new tsar's conservatism and also the Lazarev Institute's redefined identity, the institution's royally appointed patron now fell under the oversight of the Education Ministry. Under the leadership of the rightist and chauvinistic Aleksandr Shishkov, the ministry scrutinized the activities of the empire's academies with reinvigorated zeal. To assuage Shiskov's potential concerns, Benkendorf assured him in April 1828: "[I am] prepared to contribute to the prospering of this broadly beneficent [*obshchepoleznogo*] Oriental nest [*rassadnika*], especially because the institute's overall aim is to provide to the youth that education which is necessary for military and civil service. Moreover, the Armenian youth living under Russian protection, who have demonstrated zealous devotion to their new homeland . . . will unite with native Russians with greater ease."[38]

Thus, Benkendorf argued that civic integration had a potential impact beyond the immediate mission of one academic institution. He also reassured the minister that the institute derived financial profit from "the entire Armenian people," whose "devoted cooperation" continued to grow.[39] The general pointed out that the Lazarev Institute "deserves special attention because it was founded by private individuals, without any [state] encouragement and without any assistance from the treasury, to the substantive benefit of the government and to the benefit of an entire nation."[40] The Education Ministry rejected several drafts of a new charter that sought rights reserved for state-sponsored educational institutions (*kazennye uchebnye zavedeniia*),[41] but relented in 1830 under the leadership of Karl von Lieven.

Satisfied with their institute's status, the Lazarevs turned to increasing the role of Armenian studies in Russian universities, taking the next step in integrating Armenians into the Russian Empire. By late 1829, Lieven learned that the Lazarevs sought to finance a "department of Armenian language and literature" at Moscow University.[42] The Armenian philanthropists offered not only to sponsor the initial efforts but also to assist in recruiting an experienced scholar of Armenian studies and, if need be, to provide "whatever academic assistance." Lieven rejected this proposal, assuring Ivan Lazarev that the Education Ministry had "already turned its attention to the necessity of studying in our country Oriental languages, including Armenian," but the resources of the imperial capital made St. Petersburg a more appropriate site for the initiation of these efforts than Moscow. Although the first chair of Armenian studies was not established at Kazan University until 1842, the Lazarevs set the foundation on which Armenology came to be accepted in Russian academia, and in 1844 Armenian became part of the curriculum at St. Petersburg University.[43]

By 1830, the Lazarevs not only had established an increasingly esteemed center of Orientology but also had taken the first steps toward introducing Armenian studies in the empire's premier universities. The institution's reputation spread beyond Russia's Armenian diaspora to attract Armenian and non-Armenian students from India and western Europe, and it facilitated its engagement with kindred foreign scholarly bodies, such as the Royal Asiatic Society in London.[44] From 1829 to 1831 alone, the institute's enrollment grew from 73 to 93 pupils, including 52 Armenians, 11 Russians, and 2 Germans.[45] The institute's faculty grew from 12–14 instructors in 1823 to 26 in 1829. Thanks to merit-based admissions, a rigorous curriculum, qualified faculty, and comfortable facilities, the Lazarev Institute began to produce young men who eventually advanced to senior positions in the tsarist political hierarchy.

The Lazarevs envisioned their academy not as an instrument of state-directed cultural Russification of Armenians, nor as a center for fortifying Armenian national identity, but rather as a dual-purpose institution that worked separately but for the government. The Lazarev Institute was never intended to be, nor did it become, a center of Armenian national (let alone nationalist) education. It focused on the schooling of Armenian-heritage pupils not to awaken their Armenianness, or to resist their acculturation, but to prepare Armenians and non-Armenians for membership in professional Russian society. The institute sought to turn natives of the Caucasus into *rossiiane* (Russian subjects) rather than *russkie* (ethnic Russians), thus allowing the students to maintain their cultural identities while giving them the tools for social mobility and advancement in the empire. As Benkendorf made clear, these goals aligned with the state's geopolitical aims, becoming one aspect of the conditional strategies that Admiral Mordvinov and other liberal statesmen came to see as imperative.

In the experience of early nineteenth-century Russian imperialism, the Lazarev Institute demonstrates that the government could choose to pursue the civic integration of non-Russians ahead of the geopolitical absorption of territory. At first reluctant, the state by the mid-1820s recognized that its objectives in the South Caucasus required the education of non-Russian and Russian agents who could advance St. Petersburg's political agenda more effectively than could military or Russifying means alone. By the end of the Second Russo-Persian War in 1828 and the annexation of Yerevan and Nakhichevan, the Russian Empire was well prepared to absorb thousands of new Caucasian natives into its social and political fold. In this context, St. Petersburg's embrace of the Lazarev Institute and the Lazarev family's vision evinced the government's dedication to adaptable methods of empire building. To understand the processes through which foreign-subject Armenians came under St. Petersburg's umbrella, an analysis of the tsar's clashes with the shah and the sultan in the late 1820s is necessary.

Old Foes, New Friends

The Second Russo-Persian War of 1826–28 and the Russo-Ottoman War of 1828–29 pitted Russia against its two imperial neighbors in the Caucasus. The former clash gave the tsars two historic Armenian centers they had pursued since 1804, the strategically advantageous Yerevan fortress and the politically powerful Ejmiatsin monastery, which sought to submit to its authority the dispersed Armenian diaspora. While capture of Yerevan, the region's second city after Tiflis, spelled full Russian dominion over the South Caucasus, control of Ejmiatsin promised extensive political and economic sway into those countries, such as the Ottoman Empire, Persia, and even India, where Russian diplomats struggled for influence while local Armenian bishops enjoyed some prominence. Geopolitical incentives, more than economic goals, motivated Russia's conflict with Persians and Ottomans in the Caucasus in the late 1820s. In these fights, St. Petersburg found ardent allies in the Armenian natives of the region.

Persia's political elite lamented the result of the First Russo-Persian War of 1804–13, when Russia wrested away six khanates and hundreds of thousands of the shah's subjects. The terms of the Treaty of Giulistan in 1813 had confirmed the superiority of Russian weapons, but Fath-Ali Shah and Crown Prince Abbas Mirza remained convinced that good timing, more than good tactics, had brought victory to their northern neighbor. Persian leaders recognized the fact that, having both expelled Napoleon's Grande Armée and defeated the Ottomans in 1812, Russia was free to devote a larger proportion of its resources to the Caucasus campaign in 1813. Determined to regain lost territories and reestablish its imperial grip on the South Caucasus, the Persian political and spiritual elite vowed to wage jihad against the northern infidels, a fateful policy that would precipitate the decline of the entire Qajar monarchy.[46] For the tsarist state, too, the Russo-Persian border redrawn at Giulistan fell short of its goals, because, after two failed Russian attempts at their conquest, Yerevan and Ejmiatsin stayed within the shah's domain. With the death of Tsar Alexander I in late 1825 and the subsequent Decembrist revolt, Persia seized the chance to catch the tsarist military off guard.

On 16 July 1826, the *sardar*, or military governor, of Yerevan attacked Russian outposts along the boundary of Russian-held Georgia and Persian-held Yerevan. Almost simultaneously, the main Persian army, led by Crown Prince Abbas Mirza, crossed the Arax River from Persia proper into the Russian-occupied khanates of Karabakh and Talysh. The Persian force advanced easily, driving back small Russian garrisons and welcoming the defections of local khans to the Persian side.[47] Within days of the attack, the shah's army had expelled or encircled all of the Russian troops stationed in Karabakh, a success that the supreme Russian commander, General Aleksei Ermolov, attributed to the collusion of local Muslims. As one small Russian contingent became encircled in the Shusha fortress, Ermolov vented to the tsar that locals had blocked narrow mountain passages to prevent the retreat of Russian troops.[48]

A veteran of the Napoleonic Wars who distinguished himself at Borodino and Paris, Ermolov assumed command of Russian forces in the Caucasus in 1816. Like many of the aristocratic officers in the tsar's army, Ermolov was an intellectual as much as a soldier, belonging to a distant age of enlightened imperialists. He was a man of "wide culture and a fluent linguist, greatly influenced by the ideas of the Encyclopedists; a writer of philosophical verse, a skilled Latinist who always kept his Livy close at hand, and who named his two sons Severus and Claudius."[49] At the same time, the general was a "quintessential frontier conqueror," who sought to subjugate the region through relentless violence and coercion.[50] His command of the Caucasus ensured that the highlanders feared, respected, and hated "Yarmul," as they called him.[51]

From the first fusillade of the Second Russo-Persian War, the theme of a clash of religions informed the perspective of senior tsarist commanders in the Caucasus. Ermolov deflected blame for the debacle from himself to the supposed duplicitousness of the region's Muslim residents. Shaken by the powerful incursion, the Russian general reported to the autocrat within days of the Persian attack: "A war aroused by religion and fanaticism has mobilized against us all Muslims and we have nothing left but Georgia."[52] Warning of the perilous situation, Ermolov pleaded for heavy reinforcements, vowing to punish the Persians by "bringing the war into their own land!"[53] To the Imperial

General Staff, Ermolov emphasized: "This war promises to be more severe than could have been expected, for it is aroused by religion."[54]

The tsar not only disagreed with Ermolov's plans for a defensive war but also pressed him to conquer new territory. Soon after the Persian invasion, the chief of the General Staff, Hans Karl von Diebitsch, ordered Ermolov to take "decisive" action against the shah's army using the Independent Caucasus Corps, a formidable force of thirty thousand men. Diebitsch and Tsar Nicholas were so confident of this army's superiority that they instructed Ermolov not only to repulse the Persian attack but also to capture the elusive Yerevan fortress, which had repelled Russian attacks in 1804 and 1808.[55] By mid-August 1826, the emperor's terse messages revealed his waning confidence in Ermolov.[56] Although Nicholas relented by sending an additional division to the Caucasus, at the head of the reinforcements he sent General Ivan Paskevich, ostensibly to provide Ermolov with "a detailed explanation of my intentions."[57]

The complex interethnic climate of the region dictated the course of the conflict. Throughout the first months of the war, Ermolov warned St. Petersburg of the local Muslims' security risk, roused not simply by religious solidarity with the invading army but also by the financial "gifts" and incentives promised by Abbas Mirza in return for cooperation.[58] Ermolov also claimed that the *sardar* of Yerevan had sent propagandistic pamphlets to village elders in tsarist territory, urging their assistance in Persia's struggle against the infidels. To "punish" the local Muslims for their collaboration with the enemy, Ermolov planned to billet his troops on their lands and in their villages until the start of a winter campaign against Karabakh. Some of Ermolov's concerns proved justified in September 1826, when local Muslims in Elisavetpol joined with the invading Persians to drive out the Russian garrison.[59] Yet Ermolov again found himself on the wrong side of the predominant view. Despite the mass insurrection at Elisavetpol, the tsar instructed Ermolov to announce a blanket amnesty to local Muslims for their cooperation with the Persians. Ermolov and his commanders were to treat them with "mercy" and avoid any semblance of "vengeance."[60] According to Diebitsch, "His Majesty is convinced that mercy and justice sooner will instill in these people a sense of loyalty to Russia than persecution and harassment, which can fan the flames of a war birthed by religious fanaticism."[61]

If in the perception of some tsarist elites local Muslims posed security risks to Russian interests in the South Caucasus, then other groups offered advantages. Tsarist officials found indigenous, religious-based support primarily among two national groups: Armenians and Georgians. As soon as hostilities flared, Russian authorities had no doubt about Armenian allegiances. When Abbas Mirza's army overran Elisavetpol in September 1826 and mobilized local

Muslims against the Russian administration, the only good news Ermolov could report to the tsar was that "all Armenians living in the district are on our side."[62] When, a few weeks later, Paskevich's forces entered Karabakh to break the siege of the Shusha fortress, the general reported to the emperor that local Armenians had facilitated his advancement by providing intelligence on the location of Persian troops.[63]

Indeed, Armenian cooperation contributed to turning the tide of the war. The first major Russian victory of the conflict took place near Elisavetpol on 13 September 1826. Two Armenians in the Persian service, one of whom tsarist sources identified as the personal Russian interpreter of Abbas Mirza, snuck into Paskevich's camp at night to warn the Russian general of an imminent attack by the Persian crown prince.[64] This information, Paskevich reported to the tsar, permitted him to launch a preemptive assault that drove the Persians from Karabakh.[65] Days later, Paskevich broke the Persian siege of Shusha and Abbas Mirza's army withdrew from Karabakh into Persia proper, tracked along the route by Armenian informants.[66]

If during the First Russo-Persian War Armenians were mainly tsarist spies and settlers, in the second clash they also assumed the role of soldiers. On entering the long-besieged Shusha fortress, Paskevich discovered that "up to 1,500 armed Armenians" had fought alongside Russian troops to withstand the Persian attack.[67] The tsarist commander of the garrison, Colonel I. A. Reutt, confirmed to Paskevich that "brave Egerians and loyal Armenians" had played an active role in defending the citadel. Moreover, the colonel reported that, at the onset of hostilities, he had witnessed local Azeris slaughter "several" Armenians outside the fortress. The Russian officer interpreted this event as a sign of Muslim resistance to the arrival of a Christian force and their fury at their Christian neighbors, whose sympathy for tsarist rule was no secret.[68] With the turning tide of the war and growing danger of a Russian invasion of the Yerevan Khanate, tsarist authorities learned that the Yerevan *sardar* intended to relocate Armenians in his territory beyond the Arax River "in order to deprive us [the Russians] of any benefits from them."[69]

Armenians mobilized both on their own and with Russian appeals. In some cases, Armenian ecclesiastical elders urged their followers to take up arms against the Persians. In late 1826, at the behest of the catholicos in Ejmiatsin (still within the Persian domain) and the Armenian archbishop of Tiflis, Armenians in and near Nakhichevan assembled a large militia, estimated by some Armenian sources to have numbered as many as six thousand mounted men.[70] While this number is likely exaggerated, it indicates the role the Armenian Church played in rallying its flock. During the Russian advance after Paskevich's victory at Elisavetpol, several Armenian militias (*opolchentsy*), some numbering as few as one hundred individuals, fought alongside the tsarist army.[71] Junior tsarist commanders in the field issued to individual Armenian militia leaders and other local supporters certifications of their assistance to the Russian army.[72] By January 1828, tsarist officers lauded Archbishop Nerses, the head of the diocese of Georgia, for gathering "approximately four hundred Armenian cavalry and eight hundred Armenian infantry" who, they said, "are prepared to fight on our side" and who "are willing to serve at their own expense."[73]

Other natives of the region, both Muslim and Christian, joined Armenians in the tsarist war effort. Georgian militias, some of them led by aristocratic young men raised after the 1801 annexation of Kartli-Kakheti, often battled alongside Azeri and Armenian units. The General Staff learned of these displays of loyalty early, directing Ermolov in the fall of 1826 to report about local Armenians' and Georgians' cooperation with Russian war efforts.[74] Always in search of new reinforcements, Ermolov in late August 1826 recruited "up to 1,800" Georgian cavalrymen, "among whom are many princes and nobles of the best names."[75] Soon a formal declaration from Tsar Nicholas to the Georgian nobility acknowledged its contribution.[76]

After Paskevich expelled Abbas Mirza from Karabakh, the Russian army targeted Yerevan. In preparation for the assault in the spring of 1827, Paskevich recruited local Muslims, Georgians, and especially Armenians. In May 1827, he boasted to Diebitsch that, within a couple of days of his initial announcement, over one hundred Armenian men volunteered for service.[77] The terms of service for these mobilizing "Armenian battalions" were publicized widely. Armenian men aged eighteen to thirty were accepted on a temporary, voluntary basis for the duration of the war with Persia, at the conclusion of which they would be disbanded. During their service, the volunteers and their wives and children were excused from all taxes. The Russian army armed and paid them, and they submitted to its authority and command structure. However, the military made efforts to assign tsarist officers of Armenian heritage to the Armenian battalions, and it permitted such commanders to issue orders in Armenian.[78] In theory, the supplies the army provided to the Armenian units were to match the support it gave ordinary Russian soldiers, and Russian field hospitals admitted all Armenians wounded in battle. The first Armenian unit, a *"druzhina"* (squad) of 117, was dispatched from Tiflis in mid-May 1827 to rendezvous with Russian forces near Ejmiatsin. A few weeks later, another unit of 100 Armenians left Tiflis to join the Russian siege of Yerevan, followed by a third, smaller unit of 67 men in August.[79] Learning of these developments from Diebitsch, Tsar Nicholas proposed that permanent Armenian military units be organized after the war.[80]

Persian authorities recognized their Armenians' solidarity with the Russians. In the encircled Yerevan Khanate, Persian officials took measures to check the potential collusion of local Armenians with the enemy, according to Armenian reports to Russian officials, which must be interpreted with particular caution given the stakes involved.[81] In early October, Armenians in Tiflis passed on to local Russian officials information that their compatriots in Yerevan had sent them. "As much as from its explicit suspicion of the Armenian people for its devotion to Russia," summarized one Armenian report, "as much as from vengeance and evil, Yerevan authorities have begun the extreme harassment of the Armenian Ejmiatsin monastery. By order of the Persian chiefs, some of the monks have already been killed, others [tortured], and moreover they have begun plundering and destroying."[82]

In another district, the local Persian commander returned from the front to confiscate the goods of local Armenian traders and to seize valuables from the local Armenian churches. The Yerevan *sardar* ordered the hanging of all Armenians within the city suspected of colluding with the enemy, and he demanded that those living outside the city "evacuate" beyond the Arax River. Their abandoned homes were razed, as were some bridges across the river.[83] Beyond the Yerevan Khanate, according to the complaints Armenians in Tiflis made to Russian authorities, tsarist-subject Armenian merchants traveling through Persia proper were detained and their goods and money confiscated.[84] However, other Armenians from Karabakh reported that Abbas Mirza had guaranteed the safe passage of Russian-subject Armenian merchants from Tabriz back to Tiflis, even providing them with an armed escort.[85]

Back in the Russian camp, tensions between Ermolov and Paskevich came to a head, exacerbated by Paskevich's triumphs. By spring 1827, Paskevich refused to continue under Ermolov's command. The emperor relieved the veteran general from his duties, promoting Paskevich to lead the Independent Caucasus Corps. Paskevich justified his promotion quickly. Within a couple of months, the tsarist army advanced to within twenty-five kilometers of the Yerevan fortress.[86] General Benkendorf's troops, meantime, captured Ejmiatsin and drove the local Persians into Yerevan, taking care to "save Armenian villages from the expulsion of residents."[87] Paskevich bragged in his journal that on his army's entrance into Armenian villages in Persian territory, they were met with "the most festive greeting, [and] in all churches liturgies were read for the welfare of the emperor and the entire august [royal] house."[88]

On 1 October 1827, Paskevich's army stormed the Yerevan citadel, capturing the city and much of its Persian garrison, including Sardar Hassan Khan.[89] Soon tsarist troops occupied Tabriz, well inside Persia proper, without a fight. Fearing the advancement of the tsar's army deeper into his realm, the shah sued for peace. On 10 February 1828, General Paskevich and Abbas Mirza signed the Treaty of Turkmenchai in the eponymous Persian village.

The terms of the treaty were generous to the victor, much as they had been at the end of the previous Russo-Persian war. The shah ceded to the tsar the Yerevan and Nakhichevan Khanates, along with the remainder of Talysh Khanate.[90] Persia affirmed the previous concessions of the Treaty of Giulistan and forever surrendered claims to territory north of the Arax River, which became the formal boundary between the Russian and Persian states. Persia also agreed to pay reparations of 20 million silver rubles and to withdraw its naval fleet from the Caspian Sea. In return, Russia pledged to return occupied Tabriz and to support Abbas Mirza as the heir to Fath-Ali. The treaty also granted a year-long window for all Persian subjects living along the new border to decide whether to stay within the shah's domain or to relocate into tsarist territory.

Even before the signing of the Treaty of Turkmenchai, Russian officials in the Caucasus turned their attention to the stirring of the Ottoman pashas across the other imperial border. Sparked in the Balkans by the Greek War of Independence and Turkey's closing of the Dardanelles to Russian ships in retaliation for Russia's participation in an anti-Ottoman coalition, the Russo-Ottoman War of 1828–29 reverberated in the Caucasus. By December 1827, Paskevich reported that Ottoman officials in districts adjacent to the Russian border had begun preparations for war. As evidence of these developments, tsarist officials in the Caucasus notified St. Petersburg that Ottoman Armenians, "more committed to us than to their government," were placed under surveillance and relocated away from the Russian border.[91] Paskevich received multiple reports about new restrictions affecting Ottoman Armenians in Anatolia, such as a prohibition on sending letters and the summons of two elders from each Armenian village to Constantinople for unclear purposes.[92] Ottoman officials, like their Persian counterparts, recognized that their Armenian subjects sought Russian patronage.

Tsarist agents strove to capitalize on these circumstances. The governor-general of Tiflis, Nikolai Sipiagin, proposed to Diebitsch in March 1828 that "with a quick foray into Turkish borders we will prevent them from relocating Armenians into internal provinces and will take advantage of the grain stocks in Kars and Akhaltsykh Districts; while our good treatment of the locals will compel them to remain in their villages and provide us with means for the successful execution of the war."[93] Another tsarist commander, General Afanasii Krasovskii, echoed this sentiment, arguing that Ottoman Armenians would support a Russian invasion of eastern Anatolia. Once the Armenians could see that tsarist forces would treat them well, pay for supplies received from the locals, and respect their properties, he reasoned, "[the Armenians,] having noticed such a dramatic contrast with the actions of their current overlords, will rush to join us; for the Turkish government has sowed so much hatred and loathing toward itself that they will eagerly facilitate a change that is beneficial to themselves."[94] Prior to Paskevich's invasion of Ottoman territory on 14 June 1828, he sought to reassure the local Ottoman subjects, both Christian and Muslim, through pamphlets. The tsarist general vowed, "[My] army will not disturb your tranquility; no Russian soldier will touch your property . . . [or] hinder the security of Muslims."[95] Despite such assurances, the Russians on their way to Kars found little more than abandoned plains: local Muslims had fled and the authorities had removed Christians, mostly Armenians, into the interior.[96]

It would be an exaggeration to claim that Armenians played a pivotal role, in the military or political sense, in the Russian expansion into the South Caucasus. According to Russian sources, Armenian and Georgian volunteer units represented only a fraction of the total forces under tsarist command. Yet, in a conflict that was often portrayed as a civilizational clash between Christendom and Islam, the actual and potential cooperation of Armenians, and other native Caucasian Christians, allowed Russia to establish itself as a new master of the South Caucasus. The Romanov state not only relied on the aid of Armenians to facilitate its advancement but also planned its future engagements around the likelihood of Armenian collaboration. When Armenian peasants from Muslim-ruled territories colonized the tsarist South Caucasus en masse they solidified their centrality to St. Petersburg's imperial policy.

Souls and Hearts: Russia Recruits Armenians from Abroad

A controversial stipulation of the Treaty of Turkmenchai reshaped the cultural, social, and economic climate of the South Caucasus.[97] Persian subjects living along the new Russo-Persian border could choose to stay in the shah's domain or emigrate into the tsar's empire, and thousands of the shah's Armenian subjects resettled into the tsar's newly expanded realm. After the Russo-Ottoman War of 1828–29, more Armenians arrived from Anatolia. In what became state policy, Russia employed Armenians from abroad to fortify its hold on the South Caucasus.

Several factors prompted the strategy of using Armenians to colonize newly annexed lands. First, the ecumenical kinship between Orthodox Russians and Apostolic Armenians, which both senior tsarist officials and Armenian peasants evoked, fed the mutual belief that Armenians "belonged" under the suzerainty of their coreligionist emperor, rather than that of his neighboring Muslim counterparts. Armenians' religious identity represented to tsarist authorities guarantees of political devotion and stability, explaining why Russians chose Armenians to "increase the [regional] population by using Christians as much as possible."[98] Armenians' collaboration with Russians during the recent war confirmed their loyalty for imperial administrators. Second, Romanov agents sought to tap Armenians' romanticized economic adeptness in order to stimulate the development of newly conquered and underdeveloped regions. Even those Persian Armenians who enjoyed a measure of commercial success looked for physical and cultural security under the Russian aegis, convinced that relative religious freedom and improved trade opportunities would ensure prosperity. The tsarist state eagerly settled incoming Armenians in regions of the South Caucasus that had been depopulated by years of warfare. Confident in their loyalty and ability, Paskevich welcomed the influx of Armenians. "Realizing the benefits that we can receive," he argued to Diebitsch, "from the settlement of untended lands by a people who are hardworking, accustomed to obedience, and loyal to us through religion," the general facilitated the large-scale immigration of Persian-subject Armenians into the South Caucasus.[99]

To oversee this formidable task, Paskevich assigned Colonel Lazar Ekimovich Lazarev, the youngest son of Ekim Lazarev. Paskevich had specifically requested Lazarev's transfer from St. Petersburg to Tiflis, recognizing not only the young officer's diligence but also the fact that "his name alone served as a guarantee to Armenians of [Russia's] sincere disposition toward them," in the words of contemporaneous historian Sergei Glinka.[100] Paskevich, too, acknowledged that the colonel's family name "enjoys the general respect of the Armenian nation."[101] To facilitate the mission, Paskevich established in Tiflis the Committee for the Resettlement of Christians (Komitet pereseleniia Khristian, hereafter Resettlement Committee) and set aside 50,000 silver rubles for this undertaking from the shah's reparations. Lazarev dispatched officers to various Armenian villages to ascertain "the true intentions of the Christians and to confirm whether they really wish to cross into our regions."[102] Paskevich impressed on Lazarev that he ought to "use no coercion, especially violent means, but only suggestions, presenting to them all the benefits of entering into the subjecthood of the most powerful Christian emperor in Europe, and the peaceful and happy life that they will enjoy under the auspices of benevolent Russian laws."[103] Lazarev also pledged to immigrating traders that they would receive "the same rights as local merchants" in their new homeland.

All resettling Christians were promised "adequate amounts" of farmland and freed from "taxes [*podati*] for six years and from rural assessments [*zem-*

skie povinnosti] for three years."[104] During the immigrants' journey, escorted by tsarist troops to prevent potential outbursts by their Muslim neighbors, the most destitute families received a onetime allowance of 10 silver rubles; Paskevich provided Lazarev with 25,000 silver rubles for this task.[105] Persian Armenians were led mainly into the newly demarcated Armenian and Nakhichevan regions, or oblasts, where the local administration, together with the Resettlement Committee, distributed land and determined other details. Only Armenians living along the new border were to be moved into Karabakh.[106]

By late May 1828, Paskevich could report to St. Petersburg that Lazarev and his officers had made tangible progress in this endeavor. Already 948 Armenian families had been resettled into Armianskaia Oblast, and 279 into Karabakh.[107] Colonel Lazarev, moreover, had assured the general that the total number of immigrants would "exceed 5,000 families." Paskevich emphasized to Diebitsch's successor at the head of the General Staff, Count Aleksandr Chernyshev, the strictly voluntary nature of the Armenian relocation, which the tsarist army carried out not only out of Russia's economic and political interests but also out of Christian benevolence. He highlighted this aspect by crediting the "oppressive Persian rule, which burdens Christians with taxes and injustices of all kinds," for the smoothness of the population transfer and also summarized the support he had received from Armenian ecclesiastical leaders, including Archbishop Nerses.[108] Despite rising costs and diminishing grain supplies in the region, both Paskevich and Lazarev continued to stress the "obvious benefit" they could bring: "Any costs that the treasury will bear now for the support of the immigrating Armenians will always be reimbursed to it with excess; for in addition to their loyalty to Russians, which experience has shown, they are famous for their tireless work ethic."[109]

Lazar Lazarev took advantage of his identity as an ethnic Armenian in the Russian service, declaring to his superiors, "To me, as a Russian officer, [this task] brings great honor, and as an Armenian, complete happiness."[110] Cognizant of his family's position as an intermediary between the Armenian diaspora and the tsarist state, the young colonel advocated to the two sides the benefits of the Armenian relocation. When the Armenian immigrants' financial problems impeded Lazarev's mission, the colonel relied on his family name to assuage their concerns. Indeed, when some Armenians hesitated to abandon their properties without financial compensation, the promises of this Russified Armenian commander helped sway them.[111] Lazarev accused Persian officials and "English agents" of spreading false rumors among Armenians about the economic and political difficulties that awaited them in Russian territory, including enserfment, crippling taxation, and onerous military service.[112]

In an effort to prevent the exodus of Armenians, whose economic contribution to the shah's treasury Russian accountants estimated at 32 million assignation rubles,[113] Persian tactics ranged from warnings to threats to promises. Lazarev claimed that Persian officials secretly prohibited their subjects from purchasing land and homes from departing Armenians, thus exacerbating their financial situation and ensuring that capital remained in Persia.[114] These efforts bore some fruit when several Armenian communities demanded Lazarev reimburse them for at least one-third of their abandoned properties' value.[115] Moreover, according to Lazarev, Muslim Persian villagers hurled insults and rocks at the emigrating Armenians, demonstrating "tremendous hatred" and often necessitating the intervention of Russian and Cossack units to protect the refugees.[116] Yet, despite such difficulties, Lazarev emphasized in his reports to St. Petersburg that Armenians relocated of their own accord without financial support beyond the 10 silver rubles per family that Paskevich had authorized.[117]

Seeing that, despite Persian efforts, numerous Armenian communities continued to abandon their homes, Crown Prince Abbas Mirza accused tsarist agents of coercing the Armenians.[118] In a case Glinka's narrative made famous,[119] Persian officials in April 1828 alerted Lazarev that a group of four hundred Armenian families had told the shah's representatives that tsarist agents had coerced them into leaving. Confident of this account's inaccuracy and accompanied by the son of a senior Persian minister, Asker Khan, Lazarev personally tracked down the Armenian party.[120] The immigrants, he reported, "unanimously declared that they are relocating voluntarily. 'We [would] rather eat Russian grass than Persian bread,' they said to the son of Asker Khan, from whom I took a written verification."[121] Neither the Armenian motivations behind such supposed statements nor the accuracy of their Russian recordings can be ascertained from the sources; however, their prominence in Russian narratives, both official and popular, indicates the Russian perception and sentiments surrounding this population transfer.

The number of Armenians who emigrated from Persia into Russian territory in the South Caucasus after the Second Russo-Persian War is difficult to determine. The archival record is incomplete in the federal archives of both Russia and Armenia because contemporary sources provided specific numbers for individual migrant groups, villages, or regions, but almost never for entire administrative territories.[122] According to Lazar Lazarev, in the three and a half months between 26 February and 11 June 1828, he facilitated the relocation of 8,249 families.[123] It appears that at least 5,000 of these families, and perhaps as many as 6,000, were directed to the Armenian and Nakhichevan regions, with the rest of the refugees sent to Karabakh starting in May because of dwindling food supplies in the other regions of the South Caucasus.[124] Glinka provides the same total number of about 8,000 families, estimating the overall number of Armenian immigrants at approximately 40,000 individuals.[125] However, some historians place the number of Persian Armenian emigrants to the tsarist South Caucasus at closer to 30,000.[126]

Russia continued to rely on foreign-subject Christians to settle newly annexed territories in the South Caucasus after it transplanted tens of thousands of Persian Armenians. Satisfied with the accomplishments of General Paskevich and Colonel Lazarev, Tsar Nicholas sought to absorb more Armenians into the borders of his realm after the Russo-Ottoman War of 1828–29. In the wake of that conflict, tsarist agents justified this policy by emphasizing the collaboration of Western Armenians with Russian forces during the war and the consequent abuse they had experienced and would experience at the hands of their Ottoman overlords and neighbors.

After the signing of the Treaty of Adrianople in September 1829, Paskevich informed the tsar that Ottoman Armenians did not celebrate the armistice announcement, demonstrating instead "justified gloom" in anticipation of the "persecutions that threaten[ed]" them.[127] The general stressed, "In these remote countries, where for so many centuries Christianity has been oppressed by an unjust yoke, [the Russian] army could fear no hostility from the Armenian and Greek populations."[128] The mistreatment of these Ottoman Christian minorities had ensured that invading tsarist forces found among the locals "zealous allies and partners." The general enumerated the ways in which Western Armenians had directly assisted Russian forces against their Ottoman foes: in Bayazet, two thousand Armenians fought alongside Russian troops; in Kars, an Armenian battalion of eight hundred mounted men protected the Russian flank; and in Erzurum, "the majority" of the local Christians, mainly Armenians, welcomed the arriving Russian forces with open arms. "Do not let it happen," the general implored the autocrat, "that Ottoman despotism takes revenge on [Armenians] for the devotion they have demonstrated to Russia."[129]

By mid-November 1829, Tsar Nicholas permitted Paskevich to resettle about ten thousand Armenian families, mainly from the Ottoman pashalik of Bayazet, to tsarist Georgia and Armianskaia Oblast.[130] Ottoman Armenians were so eager to emigrate, claimed Paskevich, that many of them did not wait for Russian financial assistance or military protection to begin their movement into Russian territory. To determine the details of their settlement, including land distribution, Paskevich established a separate administrative organ in Tiflis. Moreover, Paskevich was so confident that Armenian relocation would bring political and economic advantages to Russia that he requested an unprecedented 1 million assignation rubles (over 250,000 silver rubles), about five times the amount he had expended on the relocation of Persian Armenians.[131] The general assured St. Petersburg: "Although the initial settlement of these people will require fairly significant costs, there is no doubt that they will be amply reimbursed by those advantages, which one can expect from this commercial and hardworking [people]."[132]

By late January 1830, about 2,500 Armenian families emigrated from Kars and its surrounding villages, settling in the vicinity of Mount Aragats.[133] Based on Armenian requests, Russian officials anticipated the imminent arrival of an additional 2,100 families from Erzurum and 3,150 families from Bayazet Pashalik. Tsarist agents directed large groups—whose exact numbers remain unclear—to Armianskaia Oblast, Georgia, and Karabakh. Yet by one Russian account from 1836, the number of Ottoman Armenian immigrants living in Armianskaia Oblast was just 5,755 individuals.[134] Though they had not done so with Persian Armenians, Russian authorities used a portion of the sultan's Armenian subjects to establish a buffer against the Ottoman Empire, seeing that polity as a continued threat, whereas Persia's expansionist ambitions had waned.

As early as November 1829, Tsar Nicholas noted Paskevich's emphasis on Armenian cooperation with the Russian army. The emperor instructed the General Staff to settle some Ottoman Armenian immigrants in Akhaltsykh and other frontier towns, where "in the form of a battalion or another military unit" they could be used "to defend our new border."[135] Soon, plans were drawn up to relocate over 2,000 Armenian families from Erzurum to Akhaltsykh.[136] The estimates of total Western Armenian repatriation to the Caucasus are as widely inconsistent as the statistics for the general Armenian population, but the most conservative guess for Ottoman Armenian immigrants is 25,000.[137] While some historians estimate that as many as 100,000 Armenians relocated from the Persian and Ottoman Empires to the tsarist domain in the late 1820s and early 1830s, the actual number is likely to be several tens of thousands less.[138]

Tsarist officials strove to provide the immigrants with "every opportunity to quickly reach a flourishing state and bring abundant benefits to Russia."[139] The immigration committee formed in Tiflis by Paskevich distributed state-owned land and communicated with Armenian leaders to ascertain details of their settlement. In February 1830, when the numbers of Ottoman Armenian immigrants exceeded Russian estimates, Paskevich granted them state-owned land in Georgia that had been allocated for Ukrainian Cossack settlers.[140] When the refugees from Bayazet proved to be nearly twice as numerous as Russians had estimated, Paskevich not only permitted them to enter Russian territory but also provided emergency food provisions from his army's military depots.[141] Within months, Russian military authorities delivered extra grain supplies to the new immigrants from other regions of the Caucasus and beyond.[142]

The absorption of new Armenians into the social and economic fabric of the South Caucasus progressed slowly. To a degree, their economic assimilation matched Russian expectations, and within a couple of years of their relocation, transplanted Armenian merchants owned numerous buildings and vending stalls in Yerevan.[143] Yet imperial administrators struggled to curb friction between the newcomers and the natives. Officials did not prevent the ethnic or national mixing of various communities, and the geographic coalescence of Persian Armenian, Ottoman Armenian, native Christian, and native Muslim groups was common. The ostensible consent of all involved parties and the availability of land were the only prerequisites for the Russian facilitation of interethnic cohabitation.[144] The Resettlement Committee, headquartered in Tiflis and with ancillary offices in Yerevan, Nakhichevan, and Abaran, facilitated negotiations between new neighbors in the South Caucasus and worked with Russian military officials and Persian and Ottoman government representatives.[145]

The Resettlement Committee tried to mediate between Muslim and Christian residents. As the Nakhichevan bureau of the Resettlement Committee grumbled in September 1828, "Not a day goes by without . . . the complaints of the immigrants about Tatars [Azeris], and the latter's about the immigrants."[146] In their objections to the influx of Christians, native Muslim residents protested that they had been "deprived of all means of farming, and thus of feeding their families in the future."[147] In Nakhichevan and elsewhere, Azeris protested at being pushed out—through either direct coercion or land redistribution—by the incoming Armenians.[148] Russian officials intervened by reducing land allotment for Armenians and stipulating that only as much land could be granted to the immigrants as they could sow at the time of their arrival. In December 1828, housing restrictions were also implemented, with one home granted to every "three or four" refugee families.[149] In theory if not in practice, senior tsarist officials in the Caucasus and St. Petersburg demanded that the Resettlement Committee "maintain the strictest supervision [to ensure that] the settlers do not inflict the slightest abuse on the indigenous residents [and] that the property of each remains inviolable," while the leaders of local native groups, "without exception," were expected to ensure that no "injustice" or "harm" befell the newcomers.[150]

Changing demographics in the South Caucasus posed ethnic, cultural, and economic challenges for the tsarist bureaucracy. As a result, policy disagreements plagued the regional administration. Not only is it doubtful that St. Petersburg's stability-seeking instructions to the Resettlement Committee were fully implemented, but internal discord among Russian officials in the South Caucasus revealed deeper schisms. One example should suffice.

The influx of Christians into the tsar's territory precipitated a concurrent exit of native Muslims into the domains of the shah and the sultan.[151] Many departing Muslims, especially from the Nakhichevan and Ordubad regions, left behind their homes and fields.[152] According to the provisions of the Treaty of Turkmenchai, the Russian state could lease out these vacant properties for its benefit, but only their owners had the right to sell them. Yet their dilapidated condition prevented the authorities from finding willing renters. In late 1828, the Resettlement Committee petitioned the regional government (*pravlenie*) of Armianskaia Oblast for permission to transfer ownership of the vacant, untended homes to the "poorest" of the relocated Armenians. However, citing the Turkmenchai Treaty, officials of the regional government rejected this request, arguing that absent Muslim owners retained rights to their abandoned properties. The Resettlement Committee repeated its appeal a year later, when no Muslims returned to claim their properties. Yet again, officials refused to grant to immigrant Armenians properties native Muslims had abandoned.[153]

To be sure, Russian authorities faced a delicate balancing act. On the one hand, the absorption of foreign-subject Armenians had become a staple of tsarist policy in the South Caucasus. Eager to populate newly annexed lands with religiously kindred and politically reliable subjects, the state attracted Armenians through various incentives. On the other hand, St. Petersburg wished to avoid any conflagration of ethnoreligious violence between Christian im-

Map 2.   The Caucasus at mid-nineteenth century, including the "Armenian region" of 1828–40.

migrants and Muslim natives. While they took no meaningful efforts to discourage Muslim emigration, Russian officials remained wary of antagonizing the indigenous population. The rejection by the regional government of the Armianskaia Oblast of the Resettlement Committee's recurrent petitions provides but one example.

As the imperial administrators came to see foreign-subject Armenians as reliable colonizers, not only did they expend significant resources to consolidate Armenian communities in the South Caucasus, but they also jeopardized relations with domestic and foreign Muslims by granting preferential treatment to the incoming Christians. Despite nominal attempts to blunt the harm this policy had on the region's native Muslims, tsarist officials from the regional to the imperial capital prioritized the absorption of Armenians. They even reassigned to Armenians land allotted to Russia's traditional colonists, Cossacks.

To some Russian political and cultural leaders, this undertaking represented a singular development. In his embellished account, Sergei Glinka hailed the relocation of Persian Armenians into Russian territory as a "hitherto unique event in the annals of the world. It was not a simple resettlement of individual people, *but a resettlement of souls and hearts.*"[154] Glinka's exaggerated narrative underscored his and the state's perception of a Russo-Armenian symbiosis. In their private and official correspondence, Paskevich, Lazarev, and other tsarist statesmen agreed that they had "opened for the state a new source of wealth," in more than the economic sense.[155] Indeed, no evidence suggests that senior tsarist officials resisted these developments; the influx of Armenians into the South Caucasus aroused resistance mainly from the region's Muslim residents. However, the autocracy viewed another section of the Armenian diaspora, the long-settled Armenian merchants of southern Russia, not as a "new source of wealth" but as a liability that threatened the social and economic hierarchy of imperial society. The experiences of Armenians in Russia proper often challenged the expectations and hopes of the Christian refugees from Muslim empires.

"Free Trade Forever and Hereditarily"

A look at Armenian tax obligations in the Caucasus and other southern Russian territories reveals the inconsistent and ambiguous economic rules governing the commerce of Russian-subject Armenians. The ramifications of the debates among imperial statesmen influenced the highest levels of the government, where Finance Minister Egor Kankrin (Georg von Cancrin) cautioned in 1827: "The question will always remain: in Russia, do Armenians possess more rights than Russians?"[156]

Armenians in Russia had received exclusive economic rights since the early modern era. Frequent visitors to Russian bazaars, Armenians from distant lands delivered rare goods from the Orient, earning special status by the second half of the seventeenth century.[157] Armenian businessmen received the right to sell silk and other raw materials in Novgorod and the northern port city of Arkhangel'sk. From 1676, Armenian merchants sent their goods to foreign markets from Arkhangel'sk, and from 1686, they began trading with Sweden through Novgorod.[158] In December 1712, the Senate took another step in encouraging Armenian economic activity in Russia by removing restrictions and mandatory inspections from Armenian merchants traveling within the Romanov domains.

Peter the Great granted Armenians exemptions from military service and other exclusive rights in 1724, leading to the growth of an Armenian community in the southern Russian city of Kizliar. Armenian immigrants from Karabakh and Zangezur rushed to establish vineyards and orchards and to engage in other agrarian commerce.[159] Peter's successors continued to present economic privileges to Armenians in Russia. In 1746, Armenian merchants in Astrakhan were allowed to trade tax-free and to establish their own court; in 1769, Astrakhan Armenians received the exclusive right to build seagoing vessels for trade in the Caspian Sea.[160] Moreover, Armenian immigrants from Crimea, whom Catherine the Great had settled in the new city of Nakhichevan on the Don River, in 1779 received the right not to enlist in the merchant guild, which freed them from that estate's taxes. Catherine decreed the Armenians "may enjoy free trade forever and hereditarily, inside and outside of the Russian state,"[161] a pronouncement that would later become a source of much headache for both Armenian businessmen and Russian bureaucrats.

Catherine's successor, Paul, extended his mother's 1779 exemptions for the Armenians of Nakhichevan-on-Don to three other southern cities. In October 1799, seeking to animate the commerce of southern provinces and to grow the populations of the strategically important Astrakhan, Kizliar, and Mozdok, Tsar Paul allowed tax-free trade for local Armenian merchants, excusing them from enrolling in merchant guilds and paying their attendant taxes. This fiat not only did not apply to non-Armenian merchants in those three cities but also omitted all Armenian traders outside Astrakhan, Kizliar, and Mozdok. By the turn of the nineteenth century, over four thousand Armenian dealers in Astrakhan, Kizliar, and Mozdok paid no taxes whatsoever.[162] Paul's successor, Alexander, initially affirmed his father's decision; however, in January 1807, Alexander canceled the exclusive rights granted to the Armenian traders of

those three cities, requiring them to enlist in merchant guilds and pay corresponding taxes within six months.[163] The emperor's motivations are unclear,
but likely he believed that, after nearly eight years, local Armenians had enjoyed sufficiently lengthy privileges to ensure their prosperity, and the time had
come to enforce uniform tax laws.

The new regulations sent shockwaves through the Armenian merchant
communities of southern Russia. Armenians complained that their businesses
ebbed and their foreign partners saw fewer financial advantages to trading with
Russian-subject Armenians.[164] An outbreak of the plague in 1807 further sti-
fled regional commerce in southern Russia and, compounded by the growing
chorus of Armenian objections to the January 1807 decree, forced Alexander I
in November 1808 to "postpone the enrollment of Armenians into guilds until
the command of the finance minister."[165] To the detriment of broader Russo-
Armenian ties, however, no decision regarding the tax obligations of Armenian merchants in Astrakhan, Kizliar, and Mozdok came for nearly two decades.
The tsarist leadership's receptiveness to Armenian petitions undermined the
state's efforts to implement uniform tax regulations and bring Armenian traders into line with general rules, resulting in unclear and temporary directives.

If the tsarist state demonstrated the first signs of rolling back the exclusive
economic rights granted to various Armenian communities as early as 1807,
the most salient manifestations of this trend appeared only in the 1820s. Yet
conflicting initiatives from St. Petersburg and their partial implementation
in the provinces yielded a multitude of ambiguous economic positions for
Russia's Armenian merchants.

Among the prominent opponents of the state's policies vis-à-vis Armenian
economic activity in the empire, General Aleksei Ermolov denounced the government's assignment of partial, temporary, and exclusive economic rights to
separate Armenian communities. In a special report to the Senate in August 1820, Ermolov argued that no more "eternal" rights ought to be granted
to new immigrants in the Caucasus, regardless of their national, ethnic, or religious ties to existing Russian-subject communities in the region.[166] "It is
[more] justified to give privileges," contended the commander of the Caucasus, "not to an entire people, not to an entire society, but only to individuals
whose immigration will bring benefits to the government, whether through
the introduction of some art or craft, or the circulation of large capital for the
revitalization of trade and industry."[167] Referring to the partial exemptions of
October 1799, the general asked, "What valid reason can there be for these
exceptions, which are insulting to other Armenians living in Georgia and our
Muslim provinces, and who are no less useful[?]"[168] Ermolov accused Armenians of Astrakhan, Kizliar, and Mozdok of evading the decree of January 1807,

which had canceled the rights granted to them in 1799. This disobedience of the tsar's orders, according to Ermolov, had been made possible by the contradictory policies of former interior minister Aleksei Kurakin, whom Ermolov accused of "shielding" Kizliar Armenians from the requirement of joining guilds and obtaining the necessary certifications for commerce. Soon, such dissension spread among other senior imperial agents and ministries.

Debates over the economic standing of Armenians in the Russian Empire penetrated the highest levels of the government and also elicited the involvement of Armenian lay and ecclesiastical leaders. By the summer of 1823, Ekim Lazarev—now the leading lay advocate of Russia's Armenians—began to petition Finance Minister Kankrin to continue Armenians' exclusive privileges.[169] Specifically, the tax obligations of Armenian merchants in Astrakhan, Kizliar, and Mozdok had remained in abeyance since the conflicting mandates of 1807, with Armenians in Astrakhan and Mozdok no longer enjoying the tax breaks of 1799, but their counterparts in Kizliar continuing to engage in tax-free commerce. The situation, according to Lazarev, had "upset" those communities and harmed their economic activities.

In justifying extended economic benefits for Armenian businessmen, Lazarev argued that Russia traded with Persia and the Ottoman Empire mainly through Armenians. At the local level, too, Armenians contributed to Russia's provinces by paying all noncommercial taxes alongside their neighbors, billeting troops on their properties at their own expense, repairing roads and bridges without the financial support of local or regional authorities, and repeatedly demonstrating their "readiness to do everything in their powers for the general good."[170] To continue this circumstance, Lazarev asked Kankrin to excuse Armenian merchants in Astrakhan, Kizliar, and Mozdok from the requirement of enlisting in the merchant guild. He also requested that Armenians be excluded from rules governing the trade of "foreigners" in Russia, arguing that such laws were intended for affluent western European entrepreneurs.

Lazarev expressed confidence that prolonged economic privileges for Armenian dealers would, in return, attract new generations of foreign-subject Armenians into the empire. The industrious immigrants would then "establish new cities and villages [and] multiply various beneficial institutions, which are particularly customary to the Armenian people. Oriental wealth will flow in abundance into the core of their new fatherland."[171] In addition to Lazarev's missives, senior Armenian ecclesiastical leaders petitioned St. Petersburg on behalf of Armenian merchants in southern Russia. Hovannes, the prelate of all Armenians in Russia and the highest-ranking member of the Armenian Church in the empire, wrote to Kankrin in June and August 1823, requesting that the privileges of 1799 be extended indefinitely.[172] This dialogue continued even after the tsar addressed these issues with an empire-wide edict.

On 14 November 1824, Tsar Alexander I decreed that all merchants operating in his empire must join guilds and pay corresponding taxes.[173] Yet the vaguely worded law created loopholes into which Armenian traders in Astrakhan, Kizliar, Mozdok, and elsewhere could potentially fall. First, the penalties for tax evasion stipulated by the new law did not apply to "Orientals, until for them special rules are reconsidered."[174] Second, the fiat ordered: "All hitherto published laws concerning visiting foreign merchants and foreigners living in Russia remain active in all respects, unless affected by this regulation." Third, the law applied to "all" merchants, "without exception," not only in Russia but also in Finland, the Polish Kingdom, Bessarabia, and Georgia; moreover, it explicitly identified Armenians (along with Tatars, Jews, Gypsies, Greeks, and other groups). However, most importantly, the law applied to "everyone in general, *as long as they do not possess specific privileges, entitling them to an exclusion from general rules, or royally granted prerogatives.*"[175]

The result was destabilizing. Authorities in the Astrakhan Treasury Chamber hesitated at first but then enforced the new statute with alacrity, forcing local Armenian dealers into guilds and assessing new taxes. When Armenians resisted, citing the rights granted to them in 1799 and extended in 1808, the provincial authorities sought St. Petersburg's clarification of the new law's applicability to the Armenian merchants of Astrakhan. The Finance Ministry in February 1825 sided with the Armenians and ordered Astrakhan authorities not to enforce the tsar's recent edict.[176] But provincial authorities in Astrakhan and other southern commercial centers applied the November 1824 law to local Armenian retailers, ignoring the decree's third stipulation and the Finance Ministry's orders. These Russian officials either were unaware of the preexisting regulations or believed them to be long expired. When Armenian businessmen in Astrakhan refused to enter into guilds and to pay new taxes, the police shut their stores and factories.[177]

Russia's broader Armenian diaspora interpreted the enforcement of the 1824 edict not as a problem limited to its merchant community but as a threat to the entire stateless nation. Lay individuals not affiliated with commerce, and also senior members of the Armenian Church, backed the struggle of Armenian businessmen in Astrakhan and elsewhere. An empire-wide campaign in 1825 sought to halt provincial authorities' enforcement of the 1824 law, pointing out that it violated the directives of the Finance Ministry.[178] Armenians who protested from Astrakhan, Kizliar, and Mozdok were joined by their compatriots in several other southern regions, including the Ekaterinoslav, Kherson, Taurida, and Caucasus Provinces.[179]

The Armenians argued that the privileges of the late eighteenth century had been granted to them "forever,"[180] that Tsar Alexander's proclamation implicitly excluded their communities because they enjoyed long-established exemptions, and that the 1824 edict had been aimed primarily at representatives of wealthy western European trade companies. These European dealers conducted wholesale commerce that benefited international firms and enriched European banks, the Armenians claimed, while Russia's Armenian retailers struggled to support their small communities and had no surplus capital for the new tax requirements.[181] Armenian petitions emphasized that their communities never had objected, and did not object, to the city and rural taxes paid by all tsarist subjects, but rather resisted enlisting in merchant guilds with their separate dues.

The Armenians of Nakhichevan-on-Don, for example, maintained that they had accomplished the tasks Catherine the Great gave them in 1779, contributing to the region's development by spreading factories, mills, stone and wooden buildings, and viniculture. These achievements justified the economic privileges granted to them, they asserted, by enriching the state treasury, whose coffers received over 120,000 rubles per year in taxes just from Nakhichevan Armenians' viniculture and fruit-growing business.[182] Moreover, individual Armenian traders ventured into countries and communities where few Russian dealers were willing or able to conduct business, especially in the backwaters of Persia and Turkey, and often jeopardized their lives and finances in search of new trade networks and customers.[183] Far from seeking an exclusive monopoly, only Armenians, they claimed, were willing to venture "with the smallest of capital into Oriental countries, to savage, obstinate, treacherous, independent peoples, [where they were] subjected to all difficulties and dangers [and] risked everything, and despite small profits, [they] returned to their new peaceful fatherland contented."[184] At the same time, Nakhichevan Armenians, unlike their Russian counterparts in neighboring towns and provinces, maintained local roads, bridges, and postal horses at their own cost; provided their own police patrols; and paid all regular city and rural duties (*povinnosti*) to the provincial and state treasuries. As one petition from October 1825 stressed, road and bridge maintenance alone had cost Nakhichevan Armenians 37,360 rubles over the previous four years.[185]

More than regional fiscal policy was at stake in these debates. The underlying question was to what degree tsarist-subject Armenians had, or should, become socially, politically, and economically assimilated into Russia. From the perspective of some tsarist authorities in St. Petersburg and the provinces, Armenian merchants by the 1820s had received ample economic privileges to compete on equal terms with their Russian counterparts. Officials in the

Astrakhan Treasury Chamber and their colleagues in Nakhichevan-on-Don often interpreted local Armenian retailers' refusal to enlist in guilds as a sign of Armenian resistance to social integration, something that reinforced stereotypes of cunning, parsimonious outsiders who looked for loopholes through which to escape the collective responsibilities all other subjects bore. As the genesis of the "Jews of the Caucasus" trope, this essentialization would haunt Russia's Armenians throughout the nineteenth century, yet they escaped much of the Jewish plight, such as the Pale of Settlement, owing to their Christianity and relatively small, and thus ostensibly less threatening, population.

Armenians viewed efforts to enforce universal fiscal policies and taxes as removing justified economic protections for minorities, whose cultural and national identities placed them at a disadvantage compared to their Russian and western European competitors. As Nakhichevan Armenians bemoaned in 1825,

> We are not able to stand on equal footing in commerce with native Russians: we are ignorant of the Russian language, laws, clerical rituals, customs of the people, of vast knowledge of European commercial practices . . . [and] lack connections to capitalists who influence trade[.] [W]e are more inclined toward Oriental trade based on simple rules; in this we are especially assisted by our knowledge of Oriental languages, customs, and rituals of these peoples, [as well as] our ties to our coreligionists, close relatives who inhabit Oriental countries.[186]

Though it could be argued that these immigrants should or could have learned the Russian language and laws after over forty years of settlement on the Don River, they relied on arguments like the above to justify their unique economic position in Russian society.

Clearly, some long-established Armenian communities in Russia felt decisively alien in their adoptive country. This sentiment was not rooted in a different sense of home, however, because the diaspora had no single location to pinpoint as its collective cradle. Rather, a sense that Armenians were unprepared for the economic changes of the modern era sowed fear among the still-unassimilated immigrant communities of the imperial provinces, where they had fewer means and incentives for full integration than their compatriots in St. Petersburg and Moscow. Maintaining a culturally distinct life, the former Armenian refugees and their descendants engaged the world around them chiefly through the commercial enterprises that, in their view, the state's new fiscal policies threatened.

Ironically, in the contemporaneous socioeconomic discourse, this partially self-perpetuated image of Armenians as nonassimilated outsiders buttressed some elite Russians' distrust of tsarist-subject Armenians. Thus, while few state officials resisted the policy of colonizing newly annexed territories with foreign-subject Armenians, certain members of Tsar Alexander's coterie opposed the state's domestic economic policies toward Armenians. In particular, senior tsarist agents feared the social and economic implications of promoting Armenian commerce by extending their former exclusive privileges. At stake, in essence, was the preeminence of the Great Russian nation within the Russian Empire, and by the third decade of the nineteenth century, Armenian merchants joined Jews and other groups that supposedly threatened to alter the social hierarchy of the polyethnic empire.

In linking Armenians and Jews, Finance Minister Kankrin cited Ermolov's assessment from 1820, when the Caucasus commander argued against partial and exclusive economic privileges for Armenians.[187] The state's "excessive patronage of these Orientals," cautioned Kankrin in January 1826, "can have negative consequences. The spirit of Oriental commerce, akin to the haggling of Jews, certainly will lead to the expulsion of Russian merchants, as General Ermolov has also noted."[188] Kankrin believed that the incentives provided to Armenians in Russia's internal provinces damaged the status of Russian merchants, who faced being squeezed out by Armenians' supposed Oriental business prowess, potentially yielding Armenian-dominated commercial centers in the Russian heartland. "In any case, one can hardly expect anything useful from cities inhabited by Armenians, Jews, Bukharans, Persians, and Persian [nomads]," insisted Kankrin, emphasizing the recent drop in tax revenue from Astrakhan, as well as the alleged decline of "some Lithuanian cities, where Jews more and more push out the Christian population."[189] This collective stereotype became well entrenched in Russian popular thought, with the ethnographer and writer Vladimir Dal' in 1861 lumping together Armenians, Greeks, Jews, and Indians as "predominantly trading peoples."[190]

In the spring of 1827, the Council of Ministers took up the issue of Armenian economic standing, yielding a heated dispute over the status of ethnonational minorities in the empire. Kankrin insisted to the other ministers that the relevant decrees Catherine, Paul, and Alexander had issued either had long expired or could no longer be justified. Kankrin focused particularly on the supposedly detrimental impact that Armenian merchants in Astrakhan had on their Russian counterparts.[191] "Cunning" Armenian dealers, the finance minister testified, feigned ignorance of the Russian language and laws to circumvent tax dues and thereby gained an unfair edge over their Russian competitors. The imminent consequence, he warned, would be that these "foreigners" would "crush" the Russians.[192] Armenians already owned more property in the city than all of the local non-Russian groups combined: from a total real estate value of 2.5 million rubles owned by non-Russian residents, Armenians held over 1.8 million rubles in real estate.[193] In a word, Kankrin demanded that all Armenian merchants in southern Russian regions, including the Caucasus, be forced to join guilds and to pay corresponding taxes.

Kankrin's colleagues acknowledged the extensive and diverse prerogatives Armenians had enjoyed for decades. They also agreed with the finance minister and some provincial governors that these privileges had often allowed local Armenian merchants to marginalize other traders, including Russians.[194] However, the Council of Ministers ruled that Alexander's empire-wide fiscal laws excluded Armenians, citing both the tsar's 1808 exemption of Armenians from his 1807 requirements and the guilds law of 1824, which omitted those "Orientals," such as Armenians, whose commerce was regulated by special guidelines. Consequently, the council found that Armenian merchants of southern Russia must remain under the pre-1807 laws governing their transactions and that provincial authorities could not force them into guilds. In acknowledging the confusion and contradiction that defined the state's introduction of the guilds law in 1824, the Council of Ministers emphasized that Tsar Nicholas I in November 1826 instructed Kankrin to undertake a revision of that law.[195]

An irritated Kankrin countered the council's decision, arguing, "[The matter at hand has] not the slightest relation to the revision of the guilds regulation, for no matter what, the question will always remain: In Russia, do Armenians have more rights than Russians?"[196] He urged that the state must enforce the requirements of 1807 and 1824 to prevent the "squeezing out" (*vytesnenie*) of Russian merchants from southern provinces. "If in former times it was necessary to provide privileges for Armenians to increase Oriental trade," the finance minister stressed, "then now [such privileges] can only become burdensome for indigenous subjects, while time has already rooted many Orientals in Russia."[197] While Kankrin's views on Armenians and Jews smacked of racism, his economic vision held that Armenians had been overly privileged, producing social inequalities that hurt regional dynamics.

His colleagues disagreed. The chairman of the Department of Economy of the State Council maintained that Armenians' arguments were justified, that they had followed proper procedure in submitting their petitions (unlike other, unspecified groups), and cited the examples of other small groups, such as "Evangelical brotherly societies," that enjoyed exclusive economic privileges in southern Russia without broader detrimental impacts.[198] He also asserted that renewing Armenian privileges would have "incomparably" more "calming" effects on southern Russia's Armenians than would implementing the requirements Kankrin urged. The chairman of the Council of Ministers, the

Department of Civil and Religious Affairs, and the Department of Laws all agreed with this view. Only the director of the Interior Ministry sided with Kankrin, who countered that the State Council alone, not the Council of Ministers, had the authority to determine whether and how a royal decree should be enforced. Tsar Nicholas I concurred, ordering that the matter be forwarded to the State Council to determine, as the monarch jotted, "whether it is fair to give immigrants *eternal* advantages over native Russians."[199] The tone of the tsar's note left little doubt as to his view on this issue.

After years of wrangling among senior statesmen and after consecutive bureaucracies passed on the question of Armenian tax obligations, the matter was finally resolved in October 1833. A decade after Ekim Lazarev and other Armenians had begun to petition the state to extend Armenian merchants' exemptions, the State Council formally rejected their appeals and ruled that all Armenian merchants in southern Russian provinces must abide by the general tax regulations governing the activities of all traders.[200] Kankrin triumphantly informed provincial governors that local Armenian businessmen were henceforth required to enroll in merchant guilds and pay corresponding taxes, for Tsar Nicholas had concurred with the State Council's proclamation that "[it is] inappropriate to provide advantages to Armenians over Russians."[201]

By the 1820s, Armenians had assumed two seemingly conflicting identities in the Russian political imagination. On the one hand, tsarist authorities actively recruited foreign-subject Armenians in Persia and Turkey to colonize the Caucasus. On the other hand, the economic success of long-settled Armenians in southern Russia—an objective of Catherine the Great and her successor—unnerved some tsarist officials, such as Ermolov and Kankrin, and threatened the social superiority of ethnic Russian elements in the provinces. These findings will not surprise readers familiar with Valerie A. Kivelson and Ronald G. Suny's explanation: "Empire was both about differentiating peoples one from another and a cosmopolitan mixing that produced hybrid combinations of colonizer and colonized."[202]

Russia's political elite viewed Armenians as simultaneously advantageous to Russian imperial goals and also threatening to the social hierarchy of the southern territories. The state's cancellation of exclusive commercial rights previous tsars had granted to Armenian merchants demonstrated the degree to which immigrant Armenians had succeeded in establishing deep roots in their new homeland and the unnerving impact this produced on some Russian statesmen. Yet Armenians were not simply a part of the imperial discourse; the nature of Russian political structures was in flux during this period. The standardizing fiscal policies of Finance Minister Kankrin embody a palpable tension between the old models—the cumbersome empires of eighteenth-century Spain and England—and the modern, post-Napoleonic powers that strove to govern their multiethnic realms with the efficiency and regularity of a nation-state.

While the state transplanted foreign-subject Armenians into the South Caucasus and provided them with economic incentives, in other southern provinces it also confronted successful Armenian merchants who it believed threatened Russian social dominance. Ironically, Armenians' economic privileges turned their proverbial mercantile prowess into reality, prompting fears that Armenian commerce was bound to crush its Russian competition. Thus, St. Petersburg pursued two seemingly contradictory policies vis-à-vis Armenians in the empire: it supported fledgling Armenian communities in the Caucasus but canceled tax exemptions for more-established Armenian groups elsewhere in Russia.

This fact evinces the complex process by which Russians came to "know" Armenians in the first third of the nineteenth century. Tsarist political elites essentialized Armenians into two broad, often complementary, categories: diligent but avaricious minorities and politically loyal but culturally insular subjects. From the government's efforts to convert the Lazarev Academy into a vocational school for merchants to Paskevich's insistence on Armenians' imminent economic rejuvenation of the South Caucasus, Russian statesmen constructed an image of a national group that could be used toward tsarist advantages. The state portrayed in a constructive manner the groups it recruited, thus justifying the human and financial resources it expended upon their absorption. Essentializing a small and still alien population permitted the state to govern and manipulate it more efficiently. The attendant stereotype of cunning businessmen was a product of Russian cultural tropes that relegated commerce to foreign—European, Jewish, "Oriental"—peoples and professed to disdain work for the sake of financial profit.

In reality, Armenian immigrants from Persia and the Ottoman Empire were no more or less diligent than their Russian, Georgian, and Muslim neighbors, but portraying them as such was in the government's interest. The same objectives prompted the Russian characterization of Armenians as political and military allies who distinguished themselves by maintaining solidarity with Russians in the face of Muslim repression. A generation after their arrival in the tsar's domain, however, Armenians in the strategically important southern Russian cities outside of the Caucasus gained a degree of economic and social prominence that piqued regional and imperial officials. But exclusive economic privileges, not inherent mercantile acumen, had granted Armenians advantages over their indigenous neighbors. Armenians of the southern cities resisted relinquishing this status not simply for financial reasons but also because they were slow to integrate into Russia's cultural fabric, employing motifs of "Oriental" distinction to justify their refusal to comply with uniform fiscal policies. As the next chapter shows, the autocracy continued to struggle to incorporate different sections of its internal Armenian diaspora during the reign of Tsar Nicholas I (1825–55), when the state sought to standardize the tax laws and the religion-related statutes governing its Armenian subjects.

CHAPTER 3

Integration and Reorientation

Religious and Economic Challenges in 1830–1856

At midcentury, Russian statesmen proffered competing visions for the social and economic role that Armenians should play in the tsarist empire. By 1830, when Russia emerged from wars with Persia and the Ottoman Empire as the new master of the Caucasus, Russo-Armenian relations centered on two spheres: religious and economic. As the Russian state absorbed the Armenian nation into the empire, the autocracy relinquished some economic and cultural control over its Armenian subjects in expectation of reciprocal political benefit. Yet in the midst of governmental reform, St. Petersburg struggled to integrate Armenians.

This chapter studies the contradictory fiscal statutes and rivalries among senior statesmen, punctuated by shifting competition and cooperation between the Orthodox and Armenian Churches, which marked the state's search for effective Armenian policies. Tsar Nicholas I (1825–55) sought standardized tax laws and religious regulations for his Armenian and other subjects as part of a broader pursuit of his own vision of a well-ordered police state, or *Polizeistaat*. Yet the encounter between Nicholaevan Russia and Armenians confirms Ann Laura Stoler's venerable argument that "imperial states operate as states of exception that vigilantly produce exceptions to their principles and exceptions to their laws."[1]

As Marc Raeff has shown, "Nicholas was narrowly conservative and afraid of bringing any radically new elements into Russia's political organization."[2]

The tsar sought small adjustments to the "machinery of government," and wished to lubricate its gears for smooth functioning, but opposed fundamental changes. To this end, the emperor tasked jurist Mikhail Speransky with codifying Russian law to clarify the legal procedures for state bureaucrats and thereby deliver "consistency, uniformity, and order."[3] But in confronting the legal loopholes into which Armenian communities in Russia fell, the Old Regime often prioritized not only juridical and fiscal uniformity but also geopolitical aims beyond Russia's frontiers. For that reason, most statesmen chose accommodation over acculturation as the method of integrating newly absorbed Armenians into the empire's political and social life.

Under Tsar Nicholas I, the state codified the activities of Orthodox and non-Orthodox groups in what one historian has termed a "project of administrative modernization."[4] Even during efforts to streamline the legal systems of governance, state policy toward the non-Orthodox often reflected Nicholas's vigilance. Indeed, new statutes and reformed administrative practices produced as many restrictions as opportunities. Under Nicholas I, the government targeted Jews for full-scale conversion more than at any other time in the nineteenth century, as John Klier has shown, subjecting them to the conscription system and the education policies of Sergei Uvarov, the architect of the Orthodoxy, Autocracy, Nationality doctrine.[5] After the Polish uprising of 1830–31, senior tsarist administrators in the northwestern provinces, as part of their anti-Polish, Russifying initiatives, sought to replace all local bureaucrats of Polish heritage with ethnic Russian officials.[6] In 1839, the state formally dissolved the Uniate Church, absorbing it into the Orthodox Church and portraying the action as a necessary de-Catholicization and de-Polonization of the northwestern borderlands.[7]

Yet the Armenian experience, distinguished by the political implications of its transregional diaspora, suggests that Nicholas's government at times pursued objectives that it considered more important than Russification and political subjugation on the periphery. In seeking to reconcile the demands of a well-regulated country with the circumstances of such imperial minorities as Armenians, the autocracy's foreign affairs imperatives often shaped its domestic policies. The Armenian Church represented a key factor in this equation. While in 1836 the state solidified the legal status of Ejmiatsin and its tsarist followers, it went no further in exerting control over Armenian religious life. Unlike Nicholas's Jewish, Georgian, and Muslim subjects, Armenians escaped the first half of the nineteenth century without experiencing extensive government interference in their material and political cultures.

National Turbulence: Imperial and Caucasian Challenges

After the Second Russo-Persian War ended in 1828, Russia consolidated its annexed lands by establishing new administrative spaces. Most of Eastern Armenia, comprising the former Persian khanates of Yerevan and Nakhichevan, became known as Armianskaia Oblast, or the Armenian region, with its center at Yerevan. The autocrat rejected sporadic Armenian calls for the establishment of an autonomous Armenia, insisting instead on the designation of an oblast for Eastern Armenia.[8] Yet, in a likely concession, the emperor appointed Armenian-heritage Major General Vasilii Bebutov commander of the territory. Pleased by his Caucasus high commissioner's accomplishments, Nicholas bestowed on General Ivan Paskevich the title *graf* Erivanskii (Count of Yerevan) and reassigned him to Warsaw, where he crushed the Polish rebellion of 1830–31.

Paskevich's successor arrived in Tiflis in October 1831. General Baron Grigorii V. Rosen had distinguished himself during the Napoleonic Wars and the recent Polish campaigns. His six years as high commissioner of the Caucasus (1831–37) focused on combating North Caucasian highlanders led by the adroit Avar warlord Imam Shamil.[9] At the same time, Rosen worked to integrate the economy and society of the South Caucasus with the rest of the country. In the mostly Muslim-populated North Caucasus, the spread of Muridism, a Sufist-political movement, challenged the tsarist hold on the region as soon as Russia emerged from wars with Persia and the Ottoman Empire in 1829. Muridism "did not recognize any worldly laws other than those laid down by the prophet Muhammed in the Shari'a."[10] Rejecting the Russian subjugation of their lands, the followers of Muridism waged a protracted jihad against the northern infidels. The Muridist movement's most deft leader, Shamil, rose to prominence in 1836, when Russian agents warily noted his success in preaching Shari'a law to the residents of Dagestan and Chechnya.[11]

Rosen's initial policies relied on force to pacify the insurgency, but the unfamiliar terrain and hostile locals impeded tsarist military success. The general sought to confiscate land used by the *gortsy* (highlanders) for agriculture and cattle rearing and to provide it to Cossack colonists. He also proposed using special border guards to cut off the highlanders' "connections" with Ottoman Turks along the Black Sea coast.[12] At a time when two indigenous insurgencies—in Poland and the North Caucasus—challenged Russian imperial rule, the nationalities policies enacted in St. Petersburg often relied on repressive tactics.

The revolt of aristocratic Poles in 1830–31 threatened Russia's grip on the western borderlands, which it had annexed in the late eighteenth century. In sending Paskevich and an army to suppress the rebellion in Warsaw, Nicholas—who crowned himself king of Poland in May 1829—signaled that he intended to crush challenges to his authority. Yet Nicholas's response to the Polish insurrection evinced the degree to which he fused personal emotions with the politics of governance.[13] Distrustful of military elites after the Decembrist uprising and suspicious that the republican cries of *Liberté, égalité, fraternité* had infected his aristocratic subjects in the peripheries, Nicholas viewed Poland, the Caucasus, and other territories as integral components of his empire and saw any tests of this arrangement as a personal affront. After his army suppressed the Polish rebels, the tsar berated the vanquished gentry: "If you stubbornly maintain your dreams of an imaginary utopia, of a separate nationality, of an independent Poland, of all these unrealistic fantasies, you can do nothing but incur grave disaster . . . for at the slightest disturbance, I will crush your city, destroy Warsaw, and of course I will not rebuild it."[14]

Nicholas took a similarly heavy-handed approach to the Georgian elites of the South Caucasus, among whom the Russian administration uncovered a conspiracy in 1832.[15] War Minister Count Aleksandr Chernyshev directed Rosen to arrest "several Georgian princes and noblemen," citing evidence of a "quite serious . . . plot" that sought Georgian independence from St. Petersburg.[16] In the summer of 1833, under the pretext that heirs of deposed Georgian royals continued to use their formal court titles in correspondence, Nicholas instructed Rosen's administration to intercept and burn their mail.[17] At the same time, the tsar worked to smooth the government's relationship with the Georgian aristocracy, sending a special envoy to Tiflis to avert a major schism. In a sanguine speech to the Georgian elite, the ambassador extraordinaire Major-General Konstantin Chevkin opined: "Having become acquainted with Georgians during the battles of the last Persian war, I have come to consider them as brothers, and believe that a Russian [*russkii*] who is devoted to his emperor must be a good Georgian, just as a loyal Georgian must be a good Russian [*rossiianin*]."[18] Yet the South Caucasus's administrative and economic incorporation into the Romanov Empire posed as many challenges for Rosen as the political resistance of Georgian elites.

Reflective of the regional and policy inconsistencies that characterized the entire imperial taxation system,[19] the deficiencies of the fiscal policies in the South Caucasus frustrated the locals. In early 1833, a survey of the population of Armianskaia Oblast revealed the residents' discontent with the local administration.[20] Armenians, Azeris, and Kurds alike complained of the slow bureaucratic processes and disparate regulations that complicated their daily lives. For example, in the first quarter century of Russian rule in the South Caucasus, tsarist overlords, wary of rattling the locals, left Georgian provinces under former Persian tax rates and allowed the regional administration to use all of the tax revenue for the benefit of the region, a deviation from standard policy in other regions.[21] In 1824, confusion ensued when officials in the South Caucasus, unlike their colleagues in neighboring districts, abandoned the household tax in favor of the poll tax. Another inconsistency had Muslim residents of the Caucasus, distrusted by the imperial authorities, pay a special military tax instead of taking part in conscription.[22]

Perhaps the key discrepancy in Russian attitudes toward Armenians arose from tsarist agents' ambiguous perception of Armenian cultural identity. From the emperor to the rank-and-file soldier, Russians labeled the indigenous peoples of the Caucasus, both Christians and Muslims, as *aziatsy* (Asiatics). Yet Armenians enjoyed a particular position in this discourse thanks to their liminal physical status and a shared religious culture, confirming that gradation of "othering" informed the Old Regime's incorporation of the Caucasus. Referring to the residents of Armianskaia Oblast, one Russian report from 1833 complained, "Most of them can be called semi-wild [*poludikimi*] people, who interpret the slowness of resolving their matters as oppression on the part of the Russian government."[23] Such tsarist sentiments, common among the administrators of the South Caucasus, consistently delineated a cultural separation between the ostensibly civilized, and European, Russians, on the one hand, and the "semi-wild" natives of the Caucasus, on the other. At the same time that Russian imperial agents engaged in cultural "othering," they remained aware of the region's delicate political situation vis-à-vis the neighboring Muslim empires. Indeed, the same report cautioned, "[Such circumstances] give our government no positive influence on the residents of the neighboring powers, who consider [such bureaucratic deficiencies] to be measures that are oppressive for Muslims."[24] Russian chauvinism patronized Armenians as *aziatsy*, but they remained familiar, "our" Asiatics.

Economic concerns also plagued the administration of Armianskaia Oblast. By early 1834, Rosen turned his attention to the province's "insignificant [tax] revenue" of 120,000 rubles per year.[25] He blamed the situation on the continuation of Persian tax practices. Inconsistent regional taxation policies also vexed the locals, who demanded a simplified system. Rosen collaborated with General Vasilii Bebutov, the commander of Armianskaia Oblast, to abolish the Persian system and compile more accurate data about local agriculture and trade. They also introduced taxes for the mostly Armenian farmers who had settled in the region four to seven years earlier and still enjoyed tax-free farming.[26] The changes "exceeded expectations," and by 1835 the province yielded

215,000 rubles in tax revenue, compared to the 120,000 collected the previous year.[27] Improved fiscal policies in the South Caucasus, however, did not relieve the deteriorating security situation in the North Caucasus and belied deeper problems with Rosen's administration. A crisis brewed beneath the surface.

In the fall of 1837, Nicholas became the first tsar since Peter the Great to visit the Caucasus.[28] Responding to a crescendo of rumors, the autocrat came to address a tangle of administrative and security deficiencies, including a corruption scheme in which the emperor's aide-de-camp and Rosen's son-in-law, Prince Alexander Dadiani, was implicated.[29] Nicholas also was eager to signal to Europe that Russia's claims to the region remained firm, despite the native insurgency and the growing commercial rivalry with British marine merchants. The monarch visited Yerevan, Tiflis, Vladikavkaz, and several other important cities. In Tiflis, the regional administration's headquarters, the tsar publicly dismissed several senior officials. The emperor also replaced Rosen with General Evgenii Golovin, reprimanding the former for his failure to quell the North Caucasus uprising and for his administration's bureaucratic shortfalls. Nicholas instructed Golovin: "Do not start anything [hoping] for luck, [for] it is better to delay until success is certain; in a word, carry out matters in such a way that, having taken a step forward, no steps are taken back."[30] But the change of officials did not affect policy. Nicholas, his ministers, and Golovin continued to pursue a military solution to Shamil's rebellion, and the region's fiscal, criminal, and civil statutes remained inconsistent, partial, and often contradictory.

This climate reflected the government's struggle to define its mission in the Caucasus. In December 1839, tsarist ministers convened to debate whether the South Caucasus "should be seen as a colony or a part of Russia."[31] Finance Minister Egor Kankrin argued that the region's social composition rendered it a colony, with only the Georgian nobility approaching the cultural pedigree of its Russian counterpart. Rosen disagreed with him, emphasizing instead the local population's vast trade networks, something the government could not risk losing through the type of colonial marginalization that the British displayed in India. Foreign Minister Karl Nesselrode also highlighted the delicate politics required to take full advantage of the region's economic offerings, but he believed that Armenians and Georgians could be "civilized" through the expansion of modern regional commerce.[32] Siding with Rosen and Nesselrode, most statesmen concurred that the South Caucasus had to be incorporated into Russia's social and political orbit.

Reflecting these efforts to integrate the Caucasus into the country, in 1840 the regional administration underwent major reshuffling. Armianskaia Oblast was abolished and its territory subsumed into the new Gruzino-Imeretinskaia *guberniia* (Georgian-Imeretian Province); the eastern portion of the Caucasus became Kaspiiskaia Oblast (the Caspian region).[33] The former was divided into eleven *uezdy* (districts), including the Yerevan and Tiflis Districts, and the latter into seven *uezdy*. Initial steps were taken to replace adat and Shari'a with Russian laws, but a backlash by some local communities prevented the full implementation of new statutes for some time.[34] Criminal cases were tried in civil rather than military courts, and the jurisdiction of civil administrators grew at the expense of their military counterparts.[35] Nevertheless, a St. Petersburg commission determined in 1842 that the state's administrative reforms had failed.

What prompted the changes of the 1840s? Even if Armenians perceived the region as their "motherland," tsarist concerns about the political implications of this circumstance did not drive the redrawing of boundaries at this point. True, the location and symbolic nomenclature of Armianskaia Oblast rendered it the de facto homeland of the Armenian people. Although the reaction of contemporaneous Armenians to the 1840 reorganization remains unclear, some modern Armenian historians have interpreted the province's dissolution as a Russian attack on Armenian nationalist dreams.[36] But these assertions are based on examples of sporadic, individual calls for Armenian activism, which hardly registered on the radar of imperial authorities in the 1840s. Economic concerns, not perceived national-political threats, guided the government's administrative reshuffling here. Organized Armenian nationalism began to endanger Romanov territorial integrity only decades later, in the 1870s and 1880s, eliciting punitive reactions from the regional and imperial authorities. Indeed, Russian sources remain mute about collective Armenian nationalism until the second half of the nineteenth century, suggesting that the key stimuli for the administrative reforms in 1840 were economic vitality and bureaucratic efficacy, rather than fears of Armenian separatism.

Frustrated with the security situation and realizing that the reorganization of 1840 was insufficient, Tsar Nicholas in 1842 replaced Golovin with General Alexander Neidgardt. The latter assumed command of the Independent Caucasus Corps at the time of Shamil's zenith and Russian authority's nadir. Neidgardt had one paramount task. "I want no conquests and [even] the thought of them consider criminal," the tsar dictated when dispatching the general to the Caucasus.[37] The pacification of the *gortsy* was the state's primary objective, followed by the improvement of the region's broader administration and bureaucracy. Moritz Wagner, a German explorer who met Neidgardt in the 1840s, described the tsarist official as "a worthy, honest man, of unsophisticated character, just and severe; endowed with sound practical sense, but without superior talent, political penetration, or knowledge of mankind—no magnanimous character, such as Yermoloff, yet an improvement on his predecessors, Rosen and Golowin."[38]

Despite Neidgardt's mission to suppress Shamil's rebellion, the government began to express openness to "political," nonmilitary solutions to the North Caucasus crisis. The region's "conquest should not be achieved only through weapons, but instead [you] must act carefully, patiently," the tsar emphasized to Neidgardt.[39] Indeed, months before Golovin's demotion, a secret memorandum recommended offering rewards and agricultural assistance to the *gortsy*.[40] The proposal argued that through economic incentives and improved relations with the natives, the government could achieve more lasting results than through perennial campaigns, stressing that Russian agents must not "offend" native sensibilities and customs.[41] But the plan also called for a divide-and-conquer strategy, using money to fan discord among Shamil's commanders, "and even to give rise to a bloody feud, forcing them to fight among each other and thus weakening them."[42] This scheme found support from such senior tsarist statesmen as War Minister Chernyshev, who argued: "The British were able to secure their sovereignty in India through political means. That way they conserved their troops and saved time in conquering the region. Should we not try this system?"[43]

By the mid-1840s, Tsar Nicholas recognized that more than a new commander was needed. Less than two years after Neidgardt's promotion, and disappointed in the general's failure to check the spread of Shamil's insurgency,[44] Nicholas turned to Count General Mikhail Vorontsov. Educated in London during his father's tenure as Catherine the Great's ambassador to England, the nobleman had served in his youth in the Caucasus under Pavel Tsitsianov.[45] The general's credentials included military distinctions in wars against the French and Ottomans and an impressive record as the governor of Novorossiia (New Russia) and viceroy of Bessarabia. In late 1844, a frustrated Tsar Nicholas, expressing his "respect and dedication" to Vorontsov, asked the general to become the first viceroy of the Caucasus.[46]

As viceroy (1845–54), Vorontsov made a real difference, because he received "enormous and extraordinary" powers to make major decisions without consulting the ministers in St. Petersburg.[47] Not since Grigorii Potemkin in Catherine's era did a Russian imperial administrator receive such carte blanche from the monarch.[48] Respected by his army and enjoying the support of War Minister Chernyshev, Vorontsov justified the tsar's trust by turning the tide against Shamil (despite some notable early disasters) and reforming the regional bureaucracy.[49] Vorontsov embraced diplomacy and economic incentives to win over disenchanted Dagestani villagers to his side, eroding Shamil's influence to such degree that the rebels posed little practical threat to Russian interests in the Caucasus when the Crimean War erupted in 1853.

To the south of the mountains, reform was the mantra of the new administration. Unlike his predecessors, Vorontsov co-opted local national elites into the regional political structure, recruiting Georgian, Armenian, and other aristocrats and community leaders.[50] He also invested in the development of the region's cultural life, establishing schools, libraries, scholarly societies, and a theater in Tiflis.[51] As a result, according to one historian, the "Georgian nobility, which fifteen years earlier had plotted to murder Russian officials and separate Georgia from the empire, made its peace with the tsarist autocracy during the viceroyalty of Vorontsov."[52] For middle-class Armenians of Tiflis and Yerevan, too, Vorontsov's changes promised a brighter future, helped by the viceroy's simplification of trade regulations, support for local students' study in St. Petersburg and Moscow (including at the Lazarev Institute), and similar enlightened policies. The viceroy's popularity among South Caucasian natives, especially elite Georgians, resulted in a statue erected to him in Tiflis. According to one scholar, through the statue locals "presented him as a father figure, placed him in an otherworldly environment, linked him to the forces of nature and the majesty of the highest mountains, and turned him into some kind of *Übermensch.*"[53] The viceroy divided the territory into new *gubernii*, including the Yerevan, Tiflis, and Baku Provinces. The Yerevan Province, which he created in 1850, resurrected and expanded the old Armianskaia Oblast. In ill health, the viceroy resigned in 1854 and died in Odessa two years later.[54]

Vorontsov trusted Armenians. He facilitated the education of Armenian youths in the empire's best academies and universities, supported the construction of new Armenian churches, and listened to the requests and suggestions of the Tiflis Armenian merchants.[55] More than his predecessors, Vorontsov stressed that "throughout the region, the Armenians are entirely devoted to us."[56] At the end of his tenure, the viceroy lauded the "unquestionable loyalty and even affection toward us of all Armenians."[57] In particular, he praised tsarist-subject Armenians' willingness to "serve against our enemies." Among the Armenian elites who volunteered for Russian service, many had performed "excellent exploits . . . [and] acquired glory and general trust." Among middle-class Armenians, too, the viceroy highlighted their mercantile successes. Unlike such predecessors as Tsitsianov and Ermolov, who faulted Armenian entrepreneurs for their perceived avarice, Vorontsov praised the broader social and economic benefits of their business acumen. "Armenians also are the government's main instrument for leases and contracts here," he summarized, "[and] competition among them reduces prices to our advantage."[58]

Vorontsov's perceptions of Armenians exemplify the tensions of the autocracy's general oscillation between Armenophilia and Armenophobia throughout the nineteenth century. In this episode, affirmations of Armenian political loyalty accompanied concerns about the social marginalization that middle-class Armenians' economic successes had produced. For all his praise, Vorontsov noted with a hint of caution that Tiflis Armenians "hold almost all [commerce] in their hands; for the Georgians, based on an ancient militant spirit and general disposition, are not capable of it."[59] Yet the Caucasus administration's facilitation of social, economic, and cultural advancement of Armenians and other natives, in line with the broader reform effort that increasingly prioritized diplomacy and economic development, represented the government's transition away from the punitive policies employed by previous regional commanders, including Ermolov and Paskevich. Armenians consolidated their position as core allies of the Russian administration, which relied on the local businesses of their middle class and the military service of their elites.

In early 1855, General Nikolai Muravev replaced Vorontsov, taking command during a particularly dangerous time for Russian imperial aims, when the Ottoman Empire, Britain, and France allied against what they saw as St. Petersburg's menacing foreign policy. While the majority of combat revolved around Crimea, the war's reverberations reached the Caucasus. As early as the summer of 1853, Shamil's rebels and Ottoman officials discussed a coordinated campaign in the Caucasus.[60] Soon Ottoman forces attacked Russia on sea and land, targeting the Black Sea coast and attempting to invade western Georgia. Shamil, meanwhile, set his sights on Tiflis. Despite these efforts, British and Ottoman plans to collaborate with North Caucasian rebels failed.[61] Tsarist forces repelled both Ottoman and highlander threats and pursued the attackers beyond Russian lines. In November 1855, the tsar's army captured Kars.

The Crimean War marked the first major Russian engagement in which well-educated and Russified Armenians became renowned members of the regular army. Less a product of state-engineered Russification than an organic result of select Armenians' melding into elite Russian circles, this trend affected small numbers of Armenians. Yet the fact that these individuals attained personal distinction within the tsarist hierarchy signaled the gradual Russian acceptance of Armenians. While thousands of Armenian peasants and middle-class laborers in Russia and the Caucasus continued to experience social marginalization and orientalist derisiveness, a select cadre of their compatriots gained prominence. For example, General Vasilii Bebutov, the former head of the disbanded Armianskaia Oblast, earned the Order of St. George (second degree) in December 1853. Another Armenian-heritage commander, Guards Colonel Mikhail Loris-Melikov, led Armenian and Tatar cavalry units against Turkish troops,[62] a modest accomplishment in a career that would culminate in his promotion to interior minister in 1880.

Thus, for much of the 1830s and 1840s, imperial Russian policy in the Caucasus revolved around the reform of the regional bureaucracy and the suppression of the North Caucasus insurgency. The shuffling of generals in Tiflis yielded few results until the creation of the Caucasian viceroyalty and the arrival of Vorontsov, whose enlightened policies effected real change. The tsarist state demonstrated political adeptness when it transitioned from one-dimensional, heavy-handed measures toward the Muslims of Dagestan and Chechnya to a reliance on a combination of Vorontsov's diplomacy and his military persistence. Coupled with the Ottoman collapse in the Caucasus, these policies forced Shamil to surrender in 1859.

Although Russia decisively lost the Crimean War, thanks mainly to the Franco-British alliance, it achieved important results in its southern domains. Tsarist troops captured the sultan's prized Kars fortress, a Pyrrhic victory quickly nullified by European diplomatic intervention. Moreover, after more than two decades of bloody resistance, Shamil capitulated, dying years later in comfortable exile in Medina.[63] Finally, Russia maintained its claim as protector of Christians under Ottoman suzerainty, a position underscored by Tsar Nicholas during his declaration of war in April 1854: "We did not and do not search for conquests, or for a dominating influence in Turkey," but rather "[we search for] the restoration of the violated rights of the Orthodox Christian subjects of the Ottoman Porte."[64] To be sure, throughout the reign of Nicholas I, the circumstances of Christian confessions, Orthodox and heterodox, were simultaneously an opportunity and a liability for domestic and foreign policy. Few dynamics illustrate this point as thoroughly as the government's dialogue with the Armenian Church, whose links to a vast diaspora presented unique considerations for St. Petersburg.

Between God and Government

Uncovering the complex, but fundamentally cooperative, nature of the ties between Ejmiatsin and St. Petersburg under Nicholas I elucidates another aspect of the Russo-Armenian symbiosis. In the 1830s, the encounter between the government and the Armenian Church underwent major transformations. In 1836, eight years after the annexation of Ejmiatsin, the state codified the rights and obligations of the Armenian Church and its followers in Russia.

While the *polozhenie* (statute) of 1836 simultaneously granted powers and placed restrictions on the catholicos, it also carried implications beyond the Armenian ecclesiastical sphere. In particular, the autocracy wished to employ Ejmiatsin to facilitate its foreign policy in the Ottoman Empire and elsewhere. Moreover, in the interests of domestic stability and out of a sense of shared ecumenical culture, the Orthodox and Armenian Churches cooperated against threats to the integrity of the Armenian confession, as long as such collaboration did not encroach on the authority of the Russian Orthodox Church.

More than a monastic institution, Ejmiatsin represented the epicenter of political initiatives for Armenians who had no state of their own. Enjoying the recognition of the vast Armenian diaspora, albeit challenged by patriarchs in Jerusalem and Constantinople, the catholicos exercised authority over Armenian communities from western Europe to southern Asia. The political implications of this circumstance rendered control over Ejmiatsin a key objective of the tsar, the shah, and the sultan. When Russia seized the complex from Persia in 1828, it gained a new tool for its foreign policy. While tsarist diplomats struggled for influence in Constantinople and Tehran, with the absorption of Ejmiatsin Russia maneuvered to advance its interests through the leverage of local Armenian bishops, who, in contrast to their oft-mistreated lay compatriots, enjoyed social and political clout in the Ottoman Empire and Persia.

FIGURE 3.   Mother See of Holy Ejmiatsin in 2014. Author's collection.

Romanov agents ruminated much about "projecting influence" into neighboring empires through Armenians, but they rarely articulated specific aims. Russian statesmen hoped eventually to have the ability to deploy non-tsarist-subject Armenians as intermediaries or saboteurs. Officials upheld a generalized idea of "influence," which could encompass, depending on author and context, diplomacy, trade, military strategy, and intelligence gathering. From gaining a better sense of regional sociopolitical trends to insider knowledge about economic conditions to nurturing future wartime allies, tsarist representatives felt that the Armenian diaspora was, or could be, a useful instrument. Because religion was the glue that bound this diaspora, the Old Regime paid special attention to Ejmiatsin.

Nerses of Ashtarak, an ambitious and nimble Armenian clergyman, played a key role in the autocracy's interaction with the Armenian Church in much of the Nicholaevan era. Born just eleven miles from Ejmiatsin, Nerses received his education and early ecclesiastical administrative training as a junior priest in Greece, Moldavia, and Wallachia before moving on to posts within the Romanov Empire, including in Odessa and Bessarabia. Nerses gained prominence as the archbishop of the important diocese of Georgia, where he served between 1811 and 1830. Russian officials noted the prelate's administrative efficiency during his tenure in Tiflis and often relied on his connections to Persian officials, especially during the Second Russo-Persian War.[65] Harboring dreams of a self-governing Armenia, Nerses cooperated with General Paskevich and Colonel Lazar Ekimovich Lazarev during the war, and at its conclusion he facilitated the resettlement of Persian Armenians into Russian territory.[66] Yet Nerses's zealous advocacy for a vaguely autonomous Armenia conflicted with the tsarist state's decision to create Armianskaia Oblast.[67] As a result, in 1830 the state effectively exiled Nerses to Kishinev, where he became the first archbishop of the Bessarabian Armenian diocese.[68] The "benign" Efrem, whom Persians had removed from Ejmiatsin during the war, returned to lead the Armenian Church.

Despite Nerses's clash with tsarist policy, he enjoyed the support of the most prominent Russian-Armenian family, the Lazarevs. Shortly after Nerses's departure from Tiflis, Khristofor Ekimovich Lazarev, the family's patriarch, corresponded with Count Alexander von Benkendorf, the architect and head of the Third Section of the Imperial Chancellery, the secret police established after the Decembrist revolt.[69] A close confidant of the tsar, Alexander von Benkendorf was the brother of tsarist general and Lazarev ally Konstantin von Benkendorf. Lazarev lobbied Benkendorf to have Nerses transferred from Bessarabia to St. Petersburg, insisting, "It is necessary for the benefit of Russia—for the good of the Armenian people."[70] The Armenian magnate argued, "No one else is capable of successfully executing all-beneficial [*obshchepoleznykh*] intentions," and he wished to see Nerses play an active role in molding the state's policy toward the newly annexed regions of the South Caucasus. In extolling Nerses, Lazarev claimed that "his personal influence, his talent, his trust, his knowledge, and [his] reasoning, dependent on the cooperation of the local—and well-disposed—civilian leadership, can contribute quite a lot in all-beneficial matters."[71]

When the incumbent catholicos, Efrem, died in early 1830, Lazarev lobbied Benkendorf to facilitate Nerses's ascension to the apex of the Armenian Church, claiming that the selection of Nerses as catholicos represented the "unified, general request of the Armenian people and the entire clergy."[72] The prelate himself petitioned the tsar for permission to return to the South Caucasus. "I have served Russia for 30 years," Nerses insisted, "[I] have demonstrated in many ways and in important matters loyalty to the [Russian] emperors, to the benefit of the government and nation, [I] have entirely justified trust, especially in wartime, [and I am] filled with the direct spirit of devotion to Russia, which is blissfully united with Armenia."[73]

Nerses thus signaled his acquiescence to Armenia's political status and made clear that he abandoned dreams of Armenian autonomy. Yet, despite his appeals and Lazarev's advocacy, Nerses spent thirteen years in Bessarabia waiting to become catholicos, ascending to the post only in 1843. In his stead, the tsarist state "insisted" on the election in 1831 of a candidate more suitable to its political goals, Hovannes.[74] A confirmation of the tsar's influence on the ecclesiastical matters of the Armenian Church, this episode—remarkable because even Lazarev's intervention proved futile—suggested that the government took Nerses's political aspirations seriously and impeded his professional advancement. However, at the same time that it protected its domestic interests by intervening in the affairs of the Armenian Church, the Romanov state also used Ejmiatsin's broad authority to advance its foreign policy.

Russia deployed Ejmiatsin to forge ties with elements in the Ottoman Empire and beyond. The autocracy's considerations of the catholicos's influence abroad necessitated a "policy of indulgence" that privileged Ejmiatsin's external prestige over its internal control, as Paul Werth has demonstrated.[75] This approach had to be balanced between, on the one hand, amplifying the catholicos's authority over foreign Armenians and, on the other hand, enforcing the domestic legal and administrative obligations of tsarist subjects. For much of the nineteenth century, the state chose to augment Ejmiatsin's standing abroad in expectation of reaping benefits within the Ottoman Empire. Until the twilight of the 1800s, generations of tsars, ministers, viceroys, and high commissioners encouraged and expected the catholicos to cement almost total leverage over the transimperial Armenian diaspora.

St. Petersburg hastened to reestablish Ejmiatsin's influence among diaspora Armenians soon after absorbing the monastery in 1828. To be sure, some distant Armenian communities celebrated the change of Ejmiatsin's imperial master. Armenians living as far away as Madras, India, declared to Khristofor Ekimovich Lazarev their readiness to financially support the church and even to emigrate to Armianskaia Oblast.[76] The wars with Persia and Turkey in 1826–29, however, had weakened the links between the Ejmiatsin catholicos and his followers in the neighboring Muslim empires, who were wary of affirming the pro-Russian prelate's authority. Ecclesiastical matters between Russian- and Ottoman-subject Armenians became further strained when Catholicos Hovannes was elected in 1831 without the participation of Ottoman Armenian delegates.[77] Moreover, two rival Armenian patriarchs in the sultan's empire, at Constantinople and Sis, sought to assume more prominent roles in Armenian religious life and to eclipse Ejmiatsin's perennial authority. In Jerusalem, too, an Armenian patriarch awaited an opportunity to outshine his rival in the South Caucasus.

Hovannes supported the integration of the Armenian nation into Russian society. The catholicos envisioned the social and political melding of Armenians into Russian everyday life, while maintaining the markers of cultural distinction, such as religious rites, that formed the cornerstones of Armenian national identity. Hovannes viewed Armenians learning Russian and observing Russian laws not as a threat to Armenian ethnocultural identity but as a means toward social, economic, and political prosperity within the empire. In backing a proposed seminary at the Lazarev Institute, Hovannes asserted: "The young Armenian clergy, having been educated in the [Armenian] national Lazarev Institute of Moscow, quickly will connect morally with native Russians and consequently will adopt the customs and laws of their new fatherland."[78] Yet foreign policy matters often overshadowed the domestic dimensions of the Russo-Armenian ecclesiastical encounter.

Caucasus high commissioner Baron Rosen supported boosting Ejmiatsin's stature abroad. He reported to Tsar Nicholas, "[Hovannes] deserves particular attention because the spread of Ejmiatsin's influence on Armenians in Turkey is quite beneficial not only for him personally but also for our government politically."[79] From his election in 1831, Hovannes and Rosen cooperated to regain the prelate's standing among Ottoman Armenians. To this end, Rosen corresponded with the tsarist Foreign, Interior, and War Ministries to achieve such goals as the Ottoman acceptance of an Ejmiatsin nuncio in Constantinople.[80] The Russian government also tasked its ambassador in Constantinople, Apollinarii Butenev, with negotiating with the Armenian patriarchs of Sis and Jerusalem and urging them to endorse Hovannes's spiritual superiority and pronounce his name during liturgy, requests that the rival patriarchs rejected.[81] "This is a very important matter," emphasized Rosen to the monarch, because the foreign patriarchs' refusal to recognize Hovannes could precipitate a chain reaction among other, particularly Persian, Armenian communities. Rosen warned that hostile powers could co-opt such ostensibly ecclesiastical schisms for political purposes.[82]

Like Persia and the Ottoman Empire, Russia's European rivals also cautiously watched the tsar's growing influence over the Armenian Church in the 1830s and 1840s. Robert Curzon, the private secretary to the British ambassador in Constantinople, stressed: "[The tsar] will not fail to pull the strings which hang loosely in the hands of the Armenian Patriarch. If he pulls them evenly and well, he will advance his interests far and wide, even in the dominions of other princes, who may hardly be aware of the influence exercised in their states from a source so distant and unobtrusive. The danger in his case is, that he may use too great violence, and break the strings from too severe a tension, raising the storm against himself which he intended to direct against others."[83] Curzon echoed the sentiments of many European statesmen when he emphasized the potential political ramifications of St. Petersburg's patronage of Ejmiatsin: "The power of which [the tsar] holds the reins is one which may be used for the advancement of the greatest or the most ignoble ends." Given such far-reaching implications, by the mid-1830s the autocracy recognized the need for a clear state policy toward the Armenian Church.

The state answered this need with the *polozhenie* of 1836.[84] The royal fiat codified Armenians' freedom of worship, granted their church control over education, and acknowledged the institutional autonomy of the Armenian Church. The decree also formalized the church's existing practice of owning land for income, and it freed Armenian clergy from taxes.[85] The new regulations took into consideration the teachings and traditions of Armenian ecumenical culture, seeking to reconcile them with the demands of the modern *Polizeistaat*. Indeed, Tsar Nicholas directed his aides to ensure that the law was based on the Armenian Church's "own ancient ordinances" while also being "brought into conformity with the legal provisions of the Russian empire."[86] In another sign of the autocracy's acceptance of the Apostolic confession, in April 1836 the elite Cadet Corps in St. Petersburg introduced Armenian religious doctrine and language courses for Armenian-heritage students.[87]

While the 1836 statute placed restrictions on the Armenian faith, it formalized the ties between St. Petersburg and Ejmiatsin, eliciting little resistance from Armenians.[88] True, Ejmiatsin became formally subordinated to the Russian emperor, despite receiving more autonomy than other national churches, such as the Georgian Orthodox Church.[89] Although ostensibly the state dropped its "insistence" on the election of a tsarist-subject catholicos,[90] the *polozhenie* required Armenian clergy and laymen from Russia *and* abroad to elect two final candidates, among whom the tsar would choose the winner. Moreover, the curriculum of church schools required the approval of the Holy Synod and the Interior Ministry. Finally, a state representative observed the Ejmiatsin Synod to ensure the church's compliance with these regulations.[91] Despite such constraints, most tsarist-subject Armenians accepted the new regulations, pleased that standardized rules now guided the Russo-Armenian relationship.

For Armenians, the *polozhenie* surpassed the ad hoc policies of the previous decades, when the autocracy affirmed the importance of Armenians to its political aims by granting economic incentives and transplanting foreign-subject Armenians to Russia. By the mid-1830s, little doubt remained that Armenians held one of the keys to Russia's foreign policy vis-à-vis the Ottoman Empire and Persia and also to its internal tranquility in the Caucasus.[92] This circumstance represented a two-way dynamic. While the Old Regime utilized Ejmiatsin to advance its interests abroad, the Armenian Church relied on the imperial government to defend its domestic interests. For example, when in 1839 a renegade Orthodox monk, Ioann Malinovskii, published a controversial book in Moscow, Hovannes not only petitioned the tsar directly, but also convinced Interior Minister Lev Perovskii that the tome contained "unfair and offensive expressions against the Armenian-Gregorian confession."[93] The catholicos sought the state's help in preventing the publication of "books or articles related to [the Armenian faith] without first consulting the supreme ecclesiastical leadership of this confession and receiving from it precise information."[94]

The Orthodox Church supported Ejmiatsin's efforts to protect its interests. The Holy Synod agreed that Malinovskii's book contained "unfair information" about the Armenian faith and directed the office of church censorship (*dukhovnaia tsenzura*) to ensure that similar items would not be published and that reprints of Malinovskii's book would be censored.[95] In a curious development, the Holy Synod "saw with comfort" that Armenian doctrine aligned with Orthodox teachings in condemning the "heresies" of Aria, Macedonia, Nestorius, Eutyches, Severian, and the Monophysites. As a result, the Holy Synod requested from Ejmiatsin a thorough explanation of Armenian dogma, promising to use it to enforce stricter censorship of religious publications that, like Malinovskii's monograph, misrepresented the Armenian canon.[96] Tsar Nicholas approved these initiatives, because at midcentury St. Petersburg had no reason to constrain the growth of the Armenian Church's standing within and beyond the empire.

This episode evinced the state's imperative of supporting the integrity of its foreign faiths. As Werth maintains, imperial Russia's "multiconfessional establishment" provided "a series of significant collective rights to recognized religious groups and rendered the foreign confessions state religions entitled to certain forms of government patronage and protection."[97] To be sure, as one official tsarist document summarized, "the dogmas and rites of the Armenian Church must be inviolable in all their fullness and purity—without deviation and without change."[98] To protect the orthodoxy of the Armenian faith and educate state censors, the Armenian Church and the Russian government discussed compiling a "simple, direct, clear, and convenient" catechism of the Armenian doctrine in Russian.[99] More tellingly, this initiative sought to highlight the kinship of the Armenian and Orthodox confessions. The government optimistically contended that "every well-meaning and enlightened" person, having read the Armenian catechism in Russian, would "understand and be convinced that the goal of Christianity is one and the same in all Christian denominations"; "that the main tenets of the faith are the same, but the small and even trivial difference is only in a few words, in outward forms and in private ceremonies"; and "that the foundational stone of the Armenian Church agrees with the Greco-Russian Church, for the dogmas are based on reason and the power of Holy Scripture."[100] In a word, in the reign of Nicholas I, the tsarist state and the Armenian Church not only derived mutual political benefit but also coordinated efforts to publicize the dogmatic ties between the two national churches.[101] Although serious discord arose in the next decades, this symbiosis lasted until the last quarter of the nineteenth century.

The Russian government maintained the integrity of Armenian religious culture to derive political advantage. While the *polozhenie* of 1836 subordinated Ejmiatsin to St. Petersburg, it privileged the Armenian Church and, by extension, the Armenian nation, at a time when few other groups in the Caucasus or elsewhere received similar concessions. For example, tsarist officials not only ended the long tradition of Georgian peasants "volunteering" for bondage and prohibited the sale of serfs without land but in 1836 also required Georgian serf owners to provide documentary evidence of serf ownership, without which the bondsmen could legally seek freedom.[102] Interpreted by many Georgian elites as a Russian attack on their historical prerogatives, such restrictions pitted aristocratic Georgians against an "alien bureaucracy" and reminded them that they remained "the servant[s] of a new master."[103] While almost no Armenians owned serfs, as a nation they avoided similar constraints on their everyday life. The Romanov Empire absorbed the Georgian Orthodox Church into its own Orthodox Church's administration as early as 1811, and hardly anyone could imagine the government bestowing on Georgians such privileges as it granted to Armenians with the *polozhenie* of 1836. The irony of the matter was that the Orthodox Georgians, by belonging to the supranational, predominant faith of the empire, enjoyed fewer entitlements than the Apostolic Armenians.

The political implications of the Armenian diaspora and the Russian perception of Armenians as loyal regional allies explain these contrasting experiences. Until the twentieth century, tsarist administrators stubbornly hoped that sympathetic Armenian clerics and community leaders in neighboring empires would augment St. Petersburg's political and economic initiatives in those countries. Within the Caucasus, too, imperial officials viewed the local Armenians as the most reliable segment of indigenous society. Russian authorities did not distinguish between native and recently transplanted Armenians in the South Caucasus, perceiving them collectively as more aligned with tsarist goals than Georgians, Azeris, or North Caucasians. The influx into the South Caucasus of ethnic Russian sectarians in the 1830s and 1840s did not recalibrate these considerations, because officials generally distrusted these "heretics" and the newcomers struggled for years to establish themselves.[104]

The tenure of Catholicos Nerses (1843–57), who succeeded Hovannes, embodied the complex relationship between the state and the Armenian Church. On the death of Hovannes, Perovskii and Neidgardt agreed on the importance of "reinforcing the domination of the Ejmiatsin patriarchal throne over the entire Armenian Church and delivering to our government the moral influence over all Armenians, [including] those outside the empire."[105] To this end, the autocracy dispatched a "special bureaucrat" to Ejmiatsin, whom it tasked with "giving the election such a direction, that the lot falls on a person worthy of imperial approval, disposed toward Russia, and enjoying equal respect among foreign and Russian Armenians, even if the patriarch elected on these bases is not a Russian subject."[106] The sources are unclear about the results of this mission, but, with or without tsarist interference, the 1843 election boded well for the autocracy.

Unanimously elected by twenty-six tsarist- and foreign-subject Armenian delegates in April 1843, Nerses finally received the tsar's approval after thirteen years of banishment as the archbishop of the Bessarabian-Nakhichevan diocese.[107] Underscoring his efforts to woo the Armenian diaspora, Nicholas sent ornate gifts—crosses and rings decorated with precious stones—to the candidates who lost the election, including the archbishop of Jerusalem and several Persian and Ottoman Armenian representatives.[108] If the emperor variably employed carrots and sticks in dealing with other ethnonational minorities, at this moment the autocrat bet on diamonds as a tool of imperialism. Prioritizing the maintenance and expansion of its position as the patron of foreign-subject Orthodox Christians, particularly of Armenians in the Ottoman Empire, the Russian government focused on enticing the Armenian diaspora. The state sought not only to nurture ties with Ejmiatsin but also to develop rapport with Ejmiatsin's rivals abroad. The new catholicos, meanwhile, proved equally crafty in maneuvering between cooperation with and autonomy from St. Petersburg and its agents.

Nerses accomplished much in meeting Russian expectations. He reestablished the submission of the Constantinople patriarch to Ejmiatsin and normalized relations with the Ottoman government in 1844.[109] Nerses also partnered with Vorontsov to found a new "commercial school" in the South Caucasus and to send Armenian and other native students to elite institutions in the two capitals, including St. Petersburg University and the Lazarev Institute of Oriental Languages in Moscow.[110] The viceroy supported the catholicos's plans for a new seminary in Ejmiatsin, insisting to the tsar that this project would yield advantages "in the political sense," for there was "no doubt that Armenians from Constantinople, India, and other parts of the Orient will send their children to Ejmiatsin for education."[111] Vorontsov extolled Nerses to the tsar in 1846, praising the prelate as "always ready and always able to help in everything useful."[112] Before his retirement, too, Vorontsov lionized Nerses as the local administration's "powerful and always prepared weapon" and assured his replacement at the head of the Caucasus, Viceroy Aleksandr Bariatinskii: "I have always found in him full readiness to assist us in everything that is useful, . . . soon you will fully confirm this."[113]

Yet Nerses also did not shy away from asserting his independence. Privately, he criticized the limitations that the *polozhenie* of 1836 placed on Ejmiatsin's powers, viewing the law as constraining the Armenian Church's historical rights. In a more egotistical display of self-interest, the catholicos targeted not only Russian but also other Armenian challenges to his authority. Nerses undermined the Ejmiatsin Synod, seeing it as a threat to his clout, and also delayed the appointment of new bishops to amplify his influence. Such actions aroused the resentment of other senior Armenian clergy, including the archbishop of the Bessarabian-Nakhichevan diocese, who complained to the imperial capital about Nerses's excesses. With no viable alternatives, St. Petersburg tolerated the bold prelate but conceded, "The unlimited despotism of Patriarch Nerses is manifest in all of his actions."[114] Despite such impediments, the state encouraged the cultural and social fortification of the Armenian faith in the empire. Already by 1837, twenty-one Armenian parish schools and 824 churches dotted the Caucasus.[115]

Indeed, at times the autocracy made legal exceptions for the Armenian Church. In 1851, Nerses complained to Vorontsov that Catholic proselytizers in the South Caucasus were converting individual Apostolic Armenians into the Catholic faith.[116] Nerses accused Catholic missionaries of targeting young and uneducated Armenians.[117] Although these efforts bore limited fruit, they compelled Ejmiatsin to seek the state's assistance.[118] Vorontsov conveyed to Interior Minister Perovskii the catholicos's request "that the Armenian-Gregorian clergy have complete freedom in returning their progeny to the core of their church."[119] Nerses not only asked for the authority to take these actions without the preliminary approval of tsarist officials but also urged the government to expel Catholic Armenian priests from the Caucasus to Poland. Apparently in a concession, he allowed for the possibility of transferring Catholic Polish clergy to Russia proper and the Caucasus, including regions populated by Armenians.[120] Nerses likely believed that Armenians would be less inclined to accept Catholicism from ethnic Polish, rather than Armenian, priests. In effect, this illustrated Ejmiatsin's implicit assumption of the interplay between ethnic and religious identities among tsarist-subject Armenians. While Nerses likely realized that the sudden influx of Catholic Armenian clergy in Poland would cause myriad logistical problems, he acquiesced to accepting Catholic Polish priests among Armenian communities, confident that Polish proselytizers would be unsuccessful among his compatriots.

Tsarist officials endorsed Ejmiatsin's efforts to "shield Gregorian Armenians from Catholicism."[121] Vorontsov lobbied Perovskii to make a legal exception in this case, allowing the Armenian Church to convert Catholic Armenians to the Apostolic confession without the onerous participation of imperial ministers. Although state law required the bureaucratic approval of all conversions between non-Orthodox Christians, Vorontsov sided with Nerses in arguing that the Armenians presented a unique case. The interior minister concurred with the viceroy and the catholicos, concluding, "With respect to the Armenian Gregorian Church, Armenian Catholics occupy an exceptional position, because they are merely the lost progeny of that ancient church."[122] The emperor signed off on these measures,[123] but retained limits on the Armenian Church's engagement with the non-Armenian natives of the Caucasus.

While the autocracy supported Ejmiatsin's reconversion of wayward Catholic Armenians, it maintained a tight grip on the Armenian Church's missionary activity. In 1853, Catholicos Nerses petitioned to allow local tsarist officials in the Caucasus, rather than the tsar and his ministers in St. Petersburg, to permit voluntary Muslim baptism in the Armenian rite.[124] The autocracy rejected this request, pointing out that between 1843 and 1852 just 109 Caucasian Muslims converted to the Armenian creed.[125] The state had equally little tolerance for Orthodox apostasy. When in 1854 news reached St. Petersburg that "several" residents of Shemakha Province (in modern Azerbaijan) had converted from "Greco-Georgian" and, reports implied, Russian Orthodoxy to the Apostolic Armenian confession, Tsar Nicholas took up the case.[126] Although zealous local authorities had convicted the defectors of apostasy, the tsar and the Interior Ministry took a gentler tack, instructing regional officials in the Caucasus to return the individuals to Orthodoxy without "constraining their personality."[127] Hence the tsarist government protected the integrity of its predominant Orthodox confession against the encroachment of otherwise favored foreign faiths.

To be sure, the state and the Orthodox Church occasionally clashed with the Armenian Church. In 1857, the Orthodox leadership foiled Ejmiatsin's attempt to expand its foothold in Moscow.[128] The dispute traced to the fundraising of the city's Armenian community, which collected money for the construction of a monastery on the grounds belonging to an Armenian cemetery. Moscow's Armenians enlisted the support of the catholicos, who corresponded with the authorities to secure approval for the new monastery. But Moscow metropolitan Filaret opposed this initiative, alerting the Holy Synod to the Armenian plans and vociferously objecting to the perceived encroachment on his jurisdiction. Filaret argued that the city's Armenian population was too small to justify a new monastery, and he maintained that the approval of the project would "make an unfavorable impression on the Orthodox people of Moscow," who "from ancient times have been especially strongly marked by the character of the dominant confession in Russia, and in the interests of general well-being [the Orthodox community of Moscow] demands the protection of its character now and in the future."[129] Even more worrisome to Filaret was the likelihood that the Roman Catholic Church, emboldened by the Armenian example, would establish monasteries in Moscow and thus threaten not only the Orthodox hold on Moscow but also all of Orthodox Russia.

Thus the Armenian Church in the second quarter of the nineteenth century operated within a conditional framework. On the one hand, it enjoyed the exclusive right to convert non-Orthodox Christians into the Armenian faith and benefited from the government's distrust of Catholic and Protestant proselytizing. On the other hand, the church had to observe its Eastern Orthodox counterpart's prerogatives, maintaining a delicate balance between promoting its interests and avoiding antagonizing the venerable Russian institution.

The complexity of the relationship between the Armenian Church and the tsarist state lay in the fact that not just domestic interests were at stake. Unique in that it exercised real influence over coreligionist communities in the Ottoman Empire, Persia, Europe, India, and beyond, the Armenian Church at Ejmiatsin brought the government of Nicholas I diverse geopolitical advantages. At the same time that statesmen in St. Petersburg relied on the catholicos to reestablish diplomatic ties with Constantinople, tsarist diplomats worked to secure foreign Armenian prelates' submission to Ejmiatsin. To facilitate this symbiotic encounter, the state kept no more than a loose hold on the Armenian clergy and laity. Yet this policy clashed with inherent Russian interests whenever the advances of the Armenian confession posed real or perceived threats to the Orthodox faith.

Overall, practically any concessions the autocracy granted to its non-Orthodox subjects in hopes of regulating their status, the empire also extended to Armenian external activities. As Robert Crews has argued, "Confessional communities that subjected the followers to divine as well as monarchical judgment provided useful forms of social discipline to complement the will of the sovereign."[130] Elsewhere, Crews has shown that the empire co-opted Muslim community leaders into its bureaucratic and cultural fabric in an effort to attain stability on its imperial periphery.[131] If, however, the government employed religious toleration as a system of control over non-Russians, in the Armenian case the state sought more than docile subjects. The opportunity to project diplomatic influence into the capitals of Eastern empires through Armenian clerics outweighed the specter of Armenian proselytizing or encroachment on traditional Orthodox spheres of influence. Thus the encounter between the tsarist state and the Armenian Church in the second quarter of the nineteenth century represented a careful calculation on each side. The codification of Armenian rights and obligations with the *polozhenie* of 1836 evinced Ann Laura Stoler's "active realignment and reformation" that was driven by geopolitical realities beyond tsarist frontiers.[132]

For the Armenian ecclesiastical leadership, even the assertive Catholicos Nerses, the vision of an independent Armenia—articulated more clearly in the second half of the nineteenth century—yielded to a desire to secure the submission of the diaspora to Ejmiatsin. Consequently, Nerses styled himself pope, not president. Unlike some of his quixotic lay compatriots, Nerses understood after his exile to Kishinev that the Russian government would tolerate no irredentist claims. An ambition of theological and, by extension, cultural and economic authority over distant Armenian communities drove the policies of the catholicos, eliciting wary glances even from the imperial overlords that sought Ejmiatsin's expanded stature. If the ecumenical relationship between the Romanov state and Armenians points to the methods of St. Petersburg's imperial project, the economic dimension of that encounter shaped Russian approaches toward Armenians equally potently.

Economic Encounters

The Romanov Empire's taxation and other fiscal policies toward large Armenian communities in the Caucasus, in Crimea, and in Astrakhan Province illustrate the extent to which Armenians' economic roles defined their rights and obligations within Russian society. The three distinct examples yield a more comprehensive understanding of the Russo-Armenian economic relationship under Tsar Nicholas I. The autocracy struggled to integrate Armenians economically into the country, issuing contradictory statutes and dithering about the expectations and realities of various Armenian communities' social roles. If at midcentury the religious aspect of Russo-Armenian ties progressed relatively smoothly, the economic dimension of the relationship stumbled on several hurdles. Indeed, no other Armenian-related matter elicited as much policy dissent among senior tsarist statesmen during Nicholas's reign. Disagreements flared between both senior and provincial tsarist officials over the socioeconomic role of Russia's Armenian population and over the political implications of that status.

This episode tells us much about that era's nationalities policies and the role of Armenians in them. First, the state sought but failed to achieve a uniform economic approach toward the Armenian communities under its dominion, reluctantly recognizing the need for distinct strategies that were dictated by historical precedents as much as by regional realities. Second, senior tsarist statesmen conceived of Armenian rights and responsibilities in starkly different ways, undercutting the notion of political solidarity within Nicholas's ruling circle. Third, these cases demonstrate the empire's difficult navigation of the process of ethnonational absorption. While some officials insisted that Armenians had received sufficient privileges to become rooted in their new homeland, other statesmen argued that continued prerogatives benefited the Russian state and their extension yielded "justice" and "fairness."

The controversy over Armenian economic policies helped the autocracy to settle on a new understanding, if not an imperial strategy, of nationalities policy. As the State Council stressed in 1848, "Privileges, at times given to foreigners settling in Russia, are necessarily reasoned with the needs and circumstances of the localities where they settle, which is why such benefits cannot and must not be the same for everyone."[133] Despite the government's efforts to standardize the collection of taxes in accord with its pursuit of an efficiently managed empire, the state's economic encounter with such non-Russian subjects as Armenians showed that no blanket policies proved practical or feasible. The government affirmed this reality when, after years of dispute, it resolved this matter by reluctantly granting permanent exemptions to some but not all Armenian communities.[134] The obdurate monarch awoke from the dream of ruling a state of efficiency to the reality of leading a state of exceptions.

The wrangling over economic strategy toward the Caucasus reflected the government's unease about the integration of that region into the Russian Empire. St. Petersburg sought, but eventually failed, to fuse its imperial territories into a cohesive budgetary framework, as Ekaterina Pravilova tells us.[135] Despite the vast cultural, political, and financial disparities between the various peripheries, including the Caucasus, Turkestan, Poland, and Finland, the government pursued a unifying economic strategy for much of the nineteenth century. But the tenure of Finance Minister Egor Kankrin (1823–44) represented an experimental deviation from this policy.

In 1827, Kankrin became the first senior Russian official to articulate an economic policy of "colonialism" toward the South Caucasus.[136] He insisted that "the government should not think about uniting [the South Caucasus] with the general state structure and should not hope to make it a part of Russia or of the Russian people [rossiiskii narod] in the moral sense."[137] Nudged by the influential finance minister, St. Petersburg began to view the region as a market for Russian products and a source of revenue, discouraging the development of local manufacturing. Kankrin decried efforts to integrate the South Caucasus into the broader Russian economic system, promoting it instead as an "Asiatic province" that could be exploited for Russia's economic benefit. By the early 1830s, Kankrin and Rosen openly argued about the financial independence of the South Caucasus. In 1832, under Kankrin's pressure and responding to reports of local corruption and mismanagement, the Council of Ministers ordered that the Finance Ministry assume tighter control over the economy of the South Caucasus. Although Rosen succeeded in delaying the implementation of the new regulations by two years, soon the region was required to send all its revenue to St. Petersburg, relying on it then to distribute it back to the administration in Tiflis.[138] Additional reforms in 1840 brought the territory under the Finance Ministry's total control. Even after the establishment of the Caucasus viceroyalty in 1844 and Vorontsov's receipt of carte blanche powers, the economy and revenues of the South Caucasus remained in the hands of the Finance Ministry in St. Petersburg.[139]

Astrakhan's Armenian community offers a valuable glimpse of the evolution of Russian economic policies toward Armenians. Astrakhan represented a strategically important and relatively large commercial center in southern Russia, and its Armenians, mostly immigrants from Persia, settled there well before the empire's annexation of the Caucasus. The community thrived, establishing its own academy in 1810 and newspaper in 1815.[140] By the 1880s, more than six thousand Armenians lived among the city's seventy-three thousand residents. The experience of Astrakhan Armenians in the mid-1830s demonstrates that even that late the autocracy had reason to maintain the exclusive economic privileges of long-settled Armenian subjects.[141] In October 1833, the State Council ruled that all Armenian merchants in southern Russian provinces must abide by the general tax regulations governing the activities of all tsarist-subject traders.[142] Kankrin, long opposed to the privileged treatment of Armenians, gleefully informed provincial governors that local Armenian businessmen were henceforth required to enlist in merchant guilds and pay corresponding taxes, for Tsar Nicholas had concurred with the State Council's proclamation that it was "inappropriate to provide advantages to Armenians over Russians."[143]

This resolution proved both temporary and incomplete. In early 1835, some Armenian merchants from Astrakhan complained to the provincial governor that, in violation of the prerogatives they had enjoyed since 1799, the Astrakhan city authorities charged them new "city and local taxes" (*gorodskie i zemskie povinnosti*) of 40 rubles per person.[144] This substantial amount was levied in addition to the standard urban tax of 2.76 rubles per person that all of the city's Armenian residents paid, irrespective of their vocation.[145] Moreover, local Armenian merchants continued to pay between 25 and 100 rubles for each trade license. Consequently, in the first half of the 1830s, some Astrakhan Armenian businessmen paid as much as 142.76 rubles per year to the city government.

The Astrakhan provincial administration (*gubernskoe pravlenie*) sided with the city's Armenian merchants.[146] It agreed that according to the relevant royal fiats of 1799 and 1825, Astrakhan Armenians were liable only for urban and merchant taxes, which they had been paying dutifully. The additional urban tax of 40 rubles was deemed unjustified because "it would involve not only the violations of the rights granted to them by the government, but also heavy burdens for them."[147] Perhaps motivated more by the fact that these taxes benefited only the city government and not the provincial administration, rather than by any sympathy for Armenians or genuine interpretation of the law, the provincial administration prohibited city officials from saddling Armenian businessmen with the new *gorodskie i zemskie povinnosti* of 40 rubles.

Hinting at the gravity with which regional and imperial authorities treated this issue, when city authorities in Astrakhan appealed the decision of the provincial administration to St. Petersburg, the Finance Ministry, the Interior Ministry, and the Senate examined the matter.[148] The review determined that, when Empress Catherine and Emperor Paul settled Armenians in Astrakhan in the eighteenth century, they had received temporary, not hereditary, economic privileges. In 1824 and 1825, the city's untaxed Armenian traders were assessed new dues, but these taxes remained below standard rates. In early 1836, imperial authorities ruled that the Astrakhan city government had the right to charge 0.25% from the city's Armenian and non-Armenian merchants, in addition to the regular urban taxes paid by all residents, but it could not assess any additional taxes from local Armenian businessmen.[149] A glimpse of the complex economic considerations informing the Russian bureaucracy's encounter with Armenians, such episodes recurred throughout the mid-1830s in Astrakhan and elsewhere as a dissonance of policies arose between the local authorities and their provincial and imperial superiors. While local agents often opposed the economic advantages enjoyed by Armenians, the imperial government maintained their privileged fiscal statuses.

Perhaps spurred by this debate, in May 1836 Tsar Nicholas I issued a decree that sought the "equalization of dues" (*uravnenie podatei*) paid by Armenians and non-Armenians in southern Russia.[150] The fiat affected tsarist-subject Armenians in Astrakhan, as well as the large Armenian communities of Crimea, including the Kherson, Taurida, and Ekaterinoslav *gubernii*. The new regulations required the "end of all hitherto . . . diverse individual, household, and land taxes" collected from Armenians and replaced them with standardized rates applicable to all tsarist subjects.[151] New, transitional tax rates applied to previously exempt communities: "Armenian burghers, regardless of their [current] obligations for city and local taxes, are to be assessed a special collection for the treasury."[152] Within ten years these "special" rates would be phased out to match the dues of their Russian and other non-Armenian neighbors. The regulations also affected "Armenian settlers," although it is unclear whether this term applied to recent or long-established immigrants. While there were some important rate adjustments, the key change was introducing poll taxes (*s dush*) and abandoning those taxes assessed from households (*s dvorov*).[153] Already murky, the situation became messy when individual regional agents deviated from the emperor's instructions.

Some provincial authorities misapplied the 1836 regulations to Armenians in their jurisdictions. The officials in Ekaterinoslav Province, for example, assessed Armenian merchants and "settlers" taxes in excess of the prescribed rates.[154] The sources do not clarify the motivation of such local bureaucrats, but despite local Armenians' complaints to the Finance Ministry, St. Petersburg took no action to rectify the situation. Yet the central government did not ignore the concerns of local Armenians when the complaints originated in strategically or economically important regions. Two Armenian communities in Crimea found powerful allies when they objected to the 1836 regulations, arguing that Catherine and Paul had bestowed on them "eternal" exemptions.[155] Mikhail Vorontsov, the governor of Novorossiia and Bessarabia (soon to become Caucasus viceroy), agreed with the Armenians in his province. With them also sided Interior Minister Dmitrii Bludov, but they faced the opposition of Finance Minister Kankrin.[156] The State Council ruled that "no privileges can be eternal" and, apparently unaware of the discrepancies in Ekaterinoslav Province and elsewhere, cited the edict of May 1836 in concluding that "the government's intention to bring all Armenians under the same regulation is obvious."[157]

Imprecise dictates, the bane of all bureaucrats, partly explain the dissonance among state and provincial officials about Armenian tax obligations. Despite the State Council's repeated declarations that "no privileges can be eternal," Tsar Nicholas I implicitly reaffirmed his predecessors' edicts from the late eighteenth century by ordering his agents to "levy taxes not on all Armenians living in Russia, but on those who are excluded from the privileges of 1799."[158] This stipulation resulted in Russian and Armenian disagreements about which communities were and were not affected by the new laws. In a word, the tax reforms of the 1830s sought de jure fiscal standardization but yielded de facto irregularities. Vexing imperial accountants and immigrant farmers alike, Armenian tax rates fluctuated from Crimea to Astrakhan to the Caucasus.

Aggrieved Armenians alerted the autocrat to this fact during his 1837 tour of the Caucasus. Representatives of the Nakhichevan Armenian community petitioned the tsar to remain under the prerogatives issued in 1779.[159] While evidence suggests that Rosen, Vorontsov, and even Police Chief Benkendorf were sympathetic to the Armenian requests, again the most acute resistance came from Finance Minister Kankrin. He found the matter "entirely disrespectful and even inappropriate," pointing out that Nakhichevan Armenians desired exemptions "while native Russian subjects pay substantially higher tax quantities."[160] For much of the Nicholaevan era, Vorontsov and Kankrin voiced directly opposing views regarding the economic responsibilities and rights of tsarist-subject Armenians.[161]

At the heart of the debate stood conflicting conceptions of Russian imperialism in general and ethnonational integration in particular. While Kankrin sought to enrich St. Petersburg's coffers through "colonial" economic policies in the South Caucasus and held pejorative views of that region's natives, Vorontsov resisted such methods and promoted Armenian and Georgian social mobility within Russian society. The finance minister needed Armenians to produce raw materials and wealth that would flow into central Russia and rebuked their supporters for seeking the "merger," "integration," and "cooperation" between those *aziatsy* and ethnic Russians. In the Caucasus Kankrin pursued glory for the metropolis, not the growth of local culture and social integration. In contrast, as Robert Geraci has stressed, Vorontsov viewed Armenians as "necessary and desirable partners who could help the region flourish."[162] Yet despite these divergent tactics, both statesmen sought to capitalize on the empire's non-Russian diversity. Vorontsov envisioned non-Russians contributing to the growth and vitality of Russia not through taxation and curtailed economic activity within a marginalized Caucasus, which was Kankrin's aim, but rather by melting into Russian social, cultural, and political life. To that end, Vorontsov dispatched Caucasian youths to universities in the two capitals and brought Russian cultural symbols to Tiflis. To either side of this debate, at issue was more than fiscal policy.

After wrangling over Armenian tax obligations in the spring of 1839, the Senate sided with the Armenians and their tsarist allies, mainly Vorontsov and former interior minister Bludov, but it focused on only some of the empire's Armenian communities. The Senate recommended that the Armenians of Karasubazar and Staryi Krym, both in Crimea, as well as Grigoriopol in modern Moldova and Nakhichevan-on-Don, remain under their former privileges and be excused from the tsar's 1836 regulations.[163] These communities were to continue paying household, not individual, taxes. Kankrin refused to sign the proposal, insisting that the Senate's decision countermanded the State Council's emphasis on the impossibility of "eternal" economic prerogatives. Instead, the finance minister proposed leaving under privileges only those Armenians who had resided in the aforementioned cities at the time the original decrees were issued, without extending those economic advantages to their descendants. Likely cognizant of this counterproposal's infeasibility, the senators remained unconvinced by Kankrin's stance.[164]

The opposing camps soon compromised. In 1840, the autocracy granted a ten-year exemption from the 1836 law to the Armenians of Karasubazar, Staryi Krym, Grigoriopol, and Nakhichevan-on-Don.[165] However, in a puzzling decision, the State Council ruled that the regime "should not mix [smeshivat'] Armenians in those regions that Russia conquered by force with those who came to us in response to the invitation of the government."[166] Evidently, the Armenian community of Astrakhan fell into the former category, leaving it under the effects of the 1836 reforms and, effectively, creating yet another legal exception.

Astrakhan Armenians protested, entreating the government to extend the same fiscal laws to them as to the Armenians of Crimea.[167] Astrakhan Armenians argued that they too had voluntarily answered the state's call for foreign settlers in the eighteenth century, colonizing Astrakhan and the northern coast of the Caspian Sea at the behest of the Russian Empire. Notably, this Armenian community sought "eternal" tax prerogatives, rather than the ten-year exemptions granted to the Armenians in Crimea, Grigoriopol, and Nakhichevan-on-Don. It also wished to continue paying taxes assessed on households rather than on individuals. In support of its position the community cited its contributions to regional economic development, mainly commercial agriculture and trade. The military governor of Astrakhan Province agreed that the Armenians in his jurisdiction were "in the same circumstances" and had "the same rights" as their compatriots in other Russian provinces.[168]

The Senate sided in part with Astrakhan Armenians. It agreed that they had settled in that city voluntarily in the eighteenth century, at which point the government had promised them taxation based on households rather than individuals.[169] Consequently, the Senate affirmed the State Council's recommendation to charge Armenian immigrants who had settled in Astrakhan in the nineteenth century just 2 rubles per household, and those who had arrived in the eighteenth century were to be assessed even lesser rates. The Interior Ministry endorsed this decision, but the Finance Ministry refused to follow suit, arguing that insufficient evidence proved that Astrakhan Armenians had voluntarily arrived in the region at the invitation of the tsarist state.[170]

Justice Minister Count Viktor Panin (1841–62) took up the issue in the spring of 1848, concluding, "The difference between the decrees granted to the Armenians of Astrakhan and the other four cities further affirms the fairness of extending to the former the power of the royally approved State Council's decision of 25 November 1840."[171] The justice minister insisted, "In all fairness, this right must now be accorded to the descendants of Astrakhan Armenians, [who were] awarded by a decree the complete freedom from taxes and who did not [benefit] from the 1840 [extension] only because they had not applied for it."[172] Panin backed Astrakhan Armenians and joined Vorontsov, Bludov, and the governor of Astrakhan against Kankrin. Among influential state actors, only the Department of the State Economy supported the finance minister's views, concluding that it was "convinced neither of the basis nor of the desirability of extending to Astrakhan Armenians the 1840 decision of the State Council."[173]

The Senate resolved the matter soon after Panin's input. Astrakhan Armenians who had settled in the city before 1799, and their direct descendants, were "not brought into the general taxation system" and were assessed instead a flat household tax of 2 silver rubles per year, in addition to the standard city and local taxes paid by all locals.[174] It appears that this regulation affected no more than four hundred individuals. The city's other Armenians, who had arrived after 1799, were to be charged the same tax rates as all other local residents, depending on their respective estates and guilds. The tsar approved this decision, bringing to an end one of the more divisive Armenian issues to affect the Russian political elite in the first half of the nineteenth century.

This controversy fed the seemingly contradictory status of Armenians in the Caucasus, where the tsarist state at once celebrated and obstructed their socioeconomic advancement. The reports of Generals Rosen and Neidgardt, two of Nicholas's commanders in the Caucasus, evince this Russian paradox. On the one hand, in 1834, Rosen resisted the attempts of three Armenian villages in the Caucasus to reclassify their estate categorization for economic purposes, arguing that the communities' financial circumstances did not justify tax breaks.[175] On the other hand, in 1836, Rosen opposed the state's plans to introduce new tariffs and other trade restrictions in the region, arguing that such constraints harmed the "welfare of the Transcaucasus."[176] Fearing that new economic restrictions would drive local Armenians to seek their profits abroad, Rosen maintained: "[Armenians] live by the trade industry, and their very loyalty to Russia is based on it. What can be expected if, because of the limitation of their trade deals, . . . they turn to resettlement in Turkey?"[177] The consequences of such a scenario, warned Rosen, would transcend the regional interests of the Caucasus economy and affect the empire's foreign affairs: "In that case, not only will the region become impoverished, [but] one cannot fail to foresee the harmful consequences in the political sense, and we will certainly lose the influence we have acquired over Armenians in Persia and Turkey, which is always needed and beneficial for us, especially in times of war with those powers."[178]

Years later, Neidgardt both lauded and cautioned against the social and economic progress made by the Armenians of the South Caucasus.[179] In a report to the tsar in July 1843, he praised local Armenians for setting a "good example" for their Georgian neighbors, whom he accused of lethargy.[180] The high commissioner emphasized, "The nature of the Armenian upper and middle classes has nothing in common with the nature of the Georgian nobility and merchantry." But his praise also contained a warning: "[Armenians] are more educated, care for the education of children, even making donations, *but all of their intellectual abilities, all their activity, is directed at [financial] acquisition.*"[181] Armenians "hold the trade in their hands," fretted Neidgardt, and they marginalized Georgians and other natives in the region's commerce. Among Tiflis's prominent businessmen, "just one . . . notable Georgian trader" could be found.[182] The city's Armenian merchants "little by little ousted from trade all other nationalities," and "to eliminate all competition they support each other through guarantees and money."[183]

To rectify this situation, which produced "disadvantages for the region as well as for the government," Neidgardt proposed recruiting "merchants and capital from Russia" to Tiflis.[184] He was confident that "Russian capital would enter into . . . competition with Armenians that is beneficial to the government, and would reduce the presently very strong importance of Armenians in all affairs and enterprises."[185] Neidgardt's proposal echoed the argument made a decade earlier by Russian economist P. Vysheslavtsov, who insisted in 1834 that "Asiatic" enterprise had left the South Caucasus's economy in a primitive state and urged Russian merchants to replace their Armenian counterparts.[186] Although Neidgardt's leadership of the Caucasus administration did not last long enough to enact these plans, his views evinced the tsarist government's simultaneous appreciation of and apprehension about the economic, social, and political implications of ostensibly exclusive Armenian advancement in Tiflis and beyond.

Despite such concerns, at midcentury the Russian political establishment conceived of middle-class urban Armenians, in the Caucasus and Russia proper, in laudatory terms. While Kankrin's orientalist wariness about Armenian entrepreneurship never faded from the Russian political imagination, within two decades of the empire's annexation of the South Caucasus tsarist officialdom recognized the broadly beneficial effects of local Armenian commerce. In 1846, the inaugural volume of the annual *Caucasus Calendar*, published by the viceroy's administration under the auspices of the imperial military establishment, emphasized the distinct socioeconomic role of local Armenians. The publication contrasted them with their main Christian neighbors in the Caucasus, Georgians, who "are generally carefree [and] fun but no strangers to hard work," although "their only occupation is agriculture."[187]

Unlike Georgians, the calendar declared, "Armenians undeniably occupy a very important place among the residents of the Transcaucasus, according to their abilities, enterprise, and pursuit of education. They have always been considered the most active toilers of the Orient."[188] Reflecting the views of most tsarist officials, the publication portrayed Armenian peasants as unremarkable and similar to their non-Armenian peasant neighbors. However, the urban, merchant communities of Armenians occupied a particular position in the Russian thinking. In the towns of the region, Armenians attained a standing where there was "no craft, no trade, in which they do not engage." The *Caucasus Calendar* insisted that, thanks in part to Russia's rescue of Armenians from their "enslavement" at the hands of their former Muslim overlords and to the "beneficial fruits of Russian rule," by midcentury Armenians had come to excel in the region's social and economic life. "Highly gifted with the spirit of entrepreneurship and an aptitude for commerce," the official publication asserted, "[Armenians] from time immemorial exclusively control the trade not only in Georgia, but also in almost all other Transcaucasian provinces. On their own they have established trade routes to Russia, which only through them traffics its goods to Georgia."[189] The publication particularly commended Armenians for securing the region's trade with such European commercial centers as Leipzig, Hamburg, Trieste, and Marseille.

The Russo-Armenian economic encounter during the reign of Nicholas I typified the government's complex ties with non-Russian groups. While the state welcomed the broader impact of urban Armenians' commercial success in Tiflis and elsewhere, it feared the social and, by extension, political implications of growing Armenian prosperity. Moreover, officials' engagement with Armenians affected the empire's perceptions of other subject nations, such as Georgians. In the Caucasus, tsarist agents applauded the broader benefits of Armenian business while hoping that the Armenian example would inspire their Georgian and other regional neighbors. Yet several administrators, such as Rosen and Neidgardt, implicitly promoted the Russian view of Armenian traders as motivated by individual and community interests that ostensibly seldom included non-Armenian elements. When in the 1830s and 1840s plans to attract Russian entrepreneurs to the South Caucasus were proposed, the underlying assumption was that ethnic Russian merchants, unlike their Armenian counterparts, engaged in morally acceptable practices that benefited the common good. And yet, in 1847, non-Russians controlled an incredible 90 percent of the tsarist empire's imports and 97 percent of its exports.[190]

The autocracy under Tsar Nicholas I struggled to reconcile the ideal of a well-regulated empire—with its implication of consistency—with the reality of ruling a singularly vast and diverse empire. Romanov administrators learned that, in practice, juridical and fiscal uniformity was impossible. The state wished to capitalize on the Armenian Church's authority in the diaspora to project influence beyond its borders. But the government also sought to standardize the economic life of its Armenian subjects, abandoning these efforts when competing visions of nationalities policy and ethnonational integration of non-Russians permeated the official discourse. In these endeavors, St. Petersburg pursued streamlined policies to achieve "uniformity and simplicity of legal relationships and categories,"[191] rather than sociopolitical equality among its subjects or their cultural Russification. When, in 1838–40, the autocracy absorbed the independent Armenian courts of Astrakhan, Kizliar, and Mozdok into the imperial judicial system, Nicholas professed a desire to see those Armenian communities "use the court and justice [system] on equal footing with our native and all other subjects."[192] But in practice the empire's ethnonational, cultural, and economic diversity made such goals impossible, as the autocracy's resurrection of abolished policies shows. For the emperor, the driving doctrine was efficiency, not egalitarianism, but by mid-century he achieved neither.

For most of the first half of the nineteenth century, the government's approach toward the Armenian diaspora revolved around the pursuit of political influence beyond Russia's borders and economic stability within its peripheral provinces. St. Petersburg tried to essentialize its Armenian subjects as Christian allies and able traders not to acculturate or wholly subjugate them but rather to deploy the domestic and external networks of their diaspora for the state's needs. The antithetical visions of senior statesmen suggest that the government struggled to grasp the various manifestations of Armenian identity. Classifying minorities—whether "diligent" Armenians, "lethargic" Georgians, or "dangerous" Muslim highlanders—allowed the state to mobilize them, or against them, to achieve its ultimate aims of vitality and stability. At the same time as it sought administrative standardization, St. Petersburg asserted non-Russian groups' inequalities by ascribing collective characteristics to them, pitting them against each other, and maintaining the dominance of the Great Russian nation among the empire's population. In another example, the government in the middle third of the nineteenth century harnessed Ukrainian ethnonational consciousness "as a powerful weapon" against the Catholic Polish nobility in the western borderlands.[193] St. Petersburg's fears of Polish political agitation outweighed the state's wariness of growing Ukrainophile sentiments, much as Vorontsov and most of his colleagues embraced Armenian economic and ecumenical autonomy despite residual concerns about maintaining ethnic hierarchies and Russian supremacy.

Perhaps the most conspicuous contradiction of such nationalities policies lay in the fact that, under Nicholas's personal approach to politics, the state equated juridical and fiscal standardization with modern governance at a time when the majority of ethnic Russians remained in bondage. Thus, a patchwork of similarly inconsistent regulations characterized Nicholas's policies toward non-Russians. The tsar dreamed of reestablishing the political order of his empress grandmother's world, one that rarely faced the challenges of post-1789 republican aspirations and national agitations.

But in the second quarter of the nineteenth century the Armenian diaspora, within and beyond the Romanov realm, sought security and prosperity, not a national state. Catholicos Nerses, politically the most influential Armenian in that era, yearned to become the pope of the diaspora, not the president of an Armenian republic. Before the rise of a concerted Armenian nationalist movement in the last decades of the century, Armenia's diaspora looked to the Russian throne for the protection and affirmation of its religious and cultural identities. To this end, it chose to cooperate with the tsarist government, albeit with periodic symptoms of discord. Few Armenians in Russia, especially those not part of the intelligentsia or the gentry, pursued social or administrative "equality" with other groups, including Russians, because they enjoyed special economic privileges. Until the 1880s, ordinary Armenians in the Caucasus and Russia prioritized personal and communal stability and growth, seeing few incentives for political agitation against their imperial overlord.

At midcentury the Russo-Armenian symbiosis remained strong. A multitude of considerations informed the tsarist state's encounter with Armenians, and tsarist statesmen weighed both economic and political factors in their interactions with Armenians. In that light, it is hardly surprising that Viceroy Vorontsov supported Armenian businessmen in a dispute with ethnic Russian industrialists in 1850,[194] because Vorontsov sought to benefit from the Armenian diaspora's political connections as much as from its economic networks. In that context, he chose to maintain constructive relations with Armenians even at the cost of ignoring the interests of ethnic Russian elements. When new imperial rivalries aroused old animosities, Nicholas's successor, Alexander II, deployed the Armenian diaspora as Russia's answer to Europe's Eastern Question.

CHAPTER 4

The Recalibration of Tsarist Policies toward Armenians inside and outside Russia, 1857–1880

The fact that international and interimperial developments often shaped Russia's encounter with Armenians became particularly conspicuous in the reign of Alexander II (1855–81). St. Petersburg acknowledged that Armenians were key to tsarist foreign policy in the East and to the Eastern Question in particular. Because Russia ruled over only a portion of the Armenian diaspora, another part of which resided in the Ottoman Empire, it had to contend with unique political circumstances. Indeed, Armenians were one of the few tsarist minority nations, if not the only such nation, who looked abroad to see their compatriots mistreated by another government. Recognizing that Armenians combined foreign with domestic advantages and liabilities for the Romanov state, the authorities maneuvered to maintain Russia's prominence in their lives.

This chapter examines the imperial officials' negotiation of delicate Armenian debates about their national identity, the state's continued partnership with Ejmiatsin in various international contexts, and the first signs of Russian hesitation about Armenian sociopolitical reliability. In its response to the Eastern Question, St. Petersburg aspired to be acknowledged as *the* political benefactor and economic patron of the Armenian diaspora, and it sought to reorient all Armenians toward Russia's orbit. Eager to capitalize on the deep social networks of Western Armenians within the sultan's domain and cognizant of their discontent, tsarist officials relied on the Armenian nation and church to advance Russian foreign policy in the East. During the Russo-Ottoman War of 1877–78, Russia continued to promote itself as the defender of the sultan's minority Christians and resettled thousands of Ottoman Armenians into tsarist territory. As the war played out on the front pages of St. Petersburg dailies, Russian liberals shined a spotlight on Armenians and revived the Eastern Question. The periodical press in the imperial capital urged the Russian government to redouble its support for foreign-subject Armenians based on past and hypothetical future political incentives, and it even pushed the state to carve an Armenian homeland out of Ottoman land. Furthermore, during the real and perceived encroachment of Western missionaries—especially British and US Protestants and French Catholics—on foreign and tsarist Armenians, Russian officials coordinated with Ejmiatsin to counteract foreign proselytizing, often without reciprocal strategic benefits.

Yet in trying to balance its influence over Armenians outside Russia with maintaining control over Armenians within the empire, St. Petersburg produced contradictory initiatives. Above all, the state worked to prevent Armenians from placing their national allegiances above their duties as civil subjects of the tsarist empire. The authorities suppressed privately conceived national Armenian institutions, prohibited the unsanctioned collection of donations for foreign-subject Armenians, and strove to prevent the Russian revolutionary movement from animating Armenian nationalism. At the heart of the matter emerged a more perceptible tension between tsarist perceptions of Armenians as useful allies or seditious troublemakers. This chapter, then, tracks some of the earliest symptoms of Eastern Armenian political activism.

For years after the Crimean War, Russia's strained relations with Britain and the Ottoman Empire revolved around Romanov concerns about outside interference in the peripheries. In the wake of the Treaty of Paris, new viceroy Aleksandr Bariatinskii (1856–62) alerted St. Petersburg to the shadowy visits of British and Ottoman military and merchant vessels to the Black Sea coast, an area populated by North Caucasian highlanders.[1] In St. Petersburg, too, members of the General Staff and senior statesmen emphasized the growing political-economic competition between Russia and Britain in the Caucasus, on the Caspian, and in Central Asia.[2]

Heeding the lessons of the Crimean defeat, Russia launched administrative and economic modernization in the Caucasus and beyond.[3] Between 1855 and 1880, military influence in the Caucasus shrank and the jurisdiction of the civilian administration expanded by 80 percent to cover almost the entire territory and 4,767,000 residents.[4] At the same time, the regional bureaucracy was trimmed, some provinces and districts amalgamated, and the authority of provincial governors boosted to expedite their work.[5] The viceroyalty's hands were fully untied in 1858 when St. Petersburg allowed it to keep all of the revenues derived from the South, but not the North, Caucasus.[6] Thus Bariatinskii received the financial carte blanche that even his powerful predecessor, Mikhail Vorontsov, had not enjoyed.[7] In 1859, the viceroy captured Shamil, the warlord of the North Caucasus highlanders, effectively ending the insurgency that for decades had drained Russian blood and rubles.[8] The stage was set for major adjustments to nationalities policies in the 1860s and 1870s.

Schooling a Diaspora

During their debates on integration, Russian policymakers and Armenian leaders increasingly considered the education of tsarist and non-tsarist Armenian youths. Before the rise of professional Armenian political organizations in the last decades of the nineteenth century, Armenian religious elders stood as the largely undisputed representatives of the Armenian nation's interests. However, the story of Russia's partnership with a particularly ambitious priest, Gavril Aivazovskii, suggests that the Russian government did not hesitate to align with socially and culturally influential Armenians who openly feuded with the established Armenian ecclesiastical hierarchy. Indeed, fissures within the Armenian national consciousness at midcentury produced new impediments and opportunities for St. Petersburg's efforts to cement the devotion of the next generations of the Armenian foreign and domestic communities.

Mechitarist monks took Gavril Aivazovskii as a child from his native Crimea to raise and educate him in Vienna.[9] Aivazovskii was the elder brother of Hovannes Aivazian, who would become a renowned marine artist better known by his Russified name of Ivan Aivazovskii. While his brother stayed in their birthplace, Gavril Aivazovskii became a lifelong scholar and priest in Europe, where he educated Armenian youths in Venice and Paris. Aivazovskii spent eight years in the latter city, where he established an academy that attracted Armenians from throughout Europe and also from Ottoman towns, Baghdad, and India. He also published a literary Armenian journal that gained equal prominence among lay and clerical diaspora Armenians. Aivazovskii's promotion of Armenian "national questions" and his resistance to Catholicism's influence on European Armenians eventually elicited the ire of the Catholic Church, which drove him out of Paris and the Mechitarist order. Expelled from Europe, Aivazovskii returned under the authority and aegis of the Ejmiatsin catholicos and the Constantinople patriarch, who lauded him for his scholarship and promotion of Armenian national interests.

Back in the tsar's domain, Aivazovskii sought to re-create his Paris academy on the Black Sea.[10] He argued that Russia's 1.5 million Armenian subjects had as much need for a national educational center as their compatriots in Europe, and he maintained that tsarist political interests demanded a national Armenian academy that would counteract Western dogmas' growing sway with Armenians. Russia's defeat in the Crimean War, Aivazovskii stressed, had eroded some of its influence among Ottoman Armenians, while at the same time the stature of British Protestantism and French Catholicism had grown to unprecedented levels among Ottoman and Russian Armenians. Equally anxious about the penetration of "alien" religious-cum-political ideologies, Armenian clerics and Russian administrators again had reason to coordinate.

In 1856, Alexander approved the plan, thanks in part to the endorsement of such tsarist officials as the Russian ambassador to France, Pavel Kiselev.[11] Although Aivazovskii had initially requested to establish the academy in Odessa, he received approval to change the location to the Crimean city of Feodosia. The emperor eagerly backed Aivazovskii's academy, met the cleric in November 1857 to laud his work, and tasked the Interior Ministry with facilitating its execution.[12] The tsar viewed the priest as an energetic, capable Armenian leader whose vision, grounded in impressive accomplishments, promised to strengthen the partnership between the Russian state and the Armenian nation, potentially allowing St. Petersburg both to counteract Western religious proselytizing and to project influence beyond its borders.

The emperor, however, overplayed his hand. Alexander sidestepped the Ejmiatsin leadership and appointed Aivazovskii the archbishop of the Nakhichevan-Bessarabian Armenian eparchy (which included Crimea), one of the largest and most profitable in the Russian Empire. State records suggest that the tsar took this decision not only to expedite Aivazovskii's project but also to allow him to use the eparchy's finances for his academy.[13] Although many tsarist and foreign Armenians supported Aivazovskii, his elevation to the head of the Nakhichevan-Bessarabian eparchy without Ejmiatsin's consent aroused ecclesiastical and even popular discontent.[14] The Armenian Church establishment, hitherto supportive of Aivazovskii, condemned what it interpreted as the government's unilateral interference in its internal affairs.

Russian sources paint a picture, prior to Aivazovskii's arrival, of a mismanaged and corrupt Nakhichevan-Bessarabian eparchy administration beset by lost or embezzled church funds and poor organization.[15] Indeed, Interior Minister Sergei Lanskoi asked Aivazovskii to address these issues, and the new archbishop made important strides in this direction, initially supported by local Armenian elders and the Ejmiatsin Synod. But Aivazovskii soon discovered that his eparchy's exhausted coffers meant that local church funds to open his academy were unavailable. To his rescue came wealthy Armenian business-man Arutiun Khalibov, who donated 50,000 silver rubles for the academy.[16] By mid-1858, Aivazovskii had secured final permission from the tsar; the min-isters of the interior, foreign affairs, and education; and the governor-general of the Novorossiisk and Bessarabian governorate.[17]

The gestation of pro-Russian attitudes among Armenian youths—foreign and tsarist—constituted a key political aim of the new academy, alongside its more standard aspirations toward enlightenment. On 12 October 1858, the Khalibov Armenian Academy of Feodosia, named for its primary benefactor, opened its doors to its first fifty students.[18] By the following academic year, the six-year school enrolled about 130 pupils, mainly from the Ottoman and Russian Armenian communities. The academy soon unveiled a publishing arm, and in 1860 it began producing a journal in Armenian, Russian, and French, continuing it after 1863 only in Armenian.[19] The aims of the journal reflected the academy's broader purpose: "the propagation of the light of science and knowledge among the Armenian people, [and] the development in [Armenians] of civil virtues and dedication to that government that pa-tronizes it."[20] The Romanov state embraced these goals, as Tsar Alexander II underscored when he visited the academy in September 1861, met with Aivazovskii and Khalibov, and commended their work.[21] The Russian govern-ment backed the academy throughout the 1860s, even propping it up with an annual subsidy of 11,000 rubles.[22]

In contrast, Ejmiatsin withdrew its backing. Not only had Aivazovskii been promoted to archbishop during an interregnum in the church leadership, but he also demonstrated more initiative than the heavily hierarchical and intransi-gent church could tolerate. Elected in 1858, new catholicos Mateos wasted no time in summoning Aivazovskii to Ejmiatsin. Although the nature of their au-dience is unknown, the fact that Mateos delayed his affirmation of Aivazovskii as the archbishop of the Nakhichevan-Bessarabian eparchy points to tension between the two clerics.[23] Despite the Russian state's and the Armenian laity's support for Aivazovskii, Mateos soon launched a multifaceted campaign against the ambitious priest.[24]

By the early 1860s, Mateos and his allies publicly denounced Aivazovskii's initiatives. A common rumor charged Aivazovskii and Khalibov with stealing church funds to finance their academy.[25] More likely, however, the secularism of such Armenian intellectuals as Aivazovskii threatened the church's preemi-nence in Armenian culture. Mateos condemned Aivazovskii for his emphasis on secular education and publishing and accused him of neglecting his duties toward the spiritual and administrative care of his flock.[26] Mateos ordered snap audits of the Nakhichevan-Bessarabian eparchy, intimidated priests who edited the Khalibov academy journal, and pressured Tiflis bookshops not to sell publications from Aivazovskii's press.[27] The academy withstood such adversity for a decade but succumbed in 1871, closing its doors and converting the facilities into a church-administered seminary.

Largely unknown to the government, the animosity between Aivazovskii and Ejmiatsin paralleled conflicting visions of Armenian identity writ large, ongoing conceptions that pitted traditional church-centered culture against the growing secularism of Armenian intellectuals.[28] The strife within Russia's Armenian community had surfaced at midcentury in the competition between publications that used the vernacular Armenian (*ashkharhabar*) and those that preferred the classical Armenian of the church (*grabar*). In modernizing Armenian culture and urging the secularization of education, Aivazovskii joined such Armenian intellectuals as writer Khachatur Abovyan, jurist Grigor Otian, and editor and novelist Hovannes Hisarian.

The Russian government stayed out of these debates as long as it perceived them as apolitical. True, the autocracy embraced the mission and role of the Khalibov academy, even though it recognized the political dangers associated with alienating the Armenian Church and its senior leadership. But the creation of national Armenian academies in Russia remained a politically controversial prospect that aroused policy disagreement among senior statesmen. The overarching tension resulted from competing visions of social integration and acculturation that the state explicitly and implicitly weighed in its policies toward Armenians.

While Petr Valuev and Aleksandr Gorchakov, the interior and foreign ministers, disagreed about promoting Ejmiatsin's interimperial stature, they supported the establishment not only of Aivazovskii's academy but also of a similar institution in Astrakhan.[29] The senior officials emphasized the mutual interests of the Russian government and the Armenian Church, entirely overlooking, intentionally or inadvertently, the serious rift between Aivazovskii and Mateos. The statesmen advocated "counteracting the Western powers' religious-political propaganda among foreign Armenians, which is as harmful to Russia as it is to the Armenian-Gregorian Church."[30] Moreover, "in order to spread and consolidate Russia's influence" on foreign-subject Armenians, and to "strengthen the moral and religious bonds" between Armenians outside and inside the Russian Empire, the ministers supported the founding of such exclusively Armenian educational centers.[31]

Unlike the Lazarev Institute, which sought to integrate Armenians into Russian society and the state by producing professional cadres for the tsarist service and private commerce, the institutions Valuev and Gorchakov supported aimed to attract Armenians from abroad, reorienting them toward Russia's orbit not through a Russian-focused curriculum but by offering subsidized education. While the interior minister remained vigilant of enabling Armenian nationalism, he cautiously favored recruiting Armenians from the Ottoman Empire, Persia, and Europe to Russia, where he hoped they could continue the long tradition of Armenian settlement of tsarist peripheries and contribute to general social and economic growth. By 1868, however, Valuev lost confidence in the Khalibov academy's ability to attract Armenians from abroad.[32]

Unique features distinguished the Khalibov academy and the proposed institution in Astrakhan.[33] First, they were intended "primarily" for foreign-subject Armenians, who received financial assistance from the Russian government. Second, all instruction was to be conducted in Armenian, and no Russian-language courses were part of the mandatory curriculum (at least for non-tsarist Armenians). Third, the schools' jurisdictional oversight would be divided between the Interior Ministry and Ejmiatsin, shutting out the Education Ministry. Finally, all tsarist-subject graduates of these academies were admitted into the lowest, fourteenth rung of the Russian Table of Ranks, while their foreign classmates entered the "personal honorary citizen" estate with hereditary rights. In addition to catering to Russia's own Armenians, the main goal of these prerogatives rested in drawing to the tsar's realm foreign, young Armenians wary of Russification but desperate for education and a better life. Comfortably ensconced in these well-supported Armenian spaces, the immigrants ostensibly would realize the advantages of the Romanov sociopolitical system and choose to become integral members of the empire's vibrant non-Russian population. Accommodation, not acculturation, drove this project.

The Education Ministry emerged as the primary opponent of this proposal and explicitly advocated the cultural assimilation of tsarist-subject Armenians. Chancellor of the ministry (and future minister) Ivan Delianov, scion of an old aristocratic Armenian family, conceded the need for "the most decisive rebuff" of Western religious and political ideas. He also agreed it was important to elevate Ejmiatsin's external prestige as part of "strengthening Russia's influence on Turkish and Persian Armenians."[34] However, the ministry resisted calls for the establishment in Russia of exclusively Armenian national academies that catered to foreign-subject Armenians. It argued that Western powers targeted Russia's Armenians as much as their foreign compatriots, and it called for a greater domestic focus on the political, cultural, and social integration of Armenians. Only the cultural assimilation of tsarist-subject Armenians could ward off nationalism and imbue their new generations with devotion to the empire. In a statement that reflected the views of many tsarist statesmen, Delianov insisted that the government

> must be solely focused on [ensuring] that [the Armenian] youth receives a common education with all of its Russian countrymen, that it is raised on the Russian language in educational facilities common for all, [raised] on Russian literature and Russian history, in the spirit of unwavering devotion to its Russian fatherland and emperor, [and thus] completely melds with all intellectual and moral interests of Russia and from childhood becomes tempered against all intrigues and agitations, as incongruous with its own well-being as with the tranquility of Russia on the southeastern periphery.[35]

In a word, the Education Ministry argued that the expansion of such institutions as the Khalibov academy would drive a wedge between Russia's Armenian subjects and the tsarist government, and it also advocated absorbing Armenian youth into the Russian social and cultural fabric. The failure to implement these policies, Delianov warned, would result in the growth of "national" ideas among tsarist-subject Armenians.

Indeed, the Education Ministry and other government agencies feared that certain state policies, such as the establishment of national academies, could arouse Armenian nationalism. The ministry cautioned that exclusive regulations that deviated from standard laws governing all *inorodtsy* (aliens) would "inevitably be interpreted as backing the national-political aspirations that are artificially excited among Armenians by hostile [foreign] policies."[36] Delianov also feared that Ottoman Armenian pupils at the proposed academies would infect their tsarist-subject classmates with anti-Russian sentiments. The result, he warned, would be an atmosphere where "a young generation of Russian Armenians, it is safe to say, would take away from the schools . . . a love not for Russia, but for a fantastical future Armenia, and would represent ardent supporters of Armenian autonomy, [which is] preached by Russia's adversaries."[37]

Russia's unique sociopolitical and ethnonational circumstances made the implementation of national academies impossible, the Education Ministry held. Delianov argued that, unlike in Austria, France, or England, in Russia distinctive factors rendered the establishment of the Khalibov academy politically counterproductive.[38] Because Russia's Armenians lived closer to their historical homeland, and also closer to the headquarters of their church, they were more likely to develop nationalist tendencies as a result of school-induced cultural consciousness. Consequently, Delianov insisted, Russia had an "obligation" to shield its Armenians from "all the political and religious machinations of its adversaries."[39] In contrast, he claimed that Western countries could afford to promote Armenian national education "without the slightest fears" precisely because of the small Armenian populations residing in those states.

In reorienting Armenians abroad toward Russia's orbit, the tsarist Education Ministry proposed a different model for reconciling Russo-Armenian domestic and foreign goals. Instead of national academies in Russia that recruited Armenians from abroad, Delianov suggested that the government provide "material and moral" sponsorship for "schools for the secular education of Armenians" in the Persian and Ottoman Empires.[40] Such institutions would strive to counteract the work of Western missionaries and political propagandists among non-Russian Armenians. They would promote the political interests of the tsarist state and the ecumenical interests of Ejmiatsin by maintaining a pro-Russian curriculum. Staffed by Russian-Armenian graduates of the empire's top universities, these schools would advertise the benefits of Russian subjecthood among foreign Armenians. Moreover, the Education Ministry insisted that Armenians from abroad should be recruited into the general-purpose academies and universities of the Russian Empire, where they could learn alongside their tsarist-subject Armenian compatriots and Russian classmates.[41] At such institutions, where no distinctions were made along ethnic or national lines, foreign Armenians would be inculcated with a spirit of political and cultural allegiance toward Russia and toward Ejmiatsin, spreading it among their compatriots upon returning to their home countries. The Education Ministry boldly predicted that Ottoman and Persian Armenian communities would send their children to be educated in Russia, producing new generations of "zealous devotees and agents of Russia in the Orient, the more they melded with the intellectual life of Russia."[42]

Delianov and his superior, education minister (and future interior minister) Count Dmitrii Tolstoi, were part of a rightist core within the state bureaucracy who longed for the rigid nationalities policies of the Nicholaevan era. Delianov, Tolstoi, and their allies, according to a historian of Bashkiria, "began to promote the Russian language as the primary means to create loyal subjects by inculcating in them the values and goals of the empire's leadership."[43] Soon these foci evolved into more intense Russification policies that prioritized language ability as the first and most important step toward cultural assimilation. By the late 1860s, Tolstoi emphasized that "education could make possible the 'rapprochement' of non-Russians with the 'native' Russian population," and in the 1870s, "Tolstoi's goal for the education of non-Russians was their 'Russification (*obrusenie*)' and 'assimilation with the Russian people' on the basis of Russian-language education."[44] These debates on identity, integration, and diaspora relations at the heart of the autocracy's encounter with Armenians continued in the 1860s in the context of a new ministerial dialogue about the domestic and international implications of Ejmiatsin's stature.

Recalibration: External Influence and Internal Control

Russia's defeat in the Crimean War aroused popular unrest, nearly bankrupted the state treasury, and humiliated the proud military, but it also spurred the new tsar to implement the Great Reforms, an unprecedented transformation of the country's judicial, military, economic, and social spheres, culminating, perhaps most famously, in the emancipation of the serfs in 1861. Alexander II introduced the reforms, as historian Larisa Zakharova has argued, to strengthen the autocracy, not to appease liberals or relax the government's grip on an inchoate civil society.[45]

As the Great Reforms transformed the empire and its sociopolitical framework, the pendulum of general Armenian nationality policy slowly swung from cooperation to confrontation. Nevertheless, espousing divergent visions of empire and wary of relinquishing authority, senior statesmen bitterly disagreed about Russia's posture toward the Armenian diaspora. In an era of reconsideration of political and social bonds, the autocracy embarked on a multifaceted endeavor to (re)define its dialogue with Armenians. As late as the third quarter of the nineteenth century, the government struggled to balance its policies between expanding its influence on Armenians abroad and maintaining control over its own Armenian subjects. While some tsarist elites backed the promotion of national Armenian institutions, other Russian officials advocated cultural assimilation. No master plan directed the government's approach.

In 1865, Tsar Alexander II initiated the most important recalibration of Russo-Armenian political ties since the *polozhenie* of 1836. Coming in the wake of the Polish uprising of 1863, the timing of the initiative suggested a new focus on tsarist minorities' connections with compatriots or coreligionists outside the Romanov Empire. Internally, too, the state grappled with the collective apostasy of baptized Tatars in Kazan Province to Islam in 1865 and 1866, straining the purportedly tolerant posture toward heterodox and non-Russian elements of "the Tsar Liberator," whose judicial reforms in 1864 had curtailed the prosecution of apostasy.[46] Between the fright of the Polish rebellion and the "great shock" of the Tatar apostasy,[47] the autocracy felt a need to reassess and, perhaps, to restructure its policies toward the equally prominent Eastern Armenians. However, an external catalyst for a Russian policy review likely contributed as much to the timing of this reappraisal.

Although official tsarist sources remain conspicuously mute about the actual or potential effects of internal Ottoman politics on Russian nationalities regulations in the mid-1860s, the parallel changes of the sultan's laws probably registered with the tsar's architects of empire. Occurring in the broader context of the Tanzimat reforms (1839–76), the modifications of state policy toward Armenians, Jews, Greeks, and other non-Turkish minorities in the late 1850s and early 1860s yielded a modicum of autonomy for that empire's Western Armenians.[48] In 1863, the Sublime Porte ratified the Armenian National Constitution and granted the Armenian National Assembly the right to engage in "conventional politics," such as "elections, voting, hearings, debates, the exchange of ideas, and decision-making processes."[49] Although, in the words of Donald Bloxham, "the Tanzimat reforms were frequently imperfectly carried out or just ignored, while the very real hardships that they sought to address even intensified in the circumstances of the mid-nineteenth century," Russian authorities probably felt compelled to respond to these developments across the border.[50]

In July 1865, under the emperor's orders, Caucasus viceroy Grand Duke Mikhail Nikolaevich, Interior Minister Valuev, and Foreign Minister Gorchakov—among the empire's most senior statesmen—convened to "coordinate the activities of their departments regarding the question of the government's relations with the Armenian church and nation."[51] Two topics in particular dominated their agenda. First, they sought to synchronize their efforts to reconcile St. Petersburg–Ejmiatsin ties with the state policy of exerting political influence over Armenians living abroad. Second, they emphasized the importance of impeding the work of foreign missionaries among Caucasian Armenians.[52] The proselytizing of outsiders troubled Romanov officials because they viewed it as an avenue for adversarial, and even friendly, powers to shake the loyalty of non-Russians. Not the potential apostasy of Armenians, which the authorities doubted was likely, but rather their embrace of new imperial patrons worried St. Petersburg.

At the heart of the debate were several interrelated questions: To what degree did the Armenian religion, a close dogmatic and liturgical cousin of Russian Orthodoxy, qualify as a "foreign faith"? How far should the government go in shielding Ejmiatsin from the encroachment of Protestant and Catholic missionaries? How could St. Petersburg best utilize the sway the Armenian Church had elsewhere, especially in the Ottoman Empire, to achieve tsarist political objectives? Which policies should the state revise in the Caucasus to achieve a balance between internal stability and external influence? How, and how far, should Armenians be incorporated into Russian political and social life? The trio of ministers each proposed different answers to these questions.

Gorchakov's warnings about the recent successes of "secret" Protestant proselytizing among Caucasian Armenians drew the attention of the viceroy and the interior minister.[53] The three men agreed on the need to cooperate with the Armenian Church to eradicate such alien doctrines among tsarist subjects. To this end, Gorchakov wished to increase his ministry's coordination with Ejmiatsin's leadership, which "by its very nature is connected to our foreign policy." In justifying a closer political partnership between the autocracy and Ejmiatsin, the foreign minister stressed the kinship of the Russian and Armenian faiths: "Although our laws place the Gregorian Church among the heterodox, it is not, strictly speaking, a heterodox church, in terms of its main dogmas and the similarity of its rites with the Orthodox Church, and deserves [our] support and protection against [foreign] propaganda."[54] The foreign minister viewed the Armenian Church as an ally of its patron empire and intended to harness what he perceived as the formidable interimperial leverage of the catholicos. Rather than a specific objective, Gorchakov pursued a general partnership with Ejmiatsin that could potentially yield tangible benefits—from diplomatic dialogue between Russians and Ottomans to new economic agreements—when and if the Romanovs called on it.

Despite important disagreements, all three statesmen agreed about the imperative of continuing to nudge Ejmiatsin along a path most favorable to tsarist foreign policy. But, while Mikhail Nikolaevich and Valuev expressed "complete agreement" with Gorchakov's need for stronger links to the Ejmiatsin leadership, they resisted his implication that the Armenian faith deserved legal declassification as a heterodox creed.[55] The viceroy and interior minister posited that the empire's existing laws for heterodox faiths protected the Armenian Church from external threats. Although they acknowledged parallel Russo-Armenian interests in combating Protestantism and Catholicism, Mikhail Nikolaevich and Valuev refused to consider the possibility of introducing a separate legal status for the Armenian religion that, in theory, would elevate its status above the standing it already enjoyed with the *polozhenie* of 1836. The viceroy and the interior minister even objected to the foreign minister's proposal to invite the catholicos to St. Petersburg and present him with a special royal commendation.[56]

The government desired a tighter grip on the affairs of the Armenian Church but recognized the potential dangers, foreign and domestic, of alienating clerical and lay Armenians. In an official proposal, the origins of which are unclear, the political elite considered introducing a special government "adviser" to the catholicos.[57] An ethnic Armenian bureaucrat, this tsarist agent would be tasked with "convincing the catholicos [to undertake] measures and courses of action that aim to dispose the [Russian] government and the

[Armenian] nation toward him and strengthen his influence abroad."[58] The adviser would lobby the catholicos to execute policies that were in line with Russian interests, focusing on Armenians both within and outside the tsarist empire. Mikhail Nikolaevich, Valuev, and Gorchakov rejected this scheme, not only doubting its efficacy but also fearing broader repercussions. The interior minister argued that the plan would "more likely elicit suspicion than sympathy from the patriarch and the Armenians themselves, which is enough reason to fear that [a tsarist adviser to Ejmiatsin], in order to acquire influence, in many cases would sacrifice the perspectives and interests of our government."[59] This scenario could precipitate "the establishment of Armenian national autonomy." Such concerns suggest that, as late as the mid-1860s, the autocracy privileged domestic control of Ejmiatsin over promoting its foreign influence.[60] But the tension between internal and external considerations that the Armenian diaspora presented to St. Petersburg remained a source of controversy for years.

Gorchakov understood this dilemma well but remained adamant. According to an official summary of the July 1865 meeting, the foreign minister stressed to his colleagues that "in light of the tremendous importance for our political interests of maintaining foreign Armenians' trust and devotion to our government," the state had to reassess its policies.[61] In particular, Gorchakov argued that in "all matters pertaining to Armenians and the Armenian Church," domestic considerations must be "subordinated" to foreign policy imperatives. Apparently confident that the merits of his stance were so clear that they required no explanation, Gorchakov did not explicate his vision for elevating Ejmiatsin's external prestige and political cachet.[62]

Valuev disagreed, likely worried about the erosion of his ministry's oversight of tsarist-subject Armenians. The critical source of disagreement lay in fears of buttressing an "artificial" sense of Armenianness that could evolve from cultural to political self-initiative. The line between Armenian religion and nationalism started to fade for some tsarist administrators, who grew increasingly concerned about the consequences of the decades-long policies of supporting the interimperial authority of the Armenian Church. The state did not face off with professional Armenian nationalist parties until the 1880s, but here emerged the first signs of Russian concerns about the entwined currents of Armenian religion and political agitation. A capable statesman with experience in managing the multiconfessional and multiethnic western borderlands, the interior minister advocated "freedom of conscience" and generally displayed a tolerant attitude toward the empire's heterodox faiths.[63] Valuev feared foreign and tsarist Armenians' pursuit of the "reestablishment of its national autonomy" and thus wished to "avoid all that which directly or indirectly could contribute to the maintenance or spread of such aspirations."[64]

The interior minister acknowledged the necessity of maintaining foreign Armenians' favorable disposition toward Russia but resisted what he interpreted as Gorchakov's attempt to assign special status to Armenians.[65] Valuev argued that tsarist laws governing all groups within the empire, including Russians and the Orthodox Church, could not be ignored, even in the interest of the "more or less conjectural" goals Gorchakov pursued. More potently, the interior minister opposed the establishment of "an exceptional position for a quite insignificant portion of the population, which the Armenians of the empire constitute."[66] Mikhail Nikolaevich sided with Valuev, positing that the elevation of Ejmiatsin's external influence could backfire by promoting the notion of Armenian exceptionality and giving the impression of preferential treatment within an imperial domain that was a kaleidoscope of nations.[67]

The ministers' disagreement reflected the anxiety the tsarist political elite felt over the unique challenges and opportunities of Armenian transimperial existence. But if the officialdom wavered in promoting Ejmiatsin's standing abroad, the domestic partnership between the Armenian Church and the Russian government appeared more clearly in other contexts, even while ties between the authorities and secular Armenian elements encountered new hurdles.

Religious Roulette

Driven by the realities of fluid geopolitics, Alexander II's government simultaneously confronted, co-opted, and cooperated with Armenians, vacillating between promoting national, quasi-secular Armenian institutions and encouraging cultural assimilation. At the same time as the state worked with the Armenian Church to stave off the influence of British, French, and US missionaries in the Caucasus, it resisted attempts by secular Armenians to form benevolent organizations. Tsarist authorities cooperated with Ejmiatsin because they feared the political consequences of the diffusion of Western faiths among their non-Russian subjects. Yet St. Petersburg did not tolerate Armenian social initiatives that could yield political, cultural, and economic autonomy.

The Armenian Church looked to the state to silence its Russian and Armenian critics. In 1856, Professor Stepanos Nazarian of the Lazarev Institute founded in Moscow an Armenian-language journal, *Hyusisapayl* (Aurora Borealis).[68] Caucasus viceroy Bariatinskii and Count Aleksei Orlov, the head of the Lazarev Institute, backed the journal's establishment, clearing the way for its approval by the Education Ministry.[69] But Nazarian, an advocate of secularism in Armenian literature and culture, turned his publication into a platform where Armenians disgruntled at the church could voice their grievances. By 1858, prominent clerics protested to the government about the journal's "malicious articles, aimed against the Armenian-Gregorian clergy in general . . . and sharp, entirely false attacks on some of the members of our senior clergy."[70] Conservative Armenian writers and church agents accused Nazarian of promoting Lutheranism and Protestantism, seeking to secularize Armenian life, and aping Western popular culture.[71] The state did not dismiss the accusations against him outright, prompting investigations of *Hyusisapayl* by the Education Ministry and the St. Petersburg censorship committee. The government even questioned the censors who had cleared the questionable articles.[72] Although the authorities finally ruled in Nazarian's favor and refused to ban his journal, their pursuit of the Armenian clergy's claims suggests an admittedly limited desire to appease the Armenian Church. The government tiptoed around the internal controversies and fissures within Armenian culture, maneuvering with only partial success to placate as many Armenians as possible.

The autocracy backed the Armenian Church more explicitly when Western religions encroached on Ejmiatsin's backyard. In 1861, eighty-one Armenians from Shemakha Province, excommunicated by the catholicos from the Armenian Church for unspecified offenses and consequently socially ostracized, sought to convert to Lutheranism.[73] While Interior Minister Valuev agreed that it was not in the autocracy's interests to permit their conversion, he also criticized the role of Catholicos Mateos in the affair. In a letter to Viceroy Bariatinskii, Valuev not only stressed the dogmatic kinship of Russian Orthodoxy and the Armenian Apostolic Church but also highlighted the latter's role in Russian foreign policy. "The Armenians," insisted the interior minister, "no matter in which country they live, always see in Russia a defender of their church and nationality—circumstances that have quite an important significance for our politics in the Orient."[74] Valuev asserted that Russia had always "shielded" Armenians, inside and outside Russia, from the efforts of Western missionaries, "who seek, with the strong assistance of Western powers, to spread Catholicism and Protestantism among Armenians, the natural result of which will be the strengthening of French and English influence at the expense of our standing in the Orient."[75]

Thus tsarist authorities fretted over the possibility that Armenian religious matters could become a conduit for outsiders' interference in Russia's imperial peripheries. Valuev believed that, should Armenians embrace Protestantism, "then likely the English government will deem it necessary to set up its consuls in several cities of the Transcaucasus, and thus will strengthen

England's influence on the natives of the Caucasus."[76] This fear reflected the government's broader concern with non-Orthodox groups' ties to outside entities. In the early 1860s, Catholic leaders in Warsaw sought to shed St. Petersburg's restrictions on their independence and links with Rome.[77] In the Caucasus, rank-and-file Muslim clerics became so disillusioned with the government's preferential treatment of a small cadre of senior Muslim clergy that they sought Persian and Ottoman "moral guidance" and facilitated the illegal sermons of foreign preachers in local mosques.[78]

Valuev blamed Catholicos Mateos for bringing a crisis on his church and the Russian government. The interior minister accused the prelate of driving small groups of his own compatriots toward Protestantism. Valuev maintained that Mateos, in a zealous effort to combat the encroachment of Western faiths, excommunicated and ostracized many Armenians for such transgressions as group scripture reading and prayer, which the catholicos interpreted as sympathy toward Protestantism.[79] Prior to his election to Ejmiatsin, Mateos, then the patriarch of Constantinople, drove "thousands" of Armenians to secede from their national church and join Protestantism, which led to English agents pressuring Ottoman authorities to establish separate legal protections for the sultan's non-Apostolic Armenians.

Now at the helm of Ejmiatsin, Valuev insisted, Mateos engaged in "the same spirit of intolerance and religious persecution, so contrary to the spirit of Christian teachings and our laws, which permit wide tolerance in matters of conscience."[80] Consequently, Valuev believed that the petition of eighty-one Armenians to convert to Lutheranism was driven less by personal conviction than by their persecution by Mateos. The minister suggested that the government reject their request but "urge" the catholicos to exercise more tolerance toward his flock, including permitting the apostates to return to the church and to congregate for private worship.[81] Valuev's record as an advocate of "freedom of conscience" suggests that he sincerely faulted Mateos's overbearing behavior for this imbroglio. In 1866, beset by impediments to his program for empire-wide religious reform, Valuev bemoaned Russia's rigidity and also listed what he viewed as the ideal goals of any government and religious hierarchy: "Respect for freedom of conscience, for personal freedom, for property rights, for a sense of propriety is completely alien to us."[82]

To be sure, few matters evoked as much cooperation between Ejmiatsin and St. Petersburg as their opposition to Western proselytizing. Throughout the reign of Alexander II, Russian officials and Armenian clerics worked together to prevent Protestant and Catholic missionaries from making inroads among Armenians living within and outside the Russian Empire. Whatever their national origin—Britain, France, Austria, Switzerland, or the United

States—foreign religious agents represented a simultaneous threat to the autocracy and Ejmiatsin. Especially after the Polish uprising of 1863, the Russian state viewed the conversion of its heterodox subjects to Western faiths as facilitating the growth of foreign political influence in the tsarist empire's periphery and beyond.[83] Given the close economic links and common national consciousness of Russian and non-Russian Armenians, the autocracy took note even whenever foreigners targeted non-tsarist-subject Armenians for proselytism. In the 1870s, Russia confronted a surprising, new rival for the hearts and souls of the Armenian diaspora: the pious emissaries of the rising US empire and a new mode of "benevolent" imperialism.

Even before the post–Civil War era of Reconstruction ended in 1877, the United States began to embrace an ideology of US globalism that had appeared only sporadically before.[84] US missionaries stood at the vanguard of the humanitarian interventionism that by the end of the century evolved into the "savior of the world" trope. Washington backed the work of its citizens in spreading the ideals of "religious liberty" in distant corners of the world, but, as historian Andrew Preston has concluded, "the American missionary enterprise was not a straightforward handmaiden of empire. The relationship between missions and imperialism was . . . a limited partnership that usually did not unfold as most of its members intended."[85] In any case, with the diplomatic assistance of US officials, motley US proselytizers promoted "freedom of worship" not only in western Europe but also among the minority communities of multiethnic, majority non-Christian polities, such as China, British-occupied Egypt, and the Ottoman Empire. "Without exception," writes Preston, "the U.S. consulates in Europe, and also in Turkey, strenuously protested the harsh treatment of Mormons and asserted their rights not only as Americans, but as Americans practicing their faith."[86]

In October 1873, the Russian consul general in the northern Persian city of Tabriz alerted St. Petersburg to the arrival of US missionaries.[87] Flush with funds and apparently enjoying the approval of Persian authorities, the US evangelists had the potential to make significant inroads among the shah's Armenian subjects. The Russian diplomat warned his superiors that local Armenian youths were particularly susceptible to the US efforts, insisting, "Many young Armenians will easily go over to Protestantism, partly out of the precariousness of their religious convictions and partly out of selfish [*korystnykh*] reasons."[88] Russian officials noted that among the recent Armenian converts, three young people were tsarist subjects. The Foreign Ministry alerted Ejmiatsin to this information, urging Catholicos Kevork IV (1866–82) to "counter Protestant propaganda among Armenians."[89] The prelate had already replaced the infirm

Armenian bishop of Tabriz with a younger and better-educated cleric and ordered the renovation of local Armenian schools.[90]

The Russian government grumbled over the presence of US missionaries outside and inside its borders throughout the 1870s and 1880s. Two organizations in particular unnerved tsarist statesmen and Armenian clergymen: the American Bible Society (ABS) and the American Missionary Society (AMS). Enjoying Washington's diplomatic backing, these entities targeted Armenians in Russia through the distribution of Armenian-language publications. As early as May 1872, the US ambassador to the Sublime Porte, George Boker, asked his Russian counterpart in Constantinople, Nikolai Ignat'ev, to secure the tsarist government's permission for the ABS to import New Testament Bibles into Russia.[91] Although the ABS published Bibles in twenty-three languages, it sought the right to import into Russia only works in modern Armenian vernacular, suggesting that the organization focused specifically on Armenian non-elites.

St. Petersburg rebuffed the United States' request but corresponded with Ejmiatsin to ascertain the position of the Armenian Church. Catholicos Kevork judged that the US texts contained "significant differences in the content and style" from Apostolic doctrine and distorted "teachings of not only the Armenian, but also the entire Eastern, Church."[92] The ministers in St. Petersburg concurred with Kevork's assessment. By late 1873, the tsarist government had coordinated with the Armenian Church to forbid the importation of Armenian-language ABS publications into the Caucasus.

Concerted Russo-Armenian efforts to stem the work of Western missionaries hardly discouraged the US government. To Washington, the diverse evangelists were agents of "modernizing" social and political currents that elevated the United States' international stature through its humanitarian concern for downtrodden minorities.[93] In early 1882, the US State Department formally asked the Russian Foreign Ministry to permit the ABS to distribute its publications in the Caucasus.[94] The US chargé d'affaires Wickham Hoffman submitted the ABS appeal to Russian officials.[95] The organization argued that it engaged in no direct proselytizing and sought equal treatment for its "legitimate business of importing into the empire and offering for sale [its publications]."[96] The organization identified tsarist-subject Armenians as its primary focus, insisting that the Russian government "forbids the [American Bible] Society to do for the Armenians of Russia what their brethren in Turkey are very willing to have done for them."[97]

The group, and by extension the US government, implied that the Christian emperor's policies toward his heterodox Christians fell short of the Muslim sultan's rule over his own Christian minorities.[98] Such accusations were particularly acerbic in the context of Russo-Ottoman antagonisms after the war of 1877–78 and the attendant anti-Armenian climate in the Ottoman Empire. In rejecting the US requests, the Russian state cited the wishes of the Armenian Church. Count Dmitrii Tolstoi, the interior minister and chief of the gendarmes, wrote to US ambassador William Hunt in March 1883: "Under Russian law, Armenian-language works of spiritual content, which are imported from abroad, are circulated in the Caucasus only with the approval of the Ejmiatsin patriarch catholicos or the Armenian-Gregorian Synod."[99] Thus the autocracy signaled its recognition of Ejmiatsin's prerogatives within the empire and its reluctance to jeopardize generally symbiotic Russo-Armenian political ties for measures that, to most Russian observers, had little value for tsarist interests.

The Russian government had fewer geopolitical reasons to fear the encroachment of US—as opposed to western European—influence in the Caucasus. Unlike Britain and France, the United States posed no immediate challenge to Russian hegemony in its southern periphery. Until the last two decades of the nineteenth century, Russo-US relations progressed amicably, underscored by St. Petersburg's support for the Union during the Civil War and its sale of Alaska in 1867.[100] As the influential newspaper *Golos* highlighted during the Congress of Berlin in 1878, with the possible exception of Germany, "there is no country in the Old or New World that elicits as much sympathy from Russia as America."[101] Ties with the United States worsened only when anti-Jewish political sentiment increased in Russia and when ideological differences broadened during the reign of the reactionary Alexander III (1881–94).[102] Thus, Russia had little to fear from any US political intrigues with Armenians but sided with Ejmiatsin against Washington as an "easy" gesture of its patronage and support of the Armenian Church.

Nevertheless, as Armenians capitalized on the privileged sociopolitical position that the state had carved for them in imperial society, the autocracy resisted Armenian social initiatives that it feared could advance nominal Armenian autonomy politically or economically. For the Romanov administration to benefit from real or perceived Armenian "devotion," it had to maintain Armenians' reliance on tsarist social and political institutions. Because national religion acted as a glue for the diaspora, which the Old Regime hoped to harness for its benefit, the government until the 1880s saw few reasons to confront Ejmiatsin. But the formation of nonecclesiastical Armenian institutions aroused Russian resistance, because officials agonized that such initiatives could evolve into politically hazardous ambitions.

In 1865, the government barred the creation of a private, secular Armenian benevolent society that promoted commercial training. A wealthy tsarist-subject Armenian businessman, Nikita Sanasarov, envisioned a philanthropic organization that would "improve the intellectual and material well-being of Armenians" in the Russian Empire.[103] Sanasarov emphasized the political benefits to Russia of ensuring that its Armenian subjects flourished, echoing the arguments the Lazarevs had made decades earlier. The businessman insisted that the organization he proposed would maintain the superiority of tsarist-subject Armenians over their external compatriots and thus ensure Russia's supremacy over its imperial rivals in the Orient. He argued that Armenians in Europe and the Near East "from time immemorial have viewed Russia as a patron of the Armenian people and [also view] their compatriots living in Russia as those who enjoy the fruits of European civilization the most."[104] Yet Turkey and the Western powers now worked to depose Russia as the benefactor of the pan-Armenian nation, threatening the tsarist empire's geopolitical interests. While the Porte recently granted new legal protections to its Armenian subjects, Sanasarov warned, "at the same time England endeavors to master the Oriental trade, which Russia from long ago has maintained with Asia through Armenians."[105]

To prevent such developments, Sanasarov asserted, Russia had to ensure that its Armenians remained intellectually and economically more advanced than their compatriots abroad. Toward this goal, the benevolent society he proposed would spread among Russian Armenians basic knowledge of commerce and business, seeking to maintain the competitive edge that past generations of Armenian merchants had enjoyed, an advantage Sanasarov believed his compatriots in Russia were losing. To achieve these aims, his group would fund vocational schools, pay students' tuitions, and publish business-related booklets.[106] The Interior Ministry's Department of Foreign Faiths supported Sanasarov's petition, agreeing that his efforts would likely carry political advantages for the empire.[107]

However, Interior Minister Valuev and the minister of education disagreed. They questioned the project's feasibility, doubted the financial stability of the program, and criticized the proposal's vagueness.[108] The notion of a privately initiated, secular benevolent society that promoted Armenian commercial training proved too radical for the autocracy. Because neither the government nor Ejmiatsin would control such an enterprise, officials feared that it would animate a self-reliant, secular Armenian identity that had fewer incentives to work within the tsarist political and social system. Yet when individual Armenians sponsored local Armenian parish schools in small villages—under Ejmiatsin's oversight—the emperor awarded to such people silver medals inscribed with "for devotion."[109] A decade and a half later, Alexander II's son and successor, Alexander III, would have a contrary stance toward Armenian parish schools.

In this era of general vigilance over non-Russian cultural initiatives, schooling in majority non-Russian regions became a particularly fraught issue. In Bashkiria, for example, by 1870, Count Tolstoi "argued that the state should demand that non-Russians learn the Russian language 'because the Eastern origin and the Mohammedan faith in no way exempt Tatars from the general state structure.'"[110] While the specific terminology applied to Bashkiria varied, Education Ministry officials "tended to look toward the full assimilation of non-Russians into Russian national culture." Although the potential advantages of the Armenian diaspora and their powerful allies in St. Petersburg probably produced a less intrusive experience for Armenians than for Bashkirs, the authorities' anxieties of Armenian cultural seclusion and cohesion radiated beyond the walls of the Education Ministry.

This fear became a recurring tension, vocalized by both imperial and regional authorities. In 1872, two Armenian businessmen from Astrakhan sought to establish an Astrakhan Armenian benevolent society. The proposed organization would "spread moral and intellectual education as well as crafts [training] among the poor Armenian children of both sexes in Astrakhan."[111] The two philanthropists had already invested over 6,000 rubles into the project, and they turned to the regional tsarist authorities to secure the final permissions. But the governor of Astrakhan criticized not only the plan but also its broader implications. In his assessment, the governor argued that the Russian government had historically erred in creating an insular Armenian community in Astrakhan that failed to integrate into its social, cultural, and economic surroundings. The governor insisted that the imperial state "artificially created in Astrakhan a privileged Armenian society, the isolation [*zamknutost'*] and orientation of which, given its legal rights, is now an anomaly in our time."[112] Consequently, the governor opposed a new Armenian academy, which would "only complicate the relationship between the [local] administration and the Armenian society." St. Petersburg concurred with this assessment, rejecting the proposed organization for the penurious children of Astrakhan Armenians.

The state's wariness of a solidifying political Armenian identity within and beyond Russia influenced its policies toward tsarist Armenians who sent remittances to their compatriots abroad. Only with the tsar's explicit approval were Armenians permitted to send such financial assistance. For example, when in early 1871 a large fire in Constantinople damaged an Armenian church, several schools, and homes, local Armenians turned to the Russian ambassador for help.[113] Through him, Ottoman Armenians petitioned the tsarist government to permit the collection of donations among the Armenians of the South Caucasus. The state conferred with Ejmiatsin, whose consent led to Tsar

Alexander II's approval of the petition. In 1874, the Armenian patriarch of Constantinople requested the help of Catholicos Kevork for the "starving" Armenians of Anatolia.[114] The autocracy again permitted Ejmiatsin to collect donations among tsarist-subject Armenians for the benefit of their compatriots in the Ottoman Empire.

Yet the autocracy interpreted as sinister any failure to seek the government's advance permission for such activity. When, in the spring of 1872, an earthquake in northern Persia damaged several local Armenian communities, they turned to Ejmiatsin for help.[115] Apparently without a precursory nod from the tsarist government, the catholicos began collecting donations among Russia's Armenians for their compatriots in Persia. Soon Russian officials in Astrakhan alerted the Interior Ministry to this unsanctioned campaign. Astrakhan governor N. N. Bippen saw in this development another symptom of nascent Armenian nationalism, emphasizing to St. Petersburg that "it will be hardly convenient in the future to permit such exclusive donations, [which] artificially buttress claims to the existence of an 'Armenian nation.'"[116] The state soon halted the campaign, finding that it deviated from the law by failing to secure the tsar's permission for fund-raising for the benefit of foreign subjects.[117]

Such incidents remind us that, throughout the nineteenth century, the tsarist empire adapted its methods of rule to govern one part of the Armenian diaspora. The government strove to delineate a sphere of influence and affiliation for Russian-subject Armenians, trying to prevent the maturation of a consciousness of a cohesive, multistate nation that transcended imperial boundaries, because such a scenario would jeopardize Russia's borders in the South Caucasus and beyond. Neither the domestic secularization of Armenians nor their church-supported interimperial bonds could be allowed to strengthen outside St. Petersburg's direct oversight if the state was to continue deploying the Armenian Church for its foreign policy. The dispersed Armenian nation's cultural kinship remained a potential liability even when the autocracy managed to harness it for its needs. Russian statesmen recognized these dangers well, emphasizing that self-initiated Armenian donation campaigns were against tsarist interests because they could have "an international significance" (*mezhdu narodnoe znachenie*).[118] However, at the same time, imperial administrators balanced these worries with the imperative of maintaining Russia's idealized image as the guardian of downtrodden Christians in the East. With the conflagration of war between Russia and the Ottoman Empire in 1877–78, the tsarist government and liberal society saw a new chance to capitalize on Armenian hopes and fears.

War and Wariness

In certain ways, the sunset of broadly symbiotic Russo-Armenian political ties began in the second half of the 1870s. Because the tsar wished to portray his empire as the champion of the sultan's oppressed minorities, Russia accepted an influx of Armenians from its imperial neighbors. However, in the government's timid embrace of these refugees, in contrast to the elaborate welcome it extended to their predecessors in the first decades of the century, we see the emergence of a new Russian hesitation about Armenian sociopolitical utility for tsarist imperialism. The state's muted consternation about Armenian nationalism that began to percolate in this decade pushed the pendulum of imperial policy and perception to the right. While the government reluctantly absorbed Ottoman Armenian immigrants during and after the Russo-Ottoman War of 1877–78, it perceived this action less as a continuation of a key colonization policy than as an obligatory nod to its domestic leftist activists and its external proclamations of Orthodox patronage.

Russian liberal society matched—and occasionally outpaced—the officialdom's focus on the conditions of the sultan's minorities, and the affairs of Ottoman Armenians prompted no less outcry than the plight of the Balkan Slavs. The influential St. Petersburg periodical *Golos*, among the most vociferous public Russian advocates for the Armenian cause, reached over twenty-two thousand subscribers on the eve of the war in 1877, securing its position among the imperial capital's esteemed dailies.[119] Throughout 1878, the newspaper rallied the government and society in support of Ottoman Armenians, whom it hailed with a mix of unabashed hyperbole and realpolitik as "the only cultured people [in Asia Minor] whose fate must be safeguarded not only in the interests of humanity, but also out of our own political considerations."[120] No major periodical advocated as much for Western Armenians during the 1878 crisis as *Golos*.

Several coalescing factors triggered the Russo-Ottoman War of 1877–78. First, Russia's defeat two decades earlier in the Crimean War rendered revenge an important if implicit aspect of tsarist foreign policy. Second, rising nationalism in the Balkans, especially among the southern Slavic subjects of the sultan, intensified while the political vitality of their imperial overlord declined. Third, the Serb insurrection against Ottoman rule in Bosnia and Herzegovina in 1875–77 aroused as much sympathy in St. Petersburg as concern in western European capitals. While historiographical attention often accents the experience of the Balkan Slavs, the role Armenians played on either side of the Russo-Ottoman imperial frontier in the Caucasus had a significant impact on public opinion and state policy in Russia.

Prince Aleksandr Gorchakov—the advocate of stronger ties between the government and Ejmiatsin—orchestrated Russia's international resurgence after its Crimean shaming. Few tsarist officials played as decisive a role in reversing Russia's diplomatic and territorial losses in the 1850s as that statesman did during the reign of Tsar Alexander II. As foreign minister (1856–82) and chancellor (1867–83), Gorchakov exercised more control over Russia's relations with its neighbors than any official in the empire. He also faced many challenges. In 1875, rebellions by Ottoman-subject Bulgarians, Bosnians, Herzegovinians, Serbs, and Montenegrins strained the Porte's hold on the Balkans, leading to Muslim-Christian atrocities and raising international concerns about a new clash between the West and Russia over the fate of the declining Ottoman state. In response to Western fears of Russian advancement, Gorchakov denied that St. Petersburg sought to conquer the sultan's territories. In an October 1876 letter to the tsarist ambassador in London, Petr Shuvalov, the chancellor asked rhetorically, "What evidence must be provided to English ministers of [our] disinterest, [which is] based not on political advantages, but on rationality and common sense?"[121]

Yet Gorchakov worked hard to reiterate Russia's self-promotion as the patron of Muslim-ruled Orthodox Christians. The chancellor emphasized the "popular and Christian sentiment in Russia, which is too close to these countries and associated with them by [too] many ties [to be] limited to academic sympathies."[122] The statesman argued that these unique considerations placed on the tsar responsibilities "that His Majesty cannot evade." But Gorchakov insisted that all of Europe had a collective obligation to prevent the bloodshed of innocent Christians: "The Eastern Question is not only a Russian question; it concerns the tranquility of Europe, of the world, and common prosperity, mankind, and Christian civilization."[123] For a senior politician who a decade earlier had tussled with his colleagues about promoting Russian interests in the Ottoman Empire through Ejmiatsin, such sentiments were not just an expedient appeal for pseudo-humanitarian interventionism. The plight of Ottoman Christians was more than a token geopolitical tool wielded by a zealous, resurgent empire. Throughout the war, tsarist agents protected Ottoman Christians and also cooperated with them against Turks. They did so most clearly in the Caucasus theater of war.

While most of the war took place in the Balkans, events in the Caucasus and Anatolia proved consequential in the postwar era. The tsar placed his brother, Caucasus viceroy Grand Duke Mikhail Nikolaevich, in command of the war effort in the Caucasus. By the end of 1877, over 113,000 tsarist officers and conscripts served in the Caucasus army, outnumbered by the nearly 642,000 men mobilized for service in the European theater.[124] The viceroy's immediate subordinate, who wielded the real authority over the military campaign in the Caucasus and Anatolia, was General Count Mikhail Loris-Melikov. An Armenian-heritage aristocrat born in Tiflis, Loris-Melikov completed his education in St. Petersburg after his expulsion from Moscow's Lazarev Institute for gluing his teacher to a chair. Decorated for his exploits against the highlanders in the North Caucasus and against the Ottomans during the Crimean War, the general also earned the tsarist political elites' respect for his managerial acumen. The viceroy trusted his general, handpicking him to spearhead Russia's thrust against the Ottoman forces in the Caucasus and granting him freedom of action. In December 1876, the Grand Duke bestowed on Loris-Melikov "complete independence" by excusing him from reporting to the War Ministry and the General Staff in St. Petersburg.[125] Essentially, Loris-Melikov had only two superiors: the Caucasus viceroy and the emperor. Such carte blanche was necessary because the general confronted enemies outside and inside the tsar's southern domain.

Some tsarist officials conceived of the Russo-Ottoman conflict as a clash between Islam and Christianity, fretting over the allegiance of tsarist-subject Muslims in the Caucasus and elsewhere.[126] Loris-Melikov was a seasoned manager of delicate religious questions, who "embraced open access to Mecca as a way to appease [Russia's] Muslims."[127] In July 1877, he warned Viceroy Mikhail Nikolaevich that the Porte "prepares for a desperate struggle, seeing it as a battle for the life and death of Islam, and recognizing that in the Asia Minor theater of war [it] seeks more important results than a successful defense."[128] The general believed that Ottoman forces aimed to invade tsarist territory in the South Caucasus, possibly Yerevan Province, and to rally local Muslims to their aid, igniting a major anti-Russian insurrection.[129] Loris-Melikov cautioned Mikhail Nikolaevich that "the Turks indeed base their upcoming offensive actions on the cooperation of the Muslims of the Transcaucasus."[130] The general alerted the viceroy that Ottoman authorities viewed their army in eastern Anatolia as "a lever for raising among their coreligionists [in tsarist territory] a tidal wave of Islam."[131] Loris-Melikov was convinced, "The Turks recognize well that their success in the Transcaucasus will deliver a blow not only to our dominion [there], but also to all our influence in the rest of Asia."[132]

If tsarist administrators suspected the allegiance of anonymous Muslims in the Caucasus, they considered, or wanted to consider, Eastern and Western Armenians a population whose devotion to the cause of the Christian emperor was beyond question. Especially for Russian officials with little experience in managing multiethnic territories, religious identity continued to serve as a definitive marker of political reliability. Western Armenians, as minority Christians surrounded by purportedly predatory Turks and Kurds, needed to do little to convince tsarist agents of their political goodwill. Although Russian concerns over Armenian national awakening surfaced before the war and tempered the enthusiasm with which the tsarist empire had previously recruited Western Armenians, the Old Regime at the onset of the war in 1877 with the Sublime Porte maintained a generally conciliatory stance toward the Armenian diaspora. This posture was grounded in a record of Armenian cooperation with Russians, Armenians' religious identity, and their geographical predicament.

Concerns about an Ottoman invasion did not prevent the tsarist army from launching its own incursions into the sultan's territory. The most successful of these attacks captured the strategically important fortress city of Kars in November 1877. Two Armenian-heritage tsarist commanders played decisive roles in the city's conquest—Loris-Melikov and General Ivan Davidovich Lazarev—aided by Western Armenian volunteers who also collaborated with Russian troops in battles at Ardahan and Erzurum.[133] In Kars, the victors took ten thousand Turkish soldiers prisoner and seized large armories and supplies.[134] With Russian forces in Anatolia and the Balkans advancing rapidly, the Porte sued for peace in the spring of 1878. In early March, the combatants signed an armistice in San Stefano, a small village near Constantinople.[135]

San Stefano galvanized nationalism among many ethnic groups. The treaty guaranteed an autonomous Principality of Bulgaria, allowing it to shed nearly five hundred years of Ottoman suzerainty. Romania gained its independence, while Serbia and Montenegro nearly doubled in size at the expense of Ottoman territories. The accord also carried important implications for Armenians, because Russia annexed much of the territory historically labeled Western Armenia, including the Ottoman provinces of Kars, Batum, Alashkert, Beyazit, Artvin, and Olti. While in most of these districts Armenians comprised a national minority, thousands of Ottoman Armenians suddenly faced the prospect of tsarist subjecthood. Such dramatic Russian gains unsettled the Western powers, which had remained on the sidelines of that imperial clash.

Politicians and the public from London to Paris to Vienna clamored against what they saw as Russia's unilateral recalibration of the European balance of power. The London newspaper *The Standard* suggested blockading the Dardanelles and occupying Egypt, while the *Daily Telegraph* went as far as urging the government to make "energetic" preparations for war.[136] The Austrian cabinet objected to the independence and expansion of Bulgaria, predicting that it would "threaten Europe with constant disturbances."[137] With the western European capitals seemingly united in their opposition to the Russian gains vis-à-vis the Ottoman Empire, German chancellor Otto von Bismarck hosted a conference of the European powers in the summer of 1878. The Congress of Berlin sought to reconcile Russia's defeat of the Ottoman Empire with the geopolitical realities of the entire European continent.

To the Russian public and statesmen, San Stefano was the rightful rejoinder to the injustices of the Crimean War, when the Western powers backed Constantinople against St. Petersburg and imposed costly concessions on Russia. When, in March 1878, news broke that the Europeans planned to debate the treaty's provisions, *Golos* echoed the sentiments of many officials when it insisted confidently: "Russia alone has shouldered the whole gigantic struggle against the enemies of the Christian religion and European civilization; the Russian people alone have paid with floods of blood for the liberation of the Christian population on the Balkan Peninsula, and only through a new war against Russia can [Russia] be forced to relinquish [its] achievements!"[138] Readers' letters to the periodical also expressed dismay at Europe's perceived preoccupation with the actions of the Romanov empire rather than the Ottoman state, accusing Western diplomats of overlooking the Sublime Porte's abuse of its Christians.[139]

Golos articulated Russia's insistence on the protection of non-Slavic Christians within the Ottoman domain. St. Petersburg sought not "conquests at the expense of its vanquished enemy," not the "destruction of the Ottoman Empire," and not the "total annihilation of every follower of the Prophet."[140] Instead, Russia demanded the "complete, definitive liberation of Christians, but not only Slavs, as they think in western Europe."[141] A clear reference to Armenians and Greeks, this declaration was meant to reaffirm Russia's support for the Ottoman Armenian population and was intended as much for domestic consumption as for external declaration. Indeed, as the Congress of Berlin approached, *Golos* grew increasingly vocal in its support of the Armenian cause. When, in April 1878, Circassian and Kurdish irregular cavalry raided several Armenian villages in eastern Anatolia, the Constantinople-based correspondent of *Golos* reported that "the Porte has paid no attention" to these abuses and that Ottoman Armenians "remain in the most critical position."[142] Citing the legal provisions of the San Stefano Treaty, the journalist urged the tsarist government to "take upon itself the protection of these unfortunate Armenians."

Russian officials—in occupied Ottoman territories, in the Caucasus, and in St. Petersburg—remained cognizant of the humanitarian, political, and logistical challenges that the Armenian dimension of the Eastern Question posed. As self-declared protectors of the sultan's Christians, Russians decades earlier had assumed a responsibility to ensure the welfare of Armenians, who, in turn, had eagerly accepted the promises of tsarist patronage. But no clear policy dictated the resettlement of threatened Western Armenian communities to Russian territory, and the post–San Stefano political uncertainty yielded an ambiguous climate in the Caucasus and occupied Anatolia. As early as March 1878, tsarist officers in seized Ottoman territories reported that San Stefano "was greeted especially joyfully by the local Christian population, in hopes that the territory we have occupied will enter into the domain of our empire and that thus they will be forever liberated from Turkish rule."[143] However, the officers reported that, with growing rumors of the Russian army's imminent withdrawal from occupied lands, local Christians, mainly Armenians, were "convinced that the Turks will not forgive them the sympathy they have demonstrated toward us since our entry" into Ottoman domains. This fear of retribution compelled a "significant portion of Christians to wish to resettle into our domains, with the adoption of Russian subjecthood."[144] Over two thousand families had already expressed this intention to Russian officers and were only waiting for instructions from them.

While Russian bureaucrats slowly drafted plans for the population transfer, Ottoman Armenians prepared for unsanctioned immigration. Tsarist representatives in Erzurum reported in April 1878 that local Christians intended to follow the withdrawing Russian army, without formal approval.[145] Although officers took "all measures to prevent" the relocation, desperate petitioners arrived at the Russian camp "daily," declaring their intention to move eastward with or without authorization. Tsarist agents warned their superiors that many families and "perhaps entire communities" of Ottoman Christians wished to become Russian subjects. These Armenians and other Christians had "most compromised themselves against the Turkish government through their complete hospitality toward Russian troops during the war" and were "convinced that no articles of peace treaties . . . will protect them from the abuse of Muslims."[146] Russian officers emphasized that the refugees were prepared to settle in tsarist domains under any conditions, waiting for neither logistical nor financial preparations to be made, because they insisted that even a life of penury would surpass the "oppression" they were certain to experience after the departure of tsarist forces. As a sign of their determination and their confidence in their imminent relocation, some Ottoman Armenian farmers refused to sow their fields.[147]

Russian representatives in the captured Ottoman territories struggled to prevent an unauthorized exodus of local Armenians into the tsarist South Caucasus. The tsar's officers insisted to Armenians that their immigration to

Russia could not be sanctioned by local military agents but could only be approved by the highest levels of the government in St. Petersburg.[148] Because signs indicated that thousands of would-be refugees were ready to flood the South Caucasus, Russian authorities searched for ways to delay the resettlement until proper diplomatic negotiations and logistical preparations could be carried out. One exasperated junior officer reported to his superiors that he was "constantly riding around, persuading and reassuring [Armenians], but nothing works, they all repeat the same thing: that they will be lost without [Russian] troops."[149] While the tsarist officialdom delayed its permission for the resettlement of Armenians, the capital's press voiced its support for Western Armenians.

Golos rallied Russian society and the state to rescue the sultan's hapless Christians and to fulfill its promises to Armenians. On the eve of the Congress of Berlin, the paper emphasized the national pedigree and ecumenical identity of Armenians, labeling them "one of the civilized nations of antiquity, part of the Greek sphere of ancient civilization."[150] Armenia's early adoption of Christianity "distinguished it from the orbit of Asiatic peoples, placed it in contradiction to their worldview, and aroused [their] hatred." Branding Armenians "an outpost of Christianity in Asia," *Golos* portrayed them as the first redoubt against the attacks of "the enemies of Christianity," implying that Armenians had earned special gratitude from the "Christian world." The paper also insisted that the Armenians of Anatolia "reside on their native soil, within the confines of ancient Armenia." Supposedly outnumbering Turks two million to nine hundred thousand in Anatolia, Armenians enjoyed no advantages, instead falling victim to a lethargic regime and marauding neighbors: "The living conditions of Armenians under Turkish rule present an outrageous picture: Armenians live among a predatory, armed population of Kurds, and not only do not receive Turkish authorities' protection from Kurdish raids, which are usually condoned by those authorities, but also are deprived of the ability to defend the honor and dignity of their family [and] the sanctity of their temples, because they are forbidden from carrying weapons."[151]

Golos also stressed that Armenians found no relief in the Ottoman judicial system, where no Christian could hope for a favorable result without the corroborating testimony of a Muslim witness, a rare occurrence because the Koran prohibits Muslims from testifying against coreligionists. The newspaper also noted that Ottoman Armenians enjoyed no hereditary property rights, unlike their Muslim neighbors. The Russian Empire, the periodical insisted, had a moral responsibility to act.

Golos argued that Armenians had been loyal Russian allies for generations, assembling militias and serving as senior officers in charge of Russian armies in past wars. While the tsar's Armenians served in his military, the sultan's Armenians demonstrated overt "sympathy" toward Russia, for which they had repeatedly paid with blood. "But never has Turkish rage against Armenians reached the stage that it did in this war," insisted *Golos*; "the systematic extermination of Armenians now constitutes the state doctrine of the Porte, *hekmeti khiukiumet* (state secret), as Turkish rulers say." *Golos* echoed the fears of Ottoman Armenians when it argued that Muslim massacres of Christians were certain to take place upon the tsarist army's withdrawal. To prevent such tragedies, *Golos* urged Russian diplomats at the Congress of Berlin to secure from the Porte concrete guarantees of protection for Ottoman Armenians.

Most strikingly, the periodical demanded the establishment of an "autonomous" Western Armenia within the Ottoman Empire, analogous to the concessions granted to Bulgaria and other Ottoman subjects in the Balkans. "Armenia has the right," declared *Golos*, "to receive the same autonomy and the same reforms as will be introduced in Bosnia, Herzegovina, and other Christian provinces of European Turkey." The newspaper emphasized both past and future Russo-Armenian cooperation: "Thus, Armenians would receive from us a just reward for that assistance, which they have provided to us in all of our wars with Turkey and Persia from the times of Peter the Great, and for those hardships and persecutions, which they have consequently endured at the hands of their Muslim rulers. Their sympathy toward us would gain a real foundation, and there is no doubt that the sympathy of such an intelligent, diligent, and large population of Asia Minor [Maloi Azii] can prove in time to be quite important."[152]

Thus, one of St. Petersburg's most widely circulated periodicals announced its unequivocal support for Ottoman Armenians, urging Romanov politicians to make the Armenian cause a key demand of their negotiations in Berlin. Western European pressure at the Congress of Berlin greatly reduced Russia's gains at San Stefano, dashing any dreams of an autonomous Western Armenia, but the newspaper's vociferous pleas underscore the Russian public's attention to the plight of Ottoman Armenians. At a time when Bulgaria and other Slavic nations attained the contours of statehood, such as constitutions, Russian liberal society included the non-Slavic Armenians in its polemics. Rather than the solidarity of ethnic fraternity that drove Pan-Slavism, liberal Russians' support for Western Armenians was grounded in notions of religious kinship and political synergy. Although this agenda did not match tsarist policy, liberals did not hesitate to publicize their support for the Armenian cause.

In August 1878, several weeks after the disappointing results of the Berlin Congress became known, 285 Armenians from Erzurum signed a letter to the editors of *Golos*. The representatives thanked the newspaper and, by exten-sion, the Russian public for their support of Ottoman Armenians.[153] They con-veyed their broader community's "feelings of immeasurable gratitude for those words of truth and defense" expressed on the pages of *Golos*. In a clear reciprocity toward the paeans of the Russian periodical, Western Armenians underscored that a "people oppressed for centuries sheds tears of gratitude to the tsar-liberator, whose all-imperial will breaks the chains of slavery, which barbarism has placed on the humble followers of Christ's teachings."[154]

Thus, the sultan's Armenian subjects signaled their acceptance of the themes—ecumenical identity and minority oppression—that *Golos* and other Russian sympathizers promoted as justifications of tsarist intervention in the Armenian cause. Ottoman Armenians embraced the often-sensationalized and melodramatic Russian characterizations of their plight, which mixed facts and apocryphal accounts. In juxtaposing their "slavery" and Christianity against the "barbarism" and ostensibly Muslim oppression committed by their impe-rial rulers and neighbors, Ottoman Armenians adroitly evoked the very themes that galvanized the Russian public and statesmen. Such efforts bore tangible fruit.

Ottoman Armenian immigration into Russian territory started before the end of the war and the finalization of the new Russo-Ottoman boundary at the Congress of Berlin. Although Russian officers in Anatolia were often con-fused about their orders, the state's abstention from forcefully preventing the immigration of Ottoman Armenians evinces St. Petersburg's decision. Con-scious of the domestic pressure and even the foreign expectation that Russia absorb Ottoman Christian refugees, the Old Regime again received Armenians in its imperial peripheries. Although this wave of Armenian settlers was less vital for securing Russia's hold on new territories than its antecedents had been in the first decades of the century, the autocracy embraced Armenian reset-tlement as an affirmation of Russia's status as a champion of Eastern Chris-tians. Indeed, more perceptibly than after Russia's wars with Persia and Turkey in the 1820s, now European diplomats and Russian journalists watched, judged, and praised or condemned such initiatives.

The Western Armenian exodus started as early as June 1877, when almost two thousand families accompanied the first withdrawing units of the tsarist army.[155] Other groups of refugees sneaked into the South Caucasus without Russian permission, prompting the governor of Yerevan to complain in July 1877 that "whole crowds" of Ottoman subjects had infiltrated his district. Soon Armenians from Erzurum, Alashkert, and other provinces moved en masse to newly annexed Kars and other former Ottoman districts.[156]

By the fall of 1878, the Russian Empire formally opened the gates for Ottoman Armenians to settle in the South Caucasus. Several semiofficial organizations sprang up in the region to facilitate the newcomers' settlement. The refugees received 20 rubles per family as well as food and lumber for construction.[157] The authorities granted supplemental financial support, usually an additional 15 rubles, to the most destitute families. The governor of Yerevan Province estimated that 50,000 rubles would be required to support the incoming refugees over the winter of 1878–79, suggesting that up to twenty-five hundred families were expected.[158] While most of the funding came from the imperial treasury, thousands of rubles poured in from private donors. If in 1872 the authorities prohibited private fund-raising for the Persian Armenian victims of an earthquake, six years later Ottoman Armenian refugees in the Caucasus reaped the benefits of an officially sanctioned, broad donation drive. Because Ottoman Armenian immigrants became tsarist subjects and the responsibility of the Romanov administration, the government supported their economic assistance without resurrecting the concerns it had in 1872 about enabling a transimperial sense of Armenianness.

The Yerevan Committee for the Relief of the Immigrants from Turkey collected money from local residents, and its benefactors included the governor of Yerevan Province, M. I. Roslavlev, who donated a modest 50 rubles to the cause.[159] Other sources of donation included newspapers and individuals in other parts of the Russian Empire and beyond, including Moscow, Kiev, Simferopol, Novorossiisk, and even Bulgaria. From mid-August 1877 to early January 1878, the Yerevan relief committee collected 4,213 rubles, and also distributed to the refugees the 3,835 rubles collected by its counterpart, the Tiflis relief committee, bringing the total amount of private donations in that four-and-a-half-month period to over 8,000 rubles.[160]

The immigrants settled in existing towns and also established new communities, such as Novobaiazet in Yerevan Province. The archival record, while partial, provides a general picture of the scale of the immigration. By January 1878, early in the Ottoman Armenian immigration process but one of the few dates for which collective population data is available, there were 2,511 individual refugees (298 families) in Ejmiatsin District; 2,509 individuals (307 families) in Novobaiazet District; 582 individuals (74 families) in Yerevan District; and 300 individuals (43 families) in Surmalinskii District.[161] These statistics are incomplete not only because Ottoman Armenians settled in other districts, too, but because subsequent waves of immigrants arrived throughout 1878. By July 1878, 7,018 Ottoman subjects, mostly Armenians, lived in Yerevan Province, receiving state assistance.[162]

In facilitating the immigration of Ottoman Armenians into its domain, Russia sought to fulfill the promises of protection that it had issued for more than a century. The state took advantage of this resettlement by bolstering its image as the defender of oppressed Christian minorities abroad. Unlike in the first half of the nineteenth century, when Armenians from Persia and the Ottoman Empire were recruited as colonizers of newly annexed and underpopulated lands, in the 1870s new motives drove the Russian absorption of foreign-subject Armenians. The immigrants became to Russian eyes less frontier colonizers than kindred allies returning under the aegis of their patron. The Armenian diaspora, then, presented both opportunities and threats to St. Petersburg's political and diplomatic ambitions. Through governing one part of the vast diaspora, the tsarist state exercised leverage in the internal affairs of its rivals. Ottoman Armenians' sympathy toward Russia allowed the autocracy further to undermine Constantinople by transplanting that important element of the regional economy from Anatolia. However, if the superstructure of the Russo-Armenian partnership appeared solid in the late 1870s, the first serious cracks in its foundation had already appeared.

Budding Armenian Activism

In the long shadow of the Crimean defeat and the Polish revolt, the state particularly feared the fusion of economically driven social agitation and nationalism in the periphery. Few imperial domains exemplified this dangerous synthesis more strikingly than the Caucasus. By the mid-1870s, the rise of European socialism, peasant populism, Russian and non-Russian nationalism, nihilism, and student radicalism challenged the foundations of the autocracy. Between 1873 and 1877 alone, over sixteen hundred tsarist subjects were implicated in subversive political movements.[163] In the spring of 1875, the Council of Ministers listened warily to the reports of the Third Section about the proliferation of antigovernment "revolutionary propaganda" throughout the empire.[164] Whereas in 1866 the secret police had uncovered early signs of socialist agitation in only four provinces, by 1875 there was evidence of such subversive movements in over thirty provinces, "indisputably proving the deficiency of the [state's] measures" and demonstrating "the necessity of more systematic countermeasures against anarchist aspirations."[165] The ministers discussed with bewilderment the apparent apathy of ordinary Russians toward the threat to public order posed by the revolutionaries, "for the achievement of whose ideals are required streams, rivers, floods of blood."[166] Although non-Russians constituted less than 5 percent of arrested revolutionaries, their

presence, and their real and imagined ties to the "outside world," elicited particular concern from St. Petersburg.

Among those detained between 1873 and 1877, the Third Section deemed
a handful of non-Russians, including Jews and Caucasians of unspecified
national origins, to be especially guilty of subversive activity.[167] The ministers
feared that foreign ideologies could infect the tsarist youth, Russian and non-
Russian, emphasizing that many subjects returned from studying in "Zurich,
Bern, and Geneva" infused with "the destructive influence of the Russian émigrés, who strive with all strength to spread anarchist principles in the state."[168]
Whether attending the lectures of such anarchist émigré ideologues as
Mikhail Bakunin in Switzerland or translating into Ukrainian illicit literature at
St. Vladimir University in Kiev, scores of tsarist-subject youths challenged the
political and social status quo.[169]

Although social, economic, and cultural circumstances in the South Caucasus distinguished it from the imperial core and the more developed western
borderlands, the political situation in Tiflis in the 1870s reflected the general
unease that characterized Russia proper. While there were fewer students and
well-educated elites in Tiflis than in St. Petersburg, Odessa, or Kiev, the local
administration feared the "transfer of political agitation" to their territory.[170]
Specifically, regional officials linked anarchist and socialist ideologies with one
group's nationalism: "The agitators take advantage . . . and help spread all
manifestations of antagonism in society, [thus we] cannot fully ignore the
clearly demonstrated . . . nationalist aspirations toward separation [*stremleniia
k obosobleniiu*] of intellectual Armenians in the Caucasus."[171]

From the Russian perspective, among the dozens of ethnonational groups
populating the South Caucasus,[172] Armenians alone possessed the distinct
factors necessary for a potential political challenge to the status quo. Their economic standing and attendant social influence in the Caucasus and elsewhere,
the domestic and foreign authority of their national church, and the diasporic
distribution of Armenians throughout Eurasia, all affected tsarist officials' perception of Armenian political aims and abilities. In the mid-1870s, imperial
administrators began to associate the revolutionary movement in Russia with
the first symptoms of Armenian political action. Soon reports from Russian
officials in the South Caucasus investigating illicit Armenian organizations
trickled into St. Petersburg ministries.

In one of the first of these notifications, dated 8 April 1875, the head of
Yerevan's provincial gendarme administration (*gubernskoe zhandarmskoe upravlenie*) alerted the Third Section that in Aleksandropol' District, police had uncovered a shadowy circle run by young Armenians.[173] Intercepted missives
revealed that the group had begun to "contemplate matters beneficial for the

[Armenian] nation, excluding government matters, which are prohibited."[174] The circle's members perceived its explicitly nonrevolutionary ethos to be so innocuous that they announced its establishment in regional Armenian newspapers. Yet at least one official report from May 1875 charged that the group was "established by Armenians with the aim of raising among their coreligionists a patriotic spirit and achieving independence."[175]

A search of the apartment belonging to the group's leader, Hambartsum Balasaniants, revealed literature published abroad and smuggled into the Russian Empire, as well as patriotic Armenian poetry, some of which was written by his brother, a student at the Aleksandropol' seminary. Although Russian investigators devoted little space to elucidating the contents of such publications, it appears that they were more Armenophilic—in the sense of celebrating Armenian antiquity, culture, and supposed national singularity—than anti-Russian, and thus not as politically subversive as some of the texts that would be discovered in the next decade.

Almost concurrently with the discovery of Balasaniants's group, local police in Aleksandropol' uncovered a more politically focused secret organization. With the ostensibly altruistic but hopelessly ambiguous name Society of the Noble Aim (Obshchestvo s blagoiu tsel'iu), the group had been founded in 1869 by a local teacher, Arsenik Krit'iants.[176] Although detected and disbanded before it could boast of any tangible accomplishments, the group has earned its place in history as "the first circle dedicated to Armenian liberation in the Russian Empire."[177] Meeting every Sunday in their furtive headquarters, which housed a library of banned Armenian publications, its members expressed a conspicuously political tone, if yet unfocused and unclear to tsarist authorities. With a notably more aggressive stance than anything theretofore seen by Russian officials, Krit'iants's writings called on the Armenian people to rediscover the fighting spirit of their ancestors and to shed the domination of the "crafty and treacherous Russians, the demented Tatars [Azeris], and the hateful Persians."[178] The group's forty-three members contributed a small weekly fee and purchased histories of Armenia published abroad, which they then distributed (often sold) to local Armenian students. Among Krit'iants's belongings, the police discovered Armenian-language texts and newspapers from abroad, including material banned by the censors, such as literature printed in 1866 in Constantinople claiming that tsarist agents engaged in the cultural Russification of Armenians.

In an early flash of Russian attention to the purported links between Armenian nationalism and religion that would soon become the crux of the state's Armenian policies, confiscated documents showed that members of Krit'iants's group had given fiery orations in Armenian churches. The audi-

ences had reacted to these appeals with "delight," displaying their receptiveness to making sacrifices for the sake of establishing poorly defined
"independence."[179] Krit'iants's correspondence with other members vented
that "the disgusting and hateful conduct of the Russians elicits [our] ire and
indignation."[180] The police noted that a portrait of Hayk, the etiological patriarch of the Armenian people, hung "in a conspicuous spot" in his school
office.[181] The Tiflis court sentenced Krit'iants to six months of incarceration
followed by two years of police surveillance. Balasaniants and his associates
received only a "strong suggestion hereafter not to allow themselves to form
any organizations without the government's permission."[182] With only a trickle
of isolated, vague, and inconclusive reports in 1875 of possible Armenian political agitation, the government moved unhurriedly in connecting the dots of
what soon emerged as a new era in Russo-Armenian political ties. With social
discontent brewing in other corners of the empire, the authorities in the capital were slow to grasp the national challenges in the Caucasus.

In December 1879, the head of the Tiflis gendarmerie notified St. Petersburg of what he interpreted as a connection between Russian socialism and
embryonic Armenian nationalism.[183] He warned that "the present emergence
of Armenian nationalist tendencies in the Caucasus" would be compounded
by the broader revolutionary movement if not checked through the "strict supervision over the spread of nationalist ideas among Armenians."[184] Officials
in Tiflis were worried: "Russian socialists . . . can easily establish here a nest
not only with banned books, but also with a printing house and an armory . . .
of course in order to act against the government."[185] The authorities identified only Armenians as a potential threat, suggesting that officials had begun
to link political subversion with Armenians.

By 1880, Tiflis became a hub for Russian and non-Russian political dissidents, attracting revolutionaries from St. Petersburg, Moscow, and universities throughout the empire.[186] The South Caucasian capital's remoteness from
the centers of imperial power, its proximity to the porous borders of the Ottoman and Persian Empires, and the city's lively cultural ambience drew diverse dissidents. The provincial gendarmerie grumbled that the Third Section
"constantly" inundated Tiflis with arrest and surveillance orders for fugitives
from Russia. Local authorities tracked daily the arrival of each intellectual and
tried to double the number of regional police stations to combat the proliferation of illicit publications, underground presses, and clandestine groups.[187]
In addition to socialist circles, provincial authorities pursued ill-defined
"political-national" tendencies among Caucasian natives. In one case, the police in Tiflis arrested a young Armenian for distributing portraits of the writer
Mikael Nalbandian,[188] an exiled socialist with ties to some of the era's leading

dissidents, including Alexander Herzen, Mikhail Bakunin, and Nikolai Ogarev. Soon the viceroy personally followed all Third Section investigations of political revolutionaries in the Caucasus.[189]

Yet the Caucasus remained but one of several imperial territories where national, social, and religious currents menaced the government's authority. More and more frequently, the Armenians of the Caucasus attracted the type of official scrutiny of their political culture and interimperial links that had vexed tsarist agents elsewhere. In the northwestern region, for example, administrators faced a multitude of national and ethnoreligious resistance movements in the last decades of the nineteenth century, especially after the Polish uprising of 1863. Catholic Poles and Jews, in particular, featured prominently in provincial and state reports about the political unreliability of local residents. Authorities' efforts to replace Polish with Russian as the language of instruction in Catholic churches and seminaries in Minsk and Kovno Provinces in the 1870s faced stiff resistance, and false rumors proliferated throughout the northwest that the introduction of Russian in traditional Catholic spaces would lead to coerced conversion to Orthodoxy.[190] In 1886, one governor-general of a northwestern province bitterly reported: "Certain parts of the population are far from giving up Polish nationalist aspirations and in the depth of their souls are always ready to behave with hostility toward all things Russian."[191] Until the turn of the twentieth century, the tsars' Armenians did not encounter such state-driven cultural and administrative persecution, but they increasingly appeared in investigations of ostensibly seditious minorities.

During the reign of Alexander II, Armenians had as many reasons to seek Russia's patronage as they had to fear its imperial grip. The Armenian Church recognized that without the state's help Western missionaries threatened its flock and its prosperity. Even the attacks of Orthodox Russians on the Armenian faith often ended in the state's backing of Ejmiatsin, signaling that the Russo-Armenian symbiosis remained intact. In this period, as throughout much of the nineteenth century, Armenians gained advantages from their association with the Russian Empire. The security and economic opportunities tsarist rule provided outweighed the absence of an independent Armenian homeland for many Eastern Armenians.

Yet the autocracy remained unprepared to provide the liberal concessions (to Russians or to non-Russians) that *Golos* and some Armenians demanded. It was not in the government's interests to precipitate consciousness of a cohesive, multistate nation that transcended imperial boundaries. Such a scenario would jeopardize Russia's borders in the South Caucasus and beyond, because Armenians could not be allowed to place their national allegiances above their civil subjecthood to the tsarist empire. Consequently, the authorities suppressed private, secular Armenian institutions, prohibited the unsanctioned collection of donations for foreign subjects, and suspected ties between the Russian revolutionary movement and Armenian activism. As the next chapter demonstrates, in the last two decades of the nineteenth century, the Russo-Armenian symbiosis faltered in the tempest of Russian reactionism and Armenian nationalism.

CHAPTER 5

The Shining of the Sabers
Ebbing Symbiosis, Rising Strife, 1881–1895

The last quarter of the nineteenth century produced a distinctly new Russo-Armenian dynamic. Official and popular Russian reactionism, bureaucratic fear of minority nationalisms, and revised political methods contributed to a dramatic—if temporary—transformation of Russia's policies toward Armenians. This chapter analyzes the tsarist responses to Armenian nationalism under the rule of Tsar Alexander III (1881–94). Despite the general Russian wariness about Armenian political activism, state agents rarely and sporadically resorted to anti-Armenian repression. To grasp the bases of St. Petersburg's unprecedented measures toward Armenians in the 1880s and 1890s, we must begin with an overview of the new tsar's political ideology.

If, from the vantage point of the long nineteenth century, the Russo-Armenian partnership appears to have soured abruptly, then in the context of the late 1870s and early 1880s the changes were more gradual. Notwithstanding the signs of Armenian agitation in the mid-1870s, the government was reluctant to end the collaboration with its oldest ally in the Caucasus. In this era, few statesmen exemplified the Armenian contribution to Romanov governance as much as Mikhail Loris-Melikov. After his exploits during the Russo-Ottoman War of 1877–78, when his forces captured the Kars fortress, Loris-Melikov rose to political prominence in the imperial capital, joining the State Council and, in February 1880, heading the Supreme Administrative

Commission. Tasked with pacifying the rising tide of social discontent among intellectuals, he received a jarring reminder of the situation's volatility during an attempt on his life just eight days after his promotion.[1]

A reformist monarchist, if not a liberal, Loris-Melikov was skilled as both a statesman and a general. Despite the pressure on him, he eschewed repressive tactics in remedying the political and social ills facing the state. A Tiflis-born son of a prominent Armenian merchant family, Loris-Melikov in April 1880 called for the reevaluation of tax obligations, the reorganization of local administration, the expansion of civil rights for such groups as the Old Believers, and even the abolition of the notorious Third Section.[2] He also collaborated with other reform-minded officials, such as Finance Minister Aleksandr Abaza, to repeal the unpopular salt tax, relax press censorship, and tighten exile regulations. Alexander II approved these measures and—based at least in part on Loris-Melikov's recommendation—removed the rightist education minister, Dmitrii Tolstoi. By August 1880, Loris-Melikov rose to interior minister and chief of the gendarmes, becoming the second most powerful man in the empire. In this position, he advocated for reformist nationalities policies throughout the empire, working "to ease the pressure on Ukrainian cultural activities and Ukrainian-language publications," among other initiatives.[3] On the morning of 1 March 1881, he met with the tsar to discuss the formation of a commission modeled on the one that two decades earlier had engineered the Great Reforms. Hours later, a bomb blast mortally injured Alexander II. His successor proved less open to the Armenian statesman's projects, compelling Loris-Melikov and other like-minded officials, including Abaza and War Minister Dmitrii Miliutin, to resign within months.

The assassination of Alexander II ended the reign of an enigmatic ruler both lauded as a liberator and derided as an autocrat. His successor, Alexander III, inherited a Russia dangerously fragmented along social, political, and ethnic lines. Alexander III saw in his father's murder proof of what he had intuited for years: the liberalization of imperial Russia over the preceding two decades had weakened the institution of the autocracy to dangerous levels.[4] Looking back before his father's era to the reign of his grandfather, "Iron Tsar" Nicholas I (1825–55), Alexander III and his camarilla renounced the Great Reforms as an unjustifiable and dangerous deviation from the Orthodoxy, Autocracy, Nationality trajectory of the prereform era. The new emperor maintained that Russia's Western tilt since the Petrine era had squandered the glory of Muscovy and had bred the Westernized society that produced regicidal radicals. Alexander's remedy for these ills relied on coerced Russification, a zealous Orthodox Church, a centralized bureaucracy, and an empowered tsar.[5]

Alexander III distrusted the liberal, Westernized aristocracy and the professionalized bureaucracy. His opposition to the legacy of the Great Reforms went beyond egotistical anxiety. Alexander believed that the progress of the state and the nation could best be guaranteed under the watchful eye of a powerful autocrat, unrestricted in his authority by cumbersome legislatures or autonomous administrators. Intent on centralizing the empire's government, in 1883 the new emperor dissolved the post of the Caucasus viceroy that had existed since 1844, replacing it with the lesser position of the high commissioner to reestablish St. Petersburg's direct rule over the territory. High commissioners enjoyed less freedom of action than viceroys because they reported not only to the monarch but also to the imperial ministers. In practically all corners of the empire, compromise yielded to confrontation as the primary mode of the nationalities policy.

For many of Russia's ethnonational minorities, Alexander III's reign brought hardship. The heir to the rejuvenated Muscovy throne increasingly saw expressions of ethnic and national identity—language, religion, education, and institutions—as threats to his empire's unity and vitality, however much his father had tolerated such things. Embracing the example of his grandfather's policies in the western borderlands, Alexander III presented the renewed Russification effort as a "defense of the national character and sovereign rights of the monarchy and the Russian people."[6] Within months of Alexander's ascension, anti-Jewish pogroms rocked parts of Ukraine and Russia's two capitals.[7] Although the government did not instigate or promote these riots, new interior minister Nikolai Ignat'ev made clear that Jews—the "conquered foe"—had received too much liberty from the previous tsar.[8]

This domestic political climate soon affected the state's external priorities. Replacing the Third Section, the new Department of Police of the Interior Ministry (also known as Okhrana) emphasized in 1881 that "the secret and systematic surveillance of Russian émigrés abroad constitutes the main task of the Russian state police."[9] In the Near East, after defeating the sultan's army in the war of 1877–78, the tsar controlled Kars and Ardahan Provinces, adding over one hundred thousand new Armenian subjects to his realm.[10] Despite the limits imposed at the Congress of Berlin, Russia continued to promote itself as the protector of Ottoman Orthodox Christians. The plight of Western Armenians elicited the attention of the Russian government, the public, and Eastern Armenians, who recalled with varying emotions the wartime slaughter of five thousand to six thousand Western Armenians in the Ottoman regions bordering Russian and Persian territory during the recent imperial conflict.[11] As the sultan's officials deployed Kurdish militias in the postwar years to maintain control over Armenian-populated districts and to provide a redoubt against Russia, Western Armenians faced a singular threat.[12] In response, Armenians on both sides of the imperial border mobilized.

The Rise of Armenian Nationalism

The manifestations of what Russians lumped under the label "Armenian nationalism" took multiple forms, and the tsarist imperial agents who often bemoaned the ambiguity of various Armenian political agendas did not always distinguish among those agendas.[13] At their broadest level, the Armenian political movements of the Russian Empire in the last quarter of the nineteenth century espoused one of three objectives. The most prominent force, because of its size and vitality, included elements in Eastern Armenia who expressed outrage at the real and imagined mistreatment of the Western Armenian population of neighboring Anatolia and sought to redress this through violence directed at Turks and Kurds. Another group of Armenians, a distinct minority of nationalists, called for the establishment of an autonomous Armenian republic within the Russian Empire, one that would enjoy the contours of statehood but also benefit from Russia's protection. The most radical faction of Armenian irredentists strove to unite Western and Eastern Armenia to establish a sovereign nation-state. This internal diversity of Armenian nationalism challenged Russian authorities, who remained especially unclear about the goals and strategies of the groups crossing into Ottoman lands from the South Caucasus.

The highly visible cross-border raids of Eastern Armenians into Ottoman territory elude neat categorization into conventional definitions of nationalism. On the one hand, the tsar's Armenians evinced cultural camaraderie with the sultan's Armenians. The two groups spoke the same language, albeit with distinct regional dialects, worshiped according to the same dogma, and traced their origins to a once-unified political state, evincing a consciousness of a shared identity.[14] However, they satisfied only two of the three components proposed by John Breuilly: they demonstrated "an explicit and peculiar character" and a primacy of self-interests and values, but did not enjoy "political sovereignty."[15]

On the other hand, most tsarist Armenians did not seek to fuse Western and Eastern Armenia into an independent nation-state. Thus, although Michael Hechter's definition of "unification nationalism" is probably the closest conceptual framework for understanding Armenians' actions, the lack of a large-scale independence discourse challenges the traditional conviction that each nationalism seeks an independent homeland.[16] Indeed, even the most prominent Armenian revolutionary party of the era, the Armenian Revolutionary Federation, or Dashnaktsutiun, conspicuously eschewed calls for the formation of an Armenian state. While some of their contemporary counterparts, such as the Hnchakian Revolutionary Party, sought the establishment of an independent Armenia under the umbrella of international socialism, the Dashnaks sought the implementation of long-promised political, social, and economic reforms in Western Armenia. Only in the early twentieth century, in the midst of a crisis in Russo-Armenian ties, did the Dashnaks turn their attention more earnestly to Eastern Armenia.[17]

Thus, my use of the term *nationalism* to refer to the actions of tsarist Armenians in the late nineteenth century emphasizes the deep role of ethnicity, which Azar Gat defines as the congruence of shared kinship and culture and considers central to the formation of nationalism.[18] Eastern Armenians' actions in the last quarter of the nineteenth century certainly display the role of a shared religious (and, more broadly, cultural) identity in the recognition of a collective kinship. Armenians defied tsarist laws and attacked Turks and Kurds not in hopes of wresting an independent Armenia from its two imperial overlords but rather out of a cultural bond and ethnonational solidarity that sought to protect Ottoman Armenians from real and imagined abuses. Indeed, some Armenian nationalist hard-liners claimed to have been so moved by the calls of the Russian press to support the oppressed Christians of eastern Anatolia, that they interpreted this as a sign of the tsarist state's tacit endorsement of its Armenian subjects' cross-border raids. Armenian nationalism did not simply emerge or awaken at the end of the nineteenth century in response to mass media advancements or repressive state policies. Rather, a collective sense of shared culture and common identity had always existed within that nation's divided communities of the Russian, Ottoman, and Persian Empires, but that shared identity became more pronounced only in the late nineteenth century as external threats decreased and the Russo-Armenian bond began to fade.

Yet, before the rise of radical Armenian political parties in the late 1880s and early 1890s, a liberal and nationalist Armenian intelligentsia defined the search for national liberation in the late 1870s. While some discontented Russian youths turned toward the peasant socialism of the Narodovoltsy, their Armenian counterparts remained more enticed by the moderate, reform-oriented proposals exemplified by the influential Tiflis newspaper *Mshak* (Cultivator) and its longtime editor, Grigor Artsruni (1872–92). *Mshak* encouraged Armenian-Russian partnership, emphasized economic growth, and denounced socialism.[19] At the same time, Artsruni rallied his compatriots across the imperial border against the injustices of the Ottoman government, urging the sultan's Armenians in July 1876 to follow the example of the rebellious Balkan Slavs: "It will be a disgrace for Armenians if they do not raise their voice in defense of their rights, at a time when other Ottoman subject nations sacrifice themselves, spilling their blood for freedom."[20] Many Armenians believed that it was time to move from words to deeds.

Frontier Raiders

Eastern Armenians maintained strong cultural and economic ties with Western Armenians, and the plight of the sultan's minority Christians became a cause célèbre among various groups in Eastern Armenian society, just as it attracted attention in Europe.[21] Whether based on legitimate or sensationalized claims of abuse, the fervor of Armenians and many Russians gathered strength in the early 1880s. Responding to the promised yet undelivered protections of the Congress of Berlin, Eastern Armenians sought to take matters into their own hands. While the Western powers delivered autonomy and political self-determination to several Balkan Slav nations, such as Bulgarians, the fate of Western Armenians remained uncertain. In that age of nationalism, political sovereignty and security became the markers of modernity.[22]

The Congress of Berlin, one historian wrote, "opened the epoch of the disintegration of empires and the multiplication of nations. The Bulgarians, Serbs, Montenegrins, Romanians, Ukrainians, Lithuanians, Jews, and others all began to claim their rights to a separate existence, justifying such rights by the unique nature of their cultures."[23] One of the key provisions of the accord called for the Ottoman government to ensure the protection of its minority Christians, including Armenians. The clause, article 61, in subsequent years acquired almost mythical gravity for Eastern and Western Armenians. The attention of purportedly "justice-loving" Europeans to the Armenian cause, mainly in the Ottoman Empire but also in Russia, remained essential to Armenian nationalists, who were keenly aware of the primacy of the Eastern Question in European capitals.[24] But a sense that Armenians' inaction hindered their salvation spread among militants as well as senior clergy. The leader of the Armenian delegation in Berlin, the former patriarch of Constantinople and future catholicos, Mkrtich Khrimian, bitterly asked his compatriots on returning from the congress: "What business did requests and petitions have in a place where weapons are what talked and where sabers shone?"[25]

In this atmosphere arose the faction of Eastern Armenian nationalists determined to aid Western Armenians. One of the earliest Russian alerts came in October 1880 from the viceroy of the Caucasus and Tsar Alexander II's brother, Grand Duke Mikhail Nikolaevich, who notified St. Petersburg about young Armenians' illegal crossing of the border from the South Caucasus into the Ottoman Empire.[26] Half a year later, in April 1881, Yerevan police detained three Armenian students who had recently run away from a private Tiflis gymnasium. Under interrogation, the youths admitted that they had intended to cross into Anatolia to join a band of so-called Van volunteers in their struggle for the protection of Armenians against Kurds.[27] Through private donations in Tiflis, the students had collected 300 rubles for the weapons and the journey, and the police report concluded that their appearance in Yerevan had "caused a strong reaction in all layers of the local Armenian population."[28] Rumors of similar incidents spread in Tiflis, Yerevan, and Aleksandropol, with administrators reporting that donations had been solicited for the funding and arming of volunteer units headed to Ottoman territories.

The delay in implementing the protections that the Congress of Berlin had stipulated for Western Armenians continued to feed the nationalistic fervor among Eastern Armenians. Through illicit pamphlets, covert meetings, and the Armenian-language press, Eastern Armenians' frustrations at the inaction of the European powers gathered momentum. Not uncommon, for example, was an anonymous letter the editor of the Armenian-language Yerevan newspaper *Psak* (Wreath) received in March 1883. Postmarked in Moscow, the letter decried the plight of the sultan's Armenian subjects and lamented that, in the five years since the Congress of Berlin, no tangible steps had been taken to enforce article 61: "We see that all articles of the Berlin Treaty have been carried out, yet the promised and tiny reforms in Armenia, according to article 61, have been left unattended. We see that Europe does not find the time to get involved in our affairs, since it already has too much work and issues that must be solved, [and thus] it has its own pressing interests. We notice all of this very clearly, yet we wait as if for a miracle from the sky."[29]

Besides equating Ottoman reforms to divine intervention, the letter reminded the reader that no nation had ever achieved "freedom" without blood and sacrifice. "Will Europe really abandon its interests," asked the author sardonically, "and for our sake make sacrifices, when we do not wish to make them for our own benefit? Do not forget that hitherto we have done nothing to attract Europe's attention to the fact that we are capable of independent self-determination [*upravliat' soboi nezavisimo*], which is one of our main weaknesses that Europe points out each time."[30]

The author's message was clear: How can Armenians—whether subjects of the sultan or the tsar—expect the position of Western Armenians to be improved, achieving what this writer vaguely presented as independence, when Armenians have not yet demonstrated to the world both the dedication and the facility for self-determination? To wait and beg for foreign intervention and eventual providence was both fruitless and unbecoming of an ancient nation, many believed. Instead, Armenians must make Europe understand that the time had come to extend to them the same privileges the Greeks had received. The only solution, then, insisted the letter's author, lay in "proving to the enlightened world that the inhabitants of Armenia have been penetrated by ideas of freedom, that they too are capable and ready to sacrifice the lives of their dear, beloved sons for the sake of freedom. Who can forget those incredible self-sacrifices through which tiny Greece returned its former independence?"[31] Eastern Armenian nationalists who focused on aiding their Ottoman compatriots often invoked such examples of the sultan's other minorities. Whether inspired by the struggles of the Greeks, Bulgarians, Albanians, or Egyptians,[32] these activists argued that the time had come to follow the actions of those nations and break away from Constantinople's "barbaric" grip. To achieve these aims, they called on Eastern Armenians in the South Caucasus to provide "material and moral support" for the cause.

Tsarist authorities disapproved of their Armenian subjects crossing into Ottoman lands. Wary of renewed hostilities with a traditional foe and seeing little to gain from Armenian political initiative, St. Petersburg dispatched Cossacks and Russian border guards to plug the porous frontier. But in the mountainous terrain, small groups of Armenians passed undetected, often terrorizing local Ottoman villagers on their way to attacking Turkish garrisons or Kurdish civilians, whom they accused of maltreating the local Armenians. Yet, despite the Russian imperial regime's clear objection to the Armenian raids into Ottoman lands, St. Petersburg breathed a sigh of relief whenever the Sublime Porte, not Russia, found itself in the crosshairs of Armenian militants.

The appeals of various nationalists—whether in the form of anonymous letters to newspapers or in speeches in churches—gave rise to several small Armenian circles in Yerevan, Tiflis, and other regional cities. Attracting the attention of local authorities, these "benevolent" societies were deemed to be *potentially* subversive yet without specific political danger to the state. In September 1883, Caucasus high commissioner Aleksandr Dondukov-Korsakov concluded that the threat of Armenian nationalism to Russian interests remained low, because the groups aimed their energies at inducing action among Western Armenians against Ottoman authorities.[33] No clear evidence yet existed, he wrote to his superiors, of similar goals on the part of Eastern Armenians, although the discovery of maps of the ancient Armenian kingdom hinted at the presence "among some South Caucasian Armenians of vague [*neiasnykh*] dreams regarding the future reestablishment of unity and political independence of both Turkish and Russian Armenia."[34] Nonetheless,

Dondukov-Korsakov found no proof of a "serious political organization" threatening Russian interests. He stressed that "the most limited number" of Armenian youths, including some teachers and publishers, could be accused of harboring unclear "dreams" and that Armenian merchants and peasants "are utterly alien to these ideas." The high commissioner proclaimed that the attempts of agitators among those groups presented "nothing dangerous" and were "devoid of any significance."[35]

For the remainder of the 1880s, Russian officials noted few instances of cross-border activities on the part of Eastern Armenians, a lull that would be broken in the following decade. Fueled by ethnoreligious conflict between Armenians and their Turkish and Kurdish neighbors in the Ottoman Empire, the steady stream of Eastern Armenians crossing into Ottoman territory or sending material help would pose major challenges for the tsarist regime. Armenian-Muslim strife within the sultan's domain had simmered long before the 1890s, with numerous Western travelers emphasizing the interethnic and interreligious conflicts they witnessed.[36] For example, decades earlier, William Francis Ainsworth, a member of the Royal Geographical Society, highlighted in a travelogue Kurdish raids of Armenian villages near Erzurum. He pointed out that local Armenians had been subject not only "to an authorized vexation and spoliation entailed by Kurdish supremacy, but also to frequent incursions of the same predatory tribes; on which occasions they drive away all their cattle, sheep, and goats, and treat the inhabitants according as they submit quietly to be left destitute, or resist this cruel system of plunder."[37]

Tsarist officials noted these abuses. In the summer of 1890, Russian diplomats in Constantinople and Erzurum alerted St. Petersburg to the rise of Armenian-Muslim violence. In one incident that June, an anonymous tip to local police in Erzurum prompted a destructive search of the city's main Armenian church for stockpiled weapons. After some damage to the walls and floors failed to produce the weapons, two mobs of Armenians and Turks clashed, leaving fifteen Armenians dead, including one Russian subject, and over two hundred injured.[38] The mob's belief that the British and French consulates sheltered Armenians aggravated the situation, resulting in armed attacks on both diplomatic missions. Consul General Clifford Lloyd barricaded himself in the British consulate, armed to the teeth. Although the Russian consulate escaped the mob's wrath that day, it was only a matter of time before these interethnic tensions in the Ottoman Empire directly affected Russian interests.

In the wake of the skirmishes in Erzurum, Ottoman Armenians disseminated in parts of the Russian South Caucasus "exaggerated" accounts of these clashes.[39] Roused by the rumors, many Eastern Armenians became convinced that both Turkish officials and civilians engaged in the abuse of their Christian Armenian minority. Small parties of Armenians, often numbering between ten to fifty men, began to cross into Ottoman lands from Russian territory to "avenge" the abuse of their compatriots. They exceeded their ostensible missions by attacking, plundering, and often murdering unsuspecting Kurdish villagers along the frontier.[40] Armenians captured by Russian border guards often freely admitted to crossing into Ottoman territory with the intention of "taking revenge on the Muslims for their abuse of Turkish Armenians."[41]

Russian responses to Armenian incursions into Ottoman lands in the 1890s demonstrate a heightened sense of urgency compared to the previous decade. Despite increased Cossack and Russian border patrols, many Armenian units continued to slip through. On 2 September 1890, Cossack border guards clashed with a unit of one hundred Armenian volunteers attempting to cross into Turkey with the intention of "taking vengeance" on the local Kurds for their abuse of Ottoman Armenians.[42] The fray left a Cossack and two Armenians dead, with the timely arrival of Russian infantry resulting in the capture of twenty-seven Armenians and a cache of arms. With men from throughout the region and beyond, including St. Petersburg, Yerevan, Tiflis, Elisavetpol, Kars, and Batumi, as well as the subjects of all three neighboring empires—Russia, Turkey, and Persia—the group's composition signaled deep cohesion among the region's Armenians. Yet not all members of this unit understood the position of the Russian authorities regarding their mission. Confusion and disagreement about Russian approval had slowed the group's advance, until several men deserted ostensibly when they realized that imperial officials had not sanctioned their task and that their outfit was hiding from Russian border patrols.[43] Later, some of these men claimed that reading pleas in Russian newspapers to help Western Armenians convinced them that officials would "look the other way" at their actions.[44]

Tsarist officials confiscated from these fighters red epaulettes stamped with the Armenian letters "M.H." Under interrogation, at least one of the captured men admitted that the abbreviation denoted "Miutiun Hayastani," or Union of Armenia.[45] This discovery pointed to the existence of a more organized, and militant, group of Armenian nationalists than Russian authorities had theretofore encountered. The missives of the group's leader, Sarkis Kukunian, who was captured during the abortive incursion against Kurds, suggested that his band of one hundred men constituted part of a broader Armenian movement rather than an isolated outburst of vengeful chauvinists. Kukunian proudly informed tsarist officials that Eastern Armenians armed Western Armenian communities not to encourage an insurrection against the sultan but rather to force the Sublime Porte, with European pressure, to honor its obligations under the Berlin Treaty. In a direct response to Mkrtich Khrimian's call after the Congress of Berlin, Kukunian contended that the attention of the European community to the plight of the Ottoman Armenians was vital for the improvement of their condition. Only the saber rattling of local Christians could solicit such attention.[46]

Not uncommon among Armenians on both sides of the imperial border, such views were expressed to Russian interrogators by other captured rebels. After traveling from St. Petersburg to Tiflis, for example, Kukunian met Akop Vartapet, the leader of a Western Armenian group who had come to the South Caucasus to solicit help from Eastern Armenians.[47] The Interior Ministry concluded that Vartapet's mission had been to gather material assistance to achieve reforms under the Berlin Treaty through terroristic action within Ottoman lands: "The entire Armenian population of Turkey, said Akop, is ready to rebel, but they have no leaders, no weapons, no material resources, which is why it is necessary to arm Turkish Armenians and to organize independent bands, spreading them throughout the Turkish empire, for a struggle against Muslims. Without a doubt this will attract the attention of European powers and with their help Turkey will be forced to comply with article 61 of the Berlin Treaty."[48]

Although Kukunian disagreed with some of Vartapet's strategies and suspected him of mismanaging donations, Kukunian shared his fellow rebel's conviction that Armenian violence against Ottoman Muslims must be employed to exact tangible reforms through the application of European pressure on Constantinople. Both men traveled from village to village, in the South Caucasus as well as in the Kars region, soliciting donations and making fiery harangues.

The ramifications of these actions for the political status of Eastern Armenians and Yerevan Province remained ambiguous to St. Petersburg. The Interior Ministry stressed that the captured Armenians "categorically deny" any intention "to establish an independent Armenian kingdom, although . . . during their first interrogation, some [of the accused] declared their dream for this organization of an independent Armenia, but one that excluded those provinces that constitute parts of Russia."[49] Other captured Armenians argued that their incursion into Turkey had been carried out as part of "a good Christian goal" and intended to attract the attention of the tsar, who, in turn, would either secure the "freedom" of the Ottoman Armenians himself or would allow his Armenian subjects to rescue their neighboring brethren.[50] Having for centuries steadfastly served as loyal subjects of the Romanovs, some Armenians claimed, they wished to see all of the sultan's Christians relocated under the tsar's aegis.

Suspicious Armenian initiatives, and the Russian scrutiny of them, transcended the political sphere and pervaded the region's cultural life. Tsarist officials pursued with zeal every reported instance of questionable nationalistic expression. In one example from Kars, Russian officials learned of the lyrics of a children's song that invited "Armenians to raise arms for the emancipation of Turkish Armenia" and described an imaginary war of independence that would result in "total Armenian victory."[51] When in 1892 several Armenian schoolchildren in Kars were observed reciting poetry with similar calls to arms, their teacher was arrested and charged with "membership in a secret Armenian organization."[52] In another incident, Russian authorities accused a Kars teacher of encouraging his students to steal gold from their parents and either use it to travel to the Ottoman Empire themselves or donate it to volunteer militia units.[53]

In November 1890, Russian officials discovered pamphlets, written in Armenian, distributed throughout Tiflis and surrounding villages.[54] Declaring that "the Armenian question now enters a new phase; long-enslaved Turkish Armenia demands freedom," the proclamations targeted Eastern Armenians. The pamphlets warned that the time for seeking independence through "cultured means" had ended and that "yesterday's slaves have become revolutionaries," and they announced that an "Armenian Revolutionary League" was prepared to shed blood for the "political and economic liberation of Turkish Armenia." They exhorted each group within the Armenian community to contribute, urging young men to "take up arms," women to "breathe soul into the holy task," the elderly to "assist with advice," the wealthy to "give material help," and the clergy to "bless the freedom fighters."

The scope of the Russian investigation into such activities reveals the Old Regime's wariness regarding the still-unclear political aspirations of its Armenian subjects. Investigations into Kukunian's and Vartapet's groups not only involved regional Russian resources in the Caucasus but also elicited the active participation of the Interior, Justice, and War Ministries in St. Petersburg. To track down suspected members of Armenian organizations, officials pursued them into "every province of the empire" and monitored suspected Armenian nationalists in such major cities as Warsaw.[55] Punishments ranged from warnings to months of solitary confinement or even exile. Most members of Kukunian's band, for example, received a month of solitary confinement followed by a year of police surveillance; the leader himself was sentenced to two months of isolation.[56]

Russian authorities struggled to define the aims and to diminish the actions of tsarist-subject Armenian militants crossing the imperial border into Anatolia. Russian officials in St. Petersburg and the Caucasus took the potential ramifications of these developments seriously, wary of destabilizing relations with the Ottoman government and apprehensive of the domestic effects of Armenian political activism. Thus, even while the most prominent factions of Armenian nationalists aimed their energies at ameliorating the plight of the sultan's Armenians, Russian administrators feared both the internal and external repercussions of this political self-initiative, mobilizing empire-wide resources to combat it. Yet statesmen in the Caucasus, such as Dondukov-Korsakov, at times had to assure their superiors in the imperial capital that the Armenian raiders posed little immediate danger to tsarist interests.

Indeed, the combination of Russian internal concerns about Eastern Armenian agitation, recently improved Russo-Ottoman ties, and Russian anxiety about European exploitation of the "Armenian Question" coalesced into a tacit shift in tsarist attitude and policy. When Kurds and Turks massacred tens of thousands of Western Armenians in the mid-1890s, the tsarist government remained conspicuously passive.[57] Michael Reynolds has summarized the international implications of these Ottoman incidents: "The great powers reminded the 'Bloody Sultan,' as European papers now referred to Abdülhamid II, of the Treaty of Berlin and their prerogative to intervene on behalf of the Armenians. When still worse massacres followed, however, Russia squelched any plans for intervention for fear that a rival might exploit the moment to its own benefit, and the great powers stood aside."[58]

The once-strong ecumenical bond between Apostolic Armenians and Orthodox Russians, so instrumental in the convergence of Armenian and Russian political aims in the first half of the nineteenth century, had frayed significantly by the late nineteenth century. Although St. Petersburg had portrayed itself as the patron of Ottoman Christians since the eighteenth century, the geopolitical realities of the Alexander III era yielded no incentives for the state to condone the actions of Armenian vigilantes. Consequently, imperial policies adapted to the rapidly changing circumstances in the Caucasus by abandoning a century of support for the Armenian cause and pursuing all manifestations of Armenian political and cultural activism.

A half century after it had allied with Armenians to conquer the South Caucasus from Persia and to establish Russian rule in the region, St. Petersburg evolved from a protector of the Armenian diaspora to another heavy-handed imperial overlord. As the erstwhile Russo-Armenian religious bond faded and political friction grew with the gestation of Armenian nationalism, the Romanov state attempted to solidify its borders without openly confronting Armenians. Because neither a rupture with the Sublime Porte nor a major showdown with Armenians served St. Petersburg's interests, the government moved cautiously. Russo-Armenian ties had transitioned from a decades-old symbiosis to a more antagonistic imperial relationship. This tension continued to swell until the early 1900s before it ebbed.

Paradoxically, a track record of Russian protection of Armenians within and beyond tsarist domains enabled the rise of Eastern Armenian vigilantism. With the threats of Persian and Ottoman subjugation long receded, thanks to Russian security and the stabilization of the South Caucasus's political status, Eastern Armenians focused their energies on the plight of their brethren across the imperial divide. A quarter century before the Armenian Genocide, the Russian government implicitly recognized Ottoman sovereignty over Western Armenians and ignored Eastern Armenians' arguments for the protection of their non-tsarist-subject compatriots.

This case demonstrates vividly the interimperial entanglements the Eastern Question produced and the vast implications of subject nationalisms. While internal Ottoman politics and the agitation of the European powers, including Russia, played major roles in these narratives,[59] the tsarist state's confrontation of Armenian nationalism in the late nineteenth century cannot be divorced from the Eastern Question. A broad variety of factors, only one of which was the plight of the Ottoman Christians, gave birth to Armenian nationalism in the Russian Empire, but the internal politics of Ottoman Turkey certainly set off far-reaching reverberations in the domain of its imperial neighbor, Russia. As early as thirty years before the collapse of the Russian and Ottoman Empires, nationalist strains between those multiethnic states' subject groups already raised the specter of a new imperial clash and dictated the course of political developments along the Russian-Ottoman borderlands as much as any other aspect of interstate rivalry. An empire's "vertical" ties to its subject nations are no less important for understanding its political behavior than its "horizontal" relations with other multiethnic states.[60] To be sure, other iterations of Armenian nationalism also challenged the tsarist state.

Unification and Independence

The most radical strain of Armenian nationalism in the South Caucasus advocated the creation of an independent nation-state that would fuse Western and Eastern Armenia. Although these irredentists could boast a less numerous membership than the groups determined to aid Ottoman Armenians, they earned their share of attention from tsarist officials in the wake of the closing of Armenian parish schools in 1885. Even before then, notifications of Eastern Armenians' growing "national awareness" and its attendant threats to tsarist interests rattled St. Petersburg. Coupled with the rise of socialism's popularity among the Armenian youth of the South Caucasus, the state monitored their activities with particular attention. The fundamental question for Russian officials remained: Which government did Armenian nationalists target?

In August 1883, the interior minister reported to the emperor that investigations of Caucasian socialist circles had revealed several nefarious Armenian nationalist tendencies.[61] Among these, the Interior Ministry outlined a revitalized effort on the part of the region's Armenian intellectuals to inculcate in their youth "aspirations toward the political revival of the Armenian people." The head of the Yerevan gymnasium took measures to check the "harmful influence" of Armenian propaganda aimed at promoting "political" thinking among the school's students. Provincial police connected this agitation to an organization of "lovers of the Armenian nationality and patriots" ("*haya-ser*" and "*azga-ser*").[62]

Several prominent local Armenians were implicated in the investigation, such as the assistant to the secretary of the Yerevan Circuit Court, Ter-Zakharov; the head of Yerevan women's schools, Hovannesiants; and the editor of the Tiflis Armenian newspaper *Mshak*, Grigor Artsruni. A search of Ter-Zakharov's home uncovered "appeals to the Armenian youth and nation," inviting them "to spill blood for the freedom of Armenia by taking part in the movement that ought to develop in the near future."[63] These writings urged Armenians of the neighboring empires to set aside any differences and to focus on the "simultaneous uprising" in both Western and Eastern Armenia. In the homes of other suspects, the police discovered evidence of cooperation between Armenian nationalists of the Russian, Ottoman, and Persian Empires, suggesting a new degree of political and diasporic cohesion. Investigators insisted that evidence pointed to a "total solidarity between Turkish and Russian Armenians, equally seeking the reestablishment of their political unity and independence."[64]

Further scrutiny of this case uncovered the genesis of the *haya-ser* and *azga-ser* groups. In the wake of the Berlin Congress, Armenians in Constantinople and other major Ottoman cities had formed organizations to prepare the empire's Armenians for increased autonomy and self-administration. Once it became clear that the provisions of article 61 were not forthcoming, these Armenian groups turned to more subversive measures, such as underground printing and calls for rebellion.[65] Discovered by Ottoman authorities, these revolutionary Armenian circles made their way into the perceived haven of the tsarist South Caucasus. However, if Western Armenians had been receptive to the bellicose appeals of the rebels, Eastern Armenians proved more reluctant, to the chagrin of the recently relocated agitators. From calling for the Ejmiatsin monastery to be moved out from under Russian control to demanding a greater role for the Armenian language, these groups initiated a rejuvenated effort to promote among South Caucasian Armenians what Russian officials labeled "patriotic aspirations." The tracing of the link between Western Armenian rebels and their new activities within Russian territory posed new challenges for tsarist officials. If hitherto they had been more familiar with their Armenian subjects crossing into Ottoman territory, now Russian authorities had to confront the threat of Armenian self-determination movements aimed at altering the status quo in the South Caucasus.

What did these groups aim to do? Russian officials often bemoaned the perceived ambiguity of Armenian goals, peppering their reports with such charges as "antigovernment," "patriotic," and "undesired wandering of minds." However, with the growing quantity of intercepted correspondence, particularly among Armenian students, the contours of specific objectives began to come into focus for state officials. In August 1883, Deputy Interior Minister Petr Orzhevskii reported to the tsar: "The existence in the higher schools of St. Petersburg, Moscow, and Kharkov of Armenian circles with social-democratic programs aimed at the achievement of federal rule in Russia, through which the dreams of Armenian patriots about the political independence of Armenia will come true, has been proved."[66] Evidence suggested, moreover, that similar circles were developing in schools in the Caucasus. Orzhevskii's report is particularly noteworthy because it is a rare example from Russian, state-produced sources of Armenian pursuits of political autonomy (in this case defined as federal rule).

Indeed, local tsarist authorities in the Caucasus often had to reassure St. Petersburg that Armenian nationalists' efforts were directed against the Ottoman, rather than the Russian, government. This reflected the fact that the links between ostensibly distinct Armenian objectives remained unclear to state officials. Although still convinced that "no serious political organization" of Armenians threatened Russian interests, Dondukov-Korsakov, the Caucasus high commissioner, reported to the justice minister in September 1883 that illicit, quasi-political Armenian circles, masquerading as benevolent or philanthropic societies but containing a "lining of a political nature," had popped up in Yerevan.[67] Nearly contradicting his earlier dismissal of these groups' potential dangers to tsarist interests, Dondukov-Korsakov summarized their main goals as "the instigation of Asia Minor Armenians against Turkish overlordship," "providing them assistance . . . as well as moral support in the form of various articles of Armenian-patriotic focus in the local press," and "the compilation of Armenian revolutionary instructions and propaganda about the unification and independence of the Armenian people."[68] The report comforted the Interior Ministry that such groups yet represented "nothing serious, due to the extremely limited number of their sympathizers and also because their objective is aimed at inciting . . . [Ottoman] Armenians against Ottoman rule." Dondukov-Korsakov concluded, "At present, there is no reason to fear the spread of similar attitudes among Russian-subject Armenians," although he ended by proposing several preemptive measures to check the growth of the embryonic and "murky ideas about the reestablishment of the political independence of the Armenian people."[69]

Tsarist ministries faced not only nationalism that the sultan's Armenian subjects imported from across the border but also its locally developed strains. By 1883, the interior minister had reason to alert the royal court to the threat of "antigovernment aims of the Armenian intelligentsia."[70] Armenian students in the South Caucasus used various means to propagate subversive material, often employing the Tiflis Armenian daily *Mshak* and the Yerevan newspaper *Psak*. The use of *Mshak* for Armenian nationalism particularly worried Russian officials given the newspaper's reach: by 1886, it boasted fourteen hundred subscribers, more than any of the other four Armenian newspapers in Tiflis.[71] In the imperial capital, too, young Armenians were accused of printing "antigovernment" material. Students from universities in the Caucasus, St. Petersburg, and Moscow were implicated in the investigations. Intercepted correspondence between one Moscow University student and his counterpart in Yerevan revealed the existence of a shadowy student group, Unity of Patriots. In June 1887, Moscow police investigated Armenian students from the Imperial Technical Institute for collecting donations for an indeterminate cause.[72] In July 1888, the Department of Police ordered the Moscow police to monitor the activities of local Armenian students known to hold secret meetings with their counterparts from St. Petersburg.[73] A student group at the St. Petersburg Forestry Institute engaged in "national questions, for which it subscribes to Armenian journals and acquires photographs of Armenian poets, 'singers of the homeland,'" although no evidence suggested that members took part in any "revolutionary activity."[74]

Less benign student circles appeared to exist in other cities. Two separate groups in Moscow, including one at prestigious Moscow University, were accused in the fall of 1888 of following a "revolutionary program." Unlike the St. Petersburg clubs, which discussed Armenian poets and collected money for individual struggling friends, the Moscow groups hosted gatherings that lauded exiled political prisoners and read banned publications.[75] Surveillance of one of these bands revealed that it sought donations, mainly from Armenian merchants of Moscow, up to ten times per year and could gather as much as 3,900 rubles per campaign. Although students constituted the core of similar circles discovered by Russian officials, there were also instances of faculty involvement. In March 1895, police intercepted letters from an Armenian in Odessa to Iurii Veselovskii, a professor at Moscow University.[76] This discovery led to the uncovering of a large organization, called Progress, with affiliated circles located in several imperial cities, including Odessa, Kharkov, and Tiflis. Members of Progress sought to "help Armenian schools through the shipment of [books for] libraries, teaching guides, etc." and strove to "encompass, as far as possible, all of Armenian society."[77]

From the perspective of the tsarist state, Eastern Armenian nationalists in the late nineteenth century sought not so much the establishment of an autonomous Armenia within the Russian Empire as the liberation, however defined, of Western Armenians from Ottoman mistreatment. How can this be explained? On the surface, the contrast between the two communities' existence explains their divergent satisfactions with the status quo: the sultan's Armenians received no security from the imperial order and regularly fell victim to their more powerful neighbors, while the tsar's Armenians not only enjoyed economic and social prominence in the South Caucasus but also earned political clout within the tsarist bureaucracy. On a less quantifiable level, however, Eastern Armenians focused on the plight of Western Armenians out of fraternal investment in the betterment of their compatriots. Aiding the sultan's Armenians without the permission of the tsarist state jeopardized tsarist Armenians' position within the imperial hierarchy, especially vis-à-vis their Georgian and Muslim neighbors in the South Caucasus. Yet a multifaceted and diverse Armenian effort risked their privileged position to achieve "national salvation." With the rise of professional revolutionary groups, these efforts took on a more cohesive form.

Professional Revolutionaries

Armenian professional revolutionary parties, like their predecessors, mainly aimed their energies at Turkey and avoided confrontation with Russia. In fact, until the late 1880s, and in many cases beyond, liberal and nationalist Eastern Armenians sought reform, not revolution.[78] Although sympathetic and supportive of Western Armenians' revolutionary actions, Eastern Armenians had no reason to seek secession from Russia. Their economic success and social preeminence had earned them resentment from non-Russian neighbors and some tsarist administrators, but these factors had also secured them an enviable socioeconomic niche in the South Caucasus. In an 1890 report to the emperor, Dondukov-Korsakov opined: "Distinguished by undeniable aptitude, a penchant for education, and the persistent pursuit of wealth through all means,

Armenians over the past thirty years have acquired a dominant economic position in the region. Having understood that whoever holds the capital and land
acquires significance and strength even in the eyes of the government, Armenians have captured in the South Caucasus almost all trade, manufacturing,
the majority of property in cities, and part of land properties [in the country-
side]."[79]

To challenge this status quo and strive for an independent nation-state
would not be proposed in earnest until the socialist Hnchak party formed in
1887. But the social revolutionary zeitgeist of Russia's multiethnic society in
the later part of the nineteenth century made the divorce of Armenian "liberation" movements from other disenchanted groups nearly impossible. Young
Eastern Armenians joined Georgian- and Russian-led socialist circles from Yerevan to St. Petersburg. In 1883, when an imperial army deserter surrendered
to Tiflis authorities in return for leniency, he exposed a large multinational socialist group operating in the South Caucasus.[80] An investigation found that
young Armenians had taken a prominent role in the group's activities, joining their Georgian socialist comrades in establishing underground networks.

Although their actions often fell beyond the purview of the tsar's agents,
the rise of Armenian professional revolutionary movements contributed to the
recalibration of Russo-Armenian ties in the last two decades of the nineteenth
century. The autocrat's reactionary nationalities policies and the international
community's continued inaction over Ottoman abuses galvanized previously
docile Armenians and birthed radical parties. These organizations boasted
well-ordered internal hierarchies and more proactive strategies, although their
objectives often were no less opaque than those of the South Caucasian student clubs.

The first such group, the Armenakan Party, arose in Van in 1885. While this
Western Armenian group "did not favor open agitation or demonstrations and
did not include Armenian independence even as a long-range objective," it
served as an important precursor to the two parties that Eastern Armenians
soon established.[81] The first of these more prolific parties appeared in 1887.
Formed in Geneva by Eastern Armenian émigrés, mainly Maro Vardanian and
her fiancé, Avetis Nazarbekian, the Hnchakian Revolutionary Party looked to
both Russian populism and Marxism for achieving Armenian liberation. With
a nod to Alexander Herzen's periodical *Kolokol* (Bell), the Armenian party took
its name from the Armenian newspaper *Hnchak* (Bell).[82] The Hnchaks, as they
came to be known, combined two of many Eastern Armenians' aims: the immediate freeing of Western Armenians and the eventual establishment of an
independent Armenian socialist state. Unlike the staunchly antisocialist Armenakan Party, the Hnchaks envisioned the cohabitation of the sultan's, the

tsar's, and the shah's Armenians under the umbrella of international social-ism.[83] Given this inclusive outlook, the Hnchaks worked with Eastern and Western Armenians equally, seeking the cooperation of all Armenians in at-taining an independent homeland. The Hnchaks gained support among vari-ous layers of regional Armenian communities, but a new party would challenge their domination.

Established in 1890 in Tiflis by Eastern Armenians, the Armenian Revolu-tionary Federation, or Dashnaktsutiun, contested the Hnchaks' goals. The Dashnaks relegated the question of an independent nation-state to a second-ary position behind the urgency of alleviating the plight of Ottoman Arme-nians. Focused on this task, the Dashnak manifesto of 1892, called the *Program*, "did not even mention the word independence. It affirmed the need for re-forms in Asiatic Turkey, but said nothing of complete separation from the Ottoman Empire."[84] In contrast to the autonomy and independence pursued by the Hnchaks, the Dashnaks sought the type of political, social, and economic reforms in Western Armenia that a dozen years earlier the Congress of Berlin had promised. Matters pertaining to Russian and Persian Armenians fell out-side the purview of the Dashnaks until the early twentieth century.

An important element, however, bound the two Armenian parties: terror-ism was their preferred tactic to achieve their contrasting objectives.[85] The Dashnaks, in particular, attacked Ottoman officials, soldiers, and even civilians, took hostages, and collaborated with other anti-Ottoman groups, such as the Bulgarian-controlled Internal Macedonian Revolutionary Organization. Un-like their less-organized and less-capable sympathizers in the South Caucasus, the Dashnaks launched attacks from Anatolian hideouts and from within Per-sian territory;[86] as a rule, they did not operate from the tsar's domain, which explains their relative absence from tsarist police records until the turn of the twentieth century.[87] Nevertheless, both the Hnchak and Dashnaktsutiun par-ties were founded by the tsar's Armenian subjects who "had never lived in Turkish Armenia for any length of time,"[88] illustrating not only this commu-nity's perennial concern for the plight of the sultan's Armenians but also the diverse political development of Eastern Armenians.

The Closing of the Parish Schools

With each discovery of an Armenian student circle with questionable aims and potentially subversive intentions, the tsarist state homed in on the perceived origin of this threat. Coupled with Alexander III's Great Russian imperial chau-vinism, the closing of the Armenian parish schools followed a broader pattern of reaction that prioritized the cultural Russification of Slavic and non-Slavic, Christian and non-Christian minorities.[89] The entrenchment of the Russian language was a favorite element of this heavy-handed policy. In internal Ufa Province, for example, the Education Ministry targeted the local Muslim youth by supplementing their existing private schools with hundreds of new secular institutions. Between 1870 and 1900, the number of state-run schools in Ufa grew about four and a half times, from 293 to 1,320.[90]

Convinced that "nationalism and a revolutionary spirit, 'patriotism and populism,' were rampant among Armenian students and had to be eradicated,"[91] officials targeted Armenian parish schools as one of the foci of Armenian cultural and political initiative. St. Petersburg viewed these schools as the epicenter of several coalescing forces: the promotion of notions of Armenian political, cultural, and religious antiquity; historical and geographical unity; and the inculcation of an inchoate but radical dissident Armenian youth. Priests and even secular teachers, imperial authorities charged, reinforced ideas of Armenian singularity—driven by Armenia's status as the first Christian nation—to promote greater cohesion and subversive "patriotism" among the students.

Aside from theological accents, Armenian schools also focused on the well-trodden myths of the nation's metahistory, highlighting the exploits and triumphs of distant kings and military commanders, and reminding students of Armenia's past territorial glory, when the nation "stretched from sea to sea." The former governor of Yerevan Province, A. A. Freze, warned: "[Armenian] parish schools inculcate in the youth a spirit of intolerance, inflated understandings of the Armenian nation and its future, a spirit of resistance to all that which is not directed at the unification and strengthening of Armenians; these schools are the disseminators of counteraction against the government's integration efforts."[92]

Armenian youths enjoyed a variety of educational options until the mid-1880s. Divided between the jurisdictions of the Education Ministry and the Armenian Church, as well as a few privately sponsored institutions, a growing number of schools provided scholastic opportunities for students from both wealthy and poor families. Growing literacy was a key component in Russia's modernization of the South Caucasus, and imperial agents assigned particular importance to education's role in maintaining a loyal populace. In February 1880, the Caucasus viceroy reiterated to Alexander II the political aims of local pedagogy: "[Teaching] must be directed in such a way that education serves not only the advancement of the spiritual development of the national masses, but [serves] also as an instrument of political unification of this region with the [Russian] government."[93] It is hardly surprising, then, that the autocracy's strategy to curb Armenian nationalism targeted Armenian parish schools.

On 16 February 1884, Tsar Alexander III issued several demands. Effectively transferring the control of the Armenian parish schools of the Caucasus to the Education Ministry, his fiat stipulated that Armenian schools must offer Russian-language instruction, relinquish control over the curriculum, report data to the ministry, and seek official approval of all decisions regarding the hiring and termination of teachers.[94] Russian authorities, moreover, gained the right to remove "unreliable" teachers. Among other suspect pedagogical tools, the new law prohibited the use of maps of ancient Armenia or hagiographies of ancient kings.[95] Maps, in particular, had commonly been seized from suspected radicals in the mid-1880s, suggesting that at least some Armenian nationalists linked their national identity to the territorial vastness and antiquity of the Armenian land.[96] When used in conjunction with foreign-published textbooks, these suspect pedagogical tools were found to be "clearly and quite strongly aimed at the education of the pupils in a sense of national separatism and hostile attitudes toward the existing order of administration," as High Commissioner Dondukov-Korsakov reported to Interior Minister Tolstoi.[97]

The emperor's decree applied to parish schools, defined as "one- and two-course institutions of general elementary learning, which are attached to churches and monasteries, and maintained either exclusively with church funds or with the assistance of the laity."[98] When the Ejmiatsin Synod failed to comply promptly with these demands, citing the recent death of the catholicos and the temporary absence of leadership until the election of his replacement, Caucasian officials in 1885 shut down five hundred schools, where nine hundred teachers had taught twenty thousand pupils.[99] Tsarist agents justified their actions by arguing that Armenian ecclesiastical authorities had resisted state educational policies since the previous decade.

In November 1873, a law covering the entire Russian Empire had required every school to teach the Russian language and, if it offered history and geography, to teach Russian history and geography (in Russian). In 1885, Russian authorities contended that Armenian clerics' protests against the 1873 policies had resulted in the introduction in July 1874 of new regulations requiring the Armenian Church to submit periodic reports about its educational activities, such as the opening and closing of schools, and the hiring and backgrounds of all teachers.[100] Russian officials charged that, despite an eventual compromise whereby the catholicos retained most of the authority over the schools, Armenian ecclesiastical leaders refused to cooperate and did not provide the required information. Thus, with the real and perceived proliferation of Armenian nationalism, compounded by a history of Armenian resistance to Russian interference in education, the imperial administration took its most radical step yet and closed the schools.

The government allowed the parish schools to reopen in 1886, despite the "total resistance" of the Armenian Church to state meddling in its education practices.[101] Yet tightened surveillance over teachers, curriculum, and even students ended Armenian hopes for a return to the relative liberty of the pre–Alexander III order. Before the authorities again closed the parish schools in 1896, new policies in the late 1880s and early 1890s brought the full weight of the government's authority to bear. In March 1889, a new law required all teachers of the Russian language, history, and geography in Armenian parish schools to hold a special license, *uchitel'skii tsenz*.[102] Any teacher found working without such certification after five years would be removed from his or her position. In March 1891, Tsar Alexander III issued a special warning to the Armenian Church to obey this law and others or face new restrictions. To drive home his message, the autocrat granted authority to the local Caucasus education curator and the head of the Caucasus civilian administration to close any schools that deviated from prescribed regulations, without the preliminary consent of ministers in St. Petersburg.

Cooperation and adaptation were not uncommon Armenian reactions to the closing of the parish schools, but the community responded mainly with both overt and furtive resistance. Patent opposition came from the new catholicos, Makarii, who in 1885 argued that the education of Eastern Armenians corresponded to broader geopolitical interests of the Romanov Empire.[103] Erudite Eastern Armenians promoted the tsar's goals not only within Russia, contended the prelate, but also in the Ottoman Empire, India, and beyond. At the same time, covert resistance took diverse forms. Within months of the first closings in 1885, privately funded underground schools popped up throughout the region.[104] As Russian authorities took to the pages of regional newspapers to announce and explain their actions, advertisements appeared alongside the official notices offering private lessons in Armenian history, literature, and geography.[105]

More irksome for Caucasus authorities were the pamphlets discovered in Tiflis in April 1885, denouncing the closing of the Armenian schools as "shameful abuse."[106] "The Russian autocracy with its customary despotism closes our schools," lamented the pamphlets, warning that the parish schools had formed an unalienable component of the Armenian Church since its inception.[107] Likening the parish schools to the sacred altar of the church, the pamphlets reminded readers: "From our past we have two sacred things left: the national church and the national schools." The anonymous writers accused the tsarist regime of declaring war on the Armenian nation: "Alexander III the Despot destroys to its foundation the Armenian school; the tsar of a giant state declares war on a tiny nation. But why are we surprised[?]" The authors charged the government with wooing small nations into Russian subjecthood, only to retract gradually these concessions and take away their rights: "What the Russian despots did to the Georgians, they are now doing to us, Armenians."

By comparing the plight of Armenians to that of other tsarist subjects, the pamphlets connected the current crisis not only to the suppression of the Georgian church and language but also to the attempted Russification of Ukrainians and Poles. "With bayonets and spurs, you, Russian despots, were unable to force the Poles to forget their language, [and] your campaigns against the Little Russian [Ukrainian] tongue likewise had completely counterproductive results," charged the Armenian letters.[108] The authors urged greater self-reliance: "Let every Armenian family represent a special Armenian school. . . . From now on, we ourselves will be our own only hope, from now on we will not trust other, especially Russian, governments, and when we, as true Armenians, carry out our holy duty, then, believe, Armenians, victory will be on the side of the righteous. Victory will be ours."[109]

Menacing Faith

The conflict over the parish schools was but the most prominent manifestation of tensions between St. Petersburg and Ejmiatsin in the last two decades of the nineteenth century. In sharp contrast to the preceding decades, the late imperial era marked the deterioration of the Russo-Armenian political symbiosis. From the imperial to the regional capital, fissures appeared. In December 1883, for example, Yerevan authorities alerted St. Petersburg to a change in local Armenian churches' practice of worship: priests no longer removed their miter or kneeled as a sign of deference to the royal Romanov family, as they had done since 1833.[110] This change, the police emphasized, could have come about only with the sanction of the Ejmiatsin leadership, apparently demonstrating the existence of "solidarity between the leaders of the Armenian agitation and senior Armenian clergy."[111] The Yerevan gendarmerie's annual report to the Department of Police in January 1884 echoed these accusations, charging senior Armenian clergy with engaging in "antigovernment" machinations. Yerevan bishop Sureniants was accused of being a "notable member of Armenian patriots [azga-ser]," but the main center of separatist aims was the Ejmiatsin monastery, where Bishops Manguni and Nerses were "distinguished [and] active members."[112] Armenian priests' publications also attracted the state's scrutiny in the mid-1880s, with numerous bans and investigations launched both by local Caucasus officials and by their superiors in St. Petersburg.[113]

Yet the geopolitical need to maintain influence over Ottoman Armenians often outweighed these domestic concerns. In the early 1880s, the autocracy focused on accruing the goodwill of the sultan's Armenians by affirming the ecclesiastical bond between the Russian and Armenian peoples. In the spring of 1883, for instance, the Russian consul in Erzurum, A. Denet, urged St. Petersburg to assist the venerable Armenian monastery Surp Karapet.[114] The tsarist diplomat asked his superiors to donate an ornate chandelier as a sign of Russia's goodwill. In stressing Surp Karapet's importance to Western Armenians, Denet compared it to the Russian reverence for similar monasteries, which "for the people are not just holy sites that serve as a source of divine benevolence, but also the embodiment of the idea of its national identity." Such a prominent position in Western Armenians' national lore made this sacred abbey a unique tool for advancing Russian political interests, Denet insisted, emphasizing that "any attention we pay to such a valuable place for the Armenian people cannot but arouse in them a burning [sense of] sympathy and gratefulness."[115] The Foreign Ministry agreed that such a sign of friendship would "in the greatest sense contribute to the revival of sympathy toward us among the majority of the Armenian people," and it determined that "a sign of the [tsar's] attention to a holy Armenian place will produce among them quite positive impressions."[116]

When foreign missionaries made inroads among Western Armenians, Alexander III's bureaucracy shelved its grievances against Ejmiatsin to join forces. In September 1887, the Constantinople patriarch alerted the catholicos to the plight of Armenians in parts of Zeitun Province in Anatolia, where famine and large-scale fires had swept through and exacerbated already dire conditions.[117] The Constantinople patriarch stressed that Catholic and Protestant missionaries had increased their activity—with notable success—taking advantage of local Armenians' economic hardships. The catholicos turned to High Commissioner Dondukov-Korsakov, who shared the two Armenian prelates' concerns and underscored to the Interior Ministry that he wished to "maintain warm relations with the senior ecclesiastical leadership of the [Armenian] Church."[118] Interior Minister Tolstoi confirmed to Alexander III that this action "completely corresponds with our interests in the East."[119] With the exception of such sporadic signs of aligned aims, overall Alexander III's reign curtailed Armenian religious autonomy.

In the spring of 1883, the autocracy reformulated its policy toward the election of the catholicos, explicitly prioritizing Russian state interests above all other considerations.[120] To ensure the "direct oversight and influence of the government" over future catholicoi, the new regulations called for reducing the number of votes from Ottoman Armenian representatives and so diminishing the leverage of "the Constantinople Armenian National Council."[121] In April 1885, the Russian-born and Russian-raised Makarii, archbishop of Nakhichevan-Bessarabia, was elected to lead Ejmiatsin by a margin of one vote.[122] Despite investigative reports that, if elected catholicos, Makarii had promised not to "hesitate to sacrifice [his] life to save his nation from the Russian yoke, for the time has come to reestablish the Armenian kingdom,"[123] the new prelate initially pleased his Russian benefactors with harangues against the impact of nationalism on the Armenian communities of the South Caucasus and admonitions against independence.

Yet tensions soon arose between Makarii and Dondukov-Korsakov over the closing of the parish schools. The high commissioner later complained to the tsar: "Despite Makarii's undoubted personal reliability and his friendliest and heartfelt relations toward me, I nevertheless was unable to turn him onto a strictly legal course."[124] The closing of the parish schools aroused recurring petitions, complaints, and resistance from Ejmiatsin, "disappointing" local Russian officials. Makarii's "remarkable intransigence" in the parish schools matter eroded what remained of the authorities' constructive modus operandi toward the Armenian Church and, by extension, much of the laity. In fact, the combination of Makarii's resistance and the continued subversive actions of lay Armenians opened a new chapter for Russo-Armenian ties. The imperial subjecthood and personal characteristics of the catholicos became secondary considerations for Russian policy, overshadowed by the activities of the secular nationalists and fear of foreign interference. An irritated Dondukov-Korsakov concluded in one report: "Apparently, the cause of such strange behavior must be discovered not in the subjecthood of the elected person to our or another government, nor in the patriarch's personal traits, but rather exclusively in that difficult situation . . . in which the patriarch finds himself surrounded by the intrigues of the Armenian intelligentsia that is hostile toward us, as well as in the persistent pressure of foreign powers."[125] This acknowledgment hardly implied a change of policy, and the state maintained its hope of using Ejmiatsin to recalibrate the political orientation of the Armenian diaspora.

The Armenian patriarch of Constantinople occupied an equally important role in Russian considerations. When Ariutin Vekhabedian, archbishop of Erzurum, was elected patriarch in early 1885, a Russian diplomat from the Constantinople Embassy reported to Foreign Minister Nikolai Giers (1882–95) that Vekhabedian's selection "can be considered fortunate for us," given that from his days in Erzurum the Armenian priest had corresponded actively with the Russian government, declaring himself to be a "zealous guardian of Armenian interests in the East, who at the same time values good relations with

Russian agents."[126] The autocracy sought to capitalize on the rivalry between the prelates of Constantinople and Ejmiatsin. As Dondukov-Korsakov advised the tsar in 1890, "In time it will be beneficial for us to take advantage of the aspirations of the Constantinople and Sis patriarchs to secede from Ejmiatsin, in order to turn the catholicos into a blind instrument of our goals [*slepoe orudie nashikh tselei*]."[127]

In a prelude to the crisis of 1903, the 1890s witnessed a new, more acrimonious dynamic between St. Petersburg and Ejmiatsin. No government edict contributed more to this circumstance than the 16 March 1891 regulations for the punishment of Armenian clergy.[128] Aiming to target low-ranking Armenian priests who "avoid carrying out the demands of the government," or who are "harmful to the state and civil order," Alexander III authorized Caucasus officials and the Interior Ministry to exile and imprison Armenian clergymen without the consent of the Ejmiatsin Synod or the catholicos. Russian imperial agents could use Armenian monasteries and "other places," within and outside the Caucasus, as penitentiaries for this purpose. Exiled priests were placed under local police supervision, prohibited from carrying out public worship or private religious services, and banned from meeting with outsiders without the consent of the police. In explaining the new law to one governor, Interior Minister Ivan Durnovo (1889–95) wrote that it was made necessary "as a result of the Armenian clergy's observed evasion of fulfilling the laws and orders of the government" and that it "has been deemed desirable especially at this time, when among our Armenians a straying [*brozhenie*] is noticed, which is aroused by the political movements of their compatriots in Turkey."[129] Regional Russian officials enforced the new law with alacrity. One of its earliest casualties was Yerevan Province priest Ter Vartan Vartanov, whom police accused of collecting among local villagers large sums of money (4,500 rubles from one village) to support young men crossing the border to join "units of Armenian volunteers rebelling against Turkish authority."[130]

Imperial officials imprisoned or banished other Armenian clergymen in the 1890s throughout the Caucasus, in Kars Province, and in internal Russian provinces. One Armenian priest from Kars, Ter Petrosiants, was arrested for receiving from known Armenian revolutionaries books banned by the censors, an offense for which he was exiled to Lenkoran for a year.[131] In Yerevan, the priest Krikor Ter Nersesiants was charged in April 1891 with recruiting young Armenians to fight in Turkey, supplying them with horses and clothing and also paying each man 20–25 rubles.[132] In another province, an Armenian priest named Ter Vaskanov was "removed" after declaring during liturgy, "His Majesty the Emperor is not our tsar, but the Russian tsar."[133] Such cases continued throughout the 1890s.[134]

Related developments in the Armenian diaspora again compelled the autocracy to reshape its policies. In contrast to the ostensibly subversive activities of low-ranking priests, a new challenge for the state emerged from Ejmiatsin's attempts to work within the imperial system. In February 1894, Catholicos Mkrtich informed Interior Minister Durnovo about the recurring pleas for aid reaching Ejmiatsin from Western Armenians.[135] Driven from their homes by famine and receiving no assistance from Ottoman authorities, Armenians of Van and Erzurum Vilayets begged the Armenian religious leader for assistance. Arguing that "when people starve to death, even political considerations give way to Christian benevolence," Mkrtich sought Russian approval, citing the policies of Alexander II, who permitted Eastern Armenians in 1880 to collect donations for their Ottoman compatriots. In response, new high commissioner Sergei Sheremetev (1890–96) made clear that Armenian political and social initiative would not be tolerated. A stern administrator who even forbade Armenians to collect alms for the poor without his approval,[136] Sheremetev believed that the donation campaigns "can hardly be considered appropriate in the political sense, given that the Armenian clergy, as well as the secular intelligentsia and especially the teachers of Armenian parish schools, most likely, will not fail to take advantage of this campaign as a convenient opportunity for tendentious agitation among the Armenian population of national-patriotic feelings."[137] Determined to prevent Ejmiatsin from overshadowing the government's authority, he feared placing the initiative behind the aid with the "current leader of their clergy, who is quite popular among Armenians."

But Sheremetev understood that, because Russian officials had previously allowed such collections for Western Armenians, their total prohibition could galvanize the population and incite renewed tension with senior Armenian clergy. Instead, Sheremetev proposed acquiescing to the request with the stipulation that donations be collected only in Armenian churches and, crucially, that the Foreign Ministry, rather than Ejmiatsin, be charged with distributing the alms to Western Armenians. The government would appear altruistic in its assistance to the starving Armenians while stripping the Eastern Armenian clergy of credit for the initiative by taking charge of the donations' distribution. The emperor and his ministers approved the high commissioner's proposal.[138]

Acrimony between the Armenian Church and Russian officials reached unprecedented levels in the last two decades of the nineteenth century. What had previously been a symbiotic partnership firmly grounded in ecumenical solidarity and parallel aims had morphed into a political conflict. Tsarist authorities linked the rise of nationalism both to the Armenian Church's senior leadership and to its low-ranking clergy. A former governor of Yerevan

Province, A. A. Freze, was unequivocal in 1892: "There is no doubt that the Armenian clergy took, and continues to take, the most lively and active part in the Armenian national-political movement."[139] Yet, to those who assumed that the darkest hour of Russo-Armenian ties had arrived, the next decade would be a thunderbolt.

Evolved Perceptions and Responses

The real and dramatized rise of Armenian political self-initiative and nationalism altered a centuries-old Russian understanding of who Armenians were, what their close association with Russia provided to the empire, and what this relationship meant for tsarist policy in the South Caucasus and beyond. Whether from Caucasus officials, the autocrat, or the periodical press, Russian reactions to the deterioration of Russo-Armenian relations shed light on the evolution of imperial Russia's perception of its Armenian subjects.

At the start of Alexander III's reign in 1881, nearly 730,000 Armenians populated the Caucasus, all but 26,000 of whom lived in the South Caucasus.[140] By 1890, through natural growth and immigration the number in the South Caucasus alone had risen to 890,000, surpassing one million by the end of the century.[141] Among the South Caucasus administrative region's (*Zakavkazskii krai*) population of nearly 4.7 million people,[142] Armenians had made conspicuous advancements in various social, economic, and even political spheres. Indeed, by the 1890s, Dondukov-Korsakov warned the tsar that Armenian economic progress threatened to marginalize Georgians and other national groups. "[Armenians'] pursuit [of land] is so strong, that into their hands will fall all estates of the impoverished Georgian nobility if the government does not come to the [Georgians'] rescue," cautioned the high commissioner.[143] Dondukov-Korsakov also pointed out: "There is no doubt that Armenians have done much for the revitalization of the province's economic life and industrial expansion, and in this regard we ought to use them, but we should not overlook their simultaneous pursuit of other aims, [nor should we] forget that for their personal gain Armenians do not stop at far from irreproachable measures."

This manifestation of the hackneyed "Jews of the Caucasus" aphorism for Armenians had been a staple of the Caucasian social milieu for generations,[144] but its increased use by the tsarist political elite signaled a shift not only in the Russian social perception of Armenians but also in the latter's political standing vis-à-vis the tsarist nationalities policy. Fellow senior officials mimicked Dondukov-Korsakov's sentiments. The head of the Holy Synod warned the Interior Ministry: "The Armenian nation possesses, like the Jews, a special ability to control the market, to take into its hands industry and trade, removing all others, and to act through deft intrigue in an environment that has insufficient strength to combat or resist it."[145] The Yerevan gendarmerie echoed this fear, reporting to St. Petersburg that Armenians, "possessing the natural tendencies of their Semitic race, are engaged exclusively in acquiring profit."[146]

The imperial leadership's growing use of this conception of Armenians, analogous to the one employed to marginalize Jews, evinced officials' new perception of the Armenian diaspora. Whereas in the early decades of the century Russian imperial administrators, seeking to expand the empire through direct Armenian cooperation, had lauded Armenians' economic success and celebrated it as a mark of Christian resilience in hostile environments, now the official understanding of Armenians had changed dramatically. While Armenian peasants were not suspected of disloyalty to the tsarist state, the intelligentsia and merchantry were deemed to "present no satisfactory guarantees of political reliability."[147] Armenians' political prominence in regional affairs compounded their potential threat. Authorities were vexed, for example, by the fact that of the Tiflis Duma's seventy vote-wielding members, fifty-four were Armenian, rendering the South Caucasus's premier city essentially "an Armenian center."[148]

Starting in the early 1880s and escalating until 1905, the government adopted a more confrontational stance toward Armenian political "deviation." Dondukov-Korsakov authored new policies in response to Deputy Interior Minister Orzhevskii's warning about the "undesired straying of the Caucasus's Armenian population, which . . . can later become harmful for the state order, having inculcated in the maturing generation a sense of separation from the general interests of the state."[149] To combat the rise of subversive Armenian movements, the high commissioner called for several interrelated policy changes. First, in a foreshadowing of the parish schools demands that the tsar would issue in a few months, Dondukov-Korsakov urged placing Armenian schools under the jurisdiction of the Education Ministry.[150] Second, he suggested instituting "strict supervision" over private Armenian societies, including benevolent and philanthropic organizations. Not only were local authorities to receive monthly financial reports from such groups, but they also would be able to shut them down. No new Armenian organizations in the Caucasus were to be permitted. Third, Dondukov-Korsakov demanded that Armenian civil servants henceforth not be assigned to regions with large Armenian communities and that Armenian bureaucrats in sensitive locales be gradually transferred away.[151] Fourth, tighter press censorship was necessary to ensure the political reliability not only of internally printed Armenian publications but also of those imported from abroad.

Tsar Alexander III ordered thirteen senior statesmen to examine Dondukov-Korsakov's proposal. The substance and even tone of their responses illustrate both the diversity of the Russian political elite's opinions on this subject and the degree to which Armenians had become indispensable to the bureaucracy of the empire. The minister of state properties hesitated to endorse the proposal and questioned its reasoning, asking for further evidence and clarification.[152] The Holy Synod's chief procurator cautioned that "Armenians are distinguished by their ability and cleverness, which is why it is not surprising that those looking for competent bureaucrats end their search with Armenians."[153] Rather than expelling all Armenian civil servants, he recommended reassigning them to secondary positions within the regional administration, ensuring their continued function but curbing their influence. The finance minister advised against a rushed removal of current Armenian officials in the Caucasus.[154] The state comptroller's office unequivocally declared that its eleven Armenian-heritage employees in the South Caucasus posed no political risk and would not be removed.[155]

Despite such dissent, the formidable Interior Ministry supported the proposed restrictions. It issued a spirited defense of the measures: "That in the Caucasus the number of believers in the idea of Armenians' national independence constantly increases, and that this movement interacts with the . . . movement of Asia Minor Armenians—none of this is subject to doubt."[156] The ministry maintained that, given the "constantly fortifying" and "prominent" position Armenians had attained in the Caucasus, the government could not afford to overlook their political activism. The growing economic advancement—"which was the main stimulus of the notion of Armenians' independent existence"—gave them unparalleled influence over regional society, and the ministry insisted it was the government's duty to prevent this influence from pervading the administrative spheres through Armenian-heritage civil servants.[157]

Yet the very backlash against Armenians signaled their important social, economic, and political position in late imperial Russia. Despite the souring of the top-level dynamic, Eastern Armenians experienced no large-scale violence, unlike their compatriots in the Ottoman Empire or such tsarist subjects as Jews. In fact, the collective Russian perception—more among the public than among state officials—continued to see Armenians as *rossiiskie*; that is, Russia's own subjects. The rise of Armenian nationalism and professional revolutionaries had blighted the constructive atmosphere of the earlier decades, but Russian society by and large continued to coexist with their Armenian neighbors and to sympathize with the plight of Western Armenians.

Indeed, only for a short but painful period at the turn of the twentieth century did an "Armenian Question" trouble late imperial Russian society.

While a "Muslim Question" and perhaps a more diluted "Jewish Question" confronted the Old Regime in the late 1800s, imperial agents never identified their Armenian subjects as a "state within a state," as the government accused Muslims of mobilizing against its authority.[158] Eastern Armenian nationalists peppered their writings with references to an "Armenian Question" but used the term to refer to the plight of Western Armenians in the Ottoman Empire. Although the administration endeavored to keep Armenian ecclesiastical and social culture within the imperial hierarchy, it refrained from implementing the types of confessional restrictions on Armenians, such as limited admission into the legal profession, as it placed on Muslims and Jews.

On the contrary, from increased scholarship on Armenian antiquity to private Russian campaigns for the support of the sultan's Armenians, Russian society embraced Armenians as *rossiiskie*. After large-scale massacres of Ottoman Armenians in the mid-1890s, a Moscow-published book, titled *Brotherly Help for the Armenian Victims in Turkey*, rallied tsarist society to come to the survivors' aid.[159] It not only condemned the "inhumane slaughter by Turks in 1894 of 10,000 peaceful Armenians in Sasun" but also celebrated Armenians' antiquity and cultural contributions. In a subsequent edition, about 120 Russian, Armenian, German, French, and English contributors presented a wide range of support for the Armenian cause. The famed Russian archeologist Nikolai Marr summarized his excavations at Ani, the ancient Armenian capital, emphasizing its rich cultural heritage.[160] An obituary of British prime minister William Gladstone repeated the late statesman's proclamation that "to serve Armenia is to serve civilization," while Lord Byron's apocryphal assertion that "Armenian is the language to speak with God" underscored the contributors' accent on Armenia's Christian identity.

Other Russian publications echoed such sentiments, highlighting the mutual benefits of the Russo-Armenian encounter. Contemporaneous historian Viktor Abaza declared, "In the moral sense, Armenians in the East rendered one of the greatest services to the Christian world, having remained the steadfast bearers of Christian light, under the most unequal multicentury struggle with pagans and Muslims."[161] Another Russian author lionized Armenians as Russia's "true sons, [who] dedicated themselves to her benefits and interests."[162] Jo Laycock has demonstrated that even distant and ostensibly disinterested British intellectuals echoed related themes, perceiving Armenia as "a cradle of civilization" and Ottoman Armenians as downtrodden European Christians in need of European rescue.[163]

Yet, in the contemporary political climate, more acerbic commentary drowned out such romanticized attestations. If Russo-Armenian religious kinship had ipso facto cemented the tiny nation's ties with the Russian Empire in the first half of the nineteenth century, Armenians no longer presented the same guarantees of political reliability and socioeconomic progress that had once made them essential colonizers. When disaffected Ottoman Armenians sought shelter in Russia in the late 1880s, the state's responses made clear that such sentiments no longer shaped imperial policy.

In April 1888, Foreign Minister Giers brought to the tsar's attention Erzurum Armenians' "indignation, entirely justified by the Porte's complete disregard of the responsibilities regarding Armenians that it had assumed as a result of the Berlin Treaty's article 61."[164] Giers enumerated the myriad ways in which Ottoman authorities and locals neglected and abused Armenians in Erzurum Vilayet, citing the reports of the Russian consulate. When Ottoman officials adjudicated cases in favor of Kurdish villagers who had raided and destroyed several Armenian villages, desperate local Armenians contemplated emigrating from Anatolia to Russia. In light of the prohibitive financial and political obstacles to such a drastic move, the besieged community chose to stay put but to convert to Orthodoxy.[165] Seeking the establishment of Russian schools and the arrival of Russian priests, the community saw salvation only in direct Russian involvement, analogous to the English protection of the Ottoman Empire's small Protestant Armenian communities. This initiative spread beyond Erzurum to neighboring Armenian settlements in Anatolia, including regions bordering Kars Province.

A suspected leader of the disaffected Erzurum Armenians, a man called Tatos, denied both to Ottoman authorities and to the local Armenian eparchy any intention to convert to Orthodoxy, but soon he appeared at the Russian consulate to ascertain the position of the tsarist government.[166] The consul general, T. Preobrazhenskii, discouraged Armenian resettlement into Russia, warning Tatos of the obligations they would face in their new homeland, including taxes and military service. Instead, the Russian diplomat urged Erzurum Armenians to form a more cohesive front through which, using legal means, to present their concerns to the Ottoman government. Undeterred, Tatos insisted that "the condition of the 10,000-Armenian population of Erzurum Vilayet is so dire, that only in resettlement in Russia does it see salvation, and should the imperial government consent, Armenians will eagerly accept all demands of Russian law."[167] Preobrazhenskii reported to St. Petersburg that nine Armenian villages from Erzurum alone, representing approximately eighteen hundred people, had joined in this request to relocate into the South Caucasus, although Tatos had omitted any mention of a conversion to Orthodoxy.

The spectrum of tsarist statesmen's responses to this challenge is also valuable for what it tells us about the broader Russian understanding of Armenian theological identity. Giers rejected Erzurum Armenians' plans, not only pointing out the unacceptability of religious conversion driven by political motivations but also arguing that such conversion would do little to alleviate their situation vis-à-vis their Muslim overlords and neighbors, potentially causing a dangerous backlash by the Armenians.[168] Moreover, Giers demonstrated greater concern for potential repercussions coming from Ejmiatsin rather than the Ottoman government, which clearly would not be pleased by Russia's real or perceived patronage of newly converted Western Armenians. "Problems," the minister feared, "will inevitably arise among our Armenian population and the Ejmiatsin clergy if we give the slightest reason to see in us a readiness to support the conversion of Turkish Armenians into Orthodoxy."[169] Yet a different consideration played the decisive role in this debate.

Giers emphasized that the relocation of Western Armenians into Russian territory contradicted broader imperial policy. The settlement, he wrote, "of the Caucasus by foreigners [*inozemtsami*] is undesired, while, on the other hand, the Christian, especially agrarian, population of the Turkish provinces bordering Russia . . . has always served as a redoubt during our wars with Turkey, and to weaken this population [by allowing them to move into the South Caucasus] would be especially dangerous because in the event of their departure the Turkish government will not fail to ensure in the abandoned places the settlement of Muslims who are hostile to us."[170] Geopolitical state priorities had always eclipsed the desires of Armenians and other imperial minorities, but the new emphasis on the "undesirability" of "foreign" elements, however defined, colonizing the Caucasus signaled a departure from earlier policies. True, the region's population had grown significantly since the Persian wars in the first decades of the nineteenth century, and little supposedly "untended" land remained, but Russia's claims of concern for the plight of Muslim-ruled Armenians had dissipated along with the tsarist state's claims to moral supremacy over its imperial rivals.[171] Giers realized this well, acknowledging that "permission for Turkish Armenians to resettle in our territory can be justified only by a sense of humanitarianism. But in state matters, such considerations can have but a secondary influence."[172]

This incident reflected a broader policy adaptation of Russian imperialism in the Caucasus and Anatolia. Corresponding to the general breakdown in Russo-Armenian ties, Romanov agents reduced their reliance on Armenians to settle the recently conquered Kars Province, hoping that in their stead Russian colonizers would arrive.[173] However, Candan Badem, after analyzing the tsarist administration of Anatolian districts captured in 1878, has concluded that, "unlike in Crimea and the northern Caucasus, the Russian administration utterly failed in colonizing the two oblasts with Russian peasants. By 1914, only about 5 percent of the permanent population (excluding troops and government officials) in the Kars oblast and less than 1 percent in the Batum oblast consisted of ethnic Russians."[174] In the past, Russian sectarians had fortified the tsar's dominion in the Caucasus,[175] but their small numbers were eagerly and successfully augmented by transplanted Eastern and Western Armenians after each Russo-Persian and Russo-Ottoman clash in the first half of the nineteenth century. However, as early as 1872, tsarist officials began to question the hitherto condoned relocation of Ottoman Christians—mainly Armenians and Greeks—to the Black Sea coast of the Caucasus.[176]

By the next decade, Dondukov-Korsakov and others charged these settlers with "maintaining a predatory and nomadic economy, exhausting the land, and moving from place to place."[177] The Old Regime gained thousands of new Armenian subjects after the Russo-Ottoman War of 1877–78 primarily through the annexation of Kars and other Ottoman districts, rather than immigration. In fact, when small bands of Armenian refugees fled from Anatolia to Russian territory without formal tsarist approval, including traversing the eastern Black Sea to settle on the Russian shores of the sea, they were forcefully deported back to Ottoman territory.[178] The Russian government instructed its diplomats in Erzurum and Trabzon to make clear to Ottoman Christians in March 1880 that unsanctioned immigration into Russia would result in their immediate repatriation. When this warning had little effect, Dondukov-Korsakov asked the Russian ambassador in Constantinople, in November 1883 and again in June 1884, to impress on the Ottoman government the need to prevent the sultan's subjects, whether Muslim or Christian, from crossing the border without authorization. Fearing that forced deportations of Ottoman refugees would have "adverse effects on our politics in the East," Dondukov-Korsakov lobbied the Foreign Ministry to check the tide of migrants.[179]

No clear evidence contradicts Dondukov-Korsakov's justification for advocating Russian rather than Armenian colonizers in the borderlands, but the contemporaneous rise of Armenian nationalism and the breakdown of the state's partnership with the Armenian diaspora cannot be discounted. The Russian administrators' ostensible reasons—lack of proper domestic economy and poor agricultural practices among newly transplanted Armenians—only strengthen the likelihood that nationalism and disrupted relations had a role. The state's waning preference for foreign Armenian settlers of recently annexed domains corresponded to its newfound mistrust of the tsar's own Armenian subjects. Officials' understanding of who Armenians were, and what their engagement (or lack thereof) with the state's imperial ambitions meant,

FIGURE 4.   An Armenian banker and his wife in Tiflis in the late 1890s. Courtesy of Natalya Tovmasyan Riegg.

had solidified by the end of the nineteenth century into opposition between a metropole and its subject nation.

Several interrelated forces in the last decades of the 1800s unraveled the mutually advantageous Russo-Armenian affiliation. The widely reactionary rule of Alexander III merged with Armenians' growing political self-initiative to sour the complex ties between the two sides. In that age of nationalism, the rise of a secular Armenian political movement and the autocracy's distrust of Ejmiatsin led to an outright indictment of Armenian antigovernment subversion. Armenian students, teachers, priests, merchants, farmers, and refugees all found themselves on the receiving end of the state's redoubled effort to maintain the cohesion and vitality of the empire, which saw itself as threatened by Armenians "straying" from once-parallel interests. Even references to the "Armenian nation" (*armianskaia natsiia*) and the "Armenian people" (*armianskii narod*) were crossed out by state censors and replaced with "Armenian society" (*armianskoe obshchestvo*),[180] further eroding the once-symbiotic partnership. As the next chapter demonstrates, the tsarist empire continued to tighten its grip on Armenians until 1905.

Yet the early stages of the deterioration of Russo-Armenian relations under Alexander III confirm that even when the autocracy confronted its non-Russian subjects' cultural and political activism, some groups continued to benefit from their associations with St. Petersburg. Even with their priests imprisoned and schools shut, Eastern Armenians collectively enjoyed the type of economic and social prosperity, as well as physical security, that decades earlier had enticed their forebears to relocate from neighboring lands. Indeed, foreign Armenians continued to seek a new life in the South Caucasus despite Russia's resistance to their immigration. Thus, even during crises of nationalities policy, the state continued to work with disaffected national minorities, presenting sufficient incentive to prevent them from splintering from St. Petersburg's patronage. However, at the turn of the twentieth century an unprecedented bitterness permeated the Russo-Armenian encounter. A new sense of danger among tsarist officials and a fear of coerced acculturation among Eastern Armenians characterized the reign of Russia's last tsar.

Chapter 6

Nadir and Normalization, 1896–1914

If during the 1800s even the most bitter Russo-Armenian conflicts were resolved relatively amicably, the new century drew Armenian blood and bullets in the Russian Empire. The nadir in St. Petersburg's political symbiosis with Armenians occurred from the late 1890s to 1905. Folksy charm and religious kinship yielded to suspicion of sedition as the primary trait of the Russian political attitude toward Armenians. The meticulously constructed partnership of the nineteenth century foundered in the storm of Russification, nationalism, revolution, and imperial turmoil. Bureaucratic meddling in Armenian life, especially its ecclesiastical dimension, aggravated by the often-tyrannical agendas of individual tsarist agents, triggered the greatest crisis of Russo-Armenian ties in the modern era. This chapter examines this disaster and the subsequent recovery of the more familiar imperial dynamic between the state and Armenians.

This oscillation between calamity and calm followed the general pattern that marked the Old Regime's posture toward other sociopolitically vocal groups and politically restive regions in the late nineteenth and early twentieth centuries. In the western provinces of the empire, from the 1860s until the dawn of much-touted Soviet supranational egalitarianism, Lithuanians, Jews, Belarusians, and Ukrainians gained confidence and success in challenging Russian and Polish regional hegemony.[1] In internal provinces like Ufa, non-Slavs who once enjoyed Russian trust came under collective suspicion at the turn of the twentieth century.[2] In Siberia and the Far East, the "formation of a sense of territorial separation among the [diverse] local population" imperiled the empire's integrity by 1900.[3]

A particular impetus behind Russia's deep but temporary reorientation toward Armenians inside and outside the empire came with St. Petersburg's recognition that its aim of projecting political influence into the Ottoman Empire through Ejmiatsin had proved largely fruitless. Even liberal ministers who shielded the Armenian Church from their more hawkish colleagues conceded by the early twentieth century that the catholicos exerted less sway on Western Armenians than he or the tsarist officialdom desired. Instead of reaping diplomatic benefits, the state anxiously watched an escalating Ottoman Armenian insurrection. Nevertheless, Russian statesmen strove to maintain the government's "prestige" in the eyes of the multimillion transimperial Armenian diaspora. In a crucial imperial periphery that abutted one of Russia's oldest rivals, officials employed variably coercion and concessions to retain Armenians' respect toward the tsarist government.

Among the roughly 9.3 million residents of the Caucasus in 1897, about 5.7 million lived in the South Caucasus.[4] This number included 1,243,000 Armenians, spread throughout the region but especially in its southwestern portion and in Yerevan Province, the heart of Eastern Armenia, where Armenians composed a majority of about 53 or 54 percent.[5] Estimates of the Ottoman Armenian population are notoriously less clear and waver by more than 1 million.[6] By one Russian governmental estimate from 1903, the Western Armenian population numbered approximately 1.4 million.[7] By formal Ottoman statistics from several years later, on the eve of World War I the sultan had 1,295,000 Armenian subjects, but the Armenian patriarch of Constantinople claimed that 2.1 million Armenians resided in the entire empire.[8] One dubious guess puts the total number of Ottoman Armenians in 1908 at 2,998,000.[9] Whatever the details, at the turn of the twentieth century the sultan's Armenians certainly outnumbered their tsarist compatriots, a point that affected the Russian government's conduct toward Ejmiatsin.

Catholicos Mkrtich Khrimian (1892–1907) played a key role in this period. Politically more active and ambitious than many of his predecessors, Mkrtich did not shy away from asserting Ejmiatsin's prerogatives within and beyond Russia. One historian hailed him as "the single most important nineteenth century figure to have entered Armenian consciousness as the bearer of the radical message of national liberation."[10] Yet Mkrtich was a practical leader, rather than a quixotic freedom fighter, and he attempted to remain above the growing rivalry between his clergy and secular revolutionaries. Concurrently, he tried to work with the system even when it threatened his power. The clever prelate found many ways to circumvent tsarist bureaucratic encroachments, but he was too pragmatic to reject St. Petersburg's patronage of Ejmiatsin. Only in 1903, finding no alternatives, did Mkrtich openly confront the government.

The turmoil of 1905 in the metropole that almost toppled the Romanov monarchy reverberated in the peripheries.[11] In the ferment of empire-wide social discontent and revolution, the state almost lost its grip on the South Caucasus in the opening years of the twentieth century. The desperate reinstatement of the Caucasus viceroyalty in 1905 restored order and led to the relative normalization of Russia's political stance toward Armenians. While aggressive tsarist policies continued to crop up periodically, the authorities and Armenians returned to the push-and-pull dynamic of the previous century. By the time of Russia's fateful entrance into World War I, the empire had generally reverted to its traditional perception of its Armenian subjects as reliable and even useful. Still, while St. Petersburg dreamed of regional influence or stability through Armenians, it articulated no answer to the Armenian Question.

Concerted Confrontation

The fragmentary signs of tsarist political disenchantment with Armenians in the 1880s were a precursor to the more concerted anti-Armenian policies of the Russian government during the first decade of rule of the last tsar, Nicholas II (1894–1917). A combination of domestic, regional, and foreign considerations spurred tsarist statesmen to adopt more assertive policies toward the Armenians under their jurisdictions. In the broadest terms, three primary causes fueled the deterioration: the policies and personalities of Russia's imperial and regional leaders, including Interior Minister Viacheslav Plehve and Caucasus high commissioner Grigorii Golitsyn; Russia's internal social instability in the imperial capital and in the Caucasus; and the Russo-Ottoman rivalry and the plight of Western Armenians.

Escalating reaction marked the tenures of successive high commissioners in the Caucasus in the late nineteenth century: Aleksandr Dondukov-Korsakov (1882–90), Sergei Sheremetev (1890–96), and Grigorii Golitsyn (1896–1904). Each man maneuvered to grow his influence in shaping Russia's nationalities policies toward the residents of the Caucasus.[12] Sheremetev even called for the restoration of the viceroyalty, which had been suspended in 1883. The fact that the infamous Golitsyn oversaw the most hostile Russian policies toward Armenians often belies the reality that his predecessor, Sheremetev, laid their foundation. Viewing them as unassimilated and unassimilable, Sheremetev equally distrusted the Ejmiatsin leadership, Ottoman Armenian refugees, and Eastern Armenian peasants and townspeople.

The Caucasus high commissioner kept Ejmiatsin on a tight leash. In March 1894, Sheremetev resisted the influx of Western Armenians seeking shelter in tsarist territory during a famine and anti-Armenian pogroms in Anatolia.[13] His administration was particularly incensed when Catholicos Mkrtich housed more than fifteen hundred foreign refugees in the Ejmiatsin monastery and surrounding Armenian villages without its approval. Brushing off the prelate's arguments that expelling the Ottoman Armenians would amount to "sending them to slaughter," Russian officials in the Caucasus cited insufficient food supplies and potential contagion as reasons for prohibiting the sheltering of foreigners.[14] Soon the Interior Ministry "asked" the catholicos "not to get involved with matters that pertain to the civilian authorities."[15]

Sheremetev's most visible attack on Armenian ecumenical life came with the closing of the Armenian parish schools in the winter of 1895–96. Initiated by the Caucasus administration, with only minimal input from the central government in St. Petersburg, the closing of the Armenian parish schools in January 1896 demonstrated an important aspect of late-imperial tsarist policy toward Armenians. The Caucasus high commissioners, Sheremetev and then Golitsyn, spearheaded the Russian government's hostile policies toward Armenians in the twilight of the nineteenth century. The emperor and his ministers in St. Petersburg usually supported—at times eagerly, at other times reluctantly—the restrictions proposed by their representatives in the Caucasus, but rarely did the imperial leadership engineer these policies.

Sheremetev insisted that he sought pedagogical and curricular control over 168 Armenian parish schools in the Caucasus in response to the Armenian Church's resistance to the law of March 1889, which required special licenses for teachers in Armenian parish schools.[16] Legally, Sheremetev exercised the power Tsar Alexander III granted him in 1891. But there is reason to believe that this action constituted retaliation for Western Armenian appeals for British help after the Hamidian massacres of 1895.[17] Ottoman Armenians looked to London for aid because, as Jo Laycock has shown, the persecution of the sultan's Armenians outraged British Armenophiles, who imagined Armenians as helpless Christians struggling against the brutality of Turks.[18] In any case, the high commissioner argued that the schools did not belong to Ejmiatsin because tuition payments and private donations sponsored them, rendering them private, not parish, schools. Demanding that Ejmiatsin "immediately" transfer oversight of the schools to the region's tsarist educational authorities, Sheremetev informed the Interior Ministry of this development only after issuing his command to Ejmiatsin.

Catholicos Mkrtich entreated Interior Minister Ivan Goremykin (1895–99) to cancel Sheremetev's order.[19] Mkrtich argued that, in accordance with long-held practices of Armenian and other non-Russian parish schools in the empire, Ejmiatsin distributed private donations to the schools and administered them itself. Rather than mandatory tuition, most private contributions to the church schools came from occasional donations by wealthy parents. Refusing to comply with Sheremetev's order, Mkrtich wrote to Goremykin, "I am perplexed how, without first informing me of the government's view of the long-existing sources of funding for Armenian church schools, now it is possible to make such a categorical demand."[20]

The Interior Ministry rejected Ejmiatsin's appeal and backed Sheremetev's decision. The Armenian Church resisted actively but continued to work within the system. Mkrtich "beg[ged]" the tsar to block Sheremetev's actions, invoking Armenians as Nicholas's "loyal subjects."[21] The catholicos also sent urgent telegrams and dispatched a senior priest to negotiate with Goremykin, who ignored the Armenian prelate in part because the catholicos sent to the capital a bishop who required a translator to speak with Russian officials.[22] The ecclesiastical leader flooded the Caucasus administration with appeals, naively warning the high commissioner that his actions "undermine the patriarch's authority."[23]

Perhaps angered by Mkrtich's refusal to comply with his orders, Sheremetev escalated the matter from a targeted punitive measure against the Armenian Church to a more wholesale restriction on Armenian ecumenical and social life. Instead of a temporary transfer of parish school oversight until Ejmiatsin met the government's demands for teacher licenses and financial disclosures, Sheremetev proposed to the Interior Ministry a permanent and complete confiscation of Armenian parish schools in the Caucasus.[24] Citing Alexander III's fiat of March 1891 as legal precedent, the high commissioner argued to his superiors that the Armenian Church had for years evaded Russian laws. To end Ejmiatsin's "schemes," to stop the perennial "wrangling" over the education of Armenian children, and to "shield the Armenian population from the quite harmful influence of these schools," Sheremetev sought the Interior Ministry's backing in January 1896 to "remove all of these schools without exception from the jurisdiction of the Armenian clergy and subordinate them, on a general basis, to the educational authority."[25]

This time Goremykin hesitated to endorse Sheremetev's plans. The interior minister broadly sympathized with the high commissioner's arguments but stopped short of signing off on the total confiscation of Armenian parish schools. Primarily concerned with maintaining social stability throughout the empire and wary of antagonizing tsarist Armenians, among whom he observed an "agitation of minds," Goremykin determined that Sheremetev's proposal was "not quite timely, especially because these schools are few and by law already exist under the supervision of the educational authority."[26] Thus, a formidable element of the capital's bureaucracy wavered in reinforcing the Caucasus administration's assault on Ejmiatsin.

The dissonance between two of Nicholas's senior agents necessitated his involvement. The tsar's views are clear from his marginalia on Sheremetev's report. As the emperor read the high commissioner's proposal, he underlined "make no concessions to the patriarch in the schools matter" and scribbled "approve" near a passage that proposed placing all Armenian schools under the authority of the Caucasus education administration.[27] Indeed, the monarch overruled the interior minister's hesitation to expand the state's oversight of Armenians not only by agreeing to the transfer of parish school control but also by endorsing Sheremetev's most radical recommendations.

In a direct rejection of the *polozhenie* of 1836, the Russian state in February 1896 moved to "confiscate from the Armenian clergy the immovable properties belonging to churches and monasteries, with compensation from the government."[28] More broadly and ominously, the emperor also consented to Sheremetev's suggestion to "increase surveillance over existing Armenian organizations."[29] Tsar Nicholas and High Commissioner Sheremetev thus established the foundation for the seizure of Armenian Church properties in 1903. By late April 1896, despite Ejmiatsin's resistance, the government claimed to control 168 Armenian parish schools from Baku to Kars.[30] To those inclined to suspect the Armenian clergy of nebulous intrigues, the elevated tensions only substantiated their misgivings about Ejmiatsin's loyalties.

In a crescendo of alerts, tsarist officials from the Caucasus warned their superiors in St. Petersburg of what they viewed as Ejmiatsin's political unreliability. Sheremetev spared no effort in enumerating to the still young tsar the supposed schemes through which the Armenian Church bypassed Russian regulations and covertly fortified Armenian youths' sense of cultural and national identity. The high commissioner decried that pupils in Armenian parish schools "practically do not study the Russian language" and that their grasp of the empire's dominant language remained "quite weak."[31] Far from seeking the integration of Armenians into Russian society, the Ejmiatsin leadership pursued "the education of a young Armenian generation along a narrow, national direction." Sheremetev intended to derail this agenda and teach the obdurate catholicos a lesson in imperial power structures. The high commissioner aspired to "compel [Ejmiatsin] to treat with respect the active laws and directives of the government and thus to paralyze the destructive influence of the Armenian clergy on its flock."[32] Firmly "convinced that only the state's strict and steadfast influence on the Armenian clergy will persuade it of the inevitability of submission to law," Sheremetev asked the tsar to approve new punitive measures.

To vigilant reactionaries such as the high commissioner, Ejmiatsin was the epicenter of Armenian nationalism. The Caucasus administration feared that the Armenian Church operated more as the shelter than the birthplace of transimperial Armenian political activism. Regional authorities grew more indiscriminate than before in pursuing all symptoms of apparent sedition, targeting equally the well-known manifestations of nationalism and the truly apolitical aspects of Armenian cultural life. Almost simultaneously with targeting parish schools in late 1895, Sheremetev prohibited Ejmiatsin from importing Armenian newspapers published abroad, including the revolutionary Dashnaks' and Hnchaks' party papers, *Droshak* (Flag) and *Hnchak*, as well as the supposedly subversive publications of Armenian émigrés, including *Masis* (Mount Ararat) from Constantinople, *Hayastan* (Armenia) from London, and *Hayk* from New York.[33] From junior priests' unprofessionalism to university-educated Armenians' embrace of the monastic life, the high commissioner saw evidence of Armenian nationalism. He believed that tsarist-subject Armenian nationalists feigned pious devotion to the national church to execute harmful political agendas away from Russian oversight.

Sheremetev cautioned the tsar that "young Armenians, on graduating from university and wishing to spread more conveniently their separatist and national ideas among their compatriots, have begun to enter the monastic order, where they are very quickly given quite prominent positions in the ecclesiastical hierarchy."[34] To Ejmiatsin's critics in the government, the Armenian Church orchestrated a charade where nationalist propaganda was camouflaged as national religion. Richard Hovannisian has demonstrated that, at least with regard to Armenian seminaries, this was not always baseless paranoia.[35] Sheremetev claimed that priests with ulterior motives so burdened their laities with financial collections in support of a future Western Armenian "uprising" that a couple of Eastern Armenian villages in Yerevan Province had professed a desire to convert to Russian Orthodoxy. Charged with hazy offenses, including "political agitation among Armenians" and "implication in the national Armenian movement," many Armenian priests were expelled from the Caucasus into internal Russian provinces.[36]

In December 1896, Prince Grigorii Golitsyn replaced Sheremetev as high commissioner in the Caucasus. History knows Golitsyn as "a man of the narrowest upbringing and outlook," an "Armenophobe," and reactionary Interior Minister Viacheslav Plehve's "creature in Transcaucasia."[37] He earned these labels. Fanatically fearful of insubordination, chauvinistically disdainful of non-Russians, and, in the words of his colleague Sergei Witte, "a misfit in the Caucasus," Golitsyn lacked tact but not zeal.[38] He scorned Armenians for what he viewed as their disproportionate political and economic sway in the region, and made flimsy overtures toward Azeris, but generally pursued a crude form of cultural and political Russification. To be sure, a fresh, empire-wide climate of distrust of non-Russians allowed reactionary statesmen in St. Petersburg and Tiflis to take markedly restrictive steps. Yet Golitsyn's policies toward Armenians overshadowed even Sheremetev's attacks on the schools.

Rightist Russians outside the government began to embrace the Caucasus administration's suspicions of Armenians with greater frequency. The widely circulated and politically influential St. Petersburg daily *Novoe vremia* (New Times) published scathing condemnations of Armenians soon after Golitsyn's arrival in Tiflis. The newspaper attacked Ejmiatsin's resistance to relinquish control over education and reported that Armenian priests preferred to "throw children out on the street rather than allow Russians into their secret hideouts."[39] While a shortage of schools plagued Tiflis, the Armenian clergy chose to shutter first-rate facilities rather than obey the government's directives for state supervision. Indeed, the newspaper suggested that the matter transcended concerns over local pedagogy and signaled a broader Armenian opposition to imperial integration. Insisting that Armenians pursued the type of cultural independence that other non-Russian groups had long abandoned,

FIGURE 5.   Tiflis in the 1890s. Library of Congress, Prints and Photographs Division, LC-DIG-ppmsc-03903.

the paper asked, "Why must the children of Jews, Tatars, Poles, and others study the Russian language, but Armenians must not?"[40] Among the nations of the South Caucasus, only Armenians refused to send their children to state-sponsored schools where Russian was the language of instruction, claimed the paper's correspondent, using the evocative nom de plume "A Russian in Tiflis."

Golitsyn intensified his predecessor's policies and crafted new measures. Just half a year after his promotion, Golitsyn convinced the State Council to issue a stern demand for Ejmiatsin to transfer oversight of Armenian parish schools to the imperial Education Ministry, rather than to the Caucasus education authority.[41] Citing the Armenian clergy's concerted opposition to tsarist regulations, the high commissioner in November 1897 suggested to the Interior Ministry that the state sequester all properties of the Armenian Church, a proposal that materialized only in June 1903. Surpassing Sheremetev's focus on implementing Russian oversight of Armenian pedagogy and curriculum in parish schools, Golitsyn set his sights on confiscating "all movable and immovable property" associated with Armenian education.[42] No longer interested in monitoring school lessons or registering teachers, the Caucasus bureaucracy sought to take physical possession of all operational and empty Armenian educational facilities.

A radical decision hitherto reserved only for Catholic schools, this step effectively collated the Armenian nation with Russia's traditional, internal and external, foes. A new imperial posture had dawned. State authorities fretted over what they judged as the imperial school system's shortcomings in the cultural Russification of non-Russian youth. In 1899, Education Minister Nikolai Bogolepov bemoaned the lackluster role of the "Russian language, Russian history, and Russian literature" in the empire's internal and peripheral provinces, where the local schools lacked a "vital, national character."[43]

In the twilight of the nineteenth century, the tsarist government's perception of Armenians shifted from the downtrodden friend to the irreverent rebel. With some notable exceptions, most statesmen from St. Petersburg to Tiflis viewed Ejmiatsin and the socioculturally active Eastern Armenian laity almost entirely with suspicion. Vigilant reactionaries criticized what they viewed as Armenians' cultural autonomy, religious hubris, social seclusion, and economic zest, but these attacks invariably led to the heart of the Russian condemnation of Armenians as politically disloyal. Wary of the Western Armenian agitation across its border, Russia feared that Ottoman Armenian nationalism and subversive zeal had infected tsarist-subject Armenians. Imperial officials had little proof that Eastern Armenians took cues from Western Armenians, but in that politically anxious zeitgeist perception trumped evidence.

Russian authorities watched nervously the desperation and strengthening radicalism of the Armenian movements in the Ottoman Empire.[44] When Sultan Abdülhamid II signed the hollow Armenian Reform Program in 1895, the Russian government hardly pushed the sultan to honor his obligations, having firmly prioritized the stability of its peripheral domains over the security of Ottoman minorities.[45] Exceeding his regular duties, Interior Minister Goremykin in October 1895 warned Catholicos Mkrtich that the realization of reforms in Anatolia depended on the cooperation of Western Armenians with Constantinople. Goremykin argued that their rebellion against the Porte only hindered their salvation, and he asked the Armenian prelate to put an end to the "Armenian troubles."[46] Some writers assert that Goremykin's colleague, the short-tenured foreign minister Aleksei Lobanov-Rostovskii (1895–96), "believed that the more massacres of Armenians there were, the 'better' it was for Russia."[47] Excepting for such atypical views, most Russian statesmen were distressed by the Western Armenian insurrection because since the early 1880s it increasingly stirred up the tsarist Eastern Armenians across the border.

Convinced that Ejmiatsin had the ability to direct Western Armenian revolutionaries, senior Russian officials in St. Petersburg held out hope of employing the Armenian Church toward their broader internal and external interests. Thus, a little more than a month before Sheremetev's Caucasus administration launched a major confrontation with Ejmiatsin, the Interior Ministry assumed, even accepted, the existence of a link between Armenian clergy and revolutionaries but still wished to harness Ejmiatsin's leverage, imploring the catholicos to "understand the position of the Russian government."[48] Unlike his successors, Goremykin viewed the connection between Ejmiatsin and Western Armenian rebels less as a strategic alliance of unified nationalists than as an intimate rapport based on shared religion and culture, which the government could tolerate out of a desire for borderlands stability. Soon, no Russian statesman entertained the idea of Ejmiatsin as an intermediary between the minorities of the tsar's and the sultan's empires.

Instead of potential diplomatic coordination, it was the cycle of violence between Western Armenians and Ottoman authorities that drew Russia's political attention in the twilight of the nineteenth century. Tsarist officials in Tiflis flooded their superiors in St. Petersburg with reports of Western Armenian liberation efforts and their cross-border links to shadowy circles throughout the tsarist South Caucasus, including in the Yerevan, Ejmiatsin, Aleksandropol, Surmalin, Akhalkalaki, and Baku Districts.[49] The authorities expressed concern, but not surprise, when they learned that the leadership of the Aleksandropol "revolutionary committee" included senior clergy of the

Armenian Church. During the Hamidian massacres in the mid-1890s, when perhaps as many as two hundred thousand Western Armenians perished, tsarist agents paid particular attention to the Zeitun uprising in the winter of 1895–96, when that town's Armenians preemptively attacked the local Turkish garrison.[50] In August 1896, when Dashnak fighters seized the Imperial Ottoman Bank in Constantinople to elicit European attention to the misery of Western Armenians, St. Petersburg had no sympathy for its erstwhile Christian allies, even after an enraged mob retaliated for the attack by massacring five thousand to six thousand Armenian residents of Constantinople.[51]

The specter of an ill-defined, but imminent, Armenian disorder haunted tsarist officials. From relatively tolerant statesmen in the capital to the most reactionary agents in the Caucasus, Russian policymakers saw revolution as a natural consequence of nationalism and thus viewed the interclass Western Armenian insurrection as a harbinger of a broad Eastern Armenian agitation that outgrew the sphere of the clergy. As one police report stressed about the tsar's Armenian subjects in 1897, "The idea of revolution has penetrated all the classes of Armenian society, those that have much wealth and those that have nothing. It has affected the rich merchant and the peasant, the townsman and the small shopkeeper, the intellectual class, and the most uneducated."[52] As the nineteenth century drew to a close, the hawkish Golitsyn gained political allies in his wholesale attack on Armenian institutions.

In line with the government's suspicion of Armenians, but in dissonance with Goremykin's efforts to deploy Ejmiatsin's influence inside Ottoman territory, in 1899 Golitsyn continued to push for the total confiscation of Armenian Church properties.[53] He cited two allegations to justify his agenda. First, Ejmiatsin had grown into a sovereign institution that ignored Russian laws. Second, the Armenian Church patronized Armenian rebels. Golitsyn grumbled, "[Ejmiatsin] is outside any government control [and] constitutes a state within a state, which unilaterally creates institutions that have not been approved by the government."[54] Equally convinced that Eastern Armenian priests aided and abetted Western Armenian rebels, he argued that this initiative would strip Ejmiatsin "of the political significance" that it currently had "as an instrument of Armenian revolutionaries."[55] Then and now, there is little concrete evidence of systematic collusion between Ejmiatsin and Armenian militants, but the sporadic symptoms of entwined religion and nationalism leave fertile ground for speculation. For example, Houri Berberian has noted that Dashnaks and Hnchaks used Armenian monasteries on the Persian-Ottoman border at the turn of the twentieth century as armories and hideouts for operations within the sultan's domain.[56]

Eager to act decisively and quickly, Golitsyn's administration logged the possessions of the Armenian Church before receiving instructions from St. Petersburg. Caucasus officials estimated that Ejmiatsin owned more than two hundred buildings and 51,300 acres of land.[57] The total value of Ejmiatsin's properties was estimated at around 3 million rubles.[58] Thus Golitsyn's administration sought the political impotence of the only legal institution that represented Armenian political authority. Until 1903, Golitsyn's superiors dithered in supporting his radical agenda—Goremykin generally sympathized with Golitsyn's plan but rejected some of its most extreme aspects, such as the confiscation of priests' personal homes.[59] Other ministers simply did not respond to the proposal, eliciting indignant missives from the frustrated high commissioner.[60] Nevertheless, at the turn of the twentieth century Armenians had no allies left in the tsarist officialdom. By 1900, the government closed all Armenian benevolent societies, libraries, and parish schools in the Caucasus, unequivocally categorizing the tsar's Armenian subjects as politically unreliable.[61] The apogee of reactionary nationalities policies had arrived.

The Secularization of 1903

The state wrested away the properties of the Armenian Church in 1903 during broader political turbulence of revolutionary upheaval, social unrest, and ethnonational strife. From rowdy street hooligans to disaffected urban workers to conspiratorial intellectuals to impoverished students, Russians and non-Russians throughout the empire contributed to general sociopolitical instability.[62] Social fissures, economic troubles, and cultural conflicts arose in spheres of life that had little to do with state politics and international or interethnic relations, underscoring the unprecedented destabilization of tsarist society well before the monarchy's demise in 1917.

The Bloody Sunday of 1905 and the defeat in the Russo-Japanese War exacerbated, rather than initiated, Russia's social and political crises.[63] In sharp contrast to the past, and future, popular displays of patriotism, Japan's attack on Russia in January 1904 hardly compelled the anguished tsarist public to rally behind the government's war effort.[64] The Revolution of 1905 forced Nicholas II to accept limitations on his authority. The tsar acquiesced to civic freedoms and the creation of a Duma, or legislative assembly, which marginally soothed the riots and mass violence raging from the boulevards of St. Petersburg and Moscow to the back alleys of Caucasian towns.[65] Socialists, anarchists, nationalists, and bandits had scores to settle.

The imperial authorities shaping Russia's nationalities policies in the early twentieth century worked and died in this climate of social and political turmoil. Interior Minister Viacheslav Plehve (1902–4) succeeded Dmitrii Sipiagin (1899–1902) after Socialist Revolutionaries assassinated the incumbent minister in St. Petersburg in April 1902. Plehve, whom colleagues remembered as "a splendid man for little things, a stupid man for affairs of state," reportedly dreamed before the conflict with Japan that a "small, victorious war" would avert revolution by galvanizing the fragmented tsarist society.[66] But Plehve did not live to see the spectacular fallacy of his prophesy, holding office even more briefly than his predecessor before another Socialist Revolutionary assassin blew him to pieces in July 1904. Yet, during his short tenure, the interior minister played an important role in recalibrating tsarist political ties with Armenians. Plehve was one element in a cumbersome bureaucracy that scrutinized non-Russians in a clumsy and often indiscriminate effort to uncover real and phantom enemies.

The tsar's Jewish, Polish, Muslim, and other minority subjects faced the government's desperate search for saboteurs and scapegoats.[67] After the Kishinev pogrom of 1903, Plehve's name became fused to accusations of state-sponsored anti-Semitism and persecution.[68] While "it was no secret that Plehve by 1903 considered the Jews to be enemies of the regime," it appears that the interior minister "did not directly foment the pogrom."[69] Nevertheless, Plehve tried to expel Jewish students from the elite Bestuzhev Higher Courses for Women in St. Petersburg, publicly targeting one of the empire's largest minorities.[70] The government continued to pursue non-Russians after the interior minister's assassination, compelling Polish intellectuals and workers from 1904 to 1907 to demand autonomy or independence.[71] Furthermore, a "paranoia" of a transimperial pan-Islamic conspiracy gripped Nicholas's government.[72] The tsar's Muslim subjects undertaking the hajj encountered new restrictions in 1903.[73] As a group whose loyalty had been questioned for decades, Armenians faced analogous efforts to quell social unrest and reestablish political control from the metropole to the periphery.

Resembling Plehve in political outlook, Golitsyn in 1903 attained the goal he had pursued since the mid-1890s. The state's seizure of Ejmiatsin's properties evinced the imperial leadership's willingness to sever the Russo-Armenian political partnership. Yet this development was neither sudden nor decisive. The denouement of a six-year campaign by Golitsyn, the 1903 confiscation did not represent the collective vision of the Russian political establishment. Rather, after years of dissension among senior statesmen, a vocal minority overcame the objections of a subtle majority. The sequestration of Armenian

Church properties eventually occurred for two core reasons. First, in an autocracy the emperor's decision carries the greatest weight. Second, the volatile political climate amplified the warnings of such reactionaries as Plehve and Golitsyn.

Golitsyn targeted Ejmiatsin from the moment he took office in December 1896, but the imperial leadership convened to discuss his agenda only in early 1900.[74] That February, Golitsyn convinced Tsar Nicholas to sanction an interministerial committee to review his proposal to confiscate Ejmiatsin's properties. Eduard Frisch, a senior member of the State Council, chaired the committee, which included Finance Minister Sergei Witte, Foreign Affairs Minister Mikhail Muravev, Justice Minister Nikolai Muravev, Interior Minister Dmitrii Sipiagin, Agriculture Minister Aleksei Ermolov, chief procurator of the Holy Synod Konstantin Pobedonostsev, and Golitsyn.[75] Pobedonostsev, derided as "the Grand Inquisitor" by liberal society, represented the officialdom's most entrenched reactionaries, having earlier condemned the promulgation of legal rights and protections for non-Orthodox religions in Russia as "one of the saddest mistakes of our government."[76] The committee approached the proposed secularization as a punitive measure against a still vague Armenian "revolutionary movement," the aims, location, and composition of which interested the ministers less than the immediate need for ethnonational stability.[77] The Caucasus high commissioner presented the confiscation of Catholic Church properties in response to Polish nationalism as practical and legal precedent, and he stressed that Ejmiatsin displayed "moral sympathy" toward Armenian separatism.[78]

Golitsyn received lukewarm support. Only Interior Minister Sipiagin backed Golitsyn's agenda as a symbolic measure to keep the autocracy's grip on Eastern Armenians. Intent on maintaining "the prestige of the government in the eyes of the Armenian population," Sipiagin feared that tsarist Armenians would interpret the state's refusal to confront Ejmiatsin as a sign of weakness.[79] The interior minister argued that the expropriation of religious properties was an oft-brandished tool of imperialism, used effectively by Russia and by its neighbors to nudge strayed minority communities back toward "correct" or "legal" paths.[80] No other statesman endorsed Golitsyn's proposal in 1900. Even the bellicose Pobedonostsev demurred.

The ministers of foreign affairs and finance denounced Golitsyn's plan. Mikhail Muravev enumerated several reasons for the proposal's incongruence with St. Petersburg's political interests.[81] His arguments evinced an ever-tenuous continuation of the nineteenth-century Russo-Armenian political symbiosis. The foreign minister emphasized that reducing Ejmiatsin's international stature boded poorly for tsarist foreign policy, which still relied on the

Armenian Church's influence abroad. Muravev reminded his colleagues of Western Armenians' well-known sympathy toward Russia and pointedly insisted that executing the secularization "without a serious reason" would deprive Russia of an important ally in the event of a new Russo-Ottoman war. Muravev argued that, internally, too, the confiscation would only backfire by radicalizing moderate members of Eastern Armenian laity and clergy. He cautioned that the seizure, instead of a cure from nationalism, was more likely to pique Armenian intellectuals who competed with the clergy for sociocultural leadership of the Armenian nation.

Finance Minister Witte concurred with Muravev. Focused on revitalizing the empire's economy, the brilliant future prime minister, a native of Tiflis, saw little benefit from punitive measures against tsarist minorities.[82] A friend of Sipiagin's, Witte disagreed with the interior minister and the Caucasus high commissioner, dismissing Golitsyn's endeavor as a "ridiculous scheme [*bezobraznaia zateia*]."[83] The finance minister's arguments were succinct: the secularization of Ejmiatsin's properties could spark a pan-Armenian "rebellion," and such hostile measures against a religious cousin were unethical. Broadly opposed to Golitsyn's nationalities policies in the Caucasus, Witte registered his disapproval in his memoirs: "Prince Golitsyn's administration in the Caucasus was noteworthy only in that he aroused the entire Caucasus against him and, indirectly, against the Russian government."[84] With the predominant opinion firmly set against Golitsyn's proposal, his efforts to capture Armenian Church properties in 1900 failed. The tsar signed off on the committee's decision, but encouraged Golitsyn and Sipiagin to maintain pressure on Ejmiatsin.

In spring 1901, the Caucasus administration took advantage of internal rivalries within Ejmiatsin's leadership to resume its pursuit of the Armenian Church.[85] "The chaotic state of affairs in Ejmiatsin," Golitsyn carped to Sipiagin, "which has been chronic for some time and occasionally requires the government's energetic involvement, now again demands special attention."[86] Golitsyn targeted Catholicos Mkrtich, whom he accused of unacceptable ambitions: "The current patriarch-catholicos, who has fully committed himself not to the role of his flock's spiritual leader but to its political driver, is growing more and more arrogant toward our government and toward the requirements of law."[87] The myopic Golitsyn showed political sagacity in attacking Mkrtich not only through the prism of Russian law but also by capitalizing on real and exaggerated discord between the catholicos and the Ejmiatsin Synod. Power struggles among Armenian Church elites no doubt affected Russian-Armenian political considerations, but here the impetus behind challenging the status quo came from Golitsyn, for whom Mkrtich's subordination to his administration became a personal cause.[88] Although even Sipiagin, one of

Golitsyn's few political allies, in June 1901 had to temper the zealous high commissioner's efforts to replace senior members of the Ejmiatsin Synod with junior Armenian priests he considered more reliable,[89] the high commissioner and the interior minister shared a distrust of the Ejmiatsin leadership.

Sipiagin held a deep suspicion of foreign-born Armenian clerics, perceiving them as corrupted by Eastern backwardness and insufficiently Russified. He fundamentally opposed the government's policy, introduced by Viceroy Aleksandr Bariatinskii in 1857, of backing an Ottoman Armenian priest for the Ejmiatsin seat. Bariatinskii had convinced the tsarist leadership that the election of a Western, rather than Eastern, Armenian to the apogee of the Armenian Church would produce myriad foreign and domestic advantages to the Russian government through strengthening the ties between Ejmiatsin and Ottoman Armenians.[90] Nearly a half century later, after several Ottoman Armenians had reigned over Ejmiatsin, Sipiagin, Golitsyn, and other reactionary statesmen argued that the foreign-born prelates had failed to deliver the benefits envisioned by Bariatinskii. The interior minister in December 1901 commiserated with the high commissioner about the purportedly duplicitous nature of the incumbent and past Ottoman-Armenian catholicoi. The officials believed that Mateos, Kevork, and Mkrtich "constantly attempted to implement [in Russia] those despotic measures, which they grew accustomed to using in their former homeland, as a result of which they were unable to demonstrate toward our law that respect which a well-ordered government has the right to demand."[91]

Sipiagin's solution was simplistic and quixotic. The government could ensure its interests only by restricting the election of the Ejmiatsin catholicos to tsarist subjects, prohibiting the participation of Ottoman and other foreign Armenians.[92] Sipiagin and other officials believed that years of Ottoman Armenian struggle against their government's de facto and de jure injustices had rendered Western Armenians less malleable and less cooperative with the agents of a "civilized" empire. The interior minister reproached the Ottoman-born Armenian catholicoi, including Mkrtich, for their shaky grasp of the Russian language and viewed it as an indication of their broader detachment from Russian culture and society. Sipiagin was convinced that the perennial tensions between the autocracy and the Armenian Church would dissolve almost instantly once "the title of catholicos is vested in a person raised in Russia, familiar with the demands of a civilized state, accustomed to obeying the regulations of the authorities, and [speaks] the Russian language."[93] Golitsyn at first insisted that a candidate's place of birth and fluency in Russian alone were insufficient guarantees of his political reliability, but less than two years later he reversed his position and backed Sipiagin's proposal.[94]

The conflict between Golitsyn and Mkrtich expanded in September 1902, when an anonymous letter landed on new interior minister Plehve's desk in St. Petersburg. Signed by "loyal Armenian subjects," the petition argued that the eighty-two-year-old prelate was unfit for his post: "The catholicos is not able to be the leader of the people, and he does not know [his] subordinates at all."[95] The authors complained of administrative and financial mismanagement and claimed that the catholicos left important eparchy leaderships vacant in a ploy to bolster his authority. In this and other anonymous letters, writers asked Plehve to pressure Mkrtich to resign, insisting that "the poor old man" was able to meet neither Armenian nor Russian needs.[96] The letters' authorship remains impossible to establish—disaffected Armenian clergy, Golitsyn's administration, and many others could have written them—but they clearly and cleverly revived past tsarist suspicions that internal conflicts in Ejmiatsin often indicated efforts by power-hungry catholicoi to shed the government's authority over them. By January 1903, Golitsyn alerted Plehve that the procurator of the Ejmiatsin Synod had taken the unusual step of protesting to him about Mkrtich's abuse of power. The catholicos allegedly violated the bylaws of the Armenian Church by sidestepping the synod's approval of senior clergy appointments and by overruling the synod's decisions regarding marriage and divorce.[97] Seeing in these reports new evidence of Mkrtich's lust for power, and also signs of Ejmiatsin's general disarray, Plehve needed little more than murky rumors to unleash Golitsyn.

The empire's sociopolitical climate and the personalities of Golitsyn and Plehve aligned to set in motion the Russian government's most potent assault on the Armenian Church in 1903. With new accusations against Mkrtich emerging, and the fiery Plehve succeeding Sipiagin, the Committee of Ministers reconsidered Golitsyn's proposal to confiscate the property of the Armenian Church.[98] The final vote was decisive: twelve members opposed the measure and five supported it.[99] Only Plehve, Golitsyn, Education Minister Grigorii Zenger, Minister of Marine Affairs Fedor Avelan, and the acting director of the General Staff, Petr Frolov, backed the plan.[100] They argued that the action was not as harsh as it could have been and that the majority of the South Caucasus's secular Armenians, peasants and townspeople who hardly benefited from Ejmiatsin's capital, were unlikely to resist the step.[101] Led by Witte, Foreign Minister Count Vladimir Lamsdorf, and former Caucasus viceroy Mikhail Nikolaevich (the tsar's granduncle), the majority of statesmen rejected the expropriation as shortsighted, counterproductive, and, ultimately, dangerous.

Count Lamsdorf encapsulated the views of the majority.[102] He saw the confiscation as ineffective, unlikely to compel the Armenian Church to follow the regulations of the government. "To the contrary," cautioned the foreign minister, "this step could elicit in the Armenian-Gregorian clergy a feeling of even greater distrust toward the government, and, as an inevitable consequence of this, it can further strengthen its spirit of opposition through various means toward the government and [strengthen its] separatist dreams."[103] Lamsdorf wisely warned that Eastern Armenian revolutionaries could find new sources of financing other than the church. The state's confrontation of Ejmiatsin could backfire by galvanizing "Armenian capitalists" to donate generously to various political organizations, including underground militias. Indeed, Lamsdorf feared that Golitsyn and Plehve's plan could spark an open rebellion among the secular layers of tsarist Armenian society against Russian authority, which would require military force to pacify.

Outside the empire, too, Lamsdorf envisioned serious consequences for the government's face-off with the Armenian Church. He acknowledged the frustratingly inconsistent record of relying on Ejmiatsin to promote Russian interests in the Ottoman domain and elsewhere abroad, but he insisted that this objective remained as important as ever. "Although we are unable to turn the catholicos into an obedient tool of our political aims," argued the foreign minister, "nevertheless we cannot fail to grant certain political significance to the supreme Armenian patriarch, who can . . . influence foreign Armenians."[104] Thus, even at the height of the state's clash with the Armenian Church, the majority of Russia's senior officials cited domestic and foreign policy imperatives for maintaining relatively amicable relations with clerical and secular Armenian communities. But in an autocracy, the monarch's view settles controversial questions.

"I agree with the opinion of the five members," the tsar announced on 12 June 1903.[105] Nicholas II authorized the Ministry of Agriculture and the Department of State Properties to seize the land and property of the Armenian Church. Effectively crippling the catholicos and the Ejmiatsin Synod, the state rendered Armenian clergy dependent on the government's patronage. The decree included all estates and other immovable properties of the church within the Russian Empire, excluding its possessions in St. Petersburg and Moscow.[106] The government would redistribute a certain percentage of profits from these properties to the Armenian Church as it saw fit. The Interior Ministry was tasked with taking over the financial affairs of the church, earmarking just 15 percent of the profits for the maintenance of the properties and the creation of a small reserve fund for emergencies.[107] By abolishing the church's financial and administrative independence, the emperor and his camarilla disarmed the catholicos and tempered Ejmiatsin's transimperial clout. Thus, six men molded the Armenian religion into little more than an extension of the tsarist bureaucracy. Why?

Overshadowed in history by 1905's war, revolution, and administrative re-shuffling, the year 1903 was a key point in Russia's nationalities policies and the tsar's posture toward the Caucasus. It marked the zenith of reactionary, Russifying efforts taken by Nicholas's inner circle, exemplified by Plehve and Golitsyn, who saw little to gain from cooperation and co-optation, but much to lose from compromise, with the empire's ethnonational minorities. Arme-nians and the Caucasus were hardly alone in absorbing this elite's clumsy pac-ification efforts. From Vilnius to Kiev, in the western borderlands Nicholas's agents struggled to contain Lithuanian, Ukrainian, Polish, and other nation-alisms, resorting to tactics analogous to those Golitsyn wielded against Arme-nians.[108] From his first day as interior minister, Plehve pursued "seditious" activity in Finland with "firm, repressive measures."[109] But the irresolute tsar's personal oscillation rendered him susceptible to lobbying, a fact most evident in his near-simultaneous proclamation of empire-wide "religious toleration" alongside the secularization of the Armenian Church.[110]

Nicholas II sided with Plehve and Golitsyn against Witte and Lamsdorf less because he heeded their warnings of Armenian plots and more due to broader ideological alignment with the interior minister and the high commissioner. The tsarist debate over Armenian nationalism and ecclesiastical autonomy took place against a backdrop of intense interministerial rivalry for influence over the tsar in general and over the nationalities policies in particular. It is no coincidence that just two months after announcing the confiscation of Ejmi-atsin's properties, Nicholas removed Witte from the Finance Ministry. In the words of Witte's biographer, the tsar "was put off by the minister of finance's views on Far Eastern policy, and . . . accepted the opinion that Witte was too well disposed toward troublesome minorities such as the Finns, the Armenians, and particularly the Jews."[111] Witte conceded that he "was too sharp" with the tsar.

Plehve's outright hostility toward Witte was no secret.[112] Aiming to eclipse the influential finance minister, the interior minister convinced the impression-able emperor that Witte fanned discontent among Armenians, other ethnon-ational minorities, and Russian students.[113] Indeed, Witte and Plehve "were at odds over Russification policies being imposed, at great political cost, on Ar-menians in the Caucasus, a region toward which Witte had an almost propri-etary feeling."[114] In his memoirs, Witte derided both of his key nemeses in the Armenian debate, Plehve and Golitsyn, recalling that the latter "was the first administrator who put into practice a narrowly nationalistic point of view . . . [and] he left the Caucasus disliked by all, including the Russians."[115] Thus, in 1903 the tsar, wary of Witte's cosmopolitanism and open to Plehve and Golit-syn's reactionary conservatism, agreed with the few against the many.

The sidelined majority of ministers grumbled. The empire's reactionary statesmen justified the use of punitive secularization as a penalty for nationalism and a panacea for revolution. Plehve had to explain the unexpected turn of events to his colleagues, resorting to political revisionism to grasp at a legal precedent. "Because our government did not desist from secularizing the ecclesiastical properties of the Georgian Orthodox Church," the interior minister argued in reference to the abolition of Georgian autocephaly in 1811 and the confiscation of that church's properties in 1869, "then simple fairness . . . demands the extension of this measure to the Armenian Church."[116] Plehve issued equally facile responses to those who raised the likelihood of a transimperial Armenian backlash and international diplomatic condemnation, insisting that in the past such concerns did not prevent the state from executing expropriation in regions "such as the western periphery and the Polish Kingdom, for example, where the political situation was, without doubt, no less unfavorable and no less complicated than in this case."[117] The reasoning was glib: if analogous tactics aimed at Orthodox Georgians and Catholic Poles ostensibly produced desired results, why not apply them to Apostolic Armenians? Golitsyn parroted his superior's stance, underscoring that six years of experience in the Caucasus had convinced him of this step's necessity.

Ecclesiastical and lay Armenians, in Russia and abroad, responded to the tsarist assault on their national church with dismay and indignation.[118] The Armenian patriarchs of Constantinople and Jerusalem wrote to Mkrtich to express solidarity and to ask for clarification of the news emerging from Russia.[119] From Illinois and Rhode Island to Egypt and Persia, the dispersed diaspora rallied behind the embattled church.[120] At the same time Armenians everywhere pressured their ecclesiastical leader to withstand the monarchy's assault. Armenians in the United States declared publicly to the catholicos: "[We] demand your resistance even to death against the unjust confiscation of our church property by the Russian government."[121] To the appeals it received from throughout the world, the tsarist bureaucracy answered consistently and curtly that the tsar's decision was "irreversible."[122]

To determine the church's response, in July and August 1903 the catholicos convened the senior leadership of the church, including the Ejmiatsin Synod and the heads of Armenian eparchies throughout the Russian Empire; the clergy demanded that Mkrtich appeal the decision to Nicholas II.[123] Lay Armenian communities within the South Caucasus, too, pressed Mkrtich "either to resign or to protest."[124] The catholicos duly complained to the emperor, "[The secularization] shakes the centuries-old foundation of my church, and I, as its leader, responsible to God and to the four million [Armenian] people that elected me to be the guardian of its inviolability, cannot remain silent."[125] Unmoved by the pleas, the tsar and the interior minister rejected the prelate's requests for a personal audience. Plehve warned Mkrtich to comply immediately and threatened that "any delay, as an act of disobedience to the Tsarist Will, will bring harsh consequences."[126]

Frustrated and under pressure from all layers of Armenian society to resist, Mkrtich ordered the clergy not to obey demands from officials and, if they insisted, simply to leave.[127] Golitsyn viewed Mkrtich's appeals as a "new trick of the Oriental politician" and instructed the governors of Caucasian provinces to confiscate Armenian property by force.[128] When priests refused to hand over the keys to the Ejmiatsin safe that held title deeds, tsarist agents obtained the papers by breaking open the safe.[129] The situation became volatile as agitated Armenian villagers and townspeople amassed uninvited in Ejmiatsin.[130] Throughout the Caucasus, Armenians rallied against the government. Armenians in Aleksandropol took to the streets to chant "Betrayal!"[131] Sensational rumors proliferated in rural communities that the confiscation was the first step in a comprehensive Russification program, whereby next the government would close Armenian churches and force every Armenian to convert to Orthodoxy.[132]

In late August, as many as eight thousand Armenian residents of Akhaltsykh protested, and soon in Elisavetpol the police opened fire on Armenian demonstrators, killing seven and injuring twenty-seven.[133] Throughout the region, disturbances and bloodshed—some of it caused by outnumbered police, some instigated by veteran Dashnak and Hnchak fighters—marked the Armenian response.[134] In Kars, Armenian residents climbed rooftops to pummel tsarist officials with rocks, requiring the intervention of hundreds of Cossacks.[135] When it appeared that Witte's and Lamsdorf's predictions of a violent Armenian break with Russia were about to materialize, even conservative commentators adopted a gentler stance. The St. Petersburg daily *Novoe vremia*, Russia's "most powerful newspaper,"[136] assured its readers that only a thin, extremist layer of the Armenian clergy animated the resistance. While in 1897 the newspaper had condemned what it viewed as the broad Armenian refusal to integrate culturally and intermingle ethnically, at the peak of the Russo-Armenian crisis in 1903 it took a milder approach, stressing that most Armenians wanted no trouble:

> On its own the Armenian popular mass in Russia is far from any agitation against the country, in which it has truly found a second homeland and flourishes to such extent that it is becoming increasingly like a plutocracy. Tell, for example, a Russian-subject Armenian to move to Persia or, even worse, to Turkey, and you will encounter the most desperate

resistance. No Armenian will want to leave Russia, this is a fact that Armenians will not deny.[137]

The bloodied Armenian villagers of the Caucasus, under fire from Cossacks and policemen, surely would have rejected this romanticized and somewhat anachronistic portrayal of their aspirations, but the newspaper captured the position of the overwhelming majority of Eastern Armenians as loyal. To be sure, the isolated skirmishes and bloodshed of late summer 1903 did not beckon a collective Armenian insurrection against Russia.[138] Yet government and society often interpreted the dramatic actions of a few radicals as manifestations of populist agitation.

The pursuit of Armenians grew into a mania for Golitsyn. In one of two rambling letters he wrote to Plehve on 14 October 1903 to enumerate the com-

Figure 6. An Armenian civil engineer and his wife and daughter in Sukhum in the early 1900s. Courtesy of Natalya Tovmasyan Riegg.

plex subterfuges of literate Armenian society, the high commissioner charged that Tiflis Armenian elites "systematically do not attend opera performances in the state theater," which to him proved the Armenian intelligentsia's "boycott" of Russian culture and served as another sign of its opposition to the tsarist regime.[139] The tone, frequency, and fervor of Golitsyn's assertions suggest that by this point the Armenian matter had grown into a personal mission for him. More so than in the past, he now suspected of seditious behavior not only Armenian clergy and revolutionaries but almost every segment of the literate Armenian population of the Caucasus.

Hours after Golitsyn drafted these letters, Hnchak revolutionaries tried to kill him.[140] Two hitmen assaulted the high commissioner as he and his wife traveled in a carriage near Tiflis. With the driver desperately attempting to evade the attackers, the two assassins held on to the flying vehicle and used every weapon at their disposal. When one assailant's revolver misfired, his accomplice pounced on the high commissioner with a dagger, stabbing at him while his prey parried the blows with his walking stick. Wounded and shocked, Golitsyn survived the attack, thanks to the chain mail vest he reportedly wore.[141] Nursing his injuries, disillusioned by the Armenian resistance to his policies and probably by what he saw as the lukewarm backing he received from St. Petersburg, Golitsyn left the Caucasus in July 1904. For modern Russo-Armenian political ties, this era was the darkest hour.

Restoration

As the political flux of 1905 altered the short remainder of imperial nationalities policies—for example, the state unshackled Ukrainian culture[142]—it also adjusted the course of the Russo-Armenian crisis. The disintegration of what for most of the nineteenth century was a political symbiosis did not serve the domestic or foreign policy imperatives of the tsarist empire, a realization that rapidly permeated the highest levels of the government at the end of Golitsyn's tenure. Consequential transformations, and reversals, in Russian policy occurred within a year of the confiscation of Ejmiatsin's properties, which was mostly completed by November 1903. Days apart in July 1904, the injured Golitsyn left his post in the Caucasus and the despised interior minister Plehve, who had already survived six assassination plots, was struck down by a bomb in St. Petersburg.[143] With two of the principal architects of the severe tsarist policies toward Armenians gone, the malleable emperor turned to statesmen who would work to repair the damage to Russo-Armenian ties done in recent years.

No person contributed more to the normalization of Russia's policies toward Armenians than Count Ilarion Vorontsov-Dashkov. A distant relative of the great viceroy Mikhail Vorontsov (and married to his granddaughter), Vorontsov-Dashkov had a thoroughly accomplished yet unremarkable career. His roots in the Caucasus were established during military service in the region in 1859–62, a pivotal period when Russia finally subdued the North Caucasus insurgency, an experience from which he drew lasting lessons and a lifelong passion for understanding the sociopolitical circumstances of Russia's southern domain.[144]

Unpretentious and capable, Vorontsov-Dashkov went on to serve in other peripheries, Turkestan in the mid-1860s and then the Russo-Ottoman War of 1877–78, where he commanded Russian cavalry and also befriended the emperor's son. After the assassination of Tsar Alexander II in 1881, Vorontsov-Dashkov headed the security of his close friend and new monarch, Alexander III. As minister of the imperial court from 1881 to 1897, he gained extensive bureaucratic and administrative experience. Member of the State Council from 1897, Vorontsov-Dashkov was generally respected for his professionalism, well regarded by elite society, and favored by successive tsars. His career's zenith arrived at a moment of political chaos in Russia. The murder of the interior minister, the debacle of the Russo-Japanese War, and the outburst of social discontent in the Bloody Sunday of 22 January 1905 were but the most prominent stimuli for Nicholas II to recalibrate his domestic and foreign policies.[145] The Caucasus did not escape the beleaguered tsar's attention.

A month after Bloody Sunday, the autocrat restored the Caucasus viceroyalty.[146] The office had existed from 1844 to 1883, when Alexander III replaced it with the lesser position of the high commissioner to reestablish St. Petersburg's direct rule over the territory. High commissioners had less freedom of action than viceroys because they reported not only to the tsar but also to the imperial ministers. In early 1905, with myriad crises swirling throughout the empire and Nicholas II as desperate for swift authority in the Caucasus as his great-grandfather, Nicholas I, had been in 1844, the tsar appointed Vorontsov-Dashkov as Caucasus viceroy. In dispatching the statesman, the emperor lamented: "To my regret, [the progress of the past decades] has been blighted by the mutual clashes of various nationalities, cases of disobedience toward authorities, and unrest that has disturbed the calm course of life" in the Caucasus.[147]

Pragmatic, measured, and erudite, Vorontsov-Dashkov in policy and personality was the complete opposite of his immediate predecessors.[148] In one of his first public announcements to the residents of the Caucasus, the viceroy emphasized that he intended to cooperate with all locals, "irrespective of faith and nationality," in his mission to restore order.[149] He made clear that he planned to employ "peaceful means" and to seek the "help of all social" segments in his task, and he also declared: "I believe in popular wisdom and I am convinced that the restless part of the population will not stand the friendly public pressure of the well-intentioned huge majority and will comply." Almost immediately, and in some cases even before Vorontsov-Dashkov arrived in Tiflis, officials sought to undo the damage done by Golitsyn's decisions. At least initially, the new viceroy benefited from a general reversal of political tides in St. Petersburg. A moderate new interior minister, Aleksandr Bulygin (who served just a few months before the tsar removed him) proposed to Vorontsov-Dashkov that the viceroy revoke Golitsyn's directive for the practically indiscriminate exile of Armenian priests suspected of sedition.[150] Throughout early and mid-1905, Vorontsov-Dashkov facilitated the return to the Caucasus of dozens of Armenian clerics who had been banished to internal provinces.[151]

One of the viceroy's strengths was his ability to contextualize for skeptical colleagues the reasons for recent Armenian troubles. Cognizant that with Golitsyn's departure Armenian disturbances subsided, but also that the government had to take additional steps to reinstate the stability of the precrisis era, Vorontsov-Dashkov showed early signs of reformist tendencies by urging Bulygin and the tsar to allow the reopening of the Armenian seminary at Shusha, which Golitsyn had shuttered in late 1903. Vorontsov-Dashkov argued that the closing of the seminary was justified "by causes that had a temporary, transient meaning" at the height of the Armenian backlash to the confiscation, but they were no longer appropriate because the outrage had abated and the closed seminary created, "without particular benefits for the government, only an additional reason for the discontent of the Armenian clergy and population."[152] For the next decade of his tenure at the helm of the Caucasus administration, Vorontsov-Dashkov demonstrated a similar inclination to portray the Armenian violence in 1903–4 as an almost valid reaction to Golitsyn's actions and to extend this argument to justify a wholesale reversal of his predecessor's policies. Emboldened by the tsar's acquiescence to the relatively minor question of the Shusha seminary, Vorontsov-Dashkov embarked in the summer of 1905 on a mission to restore the possessions of the Armenian Church.

In pushing for the return of Ejmiatsin's property, the viceroy revealed a nuanced understanding of the region's history and the particular considerations of its ethnonational fabric. Vorontsov-Dashkov did not mince words in telling the director of the Chancellery of the Committee of Ministers, Baron Emmanuil Nolde, that decades of abusive Russian policies toward Armenians had produced the recent crisis.[153] The viceroy was adamant: "The repressive measures taken systematically against the Armenian Church and the Armenian population over the past two decades, culminating in the confiscation of church schools and properties into the Treasury's possession, have elicited the general discontent of the Armenian clergy and population and the energetic terroristic activity of Armenian revolutionary committees, which has driven the region into a very alarming condition."[154] Vorontsov-Dashkov viewed the recent events as an affirmation of Witte's and Lamsdorf's warnings. The viceroy insisted that the June 1903 fiat backfired by galvanizing an Armenian insurgency that had been ebbing up to that point: "Armenian revolutionary committees, originally birthed by the Turkish abuses of the local Armenians and their desire for liberation from the Muslim yoke, took advantage of the turmoil and ferment that this decree caused in the [tsarist] Armenian population."[155] Before Russia's assault on Ejmiatsin, claimed Vorontsov-Dashkov, voluntary donations to Armenian rebels had practically dried up, forcing the Dashnaks, Hnchaks, and others to resort to extortion and violence to finance their agenda. This circumstance, "of course," could not have continued indefinitely, and soon the revolutionary groups "would have disappeared due to the lack of resources." The June 1903 decree, however, "infused the Armenian revolution with new strength and returned it to popularity."

Vorontsov-Dashkov promoted a new vision of Russian imperialism in the Caucasus. He not only advocated the restoration of Ejmiatsin's inviolability but also called for a transformation of Russia's posture toward the natives of the South Caucasus.[156] The viceroy maintained that Golitsyn's actions, far from an aberrant incident, were a culmination of almost a quarter century of Russification efforts directed at "denationalizing" (denatsionalizirovat') Armenians. The government erred in the early 1880s, argued Vorontsov-Dashkov, when it "took a sharp turn" in policy by introducing high commissioners, restricting the recruitment of Armenians into the regional administration, and insisting on their cultural assimilation. After the abolition of the viceroyalty in 1883, "The 'Russification of the territory' became the state program. Only a denationalized native was considered trustworthy." The viceroy accurately recalled how bureaucrats came to scrutinize previously tolerated expressions of cultural identity as suspect indicators of subversive machinations. "Knowledge of the Armenian language, the reading of Armenian books, [and] the attendance of Armenian theater became interpreted as 'separatism,' which had to be suppressed," he summarized.[157]

Russian imperialism, Vorontsov-Dashkov averred, had functioned more smoothly and fruitfully when it relied on the participation of Caucasus natives in its mission. At midcentury, under the leadership of Viceroys Vorontsov, Bariatinskii, and Mikhail Nikolaevich, Russia had recruited Armenians into the local bureaucracy and cooperated with them to identify and pursue mutual goals. Armenians' proverbial reliability and work ethic rendered them prominent elements of the tsarist political machinery. But after 1883, Armenians and other Caucasus natives lost the trust of tsarist imperial agents—practically inexplicably so, in Vorontsov-Dashkov's view—and became increasingly marginalized by the Russian authorities. Sidelined and suspected of sedition, Eastern Armenians began to sympathize more openly with the Western Armenian rebellion, gradually leading to the radicalization of certain segments of tsarist Armenian society. Indeed, the viceroy insisted that misguided Russian policies pushed some Eastern Armenians to extremism: "The connection of events explains how a sober, practical, prudent Armenian people could get carried away by a revolutionary movement. It is impossible to denationalize a people that has existed for several thousands of years, one that has a history, engages primarily in agriculture, possesses a distinct culture, literature, newspapers, and theater. Once a people has a known purpose, it will always manage to satisfy it."[158]

The viceroy's portrayal of Armenians, idealized and skewed in its own way, conjured up the Russian perceptions of Armenians that had been prevalent for much of the nineteenth century. To restore order in the Caucasus, reclaim Armenian political loyalty, and end their dabbling with rebellion, the state had to abandon any semblance of coerced assimilation, which had proved so debilitating for St. Petersburg's interests. The seasoned statesman insisted, "The Armenian revolution in the Caucasus was created by the system of 'Russification.' To placate the Armenian people, therefore, it is necessary to return to the system practiced by" the viceroys from 1844 to 1883.[159]

Beyond canceling the confiscation of Ejmiatsin's properties, Vorontsov-Dashkov asked Nicholas II to approve additional conciliatory measures intended to offset the damage done to Russo-Armenian ties in recent years. He urged that all closed Armenian schools reopen and that Ejmiatsin receive the right to establish new parish schools, under the government's oversight, while the state helped these schools reclaim their standings as centers of Armenian culture. On 1 August 1905, sitting in the Peterhof palace outside his capital, the taciturn emperor scribbled on the viceroy's proposal, "Agreed."[160]

The tsar's volte-face occurred because he conceded that the agenda pursued by Golitsyn and Plehve had yielded more instability than tangible benefits. The autocrat granted the viceroy carte blanche in repairing relations with his Armenian subjects, and soon Vorontsov-Dashkov cautiously reported that the Armenian agitation had subsided in response to the restoration of Ejmiatsin's possessions.[161] From the imperial capital, Interior Minister Petr Durnovo (1905–6) ensured that the Armenian properties located outside the Caucasus viceroy's jurisdiction were duly returned.[162] In another sharp break with his predecessor's behavior, the viceroy communicated cordially with Catholicos Mkrtich, promising the restoration of the Armenian Church's inviolability while stipulating permanent Armenian tranquility.[163] By late September 1905, the last Armenian priest exiled by Golitsyn returned home.[164]

Up through his retirement in 1915, Vorontsov-Dashkov steadfastly pursued the restoration of Russia's precrisis relations with Armenians. He generally enjoyed the support of the tsar and the ideological alignment of such senior officials as the short-tenured interior ministers Bulygin and Durnovo. But the normalization of the tsarist engagement with Armenians in the years prior to the Great War periodically encountered both state-constructed and indigenously grown hurdles. First, despite the ostensible independence of the viceroy, the political and personal vicissitudes of St. Petersburg's elites often affected the work of the Caucasus administration. In October 1905, the embattled tsar brought Witte back to the spotlight to bridge the abyss between government and populace, leading to the establishment of Russia as a de jure constitutional monarchy and Witte as the country's first prime minister. However, the maverick politician served just six months before the autocrat again pushed him out. Witte's most prominent successor, the feisty Petr Stolypin, proved less supportive of Vorontsov-Dashkov's tactics.[165]

Second, reflecting the near chaos of Russia proper, ethnic violence erupted between Armenians and Azeris in Baku.[166] Entrenched ethnoreligious animosities, simmering for generations under the surface, exploded to overwhelm Vorontsov-Dashkov's administration.[167] The Armenian-Azeri "war" in 1905–6, when thousands of people perished, delayed the viceroy's ambitious reforms, blighted his reputation in St. Petersburg as a skillful manager, and incurred Stolypin's scorn.[168] The violence also reenergized Armenian nationalists and generated new Russian doubts about Armenian reliability. While the restoration of Ejmiatsin's properties in 1905 appeased the majority of Armenian clergy, bourgeoisie, and peasantry, it did not quell the agitation of the Armenian revolutionaries, who continued to target tsarist officials for several years.[169] Dashnaks blamed Russians for fanning anti-Armenian enmity among Azeris in what they interpreted as a divide-and-rule strategy, and a series of Armenian assassination attempts on tsarist officials inside and outside the Caucasus rocked the fragile peace that Vorontsov-Dashkov had established. The key challenge to the normalization of Russo-Armenian ties after the crisis of 1903, however, came when the Armenian Church once again became entangled in a consequential policy debate among senior tsarist agents.

Catholicos Mkrtich died (of natural causes) in late October 1907. Esteemed by Armenians, despised by reactionary Russians, and tolerated by progressive tsarist officials, the prelate had presided over, and played a key part in, the most acute breakdown of Russo-Armenian political relations in modern history. The opening of a vacancy at Ejmiatsin's apex stirred the government to reevaluate the role of the Armenian religion, its leader, and the Armenian nation, in the empire. The new controversy emerged within the context of Stolypin's interference in Vorontsov-Dashkov's administration, when the powerful Stolypin, who in July 1906 replaced Witte and Durnovo as both prime minister and interior minister, faulted the viceroy for his inability to stem the ethnic violence in the Caucasus.[170]

A "reforming conservative," Stolypin in the evaluation of one historian has the distinction of being the only statesman to have "ever been the object, at one and the same time, of as much uncritical adulation and unrestrained vilification."[171] Some contemporaries derided him for his supposed coldheartedness and lust for power, while others lionized him for his intrepid, devoted leadership of Russia during one of its deepest modern calamities. Yet in the matter of Armenian affairs, there is less ambivalence about his motivations. To the prime minister, the ongoing terrorism of the Dashnaks after the government's reconciliation with the Armenian Church illustrated the general unreliability of the Armenian nation. By February 1907, Stolypin criticized Vorontsov-Dashkov for his failure to end the ethnic conflicts and, perhaps more worrisome for St. Petersburg, the worker strikes that had crippled the Baku oil industry. When Mkrtich died, animosity already characterized the ties between the prime minister and the viceroy.[172] In the death of the catholicos, Stolypin saw a chance to reorient permanently the government's posture toward Armenians.

The prime minister believed that decades of failed efforts to woo foreign Armenians by patronizing Ejmiatsin had proved the futility of Russia's nineteenth-century conciliatory policies toward the Armenian faith.[173] Adamant that reciprocal political benefits had not followed Russia's support of Armenians, he sought in December 1907 to reduce Ejmiatsin's legal and social status. In a remarkable echo of Golitsyn's arguments from years earlier, Stolypin demanded that the government restrict, not amplify, Ejmiatsin's international stature:

> The universal significance [*vselenskoe znachenie*] of the Ejmiatsin catholicos has quite conspicuously expanded his spiritual-political jurisdiction, creating for him the right to interfere in the affairs of foreign Armenians [and] to serve as their petitioner in front of our and other governments. This characteristic of the Ejmiatsin patriarch's activity has inevitably led to the creation for him of a special privileged status, which in cases where it is necessary prevents to some degree [our] ability to treat him as a simple seditious bishop.[174]

Stolypin traced the roots of what he viewed as misguided tsarist policies toward Armenians to the *polozhenie* of 1836. The codification of the Armenian Church's rights and obligations vis-à-vis Russian domestic and foreign policy had "artificially restored Ejmiatsin as the spiritual and political center of the Armenian people." As the main official tasked with hunting the sources of subversive currents then gestating in Russia, Stolypin believed that those concessions had "silently recognized the catholicate's ability to unite around it various Armenian parties of local and foreign origin and thereby facilitated the penetration of socialist ideas alien to the Armenian people."[175] The prime minister warned that Eastern Armenians' flirtation with foreign and domestic revolutionaries would end only once the catholicos was "deprived of his universal significance and brought within strictly defined boundaries of law."[176] The Russian ambassador in Constantinople, Ivan Zinov'ev, backed Stolypin's agenda.[177]

The viceroy fired back that he "most categorically" protested Stolypin's proposal.[178] He tied the new scheme to Golitsyn's "aimless measures" and stressed that only recently had Armenian agitation at the high commissioner's repressive policies subsided. Vorontsov-Dashkov saw in Stolypin's agenda echoes of the outdated and, in his view, discredited imperial methods that had elicited so much resistance from Caucasus natives. With just a couple of years of relative rapprochement between Armenians and the tsarist state, he feared that a new assault on their faith would "create in them again enemies of the Russian government by uniting them against it on the basis of national or religious insults."[179] Not only would offending their ecclesiastical leader "agitate all Armenians in general," but also the government simply had no way of enforcing such a directive. Vorontsov-Dashkov moreover cautioned that the natural consequence of Ejmiatsin's demotion would be the elevation of the Constantinople Armenian patriarchate, a development that in no scenario benefited Russia's foreign policy interests.

The viceroy's arguments were impassioned: "I regard our legislation on the Armenian-Gregorian Church . . . to be imbued with such governmental wisdom, aimed at protecting Russian interests in the Transcaucasus and the Near East through Armenians, that all goals unrealized by it I am inclined to explain by the measures that were subsequently taken to restrain the rights granted to the Armenian clergy by the [*polozhenie* of 1836], which served only as spokes in the wheels of the Russian government, precluding the realization of expected successes."[180] Vorontsov-Dashkov became a bulwark against the return of the recently abandoned Russification tactics. "Time has demonstrated," he believed, that the government's interference in "minor" Armenian issues, "instead of giving us, through the catholicos, influence over

Turkish Armenians, has alienated the Armenians of Russia from us, pushing even their more conservative elements toward revolution."[181]

In addition to distinct impressions of previous Russian strategies, their results, and divergent visions for future policies, a key source of the conflict arose from Russian disagreements over the nature of the catholicos's "universal significance." As Vorontsov-Dashkov only hinted, the real effects of the state's promulgation of new laws regarding the Armenian Church were far from certain because in that volatile climate the government could hardly enforce such regulations without sparking a new, perhaps bloodier, showdown. There is no evidence that Stolypin—above all concerned with "pacifying" the broadly agitated tsarist society—advocated the use of force to modify the Armenian Church's position. If the Ejmiatsin catholicos indeed enjoyed "universal significance," then nothing guaranteed that a new Russian legislation would or could hamper it, especially in light of Stolypin's and Golitsyn's repeated attestations that former efforts failed to amplify Ejmiatsin's clout in the Ottoman Empire.

The viceroy found a strong ally in Foreign Minister Aleksandr Izvolskii (1906–10).[182] Lambasted by rightist colleagues for what they charged was his fixation on Russia's image abroad,[183] Izvolskii, like Vorontsov-Dashkov, tended to look at the big picture. He struck at the heart of the matter by emphasizing that the catholicos's "universal significance" rested less on the policies of any government than on the canonical teachings of the Armenian faith and that it remained fortified by the consciousness of the Armenian people.[184] Izvolskii asserted that the Russian state had less influence on Ejmiatsin's transimperial stature than Stolypin believed, because Armenian theological doctrine underpinned the notion that the leader of the Armenian Church enjoyed spiritual and, by inevitable extension, political authority across state borders.

Vorontsov-Dashkov and Izvolskii saw a fact that was lost on Stolypin and Golitsyn. Ejmiatsin held the diaspora together, rather than advocating for an independent Armenia. The ecclesiastical leadership desperately promoted Ejmiatsin as the Vatican of the Armenian nation, not the Rome of an Armenian state. Various tsarist officials (mis)interpreted the ambitions of the Armenian clergy differently, seeing, alternatively, dangers or benefits from the catholicoi's transimperial aspirations.

The foreign minister challenged the prime minister's historical portrayal of Russia's efforts to expand Ejmiatsin's influence on Western Armenians. He argued that every tsarist action elicited a reciprocal Ottoman reaction meant to counteract Russia's efforts. Pointing to the Armenian National Constitution of 1863, Izvolskii posited that, particularly after the Crimean War, Constantinople issued its own privileges to clerical and lay Western Armenian communities to secure their loyalty to the Sublime Porte.[185] Moreover, the expansion of Ejmiatsin's authority naturally clashed with the self-interests of the Constantinople patriarchate, creating a rivalry that gestated outside the interference of imperial overlords. Izvolskii's point was that neither Russian strategies nor the actions of successive Ejmiatsin catholicoi alone could be blamed for the admittedly disappointing endeavor to project Russian influence on Ottoman Armenians. Using the same terminology but antithetical reasoning as Interior Minister Sipiagin in 1900, Foreign Minister Izvolskii stressed that at stake was the government's "prestige" in the eyes of the Armenian diaspora. The inviolability of the *polozhenie* of 1836 had to be maintained in order to safeguard the government's hard-fought but fragile status among Armenians. That law, he argued, "constitutes a famous political program; if it has not been achieved, or even in certain parts is not achievable without a radical change of the political situation, then this by no means suggests that this political program should be abandoned."[186]

Moving beyond the immediate question of Ejmiatsin's status, Izvolskii rejected Stolypin's wholesale portrayal of Armenians as seditious. The foreign minister cited the conclusions of the chief of the General Staff, who two months earlier had reported in no uncertain terms, "The Armenians are the only part of the Caucasus population on whose unconditional loyalty we can count."[187] Izvolskii's conclusion was unequivocal: Stolypin's proposal would be a "direct violation of Russian state interests."[188] After nearly a year of sharp debates among tsarist statesmen, in October 1908 the Council of Ministers ruled that decisive policy changes could be implemented only with the coordination of a new catholicos, rather than during an interregnum.[189] Only through dialogue with the ecclesiastical leader of Armenians could the government settle persistent controversies over the catholicos's compliance with tsarist laws, his authority to evade the "legal" demands of Russian administrators, his relationship with the Ejmiatsin Synod, his fluency in Russian, and other issues.[190]

The Old Regime backed off its pursuit of Armenian clergy and resumed the hunt for Dashnaks and Hnchaks.[191] Spurred on by the prime minister, the authorities arrested hundreds of suspected Armenian revolutionaries between 1908 and 1910, but later acquitted most of them.[192] Divergent strategies continued to sow animosity between Stolypin and Vorontsov-Dashkov. The prime minister viewed the Dashnaks as the main threat to the stability of the South Caucasus and pushed for their decisive defeat. The viceroy argued that the recent reconciliation between the state and the Armenian Church had eroded the base of the Dashnaks' social and economic support and that the government would eradicate them completely by securing the full favor of Armenian society. When Stolypin's heavy-handed approach prevailed, some diehard Armenian militants fled to Persia and took part in the Iranian Constitutional Revolution.[193] By 1911, according to one historian, "Stolypin was pleased that one of the strongest organizations [the Dashnaktsutiun] in a troubled region was added to the casualty list in his successful drive against the revolutionary movement," while the Hnchaks "lost their organization in the Caucasus and were not considered a threat by the tsarist administration."[194]

After a Socialist Revolutionary killed Stolypin in September 1911 and the First Balkan War (1912–13) erupted, the state's once-familiar Armenian policies returned to the foreground. Manoug Somakian has observed that "Russia energetically took the initiative in reviving the question of Turkish Armenia. It is curious that Russia, for whom in 1895 the question of Armenian reforms had been utterly distasteful, should in late 1912 be the protagonist in resurrecting it."[195] Scrambling to capitalize on Ottoman frailty, Russia reverted to its historical portrayal of itself as the champion of the Armenian diaspora. From 1912 through the beginning of World War I, the tsarist Foreign Ministry insisted that eastern Anatolia "should remain under Ottoman sovereignty, but with the addition of international oversight to uphold the rights of Christians in the region."[196]

Still, Stolypin's successors continued to question the viceroy's handling of the Caucasus in general and his Armenian policies in particular. Interior Minister Aleksandr Makarov (1911–12) revived St. Petersburg's dissatisfaction with the legal status of the Armenian Church.[197] Four years after the above resolution of the Council of Ministers, in October 1912 Makarov voiced frustration that no progress had been made in tightening Russia's authority over the Armenian faith, and he pushed Vorontsov-Dashkov to resurrect the discussion. Perhaps aware of the viceroy's now clear reputation as a defender of Ejmiatsin's prerogatives, the interior minister claimed that even some layers of the Armenian population supported the modification of their church's status and traditions. Pinpointing the process of the catholicos's election, Makarov argued: "According to the acknowledgment of some segments of Armenian society, [the election process] has in general become outdated and requires a corresponding revision."[198]

Makarov's main grievance with the election, a vestige of Russian concerns from the early 1880s, stemmed from the uneven sway that Western and Eastern Armenians held in choosing the catholicos. Because there were more Western than Eastern Armenians, and also because Armenian dioceses in the two states were organized differently, the Ottoman Empire contained forty-seven Armenian eparchies, while Russia had just six. During voting, Western Armenian delegates outnumbered their Eastern Armenian compatriots ninety-four to twenty-seven.[199] "Under these conditions," complained the interior minister, "elections usually depend completely on the wishes of Turkish Armenians; Russian Armenians, despite the fact that Ejmiatsin exists within Russia and in a legally defined relationship with the Russian government, play a secondary role in the elections."[200] He sought the "equalization" of Western and Eastern Armenian votes, cryptically cautioning, "From the perspective of state interests, Turkish delegates are particularly inclined to bring undesirable foreign political tendencies to the election." Unlike Stolypin, Makarov had no illusions of introducing these changes without the participation of the Armenian Church. He asked Vorontsov-Dashkov to discuss the issue with new catholicos Kevork V (1911–30), assuming that Kevork would favor a proposal ostensibly aimed at the "fair maintenance of the rights of Russian Armenians."[201] But the viceroy had no interest in a new controversy over Ejmiatsin's status. Simply ignoring the Interior Ministry's multiple missives or responding with terse excuses, he stalled this matter through his retirement in 1915.[202] Why did Vorontsov-Dashkov emerge as the most vociferous advocate of Armenians in late imperial Russia?

Vorontsov-Dashkov was a student of the ethnocultural, political, and social currents that shaped and reshaped Russia's ties to the Caucasus in the second half of the nineteenth century, and he evinced a tendency to learn from his predecessors' mistakes. He understood quickly that an untenable power relationship between the tsarist administration in Tiflis and the nominal head of the Armenian nation in Ejmiatsin, aggravated by the authorities' fear of losing control over Armenians, had cursed Russia with its own "Armenian Question." With the return of St. Petersburg's direct rule over the Caucasus, coinciding with the rise of Armenian nationalism, the state implemented repressive measures and also adopted a more dismissive attitude toward the senior representatives of the Armenian nation. Vorontsov-Dashkov believed that tsarist agents, from bureaucrats in Tiflis to the Holy Synod in St. Petersburg, alienated the catholicos and his followers through their "lack of tact" and what can be described as orientalist arrogance of imperialists toward subjects they considered inferior.[203]

The veteran statesman saw nothing sui generis in the Armenian agitation. He reported plainly to Nicholas II in 1913: "Of course, there are revolutionary parties among Armenians, just as they exist within Russia, but to speak of the Armenian people's revolutionary nature is just as odd as to suspect the Russian people of lacking loyalty to their monarch."[204] Thoughtful and balanced, the viceroy neither absolved Armenian extremists of terrorism nor satisfied himself with a passive maintenance of the status quo, where the empire deepened its conflict with Armenians in response to the actions of a militant minority. Vorontsov-Dashkov dismissed the Armenian revolutionary parties of the Dashnaks and Hnchaks as isolated to the Ottoman Empire, as an inconsequential minority of tsarist subjects, or as fleeting outbursts of rightful indignation at Golitsyn's abuses. For several years, the viceroy repeated to the emperor the same conclusion: "There is no separatism among the Armenians of the Caucasus."

Vorontsov-Dashkov and a handful of like-minded statesmen, such as Foreign Minister Izvolskii, saw that the Armenian Church was the glue that held the diaspora together, rather than the oil that lubricated the gears of an independence movement. Ejmiatsin, the viceroy realized, struggled to maintain its prominence in Armenian cultural life, fighting off secular intellectualism and European political activism as conduits of collective identity. Vorontsov-Dashkov supported tsarist Armenians because he accurately believed that their majority remained devoted to the Russian Empire. "Any attempt to accuse the [entire] Armenian nationality of separatism," he argued, "crumbles against the real facts, which prove, to the contrary, the loyalty of Armenians to Russia." With a boldness that only experience and accomplishment accord, the viceroy wrote to the tsar, "The grandiose plans [for defeating] the Dashnaktsutiun party, which were supposed to prove the revolutionary nature of an entire people and which were planned in ill-informed St. Petersburg despite my presentations . . . ended with a poof" and the unimpressive conviction of just thirty Armenians from throughout the Caucasus.[205] The viceroy understood nationalism's challenge to empire, but also remained cognizant that in the South Caucasus, the majority of the outnumbered Christians—with the conspicuous exception of their extremist, revolutionary elements—recognized the lack of viable alternatives.

Vorontsov-Dashkov displayed this reasoning when defending Georgians, who faced fewer but equally dubious accusations of separatism. The statesman concluded, "Armenians and Georgians clearly and realistically understand that without Russia they will be consumed by Muslims."[206] What hope could less-quixotic Armenians and Georgians entertain of independent statehood at the intersection of three empires and adjacent to diverse, often predatory highlanders of the North Caucasus? While Vorontsov-Dashkov echoed the orientalist derisiveness of his predecessors by accusing anonymous Muslims of the Caucasus of "flashes of religious fanaticism," he declared that few symptoms of insurgency had appeared within the Muslim districts in his jurisdiction and that both pan-Islamism and pan-Turkism had fizzled as conduits of collective identity in the region.[207] The tsar's Muslim subjects in the Caucasus, claimed the viceroy, demonstrated a "dispassionate" reaction to the recent Balkan wars, where Muslim-Christian ethnoreligious violence dominated the narrative.[208]

But the Russian Empire, including the Caucasus, was not to evade the conflagration of total war that soon enveloped Europe.[209]

The entanglement of imperialism and nationalism, what Dominic Lieven terms "the key dilemma of modern empire," drew Russia into World War I and also led to the demise of tsarism.[210] Soon after the conflict's opening in August 1914, Europe's largest clash since the Napoleonic Wars reached the Caucasus. Determined to redress the losses it suffered in 1878, the Sublime Porte targeted Kars and Russia's Black Sea coast of the Caucasus.[211] Western Armenia emerged as a key arena for the battle between the two empires. The Young Turk government identified its Armenian subjects as disloyal and took steps to prevent internal sabotage.[212] Ottoman authorities placed under surveillance Western Armenian cultural and social elites, discharged all Armenian policemen, and allowed anti-Armenian pogroms to spread in Anatolia.[213] Nearby, in the tsar's realm, Eastern Armenians watched anxiously.

At the start of World War I, Catholicos Kevork saw both opportunity and peril. Decades of abuses of Western Armenians, condoned or carried out by Ottoman authorities, left no doubt for the Armenian ecclesiastical leadership in 1914 that the nation faced a moment of unprecedented danger but also chance. Despite the hurdles of the recent era, the Russian state remained the main hope of Eastern Armenians for liberating their brethren across the border. In November 1914, in a remarkable premonition of the approaching calamity, Kevork warned Vorontsov-Dashkov: "There is no doubt that the horrors that have begun will in the near future entail innumerable and untold devastations for the long-suffering Armenian people."[214] The prelate predicted the terror that awaited Western Armenians from Ottoman authorities, state forces, and irregular militias.[215] At the same time, the catholicos expressed hope that "this war will finally resolve the Eastern Question and settle the centuries-long torment of the Armenians." To this end, he stressed Eastern Armenians' dedication to the tsarist war effort and urged Russia to liberate Western Armenia.[216]

Kevork's petition came at a time of deep divisions between Eastern and Western Armenians and also within the besieged Western Armenian community.[217] Despite the early signs of ethnic violence directed at them in Anatolia, by and large Ottoman Armenians remained ambivalent about whether their security was guaranteed by supporting the tsar or propping up the sultan.[218] Dashnaks resisted the calls of Eastern Armenians to ally with Russia and also dismissed the French prime minister's request to "help the Entente." One Dashnak leader rejected the portrayal of Russia as the savior of Armenians, accusing tsarist imperialists of having "set out to conquer the Armenians' lands." "Their hearts will not grieve if Armenian blood once again flows abundantly here and there," he warned.[219] Peter Holquist is clear about the role of the sultan's Armenian civilians: "Most Ottoman Armenians, it must be stressed, did not take part in either Armenian revolutionary formations or join the small number of Russian-sponsored Armenian military formations."[220] Nevertheless, according to Ronald G. Suny, "To those who saw the Armenians as traitors it did not matter that far more Ottoman Armenians joined the Ottoman army and fought against Russia until they were disarmed and sent to serve in labor battalions."[221]

At this juncture Catholicos Kevork, claiming to speak for all Eastern Armenians, called on Russia to annex Western Armenia and then to grant it "autonomy."[222] He promised Vorontsov-Dashkov that the tsar's Armenians would assist their patron empire in this mission, contending, "After patriotic statements, the Armenians are moving from words to deeds, rising as one to defend Russia's interests [and] to help the valiant Russian troops, sparing neither their lives nor resources."[223] Kevork declared with pomp that by wresting Western Armenia from Constantinople, St. Petersburg would complete "its historical mission of liberating the Christian nations that for centuries have languished under the Turkish yoke."[224] To this end, he asked the viceroy to publicize Ejmiatsin's call to arms among Western Armenians "from the name of the emperor," promising them tsarist protection and autonomy in return for cooperation.

Revealing the diplomatic touch that earned him admirers and detractors, Vorontsov-Dashkov judged Kevork's proposal generally acceptable, but

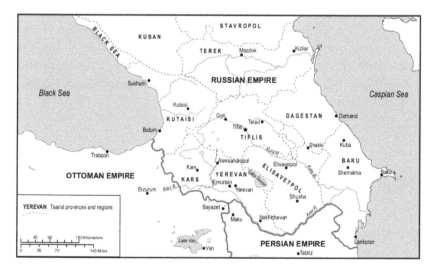

MAP 3. The Caucasus in 1914.

rejected its more specific aims.[225] He consulted the Foreign Ministry about the catholicos's request while making clear that Kevork's identification of particular boundaries for the proposed autonomous Armenia could not be settled without the participation of Russia's wartime allies. In a certain sense, the Foreign Ministry's response in November 1914 reflected the history of Russo-Armenian encounters. "The fate of the Turkish Armenian people is so closely linked to our victories," wrote the tsar's diplomats pragmatically, "that it has no choice, and it naturally must seek by all means our ultimate victory, which will be significantly easier for us with the active cooperation of the local population."[226] The success or failure of Russia's new imperial venture, in this rationale, determined the future of Ottoman Armenians. In a tragically ironic twist of history, in December 1914, just four months before the start of the Armenian Genocide, Nicholas II replied to Kevork: "Tell your flock, Holy Father, that a most brilliant future awaits the Armenians."[227]

Rather than seeking territorial seizure, the Russian government formally maintained its demand for the implementation of the long-promised reforms in Western Armenia.[228] At that chaotic moment, it possessed neither palpable incentives nor the immense resources that Kevork's scheme required. St. Petersburg felt that Ejmiatsin's plan served only Armenian interests, seeking to cement at the start of the war Russia's obligations toward Ottoman Armenians. Diplomatic officials also feared that Kevork's proclamation could alienate the Muslim residents of Anatolia, especially Kurds, who had already allied with Russia, as well as the Muslims of the Caucasus. Unconcerned by the fact that the majority of Western Armenians, led by a fiery Dashnak core, declined to align itself openly with tsarist interests, Russia remained confident of Ottoman Armenians' general favor, but concluded that Kevork's announcement could be issued only if a similar declaration was made to Kurds, which was unfeasible.[229] In the end, Armenians remained too small a factor for the Romanov Empire to adjust its terminal course. The Armenian Question received no Russian answer.

Conclusion

At times fumbling for effective strategies and at other times maneuvering dexterously, the tsars' administrators, through trial and error, retained Armenians as a loyal service minority. Armenians cooperated with tsarist aims through much of the nineteenth century because Russia represented a real and idealized guarantor of Armenian security and prosperity. Whether subjects of the sultan and the shah or inhabitants of Russian cities far from the Caucasus, Armenians worked with, and within, the Romanov system to attain a better life. At times they found that they had misplaced their dreams and zealous tsarist agents occasionally restrained Armenian material and spiritual culture. Overall, the Russian Empire's Armenian project yielded more triumphs than defeats, but the results were as mixed as the mechanisms of tsarist imperialism.

If the Russo-Armenian encounter appears permeated with inconsistencies and contradictions, then that reflects primarily the nature of imperial rule itself. This deduction emerges from ground now well tilled by the practitioners of "new imperial history," who have effectively shattered notions of systematized central imperial policies and precise metropole-periphery relationships.[1] These efforts have helped us to "demythologize the vision of empire as a rationally organized and smoothly governed space."[2] Valerie A. Kivelson and Ronald G. Suny agree that the Russian Empire "was a polity built deliberately on jury-rigged particularism, on special arrangements, differentiated rules, demands, and concessions, geared to hold a kaleidoscopic miscellany together, loosely, under the tsarist double-headed eagle."[3] Indubitably, imperial governance was messy, unequal, and full of possibilities and pitfalls.

Gradations of geopolitical "success" depend on our understandings of imperial aims. If the architects of the empire sought to craft not just loyal but also docile subjects out of minorities, then Russia's engagement with Armenians ended in failure after a promising start. Eight decades of fruitful dialogue gave way to more than three decades of distrust and nationalist tension. However, if the primary goal of Russian imperialism was to absorb new groups into the empire and through them to increase the economic and sociopolitical vitality of government and periphery, then Russia's recruitment of Armenians delivered tangible benefits to both sides.

Through partnership with such subject groups as Armenians, the Romanov Empire could link foreign policy goals to domestic growth. Ekaterina Pravilova has traced how, throughout the nineteenth century, St. Petersburg prioritized its external expansion and influence at the expense of its internal development.[4] But Russia gained in the Armenian diaspora a versatile and willing tool for working toward both of these objectives. It was an alliance grounded in religious kinship and sociopolitical realities. Except for fleeting but painful periods of reactionary vigilance, when the state apparatus perceived Armenians as inveterately disloyal, the tsars' inclusion of Armenians in the imperial project was decidedly symbiotic.

Administrators conceptualized the South Caucasus as a space distinct from Russia proper in almost every way, but welcomed some of its natives, such as Armenians, into the political project. Thus, in this episode of tsarist imperialism, statesmen relaxed their orientalist distancing between Russians and non-Russians, strategically integrating natives into the imperial civic and political fabric. Well past the defeat of the North Caucasus insurgency in the 1860s, tsarist agents kept a wary eye on the Muslims of the North Caucasus, as well as their Ottoman and Persian rivals, leading the majority of statesmen to pursue alliances with (mainly Christian) native allies in the South Caucasus. From Tsitsianov to Vorontsov-Dashkov, these architects of empire understood, and often had to convince their colleagues, that indigenous cooperation was (a) key to maintaining Russia's regional hegemony in the Caucasus. Traditional dichotomies of power and resistance inevitably overlook the important cases of indigenous agency in imperial projects. Indeed, recent research has only dented the prevailing "crisis paradigm" of Russian imperial history, which continues to play an outsize role in narratives of the Romanovs' complex political and cultural ties with non-Russian subject groups.

To speak of the tsars' imperial project is to speak of a variable dialogue that drew as much direction from the agency of non-Russian subjects as from any state-drawn blueprints. No major ethnonational group, especially those with populations over one million, experienced the period 1801–1914 without dramatic oscillations of Russian policies that, at first blush, seem arbitrary or experimental. To rule approximately 130 nationalities, St. Petersburg had to expand the categories of *russkie* and *rossiiane*, at times fretting over, and at other times capitalizing on, its diversity. Taking a comparative glance at the Armenian case reveals the intertwined roles of several key themes in the Russian Empire's nationalities policies, such as religion, assimilation, and transimperial links.

Unlike many tsarist minorities, including certain Christians, Slavs, and Muslims, Eastern Armenians experienced official scrutiny inconsistently. A combination of factors, which in various contexts outshone one another, secured for Armenians a distinct position as being politically desirable. These circumstances included the familiarity of their faith, perceived degree of social, political, or cultural integration, and the actual or potential contributions to the state's priorities. Keeping in mind that imperial differences are neither quantitative nor qualitative, we can conclude that the Russo-Armenian encounter was unique in some ways, but not so in others.

One of the key features of the Armenian experience—its diasporic distribution between the Russian, Ottoman, and Persian Empires—stands out as a distinctive factor because few, if any, other tsarist minorities had such extensive connections to conationals residing, and suffering, in other states. Moreover, the peculiar nature of this diaspora factored into Russia's political equations. On the one hand, the tsar's Armenians embraced as their brethren large numbers of foreign citizens or subjects; on the other hand, no country courted Eastern Armenians or offered them a better life than could imperial Russia.

Aspects of the Armenian diaspora rendered its case atypical, but the Romanovs' desire to harness the transregional and transimperial bonds of their minorities was rather routine. In the first half of the 1800s, St. Petersburg's geopolitical calculations encouraged the connections of Volga-Ural Muslims to coreligionist communities in Transoxiana, the Kazakh steppe, Crimea, and even Ottoman borderlands.[5] However, while the Crimean War catalyzed the government's fears "about 'trustworthiness' and 'alienation' of Muslims in the Crimea and Volga regions," Armenian-heritage officers led Russian troops, and Viceroy Vorontsov proclaimed the "unquestionable loyalty and even affection" toward Russia of all Armenians.[6] As far away from Crimean battlefields as the Volga-Ural region, rumors swirled that the Orenburg mufti had secretly ordered the local mullahs to pray for the sultan's victory.[7] Not even statesmen most hostile to Ejmiatsin ever accused the catholicoi of entreating God to aid Russia's enemies.

In the Crimean clash, as well as other conflicts occasionally labeled "holy wars" by Russians and their adversaries, the lines between religious identity and political resistance often meandered in the rushed calculations of officials. In the North Caucasus in the 1860s, for example, "Circassians were targeted for expulsion less because they were Muslims than because they were perceived to be inveterately hostile to tsarist rule."[8] By contrast, Armenians benefited from the dual advantages of Christianity and political partnership. If the suspicions of some officials about a tryst between Armenian religion and nationalism echoed analogous cases from other territories and periods, then the Russian emperors never censured the catholicoi directly. After the Polish rebellion of 1863, for example, Tsar Alexander II scolded Pope Pius IX: "This union of the servitors of religion with the instigators of disorders, a threat to society, is among the most scandalous facts of our time."[9]

Russia's expansion into Central Asia produced the same, and different, questions that imbued the Russo-Armenian conversation. As Romanov borders crept into the steppe in the mid-nineteenth century, imperial agents relied on the knowledge of Kazakh intermediaries to understand their new domains, a practice they had honed decades earlier in the South Caucasus.[10] This "uneven dialogue" between Russian officials and Kazakh locals faltered, but did not fail, under Alexander III. Yet, if this aspect of the Russo-Kazakh encounter reminds us of the early stages of the Russo-Armenian partnership, then the sharp contrasts of religion and settler colonialism in Central Asia are more obvious. By the late 1880s, some Kazakh intellectuals insisted that Kazakhs resisted Christianity because they associated that faith with surly Russian officers and ravenous Slavic colonists.[11] Indeed, from the tsarist perspective, the social transformations of the Great Reforms amplified the empire's "Muslim Question," which scrutinized Muslim subjects' real and alleged reluctance to assimilate into "Russian" society.[12] By the last quarter of the century, the once-unmolested Volga-Ural Muslims, like many of their coreligionists, as well as Armenians, experienced direct Russian interference in their spiritual and material lives.

Still, some zealous tsarist functionaries never abandoned dreams of "civilizing" Russia's Muslims by making them "Russian and Orthodox."[13] Armenians almost never starred in this fantasy, thanks to their Christianity and perceived integration. If official attitudes toward Tatars of the Kazan region corresponded to the Russian perceptions of their degree of assimilation—with less integration producing more Russifying measures—then Armenians endured such hardship much less systematically.[14] To be sure, the state's engagements with the varied subjects who practiced Islam were as multifaceted as its dialogues with the agents and the adherents of the Armenian Church. When Konstantin Kaufman, the first governor-general of Turkestan, sought to eradicate the "fanatical mood" of the Muslims in his jurisdiction by "denying Muslim leaders any role in the public life of the region," he incongruously emerged as a defender of the Muslim private sphere and also a champion of unhindered pilgrimage to Mecca.[15] These ostensibly conflicting measures become clearer when we recall Alexei Miller's proposition that St. Petersburg's nationalities policies often prioritized political stability and imperial vitality over acculturation, especially in the first half of the nineteenth century.[16]

Muslims were not the only, or even the primary, targets of Russian rightists, Pan-Slavists, and Orthodox elites, but they had fewer Russian allies than the Armenians because "knowledge of the Russian language and membership in the Orthodox Church became more urgent priorities in an age when states reorganized along national lines appeared to define the future of Europe."[17] Even social and cultural assimilation, however, rarely trumped religious identity as a marker of sociopolitical belonging. If privileged Armenians and Jews engaged in "selective integration," which facilitated their social mobility, then the broader Jewish community's legally prescribed restriction to the Pale of Settlement and its exposure to outbursts of wholesale violence easily distinguish the Jewish experience from the Armenian one.[18] Furthermore, we have seen from the Georgian example that even intimate religious kinship and romanticized aristocratic fraternity could be insufficient facilitators of political symbiosis.

In the late imperial era, the entwined questions of transimperial connections and foreign patrons vis-à-vis Armenians and other groups acquired new weight. Even when St. Petersburg shelved its schemes for instrumentalizing the Armenian diaspora for its geopolitical goals, few officials saw a need to cut off Eastern Armenians from outside entities. Notwithstanding the attestations of some Dashnak and Hnchak activists, it was difficult to envisage an Armenian future outside the Russian aegis. Tsarist authorities recognized that no European power vied with them for the patronage of the Armenians.

By contrast, elsewhere the state feared the bonds between its non-Russian subjects and foreign capitals or churches, a concern traditionally manifested by the adherence of the Polish gentry to the Vatican. Such anxieties became most acute by the early 1880s, when Russian agents and social elites imagined "a transregional Islamic conspiracy organized by the Ottoman sultan and caliph in order to unite world Muslims under caliphal authority."[19] To the bureaucrats tasked with maintaining tranquility and security, all interstate links were no more equal than the nations within the empire: some peoples' connections to the outside world were a liability to be curtailed, rather than an advantage to be cultivated.

Accommodation, not assimilation, guided the tsarist approach toward Armenians.[20] Russian chauvinism patronized Armenians as *aziatsy*, but they remained familiar, "our" Asiatics. Religious kinship between Oriental Orthodox Armenians and Eastern Orthodox Russians was an enduring cultural link that undergirded the political bond between these imperial actors, even when Armenian clerics and Russian bureaucrats required translators at their meetings. Many statesmen branded Armenians as distinctly non-European and some agents denigrated Armenian villagers as "semi-wild," but the government saw few incentives for their coerced assimilation or total subjugation. Instead, St. Petersburg unfurled variedly successful efforts to use Armenians in its governance of the Caucasus and to advance its foreign policies.

While the autocracy pursued a quintessential "civilizing mission" in the Far East and displayed prejudice toward the long-absorbed Jews,[21] it generally tolerated displays of Armenian cultural identity because more important priorities vis-à-vis Armenians informed its agenda. Even during the reactionary era of Tsar Nicholas I, the government granted Ejmiatsin exclusive powers, such as the conversion of non-Orthodox Christians into the Armenian faith. The combination of religious affiliation and parallel political interests explains this circumstance.

In the twilight of the Romanov dynasty, when empire-wide social "pacification" became the mantra of beleaguered officials, a new Russian conception of Armenians emerged. Reactionaries agonized over what they painted as Russia's own "Armenian Question," carelessly associating the terrorism of a few with the populism of the many in a misguided effort to collate the revolutionary agitations of the divided Armenian diaspora. But as the penultimate viceroy of the Caucasus lectured the emperor, to speak of an "Armenian Question" in Russia was to project the internal circumstances of the Ottoman Empire into Russia. Undeniably, small elements of Eastern Armenian society, conspicuous for their polemical nationalism and bloody exploits, vexed tsarist as well as Ottoman statesmen; however, it is hardly possible to trace the contours of an "Armenian Question" in Russia that is more than a brief flash in the *longue durée* of modern Russo-Armenian ties. To apply that term to the tsarist empire's domestic political tensions is both to ignore the specific context of a key but fleeting era in Russia and to misunderstand its implications for Ottoman history. The idea that an "Armenian Question" bedeviled successive Russian imperial administrators does not withstand the test of a broad examination.

The government sought at most what Theodore Weeks terms the "civic Russification" of Armenians, but more consequential than debating the state's uneven efforts to Russify Armenians is the point that St. Petersburg had little reason to pursue the "cultural," "administrative," or "unplanned" variations of Russification that Edward C. Thaden has identified.[22] Until the late nineteenth century, Russia hoped to derive geopolitical benefits from its patronage of the Armenian diaspora, obviating a need for, or potential benefits of, active or even passive acculturation measures toward Armenians. Reactionary agents grumbled that the catholicoi did not speak Russian and that Armenian clergy did not teach it in parish schools, ostensibly demonstrating their resistance to integration, but most statesmen dismissed such concerns because they prioritized administrative efficacy over cultural assimilation. The tsarist foci of stability and external influence rendered comprehensive attempts at altering Armenian cultural identity inherently risky, something the government conceded after the bloody but short experiment with expropriating the holdings of the Armenian Church in 1903.

Politically, Russia's Armenians became fully Russified; that is, their majority embraced a collective identity as tsarist subjects and residents of the Russian Empire. Culturally, however, they maintained the hallmarks of their ethnoreligious identity and faced only episodic and ultimately futile attempts at the state-driven cultural Russification that extreme Russian rightists advocated. In the minds of late-imperial Russian tsars and their ministers, it was the government's imperative to Russify certain national groups to counteract the influence of external forces on them, such as the efforts to "de-Polonize" the Belarusians, Lithuanians, and Ukrainians. Yet because "the Russian state never had the resources to launch a thorough-going program of cultural russification,"[23] it had to select its targets carefully. Unlike the circumstances surrounding the non-Russians of the western provinces, neither foreign patrons nor Armenian nationalists could guarantee for Eastern Armenians a better political situation.

Thus, even after the crisis of 1903, the tsar's Armenians continued to work within the Russian political system that had recently turned its back on them, with the goal of securing the liberation of Western Armenians from Ottoman rule. Because St. Petersburg had few geopolitical incentives and perhaps fewer resources to attain this goal, it ignored these appeals, leaving scores of Armenians to perish in the first genocide of the twentieth century. Yet this fact must not detract from the century of political symbiosis between Armenians and the Russian Empire.

Armenians may have been a pawn in an imperial game, but through adroit maneuvering Eastern Armenians survived the brutal age of imperialism at the threshold of three expansionist empires, emerging as an independent state in 1991. Over the course of the nineteenth century, Eastern Armenians sought out Russia's security, profited from domestic and foreign trade beyond the Caucasus, gained access to European education and culture, and, despite some Russian resistance, maintained the inviolable features of their national culture, such as religion, which often mitigated the lack of political independence. In sharp contrast to the long hardship of Western Armenians, Eastern Armenians found the better life that their ancestors had sought. Thus, the pawn remained standing after the checkmate.

NOTES

Introduction

1. The terms *rossiiane* (Russian subjects) and *russkie* (ethnic Russians) became more common later in the nineteenth century. These terms distinguish political and ethnic categories of belonging. *Russkie* denotes members of the Russian nation, while *rossiiane* indicates inhabitants of the Russian state, irrespective of their ethnic or national identity. Eric Lohr examines these themes in *Russian Citizenship: From Empire to Soviet Union* (Cambridge, MA: Harvard University Press, 2012).

2. Sebouh David Aslanian, *From the Indian Ocean to the Mediterranean: The Global Trade Networks of Armenian Merchants from New Julfa* (Berkeley: University of California Press, 2014), 82.

3. Evgenii V. Anisimov, *The Reforms of Peter the Great: Progress through Coercion in Russia*, trans. John T. Alexander (Armonk, NY: M. E. Sharpe, 1993), 260.

4. Terry Martin shows that the early architects of Soviet nationalities policies admitted Armenians into an exclusive club: "Only the Russians, Ukrainians, Georgians, Armenians, Jews, and Germans were deemed 'advanced' and were grouped together as western nationalities." Terry Martin, *The Affirmative Action Empire: Nations and Nationalism in the Soviet Union, 1923–1939* (Ithaca, NY: Cornell University Press, 2001), 23.

5. For Armenians as a diaspora, see Khachig Tölölyan, "Elites and Institutions in the Armenian Transnation," *Diaspora: A Journal of Transnational Studies* 9, no. 1 (2000): 107–35, especially 116–24.

6. Vazgen Voskanian, "Drevniaia Rus' i Armeniia," *Lraber hasarakakan gitowt'yownneri*, no. 1 (1983): 51–60. Voskanian cites this collection: *Istoricheskie sviazi i druzhba ukrainskogo i armianskogo narodov*, 3 vols. (Yerevan: Izdatel'stvo Akademii nauk Armianskoi SSR, 1961; Kiev: Naukova dumka, 1965; Yerevan: Izdatel'stvo Akademii nauk Armianskoi SSR, 1971).

7. I borrow the concept of "threads of empire" from Charles Steinwedel, *Threads of Empire: Loyalty and Tsarist Authority in Bashkiria, 1552–1917* (Bloomington: Indiana University Press, 2016).

8. Robert Geraci has rightly lamented that "in the many works published on the imperial dimension of Russian history during the past decade, it is often the mechanical or 'nuts and bolts' aspects of the empire's administration that are least discussed." Robert Geraci, "On 'Colonial' Forms and Functions," *Slavic Review* 69, no. 1 (2010): 180.

9. Nancy Shields Kollmann, *The Russian Empire, 1450–1801* (New York: Oxford University Press, 2017), 3.

10. One example of research on vast, diverse minority groups within the tsarist empire that highlights the complexities of accommodation, differentiation, assimilation, and resistance is Mustafa Tuna, *Imperial Russia's Muslims: Islam, Empire, and European Modernity, 1788–1914* (Cambridge: Cambridge University Press, 2015).

11. Marina Mogilner, "New Imperial History: Post-Soviet Historiography in Search of a New Paradigm for the History of Empire and Nationalism," *Revue d'études comparatives Est-Ouest* 45, no. 2 (2014): 35.

12. For examples of Russian cooperation with non-Russian national, and even nationalist, movements against third parties, see Faith Hillis, "Ukrainophile Activism and Imperial Governance in Russia's Southwestern Borderlands," *Kritika* 13, no. 2 (2012): 301–26; Theodore Weeks, "Russification and Lithuanians, 1863–1905," *Slavic Review* 60, no. 1 (2001): 96–114. Cooperation between state officials and religious elites is key to Paul Werth, *The Tsar's Foreign Faiths: Toleration and the Fate of Religious Freedom in Imperial Russia* (New York: Oxford University Press, 2014).

13. Alexander Morrison, "Review Essay: Muslims and Modernity in the Russian Empire," *Slavonic and East European Review* 94, no. 4 (2016): 718.

14. For a broad overview, see Alexei Miller and Erik R. Scott, "Nation and Empire: Reflections in the Margins of Geoffrey Hosking's Book," *Kritika* 13, no. 2 (2012): 419–28. For imperial Russia's cloudy divisions between metropole and colony, see Willard Sunderland, "The 'Colonization Question': Visions of Colonization in Late Imperial Russia," *Jahrbücher für Geschichte Osteuropas* 48, no. 2 (2000): 210–32; Paul Werth, "From Resistance to Subversion: Imperial Power, Indigenous Opposition, and Their Entanglement," *Kritika* 1, no. 1 (2000): 21–43; and Alexander Morrison, "Metropole, Colony, and Imperial Citizenship in the Russian Empire," *Kritika* 13, no. 2 (2012): 327–64.

15. For another example of such a "national case study," see Alexei Miller, *The Ukrainian Question: The Russian Empire and Nationalism in the Nineteenth Century* (Budapest: Central European University Press, 2003).

16. Ann Laura Stoler and Carole McGranahan, "Introduction: Refiguring Imperial Terrains," in *Imperial Formations*, ed. Ann Laura Stoler, Carole McGranahan, and Peter C. Perdue (Santa Fe, NM: School for Advanced Research Press, 2007), 8.

17. Stoler and McGranahan, "Introduction: Refiguring Imperial Terrains," 9, 12.

18. Valerie A. Kivelson and Ronald G. Suny, *Russia's Empires* (New York: Oxford University Press, 2017), 133.

19. Among the practitioners of the "imperial cohesion" angle have been Dominic Lieven and Kimitaka Matsuzato. See Dominic Lieven, *Empire: The Russian Empire and Its Rivals* (New Haven, CT: Yale University Press, 2002); and Kimitaka Matsuzato, introduction to *Imperiology: From Empirical Knowledge to Discussing the Russian Empire*, ed. Kimitaka Matsuzato (Sapporo: Slavic Research Center, Hokkaido University, 2007), 12–13.

20. For example, see Robert Crews, *For Prophet and Tsar: Islam and Empire in Russia and Central Asia* (Cambridge, MA: Harvard University Press, 2009).

21. Steinwedel, *Threads of Empire*, 5.

22. Nicholas Breyfogle, "Enduring Imperium: Russia / Soviet Union / Eurasia as Multiethnic, Multiconfessional Space," *Ab Imperio*, no. 1 (2008): 100.

23. Onur Önol, *The Tsar's Armenians: A Minority in Late Imperial Russia* (London: I. B. Tauris, 2017). Önol's book examines the years 1903–14.

24. Z. T. Grigorian, *Prisoedinenie Vostochnoi Armenii k Rossii v nachale XIX veka* (Moscow: Izdatel'stvo sotsial'no-ekonomicheskoi literatury, 1959); G. M. Kazarian, ed.,

Prisoedinenie Vostochnoi Armenii k Rossii i ego istoricheskoe znachenie: Sbornik statei (Yerevan: Erevanskii gosudarstvennyi universitet, 1978).

25. S. A. Ter-Avakimova, *Armiano-russkie otnosheniia v period podgotovki persidskogo pokhoda* (Yerevan: Izdatel'stvo Akademii nauk Armianskoi SSR, 1980); *Druzhba naveki: Materialy prazdnovaniia 150-letiia vkhozhdeniia Armenii v sostav Rossii* (Yerevan: Hayastan, 1980); A. M. Pogosian, *Karsskaia oblast' v sostave Rossii* (Yerevan: Hayastan, 1983); M. G. Nersisian, ed., *Iz istorii vekovoi druzhby* (Yerevan: Izdatel'stvo Akademii nauk Armianskoi SSR, 1983).

26. B. P. Balaian, *Diplomaticheskaia istoriia russko-iranskikh voin i prisoedineniia Vostochnoi Armenii k Rossii* (Yerevan: Izdatel'stvo Akademii nauk Armianskoi SSR, 1988); V. G. Gukasian, *Konstantinopol'skie armiane i natsional'no-prosvetitel'skoe dvizhenie 30–60-kh godov XIX veka* (Yerevan: Izdatel'stvo Akademii nauk Armianskoi SSR, 1989); V. G. Tunian, *Vostochnaia Armeniia v sostave Rossii, 1828–1853 gg.* (Yerevan: Hayastan, 1989).

27. V. G. Tunian, *Echmiadzinskii vopros v politike Rossii, 1873–1903 gg.* (Yerevan: Erevanskii gosudarstvennyi universitet, 2002); B. T. Ovanesov and N. D. Sudavtsov, *Voenno-administrativnaia deiatel'nost' armian v Rossiiskoi imperii na Kavkaze* (Stavropol: Nairi, 2008); V. G. Tunian, *Politika samoderzhaviia Rossii v Zakavkaz'e XIX–nach. XX vv.*, 6 vols. (Yerevan: Chartaraget, 2006–2008, 2010); A. Zh. Oganesian, *Rossiia i armiane: Uroki istorii i realii* (Yerevan: Erevanskii gosudarstvennyi universitet, 2015).

28. Ronald G. Suny, *The Making of the Georgian Nation* (Bloomington: Indiana University Press, 1994).

29. Austin Jersild, *Orientalism and Empire: North Caucasus Mountain People and the Georgian Frontier, 1845–1917* (Montreal: McGill-Queen's University Press, 2002); Nicholas Breyfogle, *Heretics and Colonizers: Forging Russia's Empire in the South Caucasus* (Ithaca, NY: Cornell University Press, 2005); Michael Khodarkovsky, *Bitter Choices: Loyalty and Betrayal in the Russian Conquest of the North Caucasus* (Ithaca, NY: Cornell University Press, 2011).

30. The broadest synthetic overviews include Manuel Sarkisyanz, *A Modern History of Transcaucasian Armenia: Social, Cultural, and Political* (Leiden: Brill, 1975); and Razmik Panossian, *The Armenians: From Kings and Priests to Merchants and Commissars* (New York: Columbia University Press, 2006).

31. Two specialized English-language studies have uncovered much about the experiences of Eastern Armenians in the nineteenth century in the Persian and Russian political contexts: George Bournoutian, *Eastern Armenia in the Last Decades of Persian Rule, 1807–1828: A Political and Socioeconomic Study of the Khanate of Erevan on the Eve of the Russian Conquest* (Malibu, CA: Undena Publications, 1982); and Lisa Khachaturian, *Cultivating Nationhood in Imperial Russia: The Periodical Press and the Formation of a Modern Armenian Identity* (New Brunswick, NJ: Transaction, 2009).

32. See, for example, Richard Hovannisian, *The Republic of Armenia*, 4 vols. (Berkeley: University of California Press, 1971–96); and Hovannisian, *The Armenian Holocaust* (Cambridge, MA: Armenian Heritage Press, 1980). See also the volumes Hovannisian edited: *The Armenian People from Ancient to Modern Times*, 2 vols. (New York: St. Martin's Press, 2004) and *Remembrance and Denial: The Case of the Armenian Genocide* (Detroit: Wayne State University Press, 1998).

33. Ronald G. Suny, *Looking toward Ararat: Armenia in Modern History* (Bloomington: Indiana University Press, 1993). Because Suny wrote this book during the turmoil of the Soviet collapse, his fieldwork in relevant archives was limited.

34. I conducted research at the Russian State Historical Archive (RGIA, St. Petersburg), the Russian National Library (St. Petersburg), the State Archive of the Russian Federation (GARF, Moscow), the Russian State Military-Historical Archive (RGVIA, Moscow), the Central Historical Archive of Moscow (TsIAM), the Russian State Library (Moscow), the National Archives of Armenia (HAA, Yerevan), and the Library of Congress (Washington, DC).

35. Khachatur Abovyan, *Rany Armenii*, trans. Sergei Shervinskii (Yerevan: Sovetakan grokh, 1977), 102, http://armenianhouse.org/abovyan/wounds-of-armenia/2.html.

36. Khachatur Abovyan, quoted in Ronald G. Suny, "Eastern Armenians under Tsarist Rule," in *The Armenian People from Ancient to Modern Times*, ed. Richard Hovannisian (New York: St. Martin's Press, 2004), 2:118.

1. The Embrace of an Empire, 1801–1813

1. For broad overviews, see Hovannisian, *The Armenian People*; and Panossian, *The Armenians*.

2. George Vernadsky, *Russia at the Dawn of the Modern Age* (New Haven, CT: Yale University Press, 1959), 209.

3. Kollmann, *The Russian Empire, 1450–1801*, 193.

4. *Sobranie aktov, otnosiashchikhsia k obozreniiu istorii armianskogo naroda* (Moscow: Lazarevskii institut vostochnykh iazykov, 1833), vol. 1, 3–4. See also George Vernadsky, *The Tsardom of Moscow, 1547–1682* (New Haven, CT: Yale University Press, 1969), pt. 2, 658.

5. *Sobranie aktov*, vol. 2 (1838), 289.

6. *Sobranie aktov*, vol. 1 (1833), 7, 290.

7. V. B. Barkhudarian, "Armianskie kolonisty v Rossii i ikh rol' v armiano-russkikh otnosheniiakh," in *Iz istorii vekovoi druzhby*, ed. M. G. Nersisian (Yerevan: Izdatel'stvo Akademii nauk Armianskoi SSR, 1983), 124–25.

8. *Sobranie aktov*, vol. 1 (1833), 27; Barkhudarian, "Armianskie kolonisty v Rossii," 126.

9. George Bournoutian, "Eastern Armenia from the Seventeenth Century to the Russian Annexation," in *The Armenian People from Ancient to Modern Times*, ed. Richard Hovannisian (New York: St. Martin's Press, 2004), 2:91.

10. Michael Khodarkovsky, *Russia's Steppe Frontier: The Making of a Colonial Empire, 1500–1800* (Bloomington: Indiana University Press, 2002), 218.

11. Basil Dmytryshyn, ed., *Imperial Russia: A Source Book, 1700–1917*, 2nd ed. (Orlando, FL: Harcourt, 1990), 109.

12. Muriel Atkin, *Russia and Iran, 1780–1828* (Minneapolis: University of Minnesota Press, 1980), 29; Yo'av Karny, *Highlanders: A Journey to the Caucasus in Quest of Memory* (New York: Macmillan, 2001), 382. Argutinskii-Dolgorukov died before being consecrated as catholicos.

13. For an analysis of Russia's heterodox subjects and their political role in the Russian Empire, see Werth, *The Tsar's Foreign Faiths*.

14. Paul Werth, "One Eastern Church or Two? Armenians, Orthodoxy, and Ecclesiastical Union in Nineteenth-Century Russia," *Journal of Orthodox Christian Studies* 1, no. 2 (2018): 193–94.

15. Thomas de Waal, *The Caucasus: An Introduction* (New York: Oxford University Press, 2010), 21.

16. De Waal, *The Caucasus*, 21.

17. Suny, *The Making of the Georgian Nation*, 38.

18. Charles King, *The Ghost of Freedom: A History of the Caucasus* (New York: Oxford University Press, 2008), 147.

19. Suny, *The Making of the Georgian Nation*, 77.

20. King, *The Ghost of Freedom*, 147–48. For the population of Tiflis throughout the nineteenth century, see Tunian, *Politika samoderzhaviia Rossii v Zakavkaz'e*, Vol. 6 (Yerevan: Chartaraget 2010), 5.

21. Quoted in Suny, *Looking toward Ararat*, 37.

22. Philip Paulucci, quoted in D. I. Ismail-Zade, *Naselenie gorodov Zakavkazskogo kraia v XIX–nachale XX v.: Istoriko-demograficheskii analiz* (Moscow: Nauka, 1991), 130.

23. Quoted in Suny, *Looking toward Ararat*, 38.

24. Suny, *The Making of the Georgian Nation*, 77.

25. Robert Ker Porter, *Travels in Georgia, Persia, Armenia, Ancient Babylonia, Etc. during the Years 1817, 1818, 1819, and 1820*, Vol. 1 (London: Longman, Hurst, Rees, Orme, and Brown, 1821), 133.

26. Suny, *Looking toward Ararat*, 38.

27. For some overviews, see Suny, *The Making of the Georgian Nation*, especially 63–64. See also King, *The Ghost of Freedom*; and de Waal, *The Caucasus*.

28. Quoted in King, *The Ghost of Freedom*, 28.

29. *Akty, sobrannye Kavkazskoiu arkheograficheskoiu kommissieiu: Arkhiv Glavnago upravleniia namestnika kavkazskago* (hereafter *AKAK*) (Tiflis: Glavnoe upravlenie namestnika kavkazskago, 1866), vol. 1, 93–96.

30. *AKAK*, vol. 1 (1866), 94–95 and 635–36.

31. *AKAK*, vol. 1 (1866), 95.

32. *AKAK*, vol. 1 (1866), 636.

33. George Bournoutian, ed., *Russia and the Armenians of Transcaucasia, 1797–1889: A Documentary Record* (Costa Mesa, CA: Mazda, 1998), 33.

34. Bournoutian, *Russia and the Armenians of Transcaucasia*, 43.

35. *AKAK*, vol. 1 (1866), 99.

36. Rossiiskii gosudarstvennyi voenno-istoricheskii arkhiv (Russian State Military-Historical Archive, RGVIA), f. 482, op. 1, d. 6, l. 2.

37. *AKAK*, vol. 1 (1866), 144–47.

38. *AKAK*, vol. 1 (1866), 168.

39. *AKAK*, vol. 1 (1866), 177–78.

40. *AKAK*, vol. 1 (1866), 179.

41. *AKAK*, vol. 1 (1866), 433.

42. Suny, *The Making of the Georgian Nation*, 59.

43. See Juan Cole, *Napoleon's Egypt: Invading the Middle East* (New York: Palgrave Macmillan, 2007). French imperial ambitions pushed Paul in 1798 to form a shaky alliance with the Porte against Napoleon.

44. By north of the Kura Alexander probably referred to the still-unconquered North Caucasus, and by north of the Arax he targeted Persian-held Eastern Armenia. See de Waal, *The Caucasus*, 39.

45. *AKAK*, vol. 2 (1868), iii and 3.

46. Alexander complained about Knorring's excessive caution and indecision. See *AKAK*, vol. 2 (1868), 3.

47. Throughout 1801 and 1802, secret reports reached St. Petersburg about Kovalenskii's supercilious behavior vis-à-vis the Georgians. See *AKAK*, vol. 2 (1868), 5–6.

48. *AKAK*, vol. 2 (1868), 20.

49. David Marshall Lang, *A Modern History of Soviet Georgia* (New York: Grove Press, 1962), 46–47. See also King, *The Ghost of Freedom*, 29.

50. *AKAK*, vol. 1 (1866), 184.

51. Walter Richmond, *The Northwest Caucasus: Past, Present, Future* (New York: Routledge, 2008), 82.

52. *AKAK*, vol. 2 (1868), 45.

53. *AKAK*, vol. 2 (1868), 45. Tsitsianov's solution to these issues was an expansion of Russian bureaucracy and judiciary in Georgia. See *AKAK*, vol. 2 (1868), 46.

54. *AKAK*, vol. 1 (1866), 406.

55. *AKAK*, vol. 1 (1866), 407.

56. *AKAK*, vol. 2 (1868), 44.

57. *AKAK*, vol. 1 (1866), 412.

58. *AKAK*, vol. 4 (1870), 109.

59. Robert H. Hewsen, *Armenia: A Historical Atlas* (Chicago: University of Chicago Press, 2001), 169.

60. Dominic Lieven, *Russia against Napoleon: The Battle for Europe, 1807 to 1814* (New York: Penguin, 2009), 33–34.

61. The tsarist court's formal declaration of a "rupture" in Russo-British relations, dated October 1807, presented a litany of grievances against London. See RGVIA, f. 846, op. 16, d. 377, ll. 1–2.

62. Lieven, *Russia against Napoleon*, 63.

63. Lieven, *Russia against Napoleon*, 67.

64. Lieven, *Russia against Napoleon*, 83.

65. *AKAK*, vol. 1 (1866), 689.

66. *AKAK*, vol. 4 (1870), 79.

67. *AKAK*, vol. 2 (1868), 4.

68. *AKAK*, vol. 2 (1868), 4.

69. For an overview of Tsitsianov's aggressive imperialism against Persian khans, see Firouzeh Mostashari, *On the Religious Frontier: Tsarist Russia and Islam in the Caucasus* (London: I. B. Tauris, 2006), 13–18. Tsitsianov's army easily overran Ganje, killing the khan and three thousand of his men. Renamed Elisavetpol in honor of the tsaritsa, the territory became part of the Russian Empire.

70. *AKAK*, vol. 2 (1868), 290.

71. Atkin, *Russia and Iran, 1780–1828*, 83.

72. Bournoutian, *Eastern Armenia*.

73. *AKAK*, vol. 2 (1868), 604.

74. *AKAK*, vol. 2 (1868), 604.

75. *AKAK*, vol. 2 (1868), 604.

76. *AKAK*, vol. 2 (1868), 614. Tsitsianov set the tribute at 80,000 rubles per year.

77. *AKAK*, vol. 2 (1868), 605.

78. *AKAK*, vol. 2 (1868), 615–16. Russian sources refer to Fath-Ali Shah by his pre-coronation name, Baba Khan.

79. *AKAK*, vol. 2 (1868), 625.

80. *AKAK*, vol. 2 (1868), 833.

81. *AKAK*, vol. 2 (1868), 833.

82. RGVIA, f. 482, op. 1, d. 200, l. 2.

83. Tsitsianov also proposed other, even more audacious strategies, such as a naval assault and invasion of eastern Persia through the Caspian Sea. See RGVIA, f. 846, op. 16, d. 4262, l. 3.

84. *AKAK*, vol. 2 (1868), 632.

85. *AKAK*, vol. 2 (1868), 943.

86. *AKAK*, vol. 2 (1868), 49.

87. *AKAK*, vol. 2 (1868), 1036–37.

88. *AKAK*, vol. 2 (1868), 1037.

89. Susan Layton, *Russian Literature and Empire: Conquest of the Caucasus from Pushkin to Tolstoy* (Cambridge: Cambridge University Press, 1994); Ewa Thomson, *Imperial Knowledge: Russian Literature and Colonialism* (Westport, CT: Greenwood Press, 2000).

90. *AKAK*, vol. 5 (1873), 10.

91. *AKAK*, vol. 3 (1869), 99–100.

92. RGVIA, f. 846, op. 16, d. 4265, ll. 25–54. See also *AKAK*, vol. 3 (1869), 237–53.

93. RGVIA, f. 846, op. 16, d. 4265, l. 29.

94. RGVIA, f. 846, op. 16, d. 4265, l. 30.

95. RGVIA, f. 846, op. 16, d. 4265, l. 34.

96. RGVIA, f. 482, op. 1, d. 19, ll. 5–49.

97. *AKAK*, vol. 3 (1869), 246.

98. The details of the Russian casualties are in RGVIA, f. 482, op. 1, d. 21, ll. 1–4.

99. RGVIA, f. 846, op. 16, d. 4265, ll. 49–50.

100. Atkin, *Russia and Iran, 1780–1828,* 125–29.

101. RGVIA, f. 846, op. 16, d. 4265, l. 17.

102. T. Kh. Akopian, ed., *Razvitie Erevana posle prisoedineniia Vostochnoi Armenii k Rossii: Sbornik dokumentov, 1801–1917 gg.* (Yerevan: Erevanskii gosudarstvennyi universitet, 1978), 50.

103. *AKAK*, vol. 3 (1869), 447–48.

104. RGVIA, f. 846, op. 16, d. 4265, ll. 45–46.

105. *AKAK*, vol. 3 (1869), 246.

106. RGVIA, f. 846, op. 16, d. 4265, l. 8.

107. *AKAK*, vol. 3 (1869), 502.

108. For reports about Russo-Persian skirmishes in the fall of 1809, see RGVIA, f. 846, op. 16, d. 4267.

109. *AKAK*, vol. 5 (1873), 60.

110. *AKAK*, vol. 5 (1873), 221–22.

111. *AKAK*, vol. 5 (1873), 121.

112. RGVIA, f. 846, op. 16, d. 4259, ch. 5, l. 117.

113. RGVIA, f. 846, op. 16, d. 4272.

114. Bournoutian, *Eastern Armenia,* 17.

115. Emanuil Dolbakian, "Otechestvennaia voina 1812 goda i armiane Rossii," *Moskovskii zhurnal* 1, no. 265 (2013), http://mosjour.ru/2017062812/.

116. Benjamin Nathans, "The Jews," in *The Cambridge History of Russia*, vol. 2, ed. Dominic Lieven (Cambridge: Cambridge University Press, 2006), 190.

117. Yohanan Petrovsky-Shtern, *Jews in the Russian Army, 1827–1917: Drafted into Modernity* (Cambridge: Cambridge University Press, 2009), 174.

118. Examples include G. A. Avetisian, *Generaly-armiane v Rossiiskoi imperii* (Yerevan: Amrots, 2007); and V. G. Krbekian, *Uchastie armian v russko-turetskoi voine 1877–1878 godov* (Yerevan: Antares, 2004).

119. *AKAK*, vol. 1 (1866), 414.

120. *AKAK*, vol. 1 (1866), 414. Paul's citation of "Armenia" should be interpreted not as a strict reference to a territory or space but as a broader designation of the Armenian people.

121. Rossiiskii gosudarstvennyi istoricheskii arkhiv (Russian State Historical Archive, RGIA), f. 13, op. 1, d. 28, ll. 1–1ob.

122. RGIA, f. 13, op. 1, d. 28, l. 6.

123. *AKAK*, vol. 1 (1866), 435.

124. *AKAK*, vol. 1 (1866), 436.

125. *AKAK*, vol. 2 (1868), 9.

126. *AKAK*, vol. 3 (1869), 235–36.

127. *AKAK*, vol. 3 (1869), 236–37.

128. *AKAK*, vol. 3 (1869), 265.

129. RGVIA, f. 482, op. 1, d. 23, ll. 1–1ob.

130. RGVIA, f. 482, op. 1, d. 131, ll. 48–49.

131. For a classic overview, see Vasilii Kliuchevskii, *Skazaniia inostrantsev o moskovskom gosudarstve* (Petrograd: Pervaia gosudarstvennaia tipografiia, 1918), 93–94. See also Sergei Platonov, *Moscow and the West*, trans. J. L. Wieczynski (Hattiesburg, MS: Academic International Press, 1972), 15.

132. S. M. Seredonin calculated Muscovy's combined Tatar, Cheremissian, and Mordvian troops in the late sixteenth century at ten thousand. See S. M. Seredonin, *Sochinenie Dzhil'sa Fletchera "Of the Russe Common Wealth" kak istoricheskii istochnik* (St. Petersburg: Tipografiia N. I. Skorokhodova, 1891), 346–47.

133. Andreas Kappeler, *The Russian Empire: A Multiethnic History*, trans. Alfred Clayton (Harlow, UK: Pearson Education, 2001), 129.

134. *AKAK*, vol. 1 (1866), 702.

135. *AKAK*, vol. 1 (1866), 287.

136. *AKAK*, vol. 1 (1866), 289–91.

137. *AKAK*, vol. 1 (1866), 292–93. More examples on 294.

138. *AKAK*, vol. 3 (1869), 235.

139. *AKAK*, vol. 3 (1869), 612.

140. *AKAK*, vol. 3 (1869), 614.

141. For example, in December 1802, Russian troops captured in Georgia an Armenian man who had fled Kartli-Kakheti two years earlier together with Prince Alexander. His interrogation revealed that Alexander had relied on him to communicate with Imeretian king Solomon and, most likely, to report information about Russian activities in Tiflis and elsewhere. See *AKAK*, vol. 1 (1866), 293.

142. *AKAK*, vol. 3 (1869), 416–17.

143. The French emissaries reached Persia by traveling through Ottoman territory, underscoring the deep anti-Russian coalition. More broadly, Napoleon aimed to attack India through Persia.

144. *AKAK*, vol. 3 (1869), 417–18. These appeals failed, and the envoys safely returned to France.

145. See R. M. Savory, "British and French Diplomacy in Persia, 1800–1810," *Iran* 10 (1972): 31–44.

146. *AKAK*, vol. 4 (1870), 707.

147. RGVIA, f. 846, op. 16, d. 4271, l. 1.

148. *AKAK*, vol. 5 (1873), 221–22.

149. *AKAK*, vol. 5 (1873), 221–22.

150. *AKAK*, vol. 5 (1873), 221–22.

151. *AKAK*, vol. 5 (1873), 230.

152. *AKAK*, vol. 4 (1870), 86.

153. *AKAK*, vol. 4 (1870), 86.

154. *AKAK*, vol. 1 (1866), 119.

155. *AKAK*, vol. 1 (1866), 119.

156. *AKAK*, vol. 1 (1866), 119.

157. *AKAK*, vol. 1 (1866), 682. This monastery's location is not clear.

158. *AKAK*, vol. 1 (1866), 538–39.

159. Bournoutian, *Russia and the Armenians of Transcaucasia*, 61–63.

160. *AKAK*, vol. 1 (1866), 542.

161. *AKAK*, vol. 1 (1866), 543.

162. Bournoutian, *Russia and the Armenians of Transcaucasia*, 65.

163. *AKAK*, vol. 1 (1866), 543.

164. *AKAK*, vol. 1 (1866), 542–43.

165. Bournoutian, *Russia and the Armenians of Transcaucasia*, 65.

166. *AKAK*, vol. 1 (1866), 544.

167. Alexander nonetheless assigned several officials to investigate whether Armenians in the South Caucasus really preferred Daniil to David. As late as the spring of 1803, Tsitsianov reported that local Armenians indeed supported Daniil over the "false patriarch" David. See *AKAK*, vol. 2 (1868), 274.

168. *AKAK*, vol. 1 (1866), 545.

169. *AKAK*, vol. 1 (1866), 547.

170. *AKAK*, vol. 1 (1866), 545.

171. For a broad overview, see Victor Taki, *Tsar and Sultan: Russian Encounters with the Ottoman Empire* (London: I. B. Tauris, 2016), 17–90.

172. *AKAK*, vol. 2 (1868), 274.

173. *AKAK*, vol. 2 (1868), 275.

174. *AKAK*, vol. 2 (1868), 275.

175. *AKAK*, vol. 2 (1868), 276.

176. *AKAK*, vol. 2 (1868), 276. In line with Tsitsianov's caution about Armenians, he also expressed concern that the recently relocated Armenians would wish to return to their former lands when his army conquered Yerevan.

177. *AKAK*, vol. 2 (1868), 276.

178. *AKAK*, vol. 3 (1869), 80.

179. RGIA, f. 733, op. 86, d. 174, ll. 2–3.

180. *AKAK*, vol. 3 (1869), 81.

181. *AKAK*, vol. 3 (1869), 81.

182. *AKAK*, vol. 3 (1869), 82.

183. *AKAK*, vol. 3 (1869), 82.

184. *AKAK*, vol. 3 (1869), 83.

185. *AKAK*, vol. 4 (1870), 173.

186. *AKAK*, vol. 4 (1870), 174–75. These were symbolic honors and commendations provided by each empire's royal court to the Armenian catholicos.

187. Ovanesov and Sudavtsov, *Voenno-administrativnaia deiatel'nost' armian.*

188. Ovanesov and Sudavtsov, *Voenno-administrativnaia deiatel'nost' armian*, 34.

189. Kappeler, *The Russian Empire*, 131.

190. Lohr, *Russian Citizenship*.

191. Alexander Morrison, "Metropole, Colony, and Imperial Citizenship in the Russian Empire," *Kritika: Explorations in Russian and Eurasian History* 13, no. 2 (2012): 330–31.

2. Armenians in the Russian Political Imagination, 1814–1829

1. *AKAK*, vol. 5 (1873), 951–53.

2. Stoler and McGranahan, "Introduction: Refiguring Imperial Terrains," 12.

3. The famed First Kazan Gymnasium would open in 1836. See Cynthia H. Whittaker, *The Origins of Modern Russian Education: An Intellectual Biography of Count Sergei Uvarov, 1786–1855* (DeKalb: Northern Illinois University Press, 1984), 210.

4. Theodore Weeks, "Russification: Word and Practice, 1863–1914," *Proceedings of the American Philosophical Society* 148, no. 4 (2004): 471–89.

5. Weeks, "Russification: Word and Practice, 1863–1914," 475. For "cultural," "administrative," and "unplanned" Russification, see Edward C. Thaden, ed., *Russification in the Baltic Provinces and Finland, 1855–1914* (Princeton, NJ: Princeton University Press, 1981), 7–9.

6. For the Lazarevs' financing of the church in 1779, see Tsatur Agaian, *Rol' Rossii v istoricheskikh sud'bakh armianskogo naroda: k 150-letiiu prisoedineniia Vostochnoi Armenii k Rossii* (Moscow: Nauka, 1978), 124. One of the earliest written references to Armenians in Moscow comes from 1390, when an Armenian merchant's vending stall burned down. Demographic statistics for Armenians in Moscow before the nineteenth century are unclear. For one overview, see Aleksandr Erkanian, "Istoriia armian Moskvy, vypusk 7," *Literaturnaia Gazeta* 41, no. 6529 (21 October 2015), http://www.lgz.ru /article/-41-6529-21-10-2015/istoriya-armyan-moskvy/.

7. Roger Bartlett, "Ropsha, an Imperial Palace," in *Personality and Place in Russian Culture: Essays in Memory of Lindsey Hughes*, ed. Simon Dixon (London: Modern Humanities Research Association, 2010), 171–72.

8. Tsentral'nyi istoricheskii arkhiv Moskvy (Central Historical Archive of Moscow, TsIAM), f. 213, op. 1, d. 1, ll. 1–3.

9. TsIAM, f. 213, op. 1, d. 1, l. 74.

10. TsIAM, f. 213, op. 1, d. 1, l. 6.

11. TsIAM, f. 213, op. 1, d. 1, ll. 1–3.

12. TsIAM, f. 213, op. 1, d. 1, l. 143.

13. Julia Disson, "Privileged Noble High Schools and the Formation of Russian National Elites in the First Part of the 19th Century," *Historical Social Research* 33, no. 2 (2008): 176.

14. David Schimmelpenninck van der Oye, *Russian Orientalism: Asia in the Russian Mind from Peter the Great to the Emigration* (New Haven, CT: Yale University Press, 2010), 9.

15. Whittaker, *The Origins of Modern Russian Education*, 20–21.

16. Whittaker, *The Origins of Modern Russian Education*, 23.

17. TsIAM, f. 213, op. 1, d. 1, l. 4.

18. TsIAM, f. 213, op. 1, d. 1, l. 4.

19. TsIAM, f. 213, op. 1, d. 1, l. 7.

20. TsIAM, f. 213, op. 1, d. 1, l. 8.

21. TsIAM, f. 213, op. 1, d. 1, l. 31.

22. Disson, "Privileged Noble High Schools," 176.

23. Disson, "Privileged Noble High Schools," 180.

24. TsIAM, f. 213, op. 1, d. 1, ll. 39–50.

25. TsIAM, f. 213, op. 1, d. 1, ll. 44–45.

26. TsIAM, f. 213, op. 1, d. 1, ll. 39–40.

27. Whittaker, *The Origins of Modern Russian Education*, 210.

28. TsIAM, f. 213, op. 1, d. 1, l. 40.

29. TsIAM, f. 213, op. 1, d. 1, l. 40.

30. TsIAM, f. 213, op. 1, d. 1, l. 92.

31. TsIAM, f. 213, op. 1, d. 1, l. 292.

32. TsIAM, f. 213, op. 1, d. 5, l. 89.

33. TsIAM, f. 213, op. 1, d. 1, l. 50.

34. TsIAM, f. 213, op. 1, d. 1, l. 50.

35. A. P. Baziiants, "Iz istorii Lazarevskogo instituta," *Izvestiia Akademii nauk Armianskoi SSR*, no. 2 (1964): 13–20, especially 15.

36. Mikhail Kalishevskii, "Lazarevskii institut—pervoe spetsializirovannoe diplomaticheskoe uchilishche," Moscow State Institute of International Relations (MGIMO) website, accessed 6 June 2016, http://www.mgimo.ru/study/dean/docs/6420/6624/document145668.phtml.

37. TsIAM, f. 213, op. 1, d. 5, ll. 163–64.

38. TsIAM, f. 213, op. 1, d. 5, l. 167.

39. TsIAM, f. 213, op. 1, d. 5, l. 168.

40. TsIAM, f. 213, op. 1, d. 5, l. 168.

41. TsIAM, f. 213, op. 1, d. 5, ll. 178–79.

42. TsIAM, f. 213, op. 1, d. 5, l. 205.

43. On the Armenian chair's establishment at Kazan University, see Robert Geraci, *Window on the East: National and Imperial Identities in Late Tsarist Russia* (Ithaca, NY: Cornell University Press, 2001), 160. Poor enrollment forced the chair to be closed in 1851. On Armenian as part of the curriculum at St. Petersburg University, see Schimmelpenninck van der Oye, *Russian Orientalism*, 168.

44. TsIAM, f. 213, op. 1, d. 5, l. 223.

45. On the institute's increased enrollment, see TsIAM, f. 213, op. 1, d. 5, l. 227. On the pupils' makeup, see TsIAM, f. 213, op. 1, d. 5, l. 184.

46. Abbas Amanat, "'Russian Intrusion into the Guarded Domain': Reflections of a Qajar Statesman on European Expansion," *Journal of the American Oriental Society* 113, no. 1 (1993): 35–56.

47. RGVIA, f. 846, op. 16, d. 4290, l. 28.

48. RGVIA, f. 846, op. 16, d. 4290, l. 39.

49. Michael Whittock, "Ermolov—Proconsul of the Caucasus," *Russian Review* 18, no. 1 (1959): 56.

50. King, *The Ghost of Freedom*, 45.

51. Whittock, "Ermolov—Proconsul of the Caucasus," 55.

52. RGVIA, f. 846, op. 16, d. 4290, l. 28.

53. RGVIA, f. 846, op. 16, d. 4290, l. 4.

54. RGVIA, f. 846, op. 16, d. 4290, l. 38.

55. RGVIA, f. 846, op. 16, d. 4290, l. 24.

56. RGVIA, f. 846, op. 16, d. 4290, l. 43.

57. RGVIA, f. 846, op. 16, d. 4290, l. 43.

58. RGVIA, f. 846, op. 16, d. 4290, ll. 53–54.

59. RGVIA, f. 846, op. 16, d. 4290, l. 85.

60. RGVIA, f. 846, op. 16, d. 4290, ll. 96–97.

61. RGVIA, f. 846, op. 16, d. 4290, ll. 96–97.

62. RGVIA, f. 846, op. 16, d. 4290, l. 85.

63. RGVIA, f. 846, op. 16, d. 4290, l. 106.

64. RGVIA, f. 846, op. 16, d. 4290, l. 109.

65. RGVIA, f. 846, op. 16, d. 4301, l. 1.

66. RGVIA, f. 846, op. 16, d. 4290, l. 139.

67. RGVIA, f. 846, op. 16, d. 4290, l. 145. Another source, less reliable for its unclear origin, gives the number of Armenian fighters inside the Shusha fortress at three thousand men: RGVIA, f. 846, op. 16, d. 894, l. 3.

68. RGVIA, f. 846, op. 16, d. 4290, ll. 147–51.

69. RGVIA, f. 846, op. 16, d. 4290, l. 284.

70. RGVIA, f. 846, op. 16, d. 894, l. 25.

71. RGVIA, f. 479, op. 1, d. 14, ll. 6, 8, and 10.

72. Hayastani azgayin arkhiv (National Archives of Armenia, HAA), f. 90, op. 1, d. 456, l. 1.

73. General Krasovskii to General Diebitsch, in Bournoutian, *Russia and the Armenians of Transcaucasia*, 282.

74. RGVIA, f. 846, op. 16, d. 894, l. 9.

75. RGVIA, f. 846, op. 16, d. 4309, l. 1.

76. RGVIA, f. 846, op. 16, d. 4309, ll. 2–3.

77. RGVIA, f. 846, op. 16, d. 4336, l. 1.

78. RGVIA, f. 846, op. 16, d. 4336, ll. 1–5.

79. RGVIA, f. 846, op. 16, d. 4336, ll. 9–14.

80. RGVIA, f. 846, op. 16, d. 4336, l. 7.

81. In theory, it was in Armenians' interest to exaggerate to Russians the abuse they experienced at the hands of Persians in order to encourage Russian intervention.

82. RGVIA, f. 846, op. 16, d. 894, ll. 6–7.

83. RGVIA, f. 846, op. 16, d. 894, ll. 11–12 and also 31.

84. RGVIA, f. 846, op. 16, d. 894, l. 3.

85. RGVIA, f. 846, op. 16, d. 894, l. 43.

86. RGVIA, f. 479, op. 1, d. 14, l. 7.

87. RGVIA, f. 846, op. 16, d. 4326, l. 137.

88. RGVIA, f. 846, op. 16, d. 4329, l. 193.

89. RGVIA, f. 479, op. 1, d. 14, ll. 14–15.

90. RGVIA, f. 479, op. 1, d. 14, l. 15.

91. RGVIA, f. 846, op. 16, d. 4329, l. 43.

92. RGVIA, f. 846, op. 16, d. 4329, l. 89.

93. RGVIA, f. 846, op. 16, d. 4329, l. 233.

94. RGVIA, f. 846, op. 16, d. 4334, l. 10.

95. RGVIA, f. 846, op. 16, d. 4643, l. 60.

96. RGVIA, f. 846, op. 16, d. 4643, ll. 60–62.

97. The stipulation became controversial in light of competing Armenian-Azeri ownership claims to the territory that Russians called Nagorno-Karabakh (Mountainous Karabakh). For an overview of the Nagorno-Karabakh conflict, and its historical bases, see Thomas de Waal, *Black Garden: Armenia and Azerbaijan through Peace and War* (New York: New York University Press, 2013), especially 313.

98. RGVIA, f. 846, op. 16, d. 978, l. 4.

99. RGVIA, f. 846, op. 16, d. 978, l. 1.

100. Sergei Glinka, *Opisanie pereseleniia armian adderbidzhanskikh v predely Rossii* (Baku: Elm, 1990), 36. Originally published in 1831 in Moscow by the Lazarev Institute of Oriental Languages.

101. RGVIA, f. 846, op. 16, d. 978, l. 13.

102. RGVIA, f. 846, op. 16, d. 978, l. 3.

103. RGVIA, f. 846, op. 16, d. 978, l. 3.

104. RGVIA, f. 846, op. 16, d. 978, l. 3.

105. RGVIA, f. 846, op. 16, d. 978, l. 5.

106. RGVIA, f. 846, op. 16, d. 978, ll. 1 and 4.

107. RGVIA, f. 846, op. 16, d. 978, ll. 13–14.

108. RGVIA, f. 846, op. 16, d. 978, l. 14. For Paskevich's summary of support from Armenian ecclesiastical leaders, see RGVIA, f. 846, op. 16, d. 978, l. 13.

109. RGVIA, f. 846, op. 16, d. 978, ll. 14–15.

110. RGIA, f. 383, op. 29, d. 539, ll. 4–4ob.

111. RGIA, f. 383, op. 29, d. 539, l. 5.

112. RGIA, f. 383, op. 29, d. 539, ll. 4ob and 8.

113. RGIA, f. 383, op. 29, d. 539, l. 4. In the late 1830s, the exchange rate equaled 3.5 assignation rubles for 1 silver ruble, but it appears that a decade earlier, in the 1820s, it was closer to 4:1.

114. RGIA, f. 383, op. 29, d. 539, l. 6.

115. Glinka, *Opisanie pereseleniia armian*, 52–53.

116. RGIA, f. 383, op. 29, d. 539, l. 7ob.

117. RGIA, f. 383, op. 29, d. 539, ll. 4ob–5ob.

118. RGIA, f. 383, op. 29, d. 539, ll. 8ob–9.

119. Glinka, *Opisanie pereseleniia armian*, 66–74.

120. RGIA, f. 383, op. 29, d. 539, l. 8ob.

121. RGIA, f. 383, op. 29, d. 539, l. 9.

122. For example, the following file contains partial data about the population of 132 villages around Yerevan in the Armianskaia Oblast: HAA, f. 90, op. 1, d. 5, ll. 2–8ob.

123. RGIA, f. 383, op. 29, d. 539, ll. 12–13.

124. See RGIA, f. 383, op. 29, d. 539, l. 9ob; and also Glinka, *Opisanie pereseleniia armian*, 87.

125. Glinka, *Opisanie pereseleniia armian*, 92.

126. Panossian, *The Armenians*, 121; Bournoutian, "Eastern Armenia," 105.

127. RGVIA, f. 846, op. 16, d. 1019, l. 3.

128. RGVIA, f. 846, op. 16, d. 1019, l. 3.

129. RGVIA, f. 846, op. 16, d. 1019, l. 3.

130. RGVIA, f. 846, op. 16, d. 1019, ll. 4–13.

131. RGVIA, f. 846, op. 16, d. 1019, l. 3.

132. RGVIA, f. 846, op. 16, d. 1019, l. 3.

133. RGVIA, f. 846, op. 16, d. 1019, ll. 12–12ob.

134. HAA, f. 90, op. 1, d. 318, l. 145ob.

135. RGVIA, f. 846, op. 16, d. 1019, l. 4.

136. RGVIA, f. 846, op. 16, d. 1019, ll. 12–12ob.

137. Bournoutian, "Eastern Armenia," 105.

138. Khachaturian, *Cultivating Nationhood in Imperial Russia*, 19; Alex Marshall, *The Caucasus under Soviet Rule* (New York: Routledge, 2010), 36.

139. RGVIA, f. 846, op. 16, d. 1019, l. 13.

140. RGVIA, f. 846, op. 16, d. 1019, l. 15.

141. RGVIA, f. 846, op. 16, d. 1019, l. 17.

142. HAA, f. 90, op. 1, d. 437, ll. 46–92.

143. HAA, f. 90, op. 1, d. 443, ll. 1ob–2.

144. HAA, f. 90, op. 1, d. 436, l. 7.

145. HAA, f. 90, op. 1, d. 435, ll. 10–14.

146. HAA, f. 90, op. 1, d. 435, l. 49.

147. HAA, f. 90, op. 1, d. 435, l. 50.

148. HAA, f. 90, op. 1, d. 435, ll. 50–50ob.

149. HAA, f. 90, op. 1, d. 435, l. 51.

150. HAA, f. 90, op. 1, d. 435, l. 51ob.

151. According to historian Razmik Panossian, "Whereas before 1828 there were 87,000 Muslims and 20,000 Armenians in the Yerevan khanate/province, after the mass migrations Armenians constituted the majority population: 65,000, as opposed to 50,000 Muslims." Panossian, *The Armenians*, 122.

152. HAA, f. 90, op. 1, d. 448, ll. 7–7ob.

153. HAA, f. 90, op. 1, d. 448, ll. 7–7ob.

154. Glinka, *Opisanie pereseleniia armian*, 49 (italics in the original).

155. RGIA, f. 383, op. 29, d. 539, l. 11.

156. RGIA, f. 571, op. 5, d. 740, l. 177.

157. Kollmann, *The Russian Empire, 1450–1801*, 193–94.

158. *Sobranie aktov*, vol. 2 (1838), 288–89.

159. Barkhudarian, "Armianskie kolonisty v Rossii," 124–25.

160. *Sobranie aktov*, vol. 1 (1833), 27; Barkhudarian, "Armianskie kolonisty v Rossii," 126.

161. RGIA, f. 571, op. 5, d. 740, l. 117.

162. *AKAK*, vol. 1 (1866), 765.

163. See RGIA, f. 571, op. 5, d. 742, ll. 99–101; and also RGIA, f. 880, op. 5, d. 386, ll. 5–8ob.

164. RGIA, f. 571, op. 5, d. 740, ll. 99–110ob.

165. RGIA, f. 571, op. 5, d. 740, ll. 99–110ob.

166. RGIA, f. 571, op. 5, d. 742, ll. 99–101.

167. RGIA, f. 571, op. 5, d. 742, ll. 99ob–100.

168. RGIA, f. 571, op. 5, d. 742, l. 100.

169. RGIA, f. 880, op. 5, d. 386, ll. 5–8ob.

170. RGIA, f. 880, op. 5, d. 386, ll. 7ob–8.

171. RGIA, f. 880, op. 5, d. 386, l. 8ob.

172. RGIA, f. 880, op. 5, d. 386, ll. 9–13ob.

173. RGIA, f. 571, op. 5, d. 740, l. 107ob.

174. RGIA, f. 571, op. 5, d. 740, ll. 107ob–108.

175. RGIA, f. 571, op. 5, d. 740, l. 108 (emphasis added).

176. RGIA, f. 571, op. 5, d. 740, l. 108.

177. RGIA, f. 571, op. 5, d. 740, ll. 108–108ob.

178. RGIA, f. 571, op. 5, d. 740, l. 109.

179. RGIA, f. 571, op. 5, d. 740, l. 109ob.

180. Specifically, they cited not only the 1799 decree but also Catherine's edict of 1779 for the Armenians of Nakhichevan-on-Don and Paul's decree of 1797 for Astrakhan Armenians. Catherine's edict had in fact stipulated that Nakhichevan Armenians were entitled to "enjoy eternal and hereditary free trade, within and outside the Russian state." See RGIA, f. 571, op. 5, d. 740, ll. 117–120ob.

181. RGIA, f. 571, op. 5, d. 740, l. 109.

182. RGIA, f. 571, op. 5, d. 740, l. 117ob.

183. RGIA, f. 571, op. 5, d. 740, l. 118.

184. RGIA, f. 571, op. 5, d. 740, l. 118.

185. RGIA, f. 571, op. 5, d. 740, ll. 118–118ob.

186. RGIA, f. 571, op. 5, d. 740, l. 120.

187. RGIA, f. 571, op. 5, d. 740, ll. 124–125ob.

188. RGIA, f. 571, op. 5, d. 740, ll. 124ob–125.

189. RGIA, f. 571, op. 5, d. 740, l. 125.

190. Vladimir Dal', *Sochineniia Vladimira Dalia: Novoe polnoe izdanie* (St. Petersburg: M. O. Vol'f, 1861), vol. 2, 262–69.

191. RGIA, f. 571, op. 5, d. 740, l. 161.

192. RGIA, f. 571, op. 5, d. 740, l. 161.

193. RGIA, f. 571, op. 5, d. 740, l. 14.

194. RGIA, f. 571, op. 5, d. 740, l. 174ob.

195. RGIA, f. 571, op. 5, d. 740, l. 176ob.

196. RGIA, f. 571, op. 5, d. 740, l. 177.

197. RGIA, f. 1152, op. 1, d. 77, l. 20ob.

198. RGIA, f. 571, op. 5, d. 740, ll. 177ob–178.

199. RGIA, f. 571, op. 5, d. 740, ll. 178ob–179 (emphasis in the original, expressed by underlining).

200. RGIA, f. 571, op. 5, d. 740, ll. 198–99.

201. RGIA, f. 571, op. 5, d. 740, l. 198ob.

202. Kivelson and Suny, *Russia's Empires*, 174.

3. Integration and Reorientation

1. Ann Laura Stoler, "Intimidations of Empire: Predicaments of the Tactile and Unseen," in *Haunted by Empire: Geographies of Intimacy in North American History*, ed. Ann Laura Stoler (Durham, NC: Duke University Press, 2006), 57.

2. Marc Raeff, *Michael Speransky: Statesman of Imperial Russia* (The Hague: Martinus Nijhoff, 1969), 324.

3. Raeff, *Michael Speransky*, 337.

4. Laura Engelstein, *Castration and the Heavenly Kingdom: A Russian Folktale* (Ithaca, NY: Cornell University Press, 2003), 50–51.

5. John Klier, "State Policies and the Conversion of Jews in Imperial Russia," in *Of Religion and Empire: Missions, Conversion, and Tolerance in Tsarist Russia*, ed. Robert Geraci and Michael Khodarkovsky (Ithaca, NY: Cornell University Press, 2001), 92–112.

6. Weeks, "Russification and Lithuanians, 1863–1905," 104.

7. Theodore Weeks, "Between Rome and Tsargrad: The Uniate Church in Imperial Russia," in *Of Religion and Empire: Missions, Conversion, and Tolerance in Tsarist Russia*, ed. Robert Geraci and Michael Khodarkovsky (Ithaca, NY: Cornell University Press, 2001), 74–75.

8. Suny, "Eastern Armenians under Tsarist Rule," 113.

9. For an overview, see Moshe Gammer, *Muslim Resistance to the Tsar: Shamil and the Conquest of Chechnia and Daghestan* (New York: Routledge, 2003). For a more thorough study, see V. A. Potto, *Kavkazskaia voina v otdel'nykh ocherkakh, epizodakh, legendakh i biografiiakh*, 4 vols. (St. Petersburg: Izdatel'stvo V. A. Berezovskogo, 1887–89).

10. Firouzeh Mostashari, "Colonial Dilemmas: Russian Policies in the Muslim Caucasus," in *Of Religion and Empire: Missions, Conversion, and Tolerance in Tsarist Russia*, ed. Robert Geraci and Michael Khodarkovsky (Ithaca, NY: Cornell University Press, 2001), 234.

11. *AKAK*, vol. 8 (1881), 356. Also see Rebecca Gould, "Imam Shamil," in *Russia's People of Empire: Life Stories from Eurasia, 1500 to the Present*, ed. Stephen M. Norris and Willard Sunderland (Bloomington: Indiana University Press, 2012), 119–21.

12. RGVIA, f. 846, op. 16, d. 6293, ll. 15–15ob.

13. Richard Wortman describes this circumstance in his *Scenarios of Power: Myth and Ceremony in Russian Monarchy* (Princeton, NJ: Princeton University Press, 2006), 120–66.

14. Gosudarstvennyi arkhiv Rossiiskoi Federatsii (State Archive of the Russian Federation, GARF), f. 672, op. 1, d. 301, l. 2. For some of the consequences for nationalities policies, see Kappeler, *The Russian Empire*, 131, 133–34; and Edward C. Thaden, *Russia's Western Borderlands, 1710–1870* (Princeton, NJ: Princeton University Press, 1985), 124.

15. *AKAK*, vol. 8 (1881), ii.

16. *AKAK*, vol. 8 (1881), 391–92. Georgian-heritage tsarist officials, such as Major-General Aleksandr Chavchavadze, were implicated in the investigation. After a brief exile, Chavchavadze was cleared and reinstated.

17. *AKAK*, vol. 8 (1881), 218.

18. *AKAK*, vol. 8 (1881), 394.

19. Yanni Kotsonis, *States of Obligation: Taxes and Citizenship in the Russian Empire and Early Soviet Republic* (Toronto: University of Toronto Press, 2014), 34.

20. *AKAK*, vol. 8 (1881), 504–5.

21. Ekaterina Pravilova, *Finansy imperii: Den'gi i vlast' v politike Rossii na natsional'nykh okrainakh, 1801–1917* (Moscow: Novoe izdatel'stvo, 2006), 249.

22. Pravilova, *Finansy imperii*, 264.

23. *AKAK*, vol. 8 (1881), 505.

24. *AKAK*, vol. 8 (1881), 505.

25. *AKAK*, vol. 8 (1881), 515.

26. *AKAK*, vol. 8 (1881), 515. Whether and why taxes were introduced remains unclear from the available sources and appears to contradict the ten-year tax exemptions that Paskevich promised to Persian- and Ottoman-subject Armenians in 1828.

27. *AKAK*, vol. 8 (1881), 515.

28. Khodarkovsky, *Bitter Choices*, 120.

29. Khodarkovsky, *Bitter Choices*, 122.

30. *AKAK*, vol. 9 (1884), iv–v.

31. Tunian, *Vostochnaia Armeniia*, 41.

32. Suny, "Eastern Armenians under Tsarist Rule," 113–14.

33. According to Russian statistics, in 1843 in the South Caucasus there were 1,483,392 residents, of whom over 979,000 lived in the Georgian-Imeretian Province. See *AKAK*, vol. 9 (1884), 604.

34. Khodarkovsky, *Bitter Choices*, 122.

35. Tunian, *Vostochnaia Armeniia*, 43.

36. For one example, see Tunian, *Vostochnaia Armeniia*, 44–45.

37. GARF, f. 672, op. 1, d. 84, l. 1.

38. Moritz Wagner, *Travels in Persia, Georgia and Koordistan; With Sketches of the Cossacks and the Caucasus* (London: Hurst and Blackett, 1856), 120.

39. GARF, f. 672, op. 1, d. 84, l. 1.

40. RGVIA, f. 846, op. 16, d. 6482, l. 2.

41. RGVIA, f. 846, op. 16, d. 6482, l. 3.

42. RGVIA, f. 846, op. 16, d. 6482, l. 3.

43. RGVIA, f. 846, op. 16, d. 6482, l. 8. Golovin agreed with Chernyshev's points but emphasized the religious "fanaticism" of Muridist rebels.

44. See the tsar's increasingly concerned messages to Neidgardt in GARF, f. 678, op. 1, d. 530, ll. 8–10.

45. Jersild, *Orientalism and Empire*, 63.

46. *AKAK*, vol. 10 (1885), i.

47. Anthony Rhinelander, *Prince Michael Vorontsov: Viceroy to the Tsar* (Montreal: McGill-Queen's Press, 1990), 143. The details of Vorontsov's appointment, including the tsar's decree, are in RGVIA, f. 846, op. 16, d. 6588, l. 2.

48. Tunian, *Vostochnaia Armeniia*, 52–53. For an overview of the tsarist administrators of southern provinces from Catherine to Alexander I, see John LeDonne, "Frontier Governors General 1772–1825," pt. 2, "The Southern Frontier," *Jahrbücher für Geschichte Osteuropas* 48, no. 2 (2000): 161–83.

49. Rhinelander, *Prince Michael Vorontsov*, 144–49.

50. King, *The Ghost of Freedom*, 86.

51. Jersild, *Orientalism and Empire*, 64.

52. Suny, *The Making of the Georgian Nation*, 75.

53. Hubertus Jahn, "The Bronze Viceroy: Mikhail Vorontsov's Statue and Russian Imperial Representation in the South Caucasus in the Mid-Nineteenth Century," *Russian History* 41, no. 2 (2014): 177.

54. The tsar promoted Vorontsov to field marshal just months before his death. See *AKAK*, vol. 10 (1885), xvii.

55. For Vorontsov's support of new Armenian churches, see RGIA, f. 1268, op. 2, d. 687, ll. 1–3.

56. *AKAK*, vol. 10 (1885), 96.

57. *AKAK*, vol. 10 (1885), 96.

58. *AKAK*, vol. 10 (1885), 97.

59. *AKAK*, vol. 10 (1885), 97.

60. King, *The Ghost of Freedom*, 89.

61. David Goldfrank, *The Origins of the Crimean War* (New York: Routledge, 2014), 294.

62. GARF, f. 672, op. 1, d. 126, ll. 16–16ob and 52.

63. On Shamil's restful retirement, see Thomas Barrett, "The Remaking of the Lion of Dagestan: Shamil in Captivity," *Russian Review* 53, no. 3 (1994): 353–66.

64. GARF, f. 672, op. 1, d. 126, l. 19.

65. George Bournoutian, *The Khanate of Erevan under Qajar Rule, 1795–1828* (Costa Mesa, CA: Mazda, 1992), 84–86.

66. RGVIA, f. 846, op. 16, d. 978, l. 13.

67. Bournoutian, *The Khanate of Erevan*, 89.

68. Paul Werth, "Imperial Russia and the Armenian Catholicos at Home and Abroad," in *Reconstruction and Interaction of Slavic Eurasia and Its Neighboring Worlds*, ed. Osamu Ieda and Tomohiko Uyama (Sapporo: Slavic Research Center, 2006), 211.

69. RGIA, f. 880, op. 5, d. 21, ll. 16–31.

70. RGIA, f. 880, op. 5, d. 21, l. 17.

71. RGIA, f. 880, op. 5, d. 21, l. 17.

72. RGIA, f. 880, op. 5, d. 21, l. 31.

73. RGIA, f. 880, op. 5, d. 21, l. 39.

74. Werth, "Imperial Russia and the Armenian Catholicos," 209. It appears that Hovannes, too, was a tsarist subject.

75. Werth, "Imperial Russia and the Armenian Catholicos," 203–35.

76. RGIA, f. 880, op. 5, d. 21, ll. 15–15ob.

77. Werth, "Imperial Russia and the Armenian Catholicos," 207.

78. RGIA, f. 880, op. 5, d. 174, l. 1ob.

79. RGIA, f. 1268, op. 1, d. 55, l. 1. The date of this report is unknown, but it appears to have been written in 1837.

80. RGIA, f. 1268, op. 1, d. 55, ll. 1–1ob.

81. RGIA, f. 1268, op. 1, d. 55, ll. 1ob–2.

82. RGIA, f. 1268, op. 1, d. 55, l. 2.

83. Robert Curzon, *Armenia: A Year at Erzeroom, and on the Frontiers of Russia, Turkey, and Persia* (London: John Murray, 1854), 209.

84. A full translation of the statute is available in Bournoutian, *Russia and the Armenians of Transcaucasia*, 350–68.

85. Panossian, *The Armenians*, 123.

86. Quoted in Werth, *The Tsar's Foreign Faiths*, 62.

87. RGIA, f. 880, op. 5, d. 344, l. 89.

88. Suny, "Eastern Armenians under Tsarist Rule," 115.

89. Suny, "Eastern Armenians under Tsarist Rule," 115.

90. Werth, "Imperial Russia and the Armenian Catholicos," 209.

91. The Ejmiatsin Synod was established in 1837 as part of the church reforms. See HAA, f. 90, op. 1, d. 353, ll. 1–4.

92. As Werth has emphasized, the *polozhenie* of 1836 was part of the state's broader effort to codify the rights and obligations of its non-Orthodox confessions in the 1830s. See Werth, "Imperial Russia and the Armenian Catholicos," 209.

93. On Hovannes's petition to the tsar, see RGIA, f. 880, op. 5, d. 179, ll. 12–18ob. The book was titled *An Addendum to the Proof of the Antiquity of the Tri-finger Service* (Dopolneniia k dokazatel'stvam o drevnosti trekhperstnogo slozheniia). Hovannes's description of the book is at RGIA, f. 880, op. 5, d. 179, l. 1.

94. RGIA, f. 880, op. 5, d. 179, l. 1. In an analogous example, in 1831 the Armenian Church worked with tsarist officials to curb the activities of the (Swiss) Basel Evangelical Society in the Caucasus. See RGIA, f. 383, op. 29, d. 557, ll. 1–12ob.

95. RGIA, f. 880, op. 5, d. 179, ll. 1–1ob.

96. RGIA, f. 880, op. 5, d. 179, l. 1ob.

97. Werth, *The Tsar's Foreign Faiths*, 4.

98. RGIA, f. 880, op. 5, d. 179, l. 6.

99. The structure and format of the Armenian catechism was modeled on the Russian Orthodox version.

100. RGIA, f. 880, op. 5, d. 179, ll. 6ob–7.

101. More evidence of the Russo-Armenian religious symbiosis in this era includes state and local permission for the expansion of Armenian churches in Moscow and St. Petersburg and the Lazarevs' construction of new Armenian orphanages in Moscow. See RGIA, f. 880, op. 5, d. 179, l. 41.

102. Suny, *The Making of the Georgian Nation*, 67.

103. Suny, *The Making of the Georgian Nation*, 68.

104. Breyfogle, *Heretics and Colonizers*, 49–117.

105. *AKAK*, vol. 9 (1884), 714.

106. *AKAK*, vol. 9 (1884), 714.

107. *AKAK*, vol. 9 (1884), 715. It is not clear whether senior representatives of foreign Armenian communities attended the election in Ejmiatsin or, as Werth suggests, merely sent written deeds and low-ranking representatives. In either case, it appears that both Ottoman and Persian Armenians participated in the 1843 election and recognized its results. See Werth, "Imperial Russia and the Armenian Catholicos," 211.

108. *AKAK*, vol. 9 (1884), 715–16.

109. Werth, "Imperial Russia and the Armenian Catholicos," 212.

110. *AKAK*, vol. 10 (1885), 842.

111. *AKAK*, vol. 10 (1885), 857.

112. *AKAK*, vol. 10 (1885), 842.

113. *AKAK*, vol. 10 (1885), 96. The viceroy and his wife maintained correspondence with Catholicos Nerses. See *Patriarkh vsekh armian Nerses V-i i kniaz' Mikhail Semenovich i kniaginia Elisaveta Ksaverievna Vorontsovy v ikh chastnoi perepiske*, ed. A. D. Eritsov (Tiflis: M. Martirosiantsa, 1898).

114. Quoted in Werth, "Imperial Russia and the Armenian Catholicos," 212.

115. Suny, "Eastern Armenians under Tsarist Rule," 117.

116. RGIA, f. 821, op. 7, d. 7, ll. 5–7ob. Also RGIA, f. 1268, op. 6, d. 44, ll. 1–1ob.

117. RGIA, f. 821, op. 7, d. 7, l. 6.

118. As Werth has pointed out, "Still, data (presumably provided by the patriarch) indicating that the persistent efforts of Catholic clergy over more than a half-century (1787–1846) had resulted in the 'enticement' of just 26 men and 21 women scarcely suggests a crisis." Werth, *The Tsar's Foreign Faiths*, 88n66.

119. RGIA, f. 821, op. 7, d. 7, l. 2.

120. RGIA, f. 821, op. 7, d. 7, l. 2ob.

121. RGIA, f. 821, op. 7, d. 7, l. 2ob.

122. RGIA, f. 821, op. 7, d. 7, ll. 16–16ob.

123. RGIA, f. 821, op. 7, d. 7, ll. 17–18ob.

124. RGIA, f. 1268, op. 7, d. 364a, ll. 1–2. Nerses justified this request by arguing that the long delay in receiving permission from the capital discouraged Muslims from converting to the Armenian faith.

125. RGIA, f. 1268, op. 7, d. 364a, l. 6.

126. RGIA, f. 821, op. 7, d. 11, ll. 1–4ob.

127. RGIA, f. 821, op. 7, d. 11, l. 7.

128. RGIA, f. 821, op. 7, d. 39, ll. 1–5.

129. RGIA, f. 821, op. 7, d. 39, l. 4.

130. Robert Crews, "Empire and the Confessional State: Islam and Religious Politics in Nineteenth-Century Russia," *American Historical Review* 108, no. 1 (2003): 59.

131. Crews, *For Prophet and Tsar*.

132. Ann Laura Stoler, "On Degrees of Imperial Sovereignty," *Public Culture* 18, no. 1 (2006): 138.

133. RGIA, f. 1152, op. 3, d. 31, ll. 50ob–51.

134. This circumstance echoes Ekaterina Pravilova's argument that an individual region's political circumstances, rather than a pan-imperial economic program, drove the implementation of fiscal and financial policies on the empire's peripheries. See Pravilova, *Finansy imperii*, 369.

135. Pravilova, *Finansy imperii*, 13.

136. Pravilova, *Finansy imperii*, 107.

137. Quoted in Robert Geraci, "Capitalist Stereotypes and the Economic Organization of the Russian Empire: The Case of the Tiflis Armenians," in *Defining Self: Essays on Emergent Identities in Russia, Seventeenth to Nineteenth Centuries*, ed. Michael Branch (Helsinki: Finnish Literature Society, 2009), 368.

138. Pravilova, *Finansy imperii*, 108–9.

139. Pravilova, *Finansy imperii*, 111. The Caucasus administration regained control over the local economy only in 1858.

140. "400 let armianskoi diaspore v Astrakhani," *Volga: Obshchestvenno-politicheskaia gazeta Astrakhanskoi oblasti*, accessed 10 November 2015, http://www.volgaru.ru/index.php?retro&article=1317.

141. For imperial tax policies for Astrakhan Armenians in the early 1830s, see RGIA, f. 571, op. 5, d. 786, ll. 1–49. For detailed overviews of the policies in the mid-1830s, see RGIA, f. 1341, op. 37, d. 2619, ll. 1–6ob; and also RGIA, f. 1341, op. 37, d. 1422, ll. 1–6.

142. RGIA, f. 571, op. 5, d. 740, ll. 198–99.

143. RGIA, f. 571, op. 5, d. 740, l. 198ob.

144. RGIA, f. 1152, op. 2, d. 42, ll. 2–8ob. The reasons for the introduction of these taxes are unclear.

145. It appears that even this tax of 2.76 rubles that all Astrakhan Armenians paid was three times as much as their non-Armenian neighbors paid.

146. RGIA, f. 1152, op. 2, d. 42, ll. 2ob–3.

147. RGIA, f. 1152, op. 2, d. 42, l. 3ob.

148. RGIA, f. 1152, op. 2, d. 42, ll. 4–9.

149. RGIA, f. 1152, op. 2, d. 42, l. 9.

150. RGIA, f. 1152, op. 2, d. 76, l. 7.

151. GARF, f. 672, op. 1, d. 302, l. 15.

152. RGIA, f. 1152, op. 2, d. 76, ll. 9–9ob.

153. For a concise overview of these changes, see RGIA, f. 1152, op. 2, d. 76, ll. 9–9ob. For a more thorough discussion, see GARF, f. 672, op. 1, d. 302, ll. 15–34.

154. GARF, f. 672, op. 1, d. 302, l. 26.

155. GARF, f. 672, op. 1, d. 302, l. 21. The communities in question were the Catholic Armenians of Karasubazar and the Apostolic Armenians of Staryi Krym, both on the Crimean peninsula.

156. GARF, f. 672, op. 1, d. 302, l. 21.

157. GARF, f. 672, op. 1, d. 302, ll. 22–22ob.

158. GARF, f. 672, op. 1, d. 302, l. 26.

159. GARF, f. 672, op. 1, d. 302, l. 27.

160. GARF, f. 672, op. 1, d. 302, l. 27.

161. GARF, f. 672, op. 1, d. 302 contains many examples of this tension, some of which I have cited throughout this section. For more instances, see ll. 27 and 29 of that file.

162. Geraci, "Capitalist Stereotypes," 368.

163. GARF, f. 672, op. 1, d. 302, l. 30.

164. GARF, f. 672, op. 1, d. 302, ll. 31 and 34.

165. RGIA, f. 1152, op. 3, d. 129, ll. 36–37.

166. RGIA, f. 1152, op. 3, d. 31, l. 6ob.

167. RGIA, f. 1152, op. 3, d. 31, ll. 7ob–9.

168. RGIA, f. 1152, op. 3, d. 31, l. 9.

169. RGIA, f. 1152, op. 3, d. 31, l. 11.

170. RGIA, f. 1152, op. 3, d. 31, l. 13.

171. RGIA, f. 1152, op. 3, d. 31, ll. 41–41ob.

172. RGIA, f. 1152, op. 3, d. 31, ll. 42ob–43.

173. RGIA, f. 1152, op. 3, d. 31, ll. 47ob–48.

174. RGIA, f. 1152, op. 3, d. 31, l. 67ob.

175. RGIA, f. 1150, op. 2, d. 4, ll. 5–8.

176. *AKAK*, vol. 8 (1881), 165–67.

177. *AKAK*, vol. 8 (1881), 166.

178. *AKAK*, vol. 8 (1881), 166.

179. RGIA, f. 1268, op. 1, d. 509, ll. 11–13ob.

180. RGIA, f. 1268, op. 1, d. 509, l. 11.

181. RGIA, f. 1268, op. 1, d. 509, l. 13ob (emphasis added). Neidgardt also supported the founding of private Armenian schools in the Caucasus. See RGIA, f. 1268, op. 1, d. 623, ll. 1–8ob.

182. RGIA, f. 1268, op. 1, d. 509, l. 13ob.

183. RGIA, f. 1268, op. 1, d. 509, ll. 13ob–14.

184. RGIA, f. 1268, op. 1, d. 509, l. 14.

185. RGIA, f. 1268, op. 1, d. 509, l. 14.

186. P. Vysheslavtsov, "Vzgliad na Zakavkaz'e v khoziaistvennom i torgovom otnoshenii ego k Rossii," *Syn otechestva* 66 (1834): 39.

187. *Kavkazskii kalendar' na 1846 god, izdannyi ot kantseliarii kavkazskogo namestnika* (St. Petersburg: Voennaia tipografiia, 1846), 140.

188. *Kavkazskii kalendar'* (1846), 140.

189. *Kavkazskii kalendar'* (1846), 140.

190. Alfred Rieber, *Merchants and Entrepreneurs in Imperial Russia* (Chapel Hill: University of North Carolina Press, 1982), 73.

191. Raeff, *Michael Speransky*, 337.

192. RGIA, f. 1268, op. 7, d. 485, l. 85. On the courts' absorption into the imperial judicial system, see RGIA, f. 1268, op. 7, d. 485, ll. 1–91.

193. Hillis, "Ukrainophile Activism and Imperial Governance."

194. Geraci, "Capitalist Stereotypes," 378.

4. The Recalibration of Tsarist Policies toward Armenians inside and outside Russia, 1857–1880

1. RGVIA, f. 846, op. 16, d. 6662, l. 46.

2. RGVIA, f. 446, op. 1, d. 37, ll. 1–3.

3. For the Great Reforms in the Caucasus, see Mostashari, *On the Religious Frontier*, 65–77.

4. GARF, f. 678, op. 1, d. 687, l. 1.

5. GARF, f. 678, op. 1, d. 687, ll. 4–5.

6. GARF, f. 678, op. 1, d. 687, ll. 36ob–37. See also GARF, f. 652, op. 1, d. 236, l. 30. The Caucasus viceroyalty also received supplemental annual funding from St. Petersburg. In contrast to the finances of the South Caucasus, which came under the viceroy's control in 1858, the imperial Finance Ministry administered the finances of the North Caucasus.

7. Pravilova, *Finansy imperii*, 116–17.

8. One of Bariatinskii's favorite junior aides, recent university dropout Ilarion Vorontsov-Dashkov, a half century later took over the viceroyalty. See D. I. Ismail-Zade, *Graf I. I. Vorontsov-Dashkov: Namestnik kavkazskii* (Moscow: Tsentrpoligraf, 2005), 34–37.

9. RGIA, f. 1268, op. 10, d. 103, ll. 15–16. The Mechitarists are Benedictine monks of the Armenian Catholic Church, established in 1717 and based in Vienna and Venice.

10. RGIA, f. 1268, op. 10, d. 103, l. 17.

11. RGIA, f. 1268, op. 10, d. 103, l. 18.

12. RGIA, f. 1268, op. 10, d. 103, ll. 19ob–20.

13. Russian synopses of this case claim that many local Armenians from Crimea petitioned the government to allow Aivazovskii to use church finances for the establishment of his academy. See RGIA, f. 1268, op. 10, d. 103, l. 18ob.

14. On Armenian support for Aivazovskii, see RGIA, f. 1268, op. 10, d. 103, l. 18. In addition to his elevation without Ejmiatsin's consent, another source of tension was Aivazovskii's plan to relocate the headquarters of the Nakhichevan-Bessarabian eparchy from Kishinev to Feodosia, where he argued it would be closer to the large Armenian communities of Crimea and Nakhichevan-on-Don. See RGIA, f. 1268, op. 10, d. 103, l. 21.

15. RGIA, f. 1268, op. 10, d. 103, ll. 22ob–24.

16. In 1862, Khalibov donated an additional 150,000 rubles for the construction of a new, larger facility for the academy. See RGIA, f. 1268, op. 10, d. 103, l. 29.

17. RGIA, f. 1268, op. 10, d. 103, l. 27.

18. RGIA, f. 1268, op. 10, d. 103, l. 27ob.

19. RGIA, f. 1268, op. 10, d. 103, l. 28ob.

20. RGIA, f. 1268, op. 10, d. 103, l. 28ob.

21. RGIA, f. 1268, op. 10, d. 103, l. 29.

22. RGIA, f. 880, op. 5, d. 278, ll. 13–15ob.

23. RGIA, f. 1268, op. 10, d. 103, ll. 32–33.

24. RGIA, f. 1268, op. 10, d. 103, l. 33ob.

25. RGIA, f. 1268, op. 10, d. 103, l. 34.

26. RGIA, f. 1268, op. 10, d. 103, ll. 35–35ob.

27. RGIA, f. 1268, op. 10, d. 103, l. 37.

28. See Suny, *Looking toward Ararat*, 23 and 59.

29. RGIA, f. 880, op. 5, d. 278, ll. 1–1ob.

30. RGIA, f. 880, op. 5, d. 278, l. 1.

31. RGIA, f. 880, op. 5, d. 278, ll. 1–1ob.

32. RGIA, f. 880, op. 5, d. 278, ll. 13–15ob.

33. RGIA, f. 880, op. 5, d. 278, l. 1ob.

34. RGIA, f. 880, op. 5, d. 278, l. 2.

35. RGIA, f. 880, op. 5, d. 278, ll. 2ob–3.

36. RGIA, f. 880, op. 5, d. 278, l. 3.

37. RGIA, f. 880, op. 5, d. 278, l. 3ob.

38. See RGIA, f. 880, op. 5, d. 278, ll. 3ob–4ob and also 9ob.

39. RGIA, f. 880, op. 5, d. 278, l. 9ob.

40. RGIA, f. 880, op. 5, d. 278, ll. 5–6.

41. RGIA, f. 880, op. 5, d. 278, ll. 6–7ob.

42. RGIA, f. 880, op. 5, d. 278, l. 10.

43. Steinwedel, *Threads of Empire*, 135.

44. Steinwedel, *Threads of Empire*, 136.

45. Larisa Zakharova, "Emperor Alexander II, 1855–1881," in *The Emperors and Empresses of Russia: Rediscovering the Romanovs*, ed. Donald J. Raleigh (Armonk, NY: M. E. Sharpe, 1996), 294–333.

46. On the apostasy in Kazan Province, see Paul Werth, *At the Margins of Orthodoxy: Mission, Governance, and Confessional Politics in Russia's Volga-Kama Region, 1827–1905* (Ithaca, NY: Cornell University Press, 2002), 147–76. On Alexander II's curtailing the prosecution of apostasy, see Agnès Nilüfer Kefeli, *Becoming Muslim in Imperial Russia: Conversion, Apostasy, and Literacy* (Ithaca, NY: Cornell University Press, 2014), 42.

47. Werth, *At the Margins of Orthodoxy*, 176.

48. For an overview of the reforms at midcentury, see Roderic H. Davison, *Reform in the Ottoman Empire, 1856–1876* (1963; repr., Princeton, NJ: Princeton University Press, 2015). For Western Armenians during the Tanzimat reforms, see Panossian, *The Armenians*, 148–53.

49. Bedross Der Matossian, *Shattered Dreams of Revolution: From Liberty to Violence in the Late Ottoman Empire* (Stanford, CA: Stanford University Press, 2014), 10.

50. Donald Bloxham, *The Great Game of Genocide: Imperialism, Nationalism, and the Destruction of the Ottoman Armenians* (New York: Oxford University Press, 2005), 42.

51. RGIA, f. 1268, op. 10, d. 103, l. 1.

52. RGIA, f. 1268, op. 10, d. 103, ll. 2–3.

53. RGIA, f. 1268, op. 10, d. 103, ll. 6–7ob.

54. RGIA, f. 1268, op. 10, d. 103, ll. 6–7ob.

55. RGIA, f. 1268, op. 10, d. 103, l. 8.

56. RGIA, f. 1268, op. 10, d. 103, ll. 10ob–11.

57. RGIA, f. 1268, op. 10, d. 103, ll. 9ob–10. It is unclear who proposed the scheme.

58. RGIA, f. 1268, op. 10, d. 103, ll. 9ob–10.

59. RGIA, f. 1268, op. 10, d. 103, ll. 10–10ob. The quoted text appears to be an official summary of his statement, rather than his own words.

60. See chapter 3.

61. RGIA, f. 1268, op. 10, d. 103, l. 11ob.

62. RGIA, f. 1268, op. 10, d. 103, l. 12.

63. Werth, *The Tsar's Foreign Faiths*, 133.

64. RGIA, f. 1268, op. 10, d. 103, l. 12ob.

65. RGIA, f. 1268, op. 10, d. 103, ll. 12–12ob.

66. RGIA, f. 1268, op. 10, d. 103, ll. 12–12ob.

67. RGIA, f. 1268, op. 10, d. 103, ll. 12ob–13.

68. RGIA, f. 821, op. 7, d. 46, ll. 5–6ob.

69. RGIA, f. 821, op. 7, d. 46, l. 7.

70. RGIA, f. 821, op. 7, d. 46, ll. 5–6ob.

71. Khachaturian, *Cultivating Nationhood in Imperial Russia*, 94–117.

72. RGIA, f. 821, op. 7, d. 46, ll. 13–19.

73. RGIA, f. 1268, op. 10, d. 111, ll. 4–8.

74. RGIA, f. 1268, op. 10, d. 111, ll. 4ob–5.

75. RGIA, f. 1268, op. 10, d. 111, l. 5.

76. RGIA, f. 1268, op. 10, d. 111, l. 7.

77. Werth, *The Tsar's Foreign Faiths*, 130.

78. Mostashari, "Colonial Dilemmas," 245–46.

79. RGIA, f. 1268, op. 10, d. 111, ll. 5–5ob.

80. RGIA, f. 1268, op. 10, d. 111, ll. 5ob–6.

81. RGIA, f. 1268, op. 10, d. 111, ll. 7ob–8. As late as September 1864, Armenians from Shemakha Province continued to seek permission to convert to Lutheranism, suggesting that Valuev's proposal failed.

82. Quoted in Werth, *The Tsar's Foreign Faiths*, 133.

83. Werth, *The Tsar's Foreign Faiths*, 153–58.

84. My discussion here is based on Andrew Preston, *Sword of the Spirit, Shield of Faith: Religion in American War and Diplomacy* (New York: Alfred A. Knopf, 2012), 175–206.

85. Preston, *Sword of the Spirit, Shield of Faith*, 185.

86. Preston, *Sword of the Spirit, Shield of Faith*, 189.

87. RGIA, f. 821, op. 7, d. 156, ll. 2–3.

88. RGIA, f. 821, op. 7, d. 156, l. 2ob.

89. RGIA, f. 821, op. 7, d. 156, l. 4ob.

90. RGIA, f. 821, op. 7, d. 156, l. 8.

91. RGIA, f. 821, op. 5, d. 999, ll. 1–2ob.

92. RGIA, f. 821, op. 5, d. 999, ll. 8–8ob.

93. Preston, *Sword of the Spirit, Shield of Faith*, 196.

94. RGIA, f. 821, op. 5, d. 999, l. 26.

95. The full text of the petition is at RGIA, f. 821, op. 5, d. 999, ll. 31–32.

96. RGIA, f. 821, op. 5, d. 999, l. 31.

97. RGIA, f. 821, op. 5, d. 999, ll. 31ob–32.

98. Western missionaries had established schools for Armenians and other minorities in the Ottoman Empire in the early stages of the Tanzimat reforms. See Bloxham, *The Great Game of Genocide*, 43.

99. RGIA, f. 821, op. 5, d. 999, ll. 57–57ob.

100. Norman E. Saul makes this argument in *Distant Friends: The United States and Russia, 1763–1867* (Lawrence: University Press of Kansas, 1991).

101. *Golos*, no. 109 (21 April 1878).

102. For the effect of Russian anti-Semitism on US foreign policy, see Preston, *Sword of the Spirit, Shield of Faith*, 203–6.

103. RGIA, f. 821, op. 7, d. 72, ll. 1–2ob; quote on l. 2.

104. RGIA, f. 821, op. 7, d. 72, l. 1.

105. RGIA, f. 821, op. 7, d. 72, l. 1ob.

106. RGIA, f. 821, op. 7, d. 72, ll. 2–2ob.

107. RGIA, f. 821, op. 7, d. 72, l. 10ob.

108. RGIA, f. 821, op. 7, d. 72, ll. 12–14.

109. HAA, f. 56, op. 1, d. 3461, l. 41.

110. Steinwedel, *Threads of Empire*, 135–36.

111. RGIA, f. 1287, op. 43, d. 502, l. 1.

112. RGIA, f. 1287, op. 43, d. 502, l. 1ob.

113. RGIA, f. 821, op. 7, d. 139, ll. 1–7.

114. RGIA, f. 1268, op. 19, d. 191, ll. 1–6.

115. RGIA, f. 821, op. 7, d. 143, ll. 2–4ob.

116. RGIA, f. 821, op. 7, d. 143, l. 1ob.

117. RGIA, f. 821, op. 7, d. 143, ll. 6–9.

118. RGIA, f. 821, op. 7, d. 143, ll. 9–9ob.

119. Louise McReynolds, *The News under Russia's Old Regime: The Development of a Mass-Circulation Press* (Princeton, NJ: Princeton University Press, 1991), 39–46.

120. *Golos*, no. 181 (2 July 1878).

121. RGVIA, f. 485, op. 1, d. 594, l. 1.

122. RGVIA, f. 485, op. 1, d. 594, l. 2.

123. RGVIA, f. 485, op. 1, d. 594, l. 2.

124. RGVIA, f. 846, op. 16, d. 8636, l. 3ob.

125. RGIA, f. 866, op. 1, d. 127, ll. 15–15ob.

126. Elena Campbell, *The Muslim Question and Russian Imperial Governance* (Bloomington: Indiana University Press, 2015), 30–31.

127. Eileen Kane, *Russian Hajj: Empire and the Pilgrimage to Mecca* (Ithaca, NY: Cornell University Press, 2015), 61.

128. RGIA, f. 866, op. 1, d. 70, l. 5.

129. RGIA, f. 866, op. 1, d. 70, ll. 6–6ob.

130. RGIA, f. 866, op. 1, d. 70, l. 5ob.

131. RGIA, f. 866, op. 1, d. 70, l. 7.

132. RGIA, f. 866, op. 1, d. 70, ll. 7–7ob.

133. Suny, "Eastern Armenians under Tsarist Rule," 127.

134. RGVIA, f. 15322, op. 1, d. 35, l. 13. Kars remained under the tsar's control until the Treaty of Brest-Litovsk in 1918.

135. The full text of the treaty is in RGVIA, f. 15322, op. 1, d. 17, ll. 1–4.

136. RGVIA, f. 15322, op. 1, d. 52, l. 251.

137. RGVIA, f. 15322, op. 1, d. 52, l. 260.

138. *Golos*, no. 61 (2 March 1878).

139. For one such example, published on the front page, see *Golos*, no. 63 (4 March 1878).

140. *Golos*, no. 70 (11 March 1878).

141. *Golos*, no. 70 (11 March 1878).

142. *Golos*, no. 97 (7 April 1878).

143. RGVIA, f. 15322, op. 1, d. 18, l. 11.

144. RGVIA, f. 15322, op. 1, d. 18, l. 11ob.

145. RGVIA, f. 15322, op. 1, d. 18, ll. 40–40ob.

146. RGVIA, f. 15322, op. 1, d. 18, l. 40ob.

147. RGVIA, f. 15322, op. 1, d. 18, l. 41.

148. RGVIA, f. 15322, op. 1, d. 18, ll. 41–41ob.

149. RGVIA, f. 15322, op. 1, d. 18, l. 59.

150. *Golos*, no. 146 (28 May 1878).

151. *Golos*, no. 146 (28 May 1878).

152. *Golos*, no. 146 (28 May 1878).

153. RGVIA, f. 15322, op. 1, d. 18, ll. 145–46. Tsarist officers in occupied territories assured their superiors that the Armenians had composed the letter without the participation of any Russian officials.

154. RGVIA, f. 15322, op. 1, d. 18, l. 146.

155. HAA, f. 94, op. 1, d. 208, l. 270.

156. RGVIA, f. 15322, op. 1, d. 18, ll. 168–72.

157. HAA, f. 94, op. 1, d. 247, ll. 1–2.

158. HAA, f. 94, op. 1, d. 207, l. 4. The exact number, of course, depends on each family's financial grant. If all 50,000 rubles were distributed to the refugees and each family received 20 rubles—which did not happen, as some received as much as 35 rubles—then the total number would be twenty-five hundred families.

159. HAA, f. 94, op. 1, d. 208, ll. 10–13.

160. HAA, f. 94, op. 1, d. 208, ll. 10–13.

161. See data for Ejmiatsin District: HAA, f. 94, op. 1, d. 207, ll. 671–78; Novobaiazet District: HAA, f. 94, op. 1, d. 207, ll. 683–690ob; Yerevan District: HAA, f. 94, op. 1, d. 207, ll. 667–669ob; and Surmalinskii District: HAA, f. 94, op. 1, d. 207, ll. 680–81.

162. HAA, f. 94, op. 1, d. 208, ll. 373–92.

163. GARF, f. 109, 3rd exped., 1877, op. 162, d. 146, l. 13.

164. GARF, f. 109, 3rd exped., 1877, op. 162, d. 146, l. 2.

165. GARF, f. 109, 3rd exped., 1877, op. 162, d. 146, l. 2ob.

166. GARF, f. 109, 3rd exped., 1877, op. 162, d. 146, l. 3ob.

167. GARF, f. 109, 3rd exped., 1877, op. 162, d. 146, ll. 15–16.

168. GARF, f. 109, 3rd exped., 1877, op. 162, d. 146, ll. 21ob–22.

169. The ministers noted warily: "However mad his teachings, Bakunin's works and the sermons of his followers have had an astounding and terrifying influence on the youth." GARF, f. 109, 3rd exped., 1877, op. 162, d. 146, l. 68ob.

170. GARF, f. 109, 3rd exped., 1879, op. 164, d. 59, l. 28.

171. GARF, f. 109, 3rd exped., 1879, op. 164, d. 59, ll. 28ob–29.

172. Population statistics for the Caucasus before the end of the nineteenth century are partial. In 1881, the entire Caucasus contained approximately 5,550,000 residents. These included 1,370,000 Russians (mostly sectarians); 1,250,000 "Turks and Tatars"; about 1,000,000 Georgians; 820,000 "Caucasian-highlander peoples"; and 730,000 Armenians. The total number of Christian peoples was about 3,070,000, with the rest (about 2,480,000) Muslim. See GARF f. 652, op. 1, d. 236, l. 23.

173. GARF, f. 109, 3rd exped., 1875, op. 160, d. 120, l. 10.

174. GARF, f. 109, 3rd exped., 1875, op. 160, d. 120, l. 13ob.

175. GARF, f. 109, 3rd exped., 1875, op. 160, d. 120, l. 24.

176. Obshchestvo s blagoiu tsel'iu is the Russian translation of the Armenian Barenapatak Enkerutiun.

177. Suny, "Eastern Armenians under Tsarist Rule," 130.

178. GARF, f. 109, 3rd exped., 1875, op. 160, d. 120, ll. 24ob–25.

179. GARF, f. 109, 3rd exped., 1875, op. 160, d. 120, ll. 46ob–47.

180. GARF, f. 109, 3rd exped., 1875, op. 160, d. 120, l. 89.

181. GARF, f. 109, 3rd exped., 1875, op. 160, d. 120, l. 88.

182. GARF, f. 109, 3rd exped., 1875, op. 160, d. 120, l. 90.

183. GARF, f. 109, 3rd exped., 1879, op. 164, d. 59, ll. 28–29.

184. GARF, f. 109, 3rd exped., 1879, op. 164, d. 59, l. 29.

185. GARF, f. 109, 3rd exped., 1879, op. 164, d. 59, l. 29ob.

186. GARF, f. 109, 3rd exped., 1880, op. 165, d. 81, ll. 4–4ob.

187. GARF, f. 109, 3rd exped., 1880, op. 165, d. 141, ll. 2–7.

188. GARF, f. 109, 3rd exped., 1880, op. 165, d. 141, ll. 7ob–8.

189. GARF, f. 109, 3rd exped., 1880, op. 165, d. 141, ll. 21–21ob.

190. Weeks, "Russification and Lithuanians, 1863–1905," 101.

191. I. S. Kakhanov, quoted in Weeks, "Russification and Lithuanians, 1863–1905," 101–2.

5. The Shining of the Sabers

1. GARF, f. 109, 3rd exped., 1880, op. 165, d. 234, ll. 1–55.

2. Ovanesov and Sudavtsov, *Voenno-administrativnaia deiatel'nost' armian*, 143.

3. Serhii Plokhy, *Lost Kingdom: The Quest for Empire and the Making of the Russian Nation* (New York: Basic Books, 2017), 151–52.

4. See Heide Whelan, *Alexander III and the State Council: Bureaucracy and Counter-Reform in Late Imperial Russia* (New Brunswick, NJ: Rutgers University Press, 1982).

5. Richard Wortman, *Scenarios of Power: Myth and Ceremony in Russian Monarchy*, Vol. 2, *From Peter the Great to the Abdication of Nicholas II* (Princeton, NJ: Princeton University Press, 2000), 237–38.

6. Wortman, *Scenarios of Power*, 2:237.

7. John Klier, *Russians, Jews, and the Pogroms of 1881–1882* (Cambridge: Cambridge University Press, 2011); I. Michael Aronson, *Troubled Waters: The Origins of the 1881 Anti-Jewish Pogroms in Russia* (Pittsburgh: University of Pittsburgh Press, 1990).

8. Wortman, *Scenarios of Power*, 2:238.

9. GARF, f. 102, 3rd d-vo, op. 77, 1881, d. 1313, ll. 1–2ob.

10. Suny, "Eastern Armenians under Tsarist Rule," 127.

11. Bloxham, *The Great Game of Genocide*, 45.

12. For an overview of the Hamidiye's threat to Western Armenians, see Janet Klein, *The Margins of Empire: Kurdish Militias in the Ottoman Tribal Zone* (Stanford, CA: Stanford University Press, 2011), 14–26.

13. For broad overviews, see Louise Nalbandian, *The Armenian Revolutionary Movement: The Development of Armenian Political Parties through the Nineteenth Century* (Berkeley: University of California Press, 1963); and Anahide Ter Minassian, *Nationalism and Socialism in the Armenian Revolutionary Movement (1887–1912)*, trans. A. M. Berrett (Cambridge, MA: Zoryan Institute, 1984).

14. Brendan O'Leary has argued that "consciousness of a shared cultural, religious or territorial identity is not of the essence of nationalism." See O'Leary, "On the Nature of Nationalism: An Appraisal of Ernest Gellner's Writings on Nationalism," *British Journal of Political Science* 27, no. 2 (1997): 207.

15. John Breuilly, *Nationalism and the State* (Manchester: Manchester University Press, 1993), 2.

16. Michael Hechter, *Containing Nationalism* (New York: Oxford University Press, 2000).

17. Houri Berberian, *Armenians and the Iranian Constitutional Revolution of 1905–1911* (Boulder, CO: Westview Press, 2001), 78–86.

18. Azar Gat, *Nations: The Long History and Deep Roots of Political Ethnicity and Nationalism* (Cambridge: Cambridge University Press, 2013).

19. Suny, "Eastern Armenians under Tsarist Rule," 130–31.

20. Quoted in Pogosian, *Karsskaia oblast' v sostave Rossii*, 37.

21. One prominent example is James Creagh, *Armenians, Koords, and Turks* (London: Samuel Tinsley, 1880); a later example is Malcolm MacColl, *England's Responsibility towards Armenia* (London: Longmans, Green, 1896).

22. Michael Reynolds, *Shattering Empires: The Clash and Collapse of the Ottoman and Russian Empires, 1908–1918* (Cambridge: Cambridge University Press, 2011), 17.

23. Jerzy Jedlicki, *A Suburb of Europe: Nineteenth-Century Polish Approaches to Western Civilization* (Budapest: Central European University Press, 1999), 260.

24. See M. S. Anderson, *The Eastern Question, 1774–1923: A Study in International Relations* (New York: St. Martin's Press, 1966).

25. The text is a paraphrase of Mkrtich Khrimian's statement from his address, known as the "Iron Ladle" speech, as recorded by a member of the audience. See "Iron Ladle by Khrimyan Hayrig," trans. William Bairamian, *The Armenite*, 4 March 2014, http://thearmenite.com/2014/03/iron-ladle-khrimyan-hayrig/.

26. GARF, f. 109, 3rd exped., 1880, op. 165, d. 707, l. 1. Mikhail Nikolaevich reported that he had taken steps to stop their actions, but not much is known about this incident.

27. Van is a city in an eponymous province in eastern Turkey.

28. GARF, f. 109, 3rd exped., 1880, op. 165, d. 707, l. 3.

29. GARF, f. 102, 3rd d-vo, op. 79, 1883, d. 172, l. 1a.

30. GARF, f. 102, 3rd d-vo, op. 79, 1883, d. 172, l. 1a.

31. GARF, f. 102, 3rd d-vo, op. 79, 1883, d. 172, l. 2a.

32. GARF, f. 102, 3rd d-vo, op. 79, 1883, d. 172, l. 2b.

33. GARF, f. 102, 3rd d-vo, 1883, op. 79, d. 700, ll. 11 and 17.

34. GARF, f. 102, 3rd d-vo, 1883, op. 79, d. 700, l. 11.

35. GARF, f. 102, 3rd d-vo, 1883, op. 79, d. 700, ll. 11ob–12.

36. According to Bedross Der Matossian, from 1862 to 1882, "immigration of the Muslim population from the Balkans and Russia increased the Ottoman Muslim population of Anatolia by at least 40 percent. A good number of these immigrants moved to the eastern provinces, to areas where Armenians lived, the majority of whom were peasants, thus creating a population imbalance and friction between the locals and the immigrants." Der Matossian, *Shattered Dreams of Revolution*, 12.

37. William Francis Ainsworth, *Travels and Researches in Asia Minor, Mesopotamia, Chaldea, and Armenia* (London: John W. Parker, West Strand, 1842), 379–80. See also T. B. Armstrong, *Journal of Travels in the Seat of War, during the Last Two Campaigns of Russia and Turkey* (London: A. Seguin, 1831), 179–85; and Horatio Southgate, *Narrative of a Tour through Armenia, Kurdistan, Persia and Mesopotamia* (New York: D. Appleton, 1840), 227–28.

38. RGVIA, f. 450, op. 1, d. 111, ll. 8–15.

39. GARF, f. 102, 3rd d-vo, 1895, op. 93, d. 1130, l. 2.

40. GARF, f. 102, 3rd d-vo, 1895, op. 93, d. 1130, l. 2.

41. GARF, f. 102, 3rd d-vo, 1895, op. 93, d. 1130, l. 6ob.

42. GARF, f. 102, 3rd d-vo, 1895, op. 93, d. 1130, ll. 8–8ob.

43. GARF, f. 102, 3rd d-vo, 1895, op. 93, d. 1130, l. 13.

44. GARF, f. 102, 3rd d-vo, 1895, op. 93, d. 1130, l. 12.

45. GARF, f. 102, 3rd d-vo, 1895, op. 93, d. 1130, ll. 8–8ob.

46. GARF, f. 102, 3rd d-vo, 1895, op. 93, d. 1130, l. 10.

47. GARF, f. 102, 3rd d-vo, 1895, op. 93, d. 1130, ll. 9ob–10.

48. GARF, f. 102, 3rd d-vo, 1895, op. 93, d. 1130, l. 10.

49. GARF, f. 102, 3rd d-vo, 1895, op. 93, d. 1130, l. 13.

50. GARF, f. 102, 3rd d-vo, 1895, op. 93, d. 1130, l. 14ob.

51. GARF, f. 102, 3rd d-vo, 1895, op. 93, d. 1130, l. 22.

52. GARF, f. 102, 3rd d-vo, 1895, op. 93, d. 1130, l. 22.

53. GARF, f. 102, 3rd d-vo, 1895, op. 93, d. 1130, ll. 23ob–24.

54. GARF, f. 102, 3rd d-vo, 1895, op. 93, d. 1130, l. 24ob.

55. GARF, f. 102, 3rd d-vo, 1895, op. 93, d. 1130, ll. 41–42.

56. GARF, f. 102, 3rd d-vo, 1895, op. 93, d. 1130, l. 30ob.

57. Christopher Walker, *Armenia: The Survival of a Nation*, 2nd ed. (New York: Routledge, 1990), 165.

58. Reynolds, *Shattering Empires*, 54.

59. For one example, see A. L. Macfie, *The Eastern Question, 1774–1923* (London: Longman, 1996).

60. Here I take a different view than Michael Reynolds, who has argued that a state's "horizontal" ties to other polities are often more important for understanding its political behavior than its "vertical" ties to its subjects. See Reynolds, *Shattering Empires*.

61. GARF, f. 102, 3rd d-vo, 1883, op. 79, d. 700, ll. 1–6ob.

62. GARF, f. 102, 3rd d-vo, 1883, op. 79, d. 700, ll. 2–2ob.

63. GARF, f. 102, 3rd d-vo, 1883, op. 79, d. 700, l. 3ob.

64. GARF, f. 102, 3rd d-vo, 1883, op. 79, d. 700, l. 4ob.

65. GARF, f. 102, 3rd d-vo, 1883, op. 79, d. 700, ll. 4ob–5.

66. GARF, f. 102, 3rd d-vo, 1883, op. 79, d. 700, l. 6.

67. GARF, f. 102, 3rd d-vo, 1883, op. 79, d. 700, l. 10ob.

68. GARF, f. 102, 3rd d-vo, 1883, op. 79, d. 700, l. 10ob.

69. GARF, f. 102, 3rd d-vo, 1883, op. 79, d. 700, l. 17ob.

70. GARF, f. 102, 3rd d-vo, 1883, op. 79, d. 700, l. 5ob.

71. GARF, f. 102, 3rd d-vo, 1887, op. 83, d. 9, ch. 24, ll. 33–33ob.

72. GARF, f. 102, 3rd d-vo, 1887, op. 83, d. 280, ll. 1–3.

73. GARF, f. 102, 3rd d-vo, 1888, op. 84, d. 297, l. 1.

74. GARF, f. 102, 3rd d-vo, 1888, op. 84, d. 297, ll. 8–8ob.

75. GARF, f. 102, 3rd d-vo, 1888, op. 84, d. 297, l. 11ob.

76. GARF, f. 102, 3rd d-vo, 1895, op. 93, d. 563, ll. 1–2.

77. GARF, f. 102, 3rd d-vo, 1895, op. 93, d. 563, ll. 4–4ob.

78. Suny, "Eastern Armenians under Tsarist Rule," 130–31.

79. GARF, f. 1099, op. 1, d. 587, l. 7.

80. GARF, f. 102, 3rd d-vo, 1883, op. 79, d. 1352, ll. 3–15.

81. Richard Hovannisian, "The Armenian Question in the Ottoman Empire 1876 to 1914," in *The Armenian People from Ancient to Modern Times*, ed. Richard Hovannisian (New York: St. Martin's Press, 2004), 2:213.

82. Hovannisian, "The Armenian Question in the Ottoman Empire," 214.

83. Nalbandian, *The Armenian Revolutionary Movement*, 169–70.

84. Nalbandian, *The Armenian Revolutionary Movement*, 169.

85. Nalbandian, *The Armenian Revolutionary Movement*, 171. Unlike these two groups, the Armenakan Party did not condone terrorism, although its individual members did not always eschew such means.

86. Berberian, *Armenians and the Iranian Constitutional Revolution*, 48–50.

87. Indeed, there are practically no references to Dashnak activities in the files of the Okhrana between 1890 and 1895.

88. Nalbandian, *The Armenian Revolutionary Movement*, 182.

89. For some overviews, see Theodore Weeks, *Nation and State in Late Imperial Russia: Nationalism and Russification on the Western Frontier, 1863–1914* (DeKalb: Northern Illinois University Press, 2008), 92–109; and Alexei Miller, *The Romanov Empire and Nationalism: Essays in the Methodology of Historical Research* (Budapest: Central European University Press, 2008), 45–66.

90. Steinwedel, *Threads of Empire*, 157.

91. Suny, "Eastern Armenians under Tsarist Rule," 129–30.

92. RGIA, f. 821, op. 7, d. 222, ll. 55–55ob.

93. GARF, f. 678, op. 1, d. 687, l. 27.

94. RGIA, f. 821, op. 7, d. 222, l. 45.

95. GARF, f. 102, 3rd d-vo, 1895, op. 93, d. 1130, l. 23.

96. Miroslav Hroch has highlighted the role of geographical divisions in the formation of nationalism. See Miroslav Hroch, *Social Preconditions of National Revival in Europe: A Comparative Analysis of the Social Composition of Patriotic Groups among the Smaller European Nations*, trans. Ben Fowkes (New York: Columbia University Press, 2000).

97. RGIA, f. 821, op. 7, d. 196, l. 16ob.

98. RGIA, f. 821, op. 7, d. 222, l. 6ob.

99. Ovanesov and Sudavtsov, *Voenno-administrativnaia deiatel'nost' armian*, 183.

100. *Novoe obozrenie*, 2 March, 1885.

101. RGIA, f. 821, op. 7, d. 222, l. 45.

102. RGIA, f. 821, op. 7, d. 222, ll. 45ob–46.

103. RGIA, f. 821, op. 7, d. 196, ll. 17ob–18.

104. Suny, "Eastern Armenians under Tsarist Rule," 129–30.

105. See, for example, *Novoe obozrenie*, 2 March 1885.

106. GARF, f. 102, 3rd d-vo, 1885, op. 81, d. 25, ch. 13, l. 1.

107. GARF, f. 102, 3rd d-vo, 1885, op. 81, d. 25, ch. 13, ll. 3–3ob.

108. GARF, f. 102, 3rd d-vo, 1885, op. 81, d. 25, ch. 13, l. 6ob.

109. GARF, f. 102, 3rd d-vo, 1885, op. 81, d. 25, ch. 13, ll. 7ob–8.

110. GARF, f. 102, 3rd d-vo, 1883, op. 79, d. 700, ll. 53–55.

111. GARF, f. 102, 3rd d-vo, 1883, op. 79, d. 700, l. 55.

112. GARF, f. 102, 3rd d-vo, 1884, op. 80, d. 88, ch. 2, l. 24ob.

113. RGIA, f. 821, op. 7, d. 182, ll. 10–48.

114. RGIA, f. 821, op. 7, d. 131, ll. 13–16ob.

115. RGIA, f. 821, op. 7, d. 131, l. 15ob.

116. RGIA, f. 821, op. 7, d. 131, l. 13ob.

117. RGIA, f. 821, op. 7, d. 131, ll. 23–32.

118. RGIA, f. 821, op. 7, d. 131, ll. 27–27ob.

119. RGIA, f. 821, op. 7, d. 131, l. 30ob.

120. RGIA, f. 821, op. 7, d. 196, ll. 3–3ob.

121. GARF, f. 1099, op. 1, d. 587, ll. 8–9.

122. GARF, f. 1099, op. 1, d. 587, l. 9.

123. GARF, f. 102, 3rd d-vo, 1883, op. 79, d. 700, l. 68.

124. GARF, f. 1099, op. 1, d. 587, l. 9.

125. GARF, f. 1099, op. 1, d. 587, ll. 9–9ob.

126. RGIA, f. 821, op. 7, d. 164, ll. 4–4ob.

127. GARF, f. 1099, op. 1, d. 587, l. 10.

128. RGIA, f. 821, op. 7, d. 206, ll. 15–15ob.

129. RGIA, f. 821, op. 7, d. 206, ll. 17–17ob.

130. RGIA, f. 821, op. 7, d. 206, ll. 27–27ob.

131. RGIA, f. 821, op. 7, d. 206, ll. 30–30ob and 54.

132. RGIA, f. 821, op. 7, d. 206, ll. 36–37.

133. RGIA, f. 821, op. 7, d. 206, ll. 58 and 72.

134. RGIA, f. 821, op. 7, d. 206, l. 205.

135. RGIA, f. 821, op. 7, d. 131, ll. 34–35ob.

136. RGIA, f. 821, op. 7, d. 206, l. 137.

137. RGIA, f. 821, op. 7, d. 131, ll. 38ob–39.

138. RGIA, f. 821, op. 7, d. 131, ll. 43–44.

139. RGIA, f. 821, op. 7, d. 222, l. 55.

140. GARF, f. 652, op. 1, d. 236, l. 24.

141. GARF, f. 1099, op. 1, d. 587, l. 7; *Bratskaia pomoshch' postradavshim v Turtsii armianam* (Moscow: I. N. Kushnerev, 1898), 254.

142. GARF, f. 1099, op. 1, d. 587, l. 4.

143. GARF, f. 1099, op. 1, d. 587, l. 7.

144. A local Caucasian proverb warned: "A Greek will cheat three Jews, but an Armenian will cheat three Greeks." See King, *The Ghost of Freedom*, 148.

145. GARF, f. 102, 3rd d-vo, 1883, op. 79, d. 700, l. 50.

146. GARF, f. 102, 3rd d-vo, 1884, op. 80, d. 88, ch. 2, ll. 18–18ob.

147. GARF, f. 1099, op. 1, d. 587, l. 7.

148. GARF, f. 1099, op. 1, d. 587, l. 8.

149. GARF, f. 102, 3rd d-vo, 1883, op. 79, d. 700, l. 8.

150. GARF, f. 102, 3rd d-vo, 1883, op. 79, d. 700, ll. 15ob–16.

151. GARF, f. 102, 3rd d-vo, 1883, op. 79, d. 700, ll. 16–16ob.

152. GARF, f. 102, 3rd d-vo, 1883, op. 79, d. 700, l. 41.

153. GARF, f. 102, 3rd d-vo, 1883, op. 79, d. 700, l. 48ob.

154. GARF, f. 102, 3rd d-vo, 1883, op. 79, d. 700, l. 45.

155. GARF, f. 102, 3rd d-vo, 1883, op. 79, d. 700, l. 51.

156. GARF, f. 102, 3rd d-vo, 1883, op. 79, d. 700, l. 43ob.

157. GARF, f. 102, 3rd d-vo, 1883, op. 79, d. 700, l. 44.

158. Crews, "Empire and the Confessional State."

159. *Bratskaia pomoshch' postradavshim v Turtsii armianam* (Moscow: K. O. Aleksandrov, 1897). The book's second edition was released the following year. On the massacres of Ottoman Armenians in the mid-1890s, see Bloxham, *The Great Game of Genocide*, 51–57.

160. Nikolai Marr, "Ani, stolitsa drevnei Armenii," in *Bratskaia pomoshch' postradavshim v Turtsii Armianam* (Moscow: I. N. Kushnerev, 1898), 197–222.

161. Viktor Abaza, *Istoriia Armenii* (St. Petersburg: Tipografiia I. N. Skorokhodova, 1888), v.

162. I. Ia. Aleksanov, *Kratkaia istoriia Armenii s pribavleniem ocherka "Armiane v Rossii"* (Rostov: Tipografiia A. I. Adamkovicha, 1884), 107.

163. Jo Laycock, *Imagining Armenia: Orientalism, Ambiguity and Intervention* (Manchester: Manchester University Press, 2009).

164. RGIA, f. 821, op. 7, d. 164, l. 28.

165. RGIA, f. 821, op. 7, d. 164, ll. 22ob–23.

166. RGIA, f. 821, op. 7, d. 164, ll. 23ob and 30.

167. RGIA, f. 821, op. 7, d. 164, l. 30ob.

168. RGIA, f. 821, op. 7, d. 164, ll. 30ob–31.

169. RGIA, f. 821, op. 7, d. 164, l. 31ob.

170. RGIA, f. 821, op. 7, d. 164, ll. 31ob–32.

171. For early notions of Russian moral superiority against its imperial competitors, see Lieven, *Empire*.

172. RGIA, f. 821, op. 7, d. 164, l. 32.

173. RGIA, f. 821, op. 7, d. 164, ll. 34–35ob.

174. Candan Badem, "'Forty Years of Black Days?' The Russian Administration of Kars, Ardahan, and Batum, 1878–1918," in *Russian-Ottoman Borderlands: The Eastern Question Reconsidered*, ed. Lucien Frary and Mara Kozelsky (Madison: University of Wisconsin Press, 2014), 245.

175. See Breyfogle, *Heretics and Colonizers*.

176. RGIA, f. 821, op. 7, d. 164, ll. 34–34ob.

177. RGIA, f. 821, op. 7, d. 164, l. 34ob.

178. RGIA, f. 821, op. 7, d. 164, ll. 34–35ob.

179. RGIA, f. 821, op. 7, d. 164, l. 35ob.

180. Ovanesov and Sudavtsov, *Voenno-administrativnaia deiatel'nost' armian*, 184.

6. Nadir and Normalization, 1896–1914

1. Weeks, *Nation and State in Late Imperial Russia*, 110–30.

2. Steinwedel, *Threads of Empire*, 182–203.

3. Anatolyi Remnev, "Siberia and the Russian Far East in the Imperial Geography of Power," in *Russian Empire: Space, People, Power, 1700–1930*, ed. Jane Burbank, Mark von Hagen, and Anatolyi Remnev (Bloomington: Indiana University Press, 2007), 445.

4. Tunian, *Politika samoderzhaviia Rossii v Zakavkaz'e*, vol. 6 (2010), 5.

5. On the number of Armenians in the Caucasus in 1897, see Suny, *Looking toward Ararat*, 82. On the Armenian majority in Yerevan Province, see Berberian, *Armenians*

and the Iranian Constitutional Revolution, 16; and Tunian, *Politika samoderzhaviia Rossii v Zakavkaz'e*, vol. 6 (2010), 5.

6. Levon Marashlian, *Politics and Demography: Armenians, Turks, and Kurds in the Ottoman Empire* (Cambridge, MA: Zoryan Institute, 1991), 36–37 and 58; Kemal H. Karpat, *Ottoman Population, 1830–1914: Demographic and Social Characteristics* (Madison: University of Wisconsin Press, 1985), 16 and 148.

7. RGIA, f. 821, op. 138, d. 72, l. 269.

8. Gerard Libaridian, *Modern Armenia: People, Nation, State* (New Brunswick, NJ: Transaction, 2011), 19.

9. Vahe A. Sarafian, "Turkish Armenia and Expatriate Population Statistics," *Armenian Review* 9, no. 3 (1956): 119.

10. Panossian, *The Armenians*, 167.

11. For an overview of the crisis of 1905 in the Caucasus, see Amiran Urushadze, "Kavkaz v kontse XIX–nachale XX v.: Problemy upravleniia i modernizatsii na iuzhnoi okraine Rossiiskoi imperii," *Quaestio Rossica* 2 (2015): 144–57, particularly 149.

12. Kimitaka Matsuzato, "General-gubernatorstva v Rossiiskoi imperii: Ot etnicheskogo k prostranstvennomu podkhodu," in *Novaia imperskaia istoriia postsovetskogo prostranstva*, ed. Ilya Gerasimov, Sergei Glebov, Alexander Kaplunovskii, Marina Mogilner, and Alexander Semyonov (Kazan: Tsentr issledovanii natsionalizma i imperii, 2004), 441.

13. RGIA, f. 821, op. 7, d. 164, ll. 50–55. For the Hamidian massacres, see Klein, *The Margins of Empire*, 26.

14. RGIA, f. 821, op. 7, d. 164, l. 52ob.

15. RGIA, f. 821, op. 7, d. 164, l. 59.

16. RGIA, f. 821, op. 7, d. 222, ll. 1–2.

17. Ronald G. Suny writes that the St. Petersburg authorities informed the catholicos that the school closings were a punishment for Armenian petitions to the British. Suny, *Looking toward Ararat*, 47.

18. Laycock, *Imagining Armenia*, 77–83.

19. RGIA, f. 821, op. 7, d. 222, ll. 3–5ob.

20. RGIA, f. 821, op. 7, d. 222, l. 5.

21. RGIA, f. 821, op. 7, d. 222, ll. 60–62.

22. Tunian, *Echmiadzinskii vopros*, 131.

23. RGIA, f. 821, op. 7, d. 222, l. 14.

24. RGIA, f. 821, op. 7, d. 222, ll. 14–15.

25. RGIA, f. 821, op. 7, d. 222, l. 15.

26. RGIA, f. 821, op. 7, d. 222, ll. 16–16ob.

27. RGIA, f. 821, op. 7, d. 222, l. 40ob.

28. RGIA, f. 821, op. 7, d. 222, l. 41.

29. RGIA, f. 821, op. 138, d. 71, ll. 1–2.

30. RGIA, f. 821, op. 7, d. 222, l. 68.

31. RGIA, f. 821, op. 7, d. 222, l. 43.

32. RGIA, f. 821, op. 7, d. 222, l. 43ob.

33. Tunian, *Echmiadzinskii vopros*, 110.

34. RGIA, f. 821, op. 7, d. 222, l. 44.

35. Richard Hovannisian, "Simon Vratzian and Armenian Nationalism," *Middle Eastern Studies* 5, no. 3 (1969): 192–220, especially 197.

36. RGIA, f. 821, op. 7, d. 206, ll. 191–205.

37. Lang, *A Modern History of Soviet Georgia*, 119; Suny, *Looking toward Ararat*, 47; Christopher Walker, *Armenia: The Survival of a Nation*, 2nd ed. (New York: Routledge, 1990), 70.

38. Sergei Witte memoirs, in *A Source Book for Russian History*, ed. George Vernadsky (New Haven, CT: Yale University Press, 1972), vol. 3, 694.

39. RGIA, f. 821, op. 7, d. 222, l. 122.

40. RGIA, f. 821, op. 7, d. 222, l. 122.

41. RGIA, f. 821, op. 7, d. 222, l. 131.

42. RGIA, f. 821, op. 7, d. 222, l. 168ob.

43. Quoted in Steinwedel, *Threads of Empire*, 158.

44. For a synthetic overview of the "Armenian Question" in the Ottoman Empire, see Panossian, *The Armenians*, 160–80.

45. Manoug Somakian, *Empires in Conflict: Armenia and the Great Powers, 1895–1920* (London: I. B. Tauris, 1995), 23–31.

46. Tunian, *Echmiadzinskii vopros*, 109.

47. Somakian, *Empires in Conflict*, 29. Historians continue to debate the authenticity of Lobanov-Rostovskii's statements about Armenians.

48. Tunian, *Echmiadzinskii vopros*, 109.

49. Tunian, *Echmiadzinskii vopros*, 108.

50. On the Hamidian massacres, see Somakian, *Empires in Conflict*, 3. On the Zeitun uprising, see Guenter Lewy, *The Armenian Massacres in Ottoman Turkey: A Disputed Genocide* (Salt Lake City: University of Utah Press, 2005), 24.

51. Ronald G. Suny, *"They Can Live in the Desert but Nowhere Else": A History of the Armenian Genocide* (Princeton, NJ: Princeton University Press, 2015), 123.

52. Quoted in Suny, *Looking toward Ararat*, 46.

53. RGIA, f. 821, op. 138, d. 71, ll. 18–20.

54. RGIA, f. 821, op. 138, d. 71, l. 20.

55. Quoted in Werth, *The Tsar's Foreign Faiths*, 161. Golitsyn's reports to Goremykin about Armenian clergy aiding Armenian rebels are in RGIA, f. 821, op. 138, d. 71, ll. 89–99ob.

56. Berberian, *Armenians and the Iranian Constitutional Revolution*, 50.

57. The official estimate was 19,000 *desiatiny* of land. One *desiatina* = 2.7 acres.

58. RGIA, f. 821, op. 138, d. 71, l. 18.

59. RGIA, f. 821, op. 138, d. 71, l. 55.

60. RGIA, f. 821, op. 138, d. 71, ll. 145–147ob.

61. Tunian, *Politika samoderzhaviia Rossii v Zakavkaz'e*, vol. 6 (2010), 6.

62. See Joan Neuberger, *Hooliganism: Crime, Culture, and Power in St. Petersburg, 1900–1914* (Berkeley: University of California Press, 1993); and Leopold Haimson, "'The Problem of Political and Social Stability in Urban Russia on the Eve of War and Revolution' Revisited," *Slavic Review* 59, no. 4 (2000): 848–75.

63. See David Schimmelpenninck van der Oye, *Toward the Rising Sun: Russian Ideologies of Empire and the Path to War with Japan* (DeKalb: Northern Illinois University Press, 2006).

64. David McDonald, *United Government and Foreign Policy in Russia, 1900–1914* (Cambridge, MA: Harvard University Press, 1992), 9.

65. Sheila Fitzpatrick, *The Russian Revolution*, 3rd ed. (Oxford: Oxford University Press, 2008), 15–39.

66. Robert K. Massie, *Nicholas and Alexandra: The Fall of the Romanov Dynasty* (New York: Modern Library, 2012), 104.

67. For one overview of Polish-Russian-Jewish conflicts in the western borderlands from the 1890s to the 1910s, see Weeks, *Nation and State in Late Imperial Russia*, 152–71.

68. Edward H. Judge, *Plehve: Repression and Reform in Imperial Russia, 1902–1904* (Syracuse, NY: Syracuse University Press, 1983), 93–121.

69. Albert S. Lindemann, *The Jew Accused: Three Anti-Semitic Affairs, 1894–1914* (New York: Cambridge University Press, 1991), 160.

70. Benjamin Nathans, *Beyond the Pale: The Jewish Encounter with Late Imperial Russia* (Berkeley: University of California Press, 2004), 298.

71. Robert E. Blobaum, *Rewolucja: Russian Poland, 1904–1907* (Ithaca, NY: Cornell University Press, 1995).

72. Tuna, *Imperial Russia's Muslims*, 199–215. See also Crews, *For Prophet and Tsar*, 330. For the influence of pan-Islamism and pan-Turkism on tsarist policies in the South Caucasus in the early twentieth century, see Önol, *The Tsar's Armenians*, 118–27.

73. Kane, *Russian Hajj*, 108.

74. RGIA, f. 821, op. 150, d. 474, ll. 2–51.

75. Tunian, *Echmiadzinskii vopros*, 155.

76. Quoted in Werth, *The Tsar's Foreign Faiths*, 145.

77. Sipiagin's report about the March 1900 debate is in RGIA, f. 821, op. 150, d. 474, ll. 1–51.

78. Tunian, *Echmiadzinskii vopros*, 155.

79. RGIA, f. 821, op. 150, d. 474, l. 2.

80. RGIA, f. 821, op. 150, d. 474, l. 2ob and 51.

81. Tunian, *Echmiadzinskii vopros*, 167.

82. For Witte's political biography, see Sidney Harcave, *Count Sergei Witte and the Twilight of Imperial Russia: A Biography* (New York: M. E. Sharpe, 2004).

83. Quoted in Tunian, *Echmiadzinskii vopros*, 157.

84. Witte memoirs, in Vernadsky, *A Source Book for Russian History*, vol. 3, 693.

85. Tunian, *Echmiadzinskii vopros*, 158–60.

86. Quoted in Tunian, *Echmiadzinskii vopros*, 161.

87. Quoted in Tunian, *Echmiadzinskii vopros*, 161–62.

88. Paul Werth has summarized the catholicos's resistance to Golitsyn's policies. See Werth, *The Tsar's Foreign Faiths*, 161.

89. Tunian, *Echmiadzinskii vopros*, 163.

90. RGIA, f. 821, op. 138, d. 80, ll. 1–7ob.

91. RGIA, f. 821, op. 138, d. 80, l. 12.

92. RGIA, f. 821, op. 138, d. 80, ll. 12–12ob.

93. RGIA, f. 821, op. 138, d. 80, l. 12.

94. For Golitsyn's views on candidates' political reliability, see RGIA, f. 821, op. 138, d. 80, ll. 14–16ob. On Golitsyn's backing of Sipiagin's proposal, see RGIA, f. 821, op. 138, d. 80, l. 19.

95. Quoted in Tunian, *Echmiadzinskii vopros*, 164.

96. Quoted in Tunian, *Echmiadzinskii vopros*, 164.

97. RGIA, f. 821, op. 138, d. 72, l. 158.

98. RGIA, f. 821, op. 138, d. 72, ll. 158–324.

99. See B. T. Ovanesov, "Rol' armianskoi tserkvi v obrazovatel'nom protsesse i sblizhenii ee s russkim pravitel'stvom (XIX–nachalo XX v.)," *Izvestiia Altaiskogo gosudarstvennogo universiteta* 4, no. 4 (2009): 206; and also Tunian, *Echmiadzinskii vopros*, 168.

100. Tunian, *Echmiadzinskii vopros*, 168.

101. RGIA, f. 821, op. 138, d. 72, l. 320ob.

102. RGIA, f. 821, op. 138, d. 72, ll. 309–310ob.

103. RGIA, f. 821, op. 138, d. 72, l. 309ob.

104. RGIA, f. 821, op. 138, d. 72, l. 310.

105. RGIA, f. 821, op. 138, d. 72, l. 324.

106. RGIA, f. 821, op. 138, d. 72, l. 323.

107. Tunian, *Echmiadzinskii vopros*, 168.

108. For overviews, see Theodore Weeks, *Vilnius between Nations, 1795–2000* (DeKalb: Northern Illinois University Press, 2015), 83; and Faith Hillis, *Children of Rus': Right-Bank Ukraine and the Invention of a Russian Nation* (Ithaca, NY: Cornell University Press, 2013), 139–77. For a broader look, see Timothy Snyder, *The Reconstruction of Nations: Poland, Ukraine, Lithuania, Belarus, 1569–1999* (New Haven, CT: Yale University Press, 2003), 31–51 and 119–22.

109. Judge, *Plehve*, 113.

110. Werth, *The Tsar's Foreign Faiths*, 201.

111. Harcave, *Count Sergei Witte*, 103.

112. Judge, *Plehve*, 62–92.

113. Harcave, *Count Sergei Witte*, 85.

114. Harcave, *Count Sergei Witte*, 96.

115. Witte memoirs, in Vernadsky, *A Source Book for Russian History*, vol. 3, 694.

116. Quoted in Tunian, *Echmiadzinskii vopros*, 169. For an overview of the Russian absorption of the Georgian Orthodox Church, see Suny, *The Making of the Georgian Nation*, 84–85.

117. Quoted in Tunian, *Echmiadzinskii vopros*, 169–70.

118. About seven hundred pages of Armenian and Russian records of Armenian responses to the 1903 confiscation are located in these three large collections: RGIA, f. 821, op. 138, d. 107; RGIA, f. 821, op. 138, d. 108; and RGIA, f. 821, op. 138, d. 109.

119. Tunian, *Echmiadzinskii vopros*, 170, 179.

120. RGIA, f. 821, op. 138, d. 108, ll. 228–32.

121. *Los Angeles Herald*, no. 355 (21 September 1903).

122. RGIA, f. 821, op. 138, d. 108, l. 253.

123. Tunian, *Echmiadzinskii vopros*, 171.

124. RGIA, f. 821, op. 138, d. 107, ll. 2–2ob.

125. RGIA, f. 821, op. 138, d. 108, l. 81.

126. RGIA, f. 821, op. 138, d. 107, l. 3.

127. RGIA, f. 821, op. 138, d. 107, ll. 6 and 51. For a thorough overview of the Armenian resistance, see Tunian, *Echmiadzinskii vopros*, 170–201. For more concise sum-

maries, see Walker, *Armenia*, 70; Suny, *Looking toward Ararat*, 92; and Werth, *The Tsar's Foreign Faiths*, 162.

128. Quote at RGIA, f. 821, op. 138, d. 107, l. 46.

129. Walker, *Armenia*, 70.

130. RGIA, f. 821, op. 138, d. 107, l. 12.

131. Tunian, *Echmiadzinskii vopros*, 171.

132. RGIA, f. 821, op. 138, d. 107, ll. 56ob–57.

133. RGIA, f. 821, op. 138, d. 107, l. 62.

134. For an overview of Dashnak and Hnchak responses to the expropriation, see Berberian, *Armenians and the Iranian Constitutional Revolution*, 77.

135. RGIA, f. 821, op. 138, d. 107, l. 59.

136. McReynolds, *The News under Russia's Old Regime*, 74.

137. RGIA, f. 821, op. 138, d. 107, l. 52.

138. Historian Onur Önol exaggerates when he writes about an "all-out Armenian rebellion against the Russian authorities" after the confiscation of 1903. Önol, *The Tsar's Armenians*, 12.

139. RGIA, f. 821, op. 138, d. 108, ll. 65–66ob.

140. RGIA, f. 821, op. 138, d. 108, l. 225.

141. Stephen F. Jones, *Socialism in Georgian Colors: The European Road to Social Democracy, 1883–1917* (Cambridge, MA: Harvard University Press, 2005), 171.

142. Plokhy, *Lost Kingdom*, 162–63. For a broader overview, see Mikhail Volkhonskii, "K 100-letiiu revoliutsii 1905–1907 gg. v Rossii: Natsional'nyi vopros vo vnutrennei politike pravitel'stva v gody pervoi russkoi revoliutsii," *Otechestvennaia istoriia* 5 (2005): 48–62.

143. Judge, *Plehve*, 232–37.

144. See Ismail-Zade, *Graf I. I. Vorontsov-Dashkov.*

145. For the crisis of 1905, see Abraham Ascher, *The Revolution of 1905: A Short History* (Stanford, CA: Stanford University Press, 2004).

146. RGIA, f. 1276, op. 19, d. 1, ll. 1–2.

147. RGIA, f. 1276, op. 19, d. 1, l. 4.

148. M. F. Florinskii, "Tsentral'naia vlast' i Kavkazskaia administratsiia v sisteme upravleniia Rossiiskoi imperii v 1905–1914 gg.," in *Tsentr i regiony v istorii Rossii: Problemy ekonomicheskogo, politicheskogo i sotsiokul'turnogo vzaimodeistviia*, ed. A. Iu. Dvornichenko (St. Petersburg: Sankt Peterburgskii gosudarstvennyi universitet, 2010), 380–81.

149. RGIA, f. 1276, op. 19, d. 1, l. 5.

150. RGIA, f. 821, op. 138, d. 109, ll. 245–47.

151. RGIA, f. 821, op. 138, d. 109, ll. 174, 191, 197, 201, 224–25, 230, and 240.

152. RGIA, f. 821, op. 138, d. 109, l. 250ob.

153. RGIA, f. 821, op. 138, d. 72, ll. 327–42.

154. RGIA, f. 821, op. 138, d. 72, l. 327. This passage is from Nolde's report to the tsar, and it is not clear whether he was quoting or summarizing Vorontsov-Dashkov's statement.

155. RGIA, f. 821, op. 138, d. 72, l. 335.

156. RGIA, f. 821, op. 138, d. 72, ll. 338–338ob.

157. RGIA, f. 821, op. 138, d. 72, l. 339.

158. RGIA, f. 821, op. 138, d. 72, l. 339.

159. RGIA, f. 821, op. 138, d. 72, l. 339ob.

160. RGIA, f. 821, op. 138, d. 72, l. 339ob.

161. RGIA, f. 821, op. 138, d. 109, l. 267.

162. RGIA, f. 821, op. 138, d. 72, l. 325.

163. RGIA, f. 821, op. 138, d. 72, l. 327ob.

164. RGIA, f. 821, op. 138, d. 109, l. 269.

165. Florinskii, "Tsentral'naia vlast' i Kavkazskaia administratsiia," 397–400.

166. See O. V. Edel'man, "Mezhnatsional'nye stolknoveniia v Baku 7–10 fevralia 1905 g. v dokumentakh Departamenta politsii," in *Russkii sbornik: Issledovaniia po istorii Rossii* (Moscow: Modest Kolerov, 2017), vol. 22, 343–412; and also Leslie Sargent, "The 'Armeno-Tatar War' in the South Caucasus, 1905–1906: Multiple Causes, Interpreted Meanings," *Ab Imperio*, no. 4 (2010): 143–69.

167. Mostashari, *On the Religious Frontier*, 101–5.

168. Urushadze, "Kavkaz v kontse XIX–nachale XX v.," 153.

169. Önol, *The Tsar's Armenians*, 36–41.

170. Abraham Ascher, *P. A. Stolypin: The Search for Stability in Late Imperial Russia* (Stanford, CA: Stanford University Press, 2001), 237–40.

171. Historian Robert Service aptly refers to Stolypin as a "reforming conservative" in Robert Service, *A History of Modern Russia from Nicholas II to Vladimir Putin*, 2nd ed. (Cambridge, MA: Harvard University Press, 2003), 16. On the assessment of Stolypin the statesman, see Ascher, *P. A. Stolypin*, 1.

172. Florinskii, "Tsentral'naia vlast' i Kavkazskaia administratsiia," 397.

173. RGIA, f. 821, op. 138, d. 90, ll. 167–181ob.

174. RGIA, f. 821, op. 138, d. 90, l. 183.

175. RGIA, f. 821, op. 138, d. 90, l. 183ob.

176. RGIA, f. 821, op. 138, d. 90, l. 184.

177. RGIA, f. 821, op. 138, d. 90, ll. 206–8.

178. RGIA, f. 821, op. 138, d. 90, ll. 193–198ob; quote on l. 193.

179. RGIA, f. 821, op. 138, d. 90, l. 193ob.

180. RGIA, f. 821, op. 138, d. 90, ll. 194–194ob.

181. RGIA, f. 821, op. 138, d. 90, l. 194ob.

182. RGIA, f. 821, op. 138, d. 90, ll. 199–205ob.

183. McDonald, *United Government and Foreign Policy in Russia*, 96.

184. RGIA, f. 821, op. 138, d. 90, l. 200ob.

185. RGIA, f. 821, op. 138, d. 90, l. 202ob.

186. RGIA, f. 821, op. 138, d. 90, l. 203.

187. RGIA, f. 821, op. 138, d. 90, l. 202.

188. RGIA, f. 821, op. 138, d. 90, l. 201.

189. For the debates in 1908, see RGIA, f. 1276, op. 4, d. 830, ll. 2–128. Tsar Nicholas II approved the ministers' decision.

190. RGIA, f. 821, op. 7, d. 306, l. 163.

191. Önol, *The Tsar's Armenians*, 43–70.

192. Hovannisian, "Simon Vratzian and Armenian Nationalism," 200.

193. Berberian, *Armenians and the Iranian Constitutional Revolution*, 6–8.

194. Önol, *The Tsar's Armenians*, 61.

195. Somakian, *Empires in Conflict*, 46.

196. Peter Holquist, "The Politics and Practice of the Russian Occupation of Armenia, 1915–February 1917," in *A Question of Genocide: Armenians and Turks at the End of the Ottoman Empire*, ed. Ronald G. Suny, Fatma Müge Göçek, and Norman M. Naimark (New York: Oxford University Press, 2011), 153.

197. RGIA, f. 821, op. 7, d. 306, ll. 169–71.

198. RGIA, f. 821, op. 7, d. 306, l. 169.

199. RGIA, f. 821, op. 7, d. 306, l. 160. Additionally, two delegates came from Persia and six from Europe and the United States.

200. RGIA, f. 821, op. 7, d. 306, l. 161.

201. RGIA, f. 821, op. 7, d. 306, l. 170.

202. RGIA, f. 821, op. 7, d. 306, ll. 172–75.

203. Vorontsov-Dashkov complained of past administrators' arrogant behavior with the catholicoi in June 1909. See RGIA, f. 919, op. 2, d. 661, l. 3ob.

204. Ilarion Vorontsov-Dashkov, *Vsepoddanneishii otchet za vosem' let upravleniia Kavkazom* (St. Petersburg: Gosudarstvennaia tipografiia, 1913), 7.

205. Vorontsov-Dashkov, *Vsepoddanneishii otchet za vosem' let*, 7.

206. Vorontsov-Dashkov, *Vsepoddanneishii otchet za vosem' let*, 9.

207. Citing Vorontsov-Dashkov's earlier reports, Önol disputes this narrative, arguing that both the viceroy and the statesmen in St. Petersburg, especially between 1905 and 1912, remained wary of pan-Islamism and pan-Turkism in the Caucasus. Önol, *The Tsar's Armenians*, 118–27. Mustafa Tuna has concluded, "We know that the global threat of pan-Islamism (or pan-Turkism) was fiction, at least until the First World War, and that no concerted Russian Muslim movement against the tsarist state ever existed." Tuna, *Imperial Russia's Muslims*, 213.

208. Vorontsov-Dashkov, *Vsepoddanneishii otchet za vosem' let*, 10.

209. For Russia's entrance into World War I, see Joshua Sanborn, *Imperial Apocalypse: The Great War and the Destruction of the Russian Empire* (New York: Oxford University Press, 2014), 21–64.

210. Dominic Lieven, *The End of Tsarist Russia: The March to World War I and Revolution* (New York: Penguin, 2016), 5.

211. Sanborn, *Imperial Apocalypse*, 87–91.

212. Taner Akçam, *The Young Turks' Crime against Humanity: The Armenian Genocide and Ethnic Cleansing in the Ottoman Empire* (Princeton, NJ: Princeton University Press, 2012), 139–48.

213. Suny, *"They Can Live in the Desert but Nowhere Else,"* 224.

214. RGIA, f. 919, op. 2, d. 767, ll. 13–13ob.

215. Akçam, *The Young Turks' Crime against Humanity*, 157–202.

216. RGIA, f. 919, op. 2, d. 767, ll. 14ob–15.

217. Hovannisian, "Simon Vratzian and Armenian Nationalism," 202–3.

218. Suny, *"They Can Live in the Desert but Nowhere Else,"* 221–24.

219. Simon Vratzian, quoted in Suny, *"They Can Live in the Desert but Nowhere Else,"* 224.

220. Holquist, "The Politics and Practice of the Russian Occupation of Armenia," 154.

221. Suny, *"They Can Live in the Desert but Nowhere Else,"* 231.

222. RGIA, f. 919, op. 2, d. 767, l. 16.

223. RGIA, f. 919, op. 2, d. 767, l. 14.

224. RGIA, f. 919, op. 2, d. 767, l. 15.

225. RGIA, f. 919, op. 2, d. 767, ll. 17–17ob.

226. RGIA, f. 919, op. 2, d. 845, l. 1ob.

227. Quoted in Richard Hovannisian, *Armenia on the Road to Independence, 1918* (Berkeley: University of California Press, 1967), 45.

228. Holquist, "The Politics and Practice of the Russian Occupation of Armenia," 153.

229. RGIA, f. 919, op. 2, d. 845, ll. 1ob–2.

Conclusion

1. See Ilya Gerasimov, Sergey Glebov, Jan Kusber, Marina Mogilner, and Alexander Semyonov, "New Imperial History and the Challenges of Empire," in *Empire Speaks Out: Languages of Rationalization and Self-Description in the Russian Empire*, ed. Ilya Gerasimov, Jan Kusber, and Alexander Semyonov (Leiden: Brill, 2009), 3–32. These scholars have, in part, built off the foundations set by Anatolyi Remnev and Andreas Kappeler.

2. Mogilner, "New Imperial History," 35.

3. Kivelson and Suny, *Russia's Empires*, 109.

4. Pravilova, *Finansy imperii*.

5. Tuna, *Imperial Russia's Muslims*, 4.

6. Campbell, *The Muslim Question and Russian Imperial Governance*, 21. For Vorontsov's proclamation, see chapter 3.

7. Campbell, *The Muslim Question and Russian Imperial Governance*, 24.

8. Werth, *The Tsar's Foreign Faiths*, 260–61.

9. Quoted in Werth, *The Tsar's Foreign Faiths*, 154.

10. Ian Campbell, *Knowledge and the Ends of Empire: Kazak Intermediaries and Russian Rule on the Steppe, 1731–1917* (Ithaca, NY: Cornell University Press, 2017).

11. Alexander Morrison, "Russian Settler Colonialism," in *The Routledge Handbook of the History of Settler Colonialism*, ed. Edward Cavanagh and Lorenzo Veracini (Abingdon, UK: Routledge, 2017), 320.

12. Campbell, *The Muslim Question and Russian Imperial Governance*, 2–9.

13. Michael Khodarkovsky, "Between Europe and Asia: Russia's State Colonialism in Comparative Perspective, 1550s–1900s," *Canadian-American Slavic Studies* 52, no. 1 (2018): 25–26.

14. Geraci, *Window on the East*.

15. Daniel Brower, "Russian Roads to Mecca: Religious Tolerance and Muslim Pilgrimage in the Russian Empire," *Slavic Review* 55, no. 3 (1996): 569. On Kaufman's support of access to the Mecca pilgrimage, see Kane, *Russian Hajj*, 64.

16. Miller, *The Romanov Empire and Nationalism*.

17. Crews, *For Prophet and Tsar*, 302.

18. On the process of "selective integration," see Nathans, *Beyond the Pale*. On the restrictions and violence the Jewish community faced, see Klier, *Russians, Jews, and the Pogroms of 1881–1882*.

19. Tuna, *Imperial Russia's Muslims*, 200.

20. In some regions of imperial Russia, including parts of the Caucasus and in Central Asia, Russia saw itself as delivering not Christian civilization but rather the benefits of European science. See Vera Tolz, *Russia's Own Orient: The Politics of Identity and Oriental Studies in the Late Imperial and Early Soviet Periods* (Oxford: Oxford University Press, 2011).

21. Mark Bassin, *Imperial Visions: National Imagination and Geographical Expansion in the Russian Far East, 1840–1865* (Cambridge: Cambridge University Press, 1999), 52–55.

22. Weeks, "Russification"; Thaden, *Russification in the Baltic Provinces and Finland*.

23. Weeks, "Russification," 476.

BIBLIOGRAPHY

Archives

GARF   Gosudarstvennyi arkhiv Rossiiskoi Federatsii

HAA   Hayastani azgayin arkhiv

RGIA   Rossiiskii gosudarstvennyi istoricheskii arkhiv

RGVIA   Rossiiskii gosudarstvennyi voenno-istoricheskii arkhiv

TsIAM   Tsentral'nyi istoricheskii arkhiv Moskvy

Published Primary Sources

Ainsworth, William Francis. *Travels and Researches in Asia Minor, Mesopotamia, Chaldea, and Armenia.* London: John W. Parker, West Strand, 1842.

Akopian, T. Kh., ed. *Razvitie Erevana posle prisoedineniia Vostochnoi Armenii k Rossii: Sbornik dokumentov, 1801–1917 gg.* Yerevan: Erevanskii gosudarstvennyi universitet, 1978.

Akty, sobrannye Kavkazskoiu arkheograficheskoiu kommissieiu: Arkhiv Glavnago upravleniia namestnika kavkazskago. 12 vols. Tiflis: Glavnoe upravlenie namestnika kavkazskago, 1866–1904.

Armstrong, T. B. *Journal of Travels in the Seat of War, during the Last Two Campaigns of Russia and Turkey.* London: A. Seguin, 1831.

Bournoutian, George, ed. *Armenians and Russia, 1626–1796: A Documentary Record.* Costa Mesa, CA: Mazda, 2001.

Bournoutian, George, ed. *Russia and the Armenians of Transcaucasia, 1797–1889: A Documentary Record.* Costa Mesa, CA: Mazda, 1998.

Bratskaia pomoshch' postradavshim v Turtsii armianam. Moscow: K. O. Aleksandrov, 1897.

Bratskaia pomoshch' postradavshim v Turtsii armianam. Moscow: I. N. Kushnerev, 1898.

Bryce, James. *Transcaucasia and Ararat: Being Notes of a Vacation Tour in the Autumn of 1876*. London: Macmillan, 1877.

Curzon, Robert. *Armenia: A Year at Erzeroom, and on the Frontiers of Russia, Turkey, and Persia*. London: John Murray, 1854.

Dal', Vladimir. *Sochineniia Vladimira Dalia: Novoe polnoe izdanie*. 8 vols. St. Petersburg: M. O. Vol'f, 1861.

Dmytryshyn, Basil, ed. *Imperial Russia: A Source Book, 1700–1917*. 2nd ed. Orlando, FL: Harcourt, 1990.

Duncan, Charles. *A Campaign with the Turks in Asia*. London: Smith, Elder, 1855.

Fraser, James Baillie. *Travels in Koordistan, Mesopotamia, Etc.: Including an Account of Parts of Those Countries Hitherto Unvisited by Europeans*. 2 vols. London: Richard Bentley, 1840.

Geary, Grattan. *Through Asiatic Turkey: Narrative of a Journey from Bombay to the Bosphorus* London: Sampson Low, Marston, Searle, and Rivington, 1878.

Heude, William. *A Voyage up the Persian Gulf and a Journey Overland from India to England, in 1817*. London: Longman, Hurst, Rees, Orme, and Brown, 1819.

Kavkazskii kalendar' na 1846 god, izdannyi ot kantseliarii kavkazskogo namestnika. St. Petersburg: Voennaia tipografiia, 1846.

Kinneir, John Macdonald. *A Geographical Memoir of the Persian Empire*. London: John Murray, 1813.

Layard, Austen H. *Discoveries in the Ruins of Nineveh and Babylon with Travels in Armenia, Kurdistan and the Desert: Being the Result of a Second Expedition Undertaken for the Trustees of the British Museum*. New York: G. P. Putnam, 1853.

MacColl, Malcolm. *England's Responsibility towards Armenia*. London: Longmans, Green, 1896.

Marr, Nikolai. "Ani, stolitsa drevnei Armenii." In *Bratskaia pomoshch' postradavshim v Turtsii armianam*, 197–222. Moscow: I. N. Kushnerev, 1898.

Mignan, Robert. *A Winter Journey through Russia, the Caucasian Alps, and Georgia; Thence across Mount Zagros, by the Pass of Xenophon and the Ten Thousand Greeks, into Koordistaun*. London: Richard Bentley, 1839.

Patriarkh vsekh armian Nerses V-i i kniaz' Mikhail Semenovich i kniaginia Elisaveta Ksaverievna Vorontsovy v ikh chastnoi perepiske. Edited by A. D. Eritsov. Tiflis: M. Martirosiantsa, 1898.

Porter, Robert Ker. *Travels in Georgia, Persia, Armenia, Ancient Babylonia, Etc. during the Years 1817, 1818, 1819, and 1820*. Vol. 1. London: Longman, Hurst, Rees, Orme, and Brown, 1821.

Sandwith, Humphry. *A Narrative of the Siege of Kars, and of the Six Months Resistance by the Turkish Garrison under General Williams to the Russian Army*. London: J. Murray, 1856.

Sobranie aktov, otnosiashchikhsia k obozreniiu istorii armianskogo naroda. 3 vols. Moscow: Lazarevskii institut vostochnykh iazykov, 1833–38.

Southgate, Horatio. *Narrative of a Tour through Armenia, Kurdistan, Persia and Mesopotamia*. New York: D. Appleton, 1840.

Telfer, John Buchan. *The Crimea and Transcaucasia: Being the Narrative of a Journey in the Kouban, in Gouria, Georgia, Armenia, Ossety, Imeritia, Swannety, and Mingrelia, and in the Tauric Range*. London: Henry S. King, 1876.

Thielmann, Max von. *Journey in the Caucasus, Persia, and Turkey in Asia*. London: John Murray, 1875.

Ussher, John. *A Journey from London to Persepolis; Including Wanderings in Daghestan, Georgia, Armenia, Kurdistan, Mesopotamia, and Persia*. London: Hurst and Blackett, 1865.

Vernadsky, George, ed. *A Source Book for Russian History*. Vol. 3. New Haven, CT: Yale University Press, 1972.

Vorontsov-Dashkov, Ilarion. *Vsepoddanneishii otchet za vosem' let upravleniia Kavkazom*. St. Petersburg: Gosudarstvennaia tipografiia, 1913.

Wagner, Moritz. *Travels in Persia, Georgia and Koordistan; With sketches of the Cossacks and the Caucasus*. London: Hurst and Blackett, 1856.

Witte, Sergei. *The Memoirs of Count Witte*. Translated and edited by Sidney Harcave. Armonk, NY: M. E. Sharpe, 1990.

Secondary Literature

Abaza, Viktor. *Istoriia Armenii*. St. Petersburg: Tipografiia I. N. Skorokhodova, 1888.

Abovyan, Khachatur. *Rany Armenii*. Translated by Sergei Shervinskii. Yerevan: Sovetakan grokh, 1977. http://armenianhouse.org/abovyan/wounds-of -armenia/2.html.

Akçam, Taner. *The Young Turks' Crime Against Humanity: The Armenian Genocide and Ethnic Cleansing in the Ottoman Empire*. Princeton, NJ: Princeton University Press, 2012.

Aleksanov, I. Ia. *Kratkaia istoriia Armenii s pribavleniem ocherka "Armiane v Rossii."* Rostov: Tipografiia A. I. Adamkovicha, 1884.

Amanat, Abbas. "'Russian Intrusion into the Guarded Domain': Reflections of a Qajar Statesman on European Expansion." *Journal of the American Oriental Society* 113, no. 1 (1993): 35–56.

Anderson, M. S. *The Eastern Question, 1774–1923: A Study in International Relations*. New York: St. Martin's Press, 1966.

Anisimov, Evgenii V. *The Reforms of Peter the Great: Progress through Coercion in Russia*. Translated by John T. Alexander. Armonk, NY: M. E. Sharpe, 1993.

Aronson, I. Michael. *Troubled Waters: The Origins of the 1881 Anti-Jewish Pogroms in Russia*. Pittsburgh: University of Pittsburgh Press, 1990.

Ascher, Abraham. *P. A. Stolypin: The Search for Stability in Late Imperial Russia*. Stanford, CA: Stanford University Press, 2001.

Ascher, Abraham. *The Revolution of 1905: A Short History*. Stanford, CA: Stanford University Press, 2004.

Aslanian, Sebouh David. *From the Indian Ocean to the Mediterranean: The Global Trade Networks of Armenian Merchants from New Julfa*. Berkeley: University of California Press, 2014.

Atkin, Muriel. *Russia and Iran, 1780–1828*. Minneapolis: University of Minnesota Press, 1980.

Avetisian, G. A. *Generaly-armiane v Rossiiskoi imperii*. Yerevan: Amrots, 2007.

Baddeley, John. *The Russian Conquest of the Caucasus*. London: Longmans and Green, 1908.

Badem, Candan. "'Forty Years of Black Days?' The Russian Administration of Kars, Ardahan, and Batum, 1878–1918." In *Russian-Ottoman Borderlands: The Eastern Question Reconsidered*, edited by Lucien Frary and Mara Kozelsky, 221–50. Madison: University of Wisconsin Press, 2014.

Baer, Brian James. "Literary Translation in the Age of the Decembrists." In *The Power of the Pen: Translation and Censorship in Nineteenth-Century Europe*, edited by Denise Merkle, Carol O'Sullivan, Luc van Doorslaer, and Michaela Wolf, 213–42. Berlin: LIT Verlag, 2010.

Balaian, B. P. *Diplomaticheskaia istoriia russko-iranskikh voin i prisoedineniia Vostochnoi Armenii k Rossii*. Yerevan: Izdatel'stvo Akademii nauk Armianskoi SSR, 1988.

Barkhudarian, V. B. "Armianskie kolonisty v Rossii i ikh rol' v armiano-russkikh otnosheniiakh." In *Iz istorii vekovoi druzhby*, edited by M. G. Nersisian, 124–35. Yerevan: Izdatel'stvo Akademii nauk Armianskoi SSR, 1983.

Barrett, Thomas. "The Remaking of the Lion of Dagestan: Shamil in Captivity." *Russian Review* 53, no. 3 (1994): 353–66.

Bartlett, Roger. "Ropsha, an Imperial Palace." In *Personality and Place in Russian Culture: Essays in Memory of Lindsey Hughes*, edited by Simon Dixon, 156–79. London: Modern Humanities Research Association, 2010.

Bassin, Mark. *Imperial Visions: National Imagination and Geographical Expansion in the Russian Far East, 1840–1865*. Cambridge: Cambridge University Press, 1999.

Bassin, Mark. "Russia between Europe and Asia: The Ideological Construction of Geographical Space." *Slavic Review* 50, no. 1 (1991): 1–17.

Baziiants, A. P. "Iz istorii Lazarevskogo instituta." *Izvestiia Akademii nauk Armianskoi SSR*, no. 2 (1964): 13–20.

Berberian, Houri. *Armenians and the Iranian Constitutional Revolution of 1905–1911*. Boulder, CO: Westview Press, 2001.

Bhabha, Homi. *The Location of Culture*. New York: Routledge, 2004.

Blobaum, Robert E. *Rewolucja: Russian Poland, 1904–1907*. Ithaca, NY: Cornell University Press, 1995.

Bloxham, Donald. *The Great Game of Genocide: Imperialism, Nationalism, and the Destruction of the Ottoman Armenians*. New York: Oxford University Press, 2005.

Bournoutian, George. "Eastern Armenia from the Seventeenth Century to the Russian Annexation." In *The Armenian People from Ancient to Modern Times*, edited by Richard Hovannisian, vol. 2, 81–107. New York: St. Martin's Press, 2004.

Bournoutian, George. *Eastern Armenia in the Last Decades of Persian Rule, 1807–1828: A Political and Socioeconomic Study of the Khanate of Erevan on the Eve of the Russian Conquest*. Malibu, CA: Undena Publications, 1982.

Bournoutian, George. *The Khanate of Erevan under Qajar Rule, 1795–1828*. Costa Mesa, CA: Mazda, 1992.

Breuilly, John. *Nationalism and the State*. Chicago: University of Chicago Press, 1985.

Breyfogle, Nicholas. "Enduring Imperium: Russia / Soviet Union / Eurasia as Multiethnic, Multiconfessional Space." *Ab Imperio*, no. 1 (2008): 75–126.

Breyfogle, Nicholas. *Heretics and Colonizers: Forging Russia's Empire in the South Caucasus*. Ithaca, NY: Cornell University Press, 2005.

Breyfogle, Nicholas, Abby Schrader, and Willard Sunderland, eds. *Peopling the Russian Periphery: Borderland Colonization in Eurasian History*. London: Routledge, 2007.

Brower, Daniel. "Russian Roads to Mecca: Religious Tolerance and Muslim Pilgrimage in the Russian Empire." *Slavic Review* 55, no. 3 (1996): 567–84.

Brower, Daniel, and Edward Lazzerini, eds. *Russia's Orient: Imperial Borderlands and Peoples, 1700–1917*. Bloomington: Indiana University Press, 1997.

Burbank, Jane. "An Imperial Rights Regime: Law and Citizenship in the Russian Empire." *Kritika: Explorations in Russian and Eurasian History* 7, no. 7 (2006): 397–431.

Burbank, Jane, and Frederick Cooper. *Empires in World History: Power and the Politics of Difference*. Princeton, NJ: Princeton University Press, 2010.

Burbank, Jane, Mark von Hagen, and Anatolyi Remnev, eds. *Russian Empire: Space, People, Power, 1700–1930*. Bloomington: Indiana University Press, 2007.

Campbell, Elena. *The Muslim Question and Russian Imperial Governance*. Bloomington: Indiana University Press, 2015.

Campbell, Ian. *Knowledge and the Ends of Empire: Kazak Intermediaries and Russian Rule on the Steppe, 1731–1917*. Ithaca, NY: Cornell University Press, 2017.

Cole, Juan. *Napoleon's Egypt: Invading the Middle East*. New York: Palgrave Macmillan, 2007.

Cooper, Frederick. *Colonialism in Question: Theory, Knowledge, History*. Berkeley: University of California Press, 2005.

Cooper, Frederick, and Ann Laura Stoler. "Tensions of Empire: Colonial Control and Visions of Rule." *American Ethnologist* 16, no. 4 (1989): 609–21.

Creagh, James. *Armenians, Koords, and Turks*. London: Samuel Tinsley, 1880.

Crews, Robert. "Empire and the Confessional State: Islam and Religious Politics in Nineteenth-Century Russia." *American Historical Review* 108, no. 1 (2003): 50–83.

Crews, Robert. *For Prophet and Tsar: Islam and Empire in Russia and Central Asia*. Cambridge, MA: Harvard University Press, 2009.

Davison, Roderic H. *Reform in the Ottoman Empire, 1856–1876*. 2015. Reprint, Princeton, NJ: Princeton University Press, 1963.

Der Matossian, Bedross. *Shattered Dreams of Revolution: From Liberty to Violence in the Late Ottoman Empire*. Stanford, CA: Stanford University Press, 2014.

De Waal, Thomas. *Black Garden: Armenia and Azerbaijan through Peace and War*. New York: New York University Press, 2013.

De Waal, Thomas. *The Caucasus: An Introduction*. New York: Oxford University Press, 2010.

Disson, Julia. "Privileged Noble High Schools and the Formation of Russian National Elites in the First Part of the 19th Century." *Historical Social Research* 33, no. 2 (2008): 174–89.

Dolbakian, Emanuil. "Otechestvennaia voina 1812 goda i armiane Rossii." *Moskovskii zhurnal* 1, no. 265 (2013). http://mosjour.ru/2017062812/.

Dolbilov, Mikhail. "Russification and the Bureaucratic Mind in the Russian Empire's Northwestern Region in the 1860s." *Kritika: Explorations in Russian and Eurasian History* 5, no. 2 (2004): 245–71.

Druzhba naveki: Materialy prazdnovaniia 150-letiia vkhozhdeniia Armenii v sostav Rossii. Yerevan: Hayastan, 1980.

Edel'man, O. V. "Mezhnatsional'nye stolknoveniia v Baku 7–10 fevralia 1905 g. v dokumentakh Departamenta politsii." In *Russkii sbornik: Issledovaniia po istorii Rossii,* vol. 22, 343–412. Moscow: Modest Kolerov, 2017.

Eklof, Ben, John Bushnell, and Larissa Zakharova, eds. *Russia's Great Reforms, 1855–1881.* Bloomington: Indiana University Press, 1994.

Ely, Christopher. *This Meager Nature: Landscape and National Identity in Imperial Russia.* DeKalb: Northern Illinois University Press, 2002.

Engelstein, Laura. *Castration and the Heavenly Kingdom: A Russian Folktale.* Ithaca, NY: Cornell University Press, 2003.

Erkanian, Aleksandr. "Istoriia armian Moskvy, vypusk 7." *Literaturnaia Gazeta* 41, no. 6529 (21 October 2015). http://www.lgz.ru/article/-41-6529-21-10-2015/istoriya-armyan-moskvy/.

Fitzpatrick, Sheila. *The Russian Revolution.* 3rd ed. Oxford: Oxford University Press, 2008.

Florinskii, M. F. "Tsentral'naia vlast' i Kavkazskaia administratsiia v sisteme upravleniia Rossiiskoi imperii v 1905–1914 gg." In *Tsentr i regiony v istorii Rossii: Problemy ekonomicheskogo, politicheskogo i sotsiokul'turnogo vzaimodeistviia,* edited by A. Iu. Dvornichenko, 380–408. St. Petersburg: Sankt Peterburgskii gosudarstvennyi universitet, 2010.

Gammer, Moshe. "The Imam and the Pasha: A Note on Shamil and Muhammad Ali." *Middle Eastern Studies* 32, no. 4 (1996): 336–42.

Gammer, Moshe. *Muslim Resistance to the Tsar: Shamil and the Conquest of Chechnia and Daghestan.* New York: Routledge, 2003.

Gat, Azar. *Nations: The Long History and Deep Roots of Political Ethnicity and Nationalism.* Cambridge: Cambridge University Press, 2013.

Gellner, Ernest. *Nations and Nationalism.* Ithaca, NY: Cornell University Press, 1983.

Geraci, Robert. "Capitalist Stereotypes and the Economic Organization of the Russian Empire: The Case of the Tiflis Armenians." In *Defining Self: Essays on Emergent Identities in Russia, Seventeenth to Nineteenth Centuries,* edited by Michael Branch, 365–79. Helsinki: Finnish Literature Society, 2009.

Geraci, Robert. "On 'Colonial' Forms and Functions." *Slavic Review* 69, no. 1 (2010): 180–84.

Geraci, Robert. *Window on the East: National and Imperial Identities in Late Tsarist Russia.* Ithaca, NY: Cornell University Press, 2001.

Geraci, Robert, and Michael Khodarkovsky, eds. *Of Religion and Empire: Missions, Conversion, and Tolerance in Tsarist Russia.* Ithaca, NY: Cornell University Press, 2001.

Gerasimov, Ilya, Sergey Glebov, Jan Kusber, Marina Mogilner, and Alexander Semyonov. "New Imperial History and the Challenges of Empire." In *Empire*

Speaks Out: Languages of Rationalization and Self-Description in the Russian Empire, edited by Ilya Gerasimov, Jan Kusber, and Alexander Semyonov, 1–32. Leiden: Brill, 2009.

Glinka, Sergei. *Opisanie pereseleniia armian adderbidzhanskikh v predely Rossii.* Baku: Elm, 1990.

Goldfrank, David. *The Origins of the Crimean War.* New York: Routledge, 2014.

Gordin, Ia. A., ed. *Kavkaz i Rossiiskaia imperiia: Proekty, idei, illiuzii i real'nost'.* St. Petersburg: Zvezda, 2005.

Gould, Rebecca. "Imam Shamil." In *Russia's People of Empire: Life Stories from Eurasia, 1500 to the Present*, edited by Stephen M. Norris and Willard Sunderland, 117–27. Bloomington: Indiana University Press, 2012.

Grigorian, Z. T. *Prisoedinenie Vostochnoi Armenii k Rossii v nachale XIX veka.* Moscow: Izdatel'stvo sotsial'no-ekonomicheskoi literatury, 1959.

Gukasian, V. G. *Konstantinopol'skie armiane i natsional'no-prosvetitel'skoe dvizhenie 30–60-kh godov XIX veka.* Yerevan: Izdatel'stvo Akademii nauk Armianskoi SSR, 1989.

Haimson, Leopold. "'The Problem of Political and Social Stability in Urban Russia on the Eve of War and Revolution' Revisited." *Slavic Review* 59, no. 4 (2000): 848–75.

Harcave, Sidney. *Count Sergei Witte and the Twilight of Imperial Russia: A Biography.* Armonk, NY: M. E. Sharpe, 2004.

Hechter, Michael. *Containing Nationalism.* New York: Oxford University Press, 2000.

Hewsen, Robert H. *Armenia: A Historical Atlas.* Chicago: University of Chicago Press, 2001.

Hillis, Faith. *Children of Rus': Right-Bank Ukraine and the Invention of a Russian Nation.* Ithaca, NY: Cornell University Press, 2013.

Hillis, Faith. "Ukrainophile Activism and Imperial Governance in Russia's Southwestern Borderlands." *Kritika: Explorations in Russian and Eurasian History* 13, no. 2 (2012): 301–26.

Hirsch, Francine. *Empire of Nations: Ethnographic Knowledge and the Creation of the Soviet Union.* Ithaca, NY: Cornell University Press, 2005.

Holquist, Peter. "The Politics and Practice of the Russian Occupation of Armenia, 1915–February 1917." In *A Question of Genocide: Armenians and Turks at the End of the Ottoman Empire*, edited by Ronald G. Suny, Fatma Müge Göçek, and Norman M. Naimark, 151–74. New York: Oxford University Press, 2011.

Hosking, Geoffrey. "The Freudian Frontier." *Times Literary Supplement*, 10 March 1995.

Hovannisian, Richard. *Armenia on the Road to Independence, 1918.* Berkeley: University of California Press, 1967.

Hovannisian, Richard. *The Armenian Holocaust.* Cambridge, MA: Armenian Heritage Press, 1980.

Hovannisian, Richard, ed. *The Armenian People from Ancient to Modern Times.* 2 vols. New York: St. Martin's Press, 2004.

Hovannisian, Richard. "The Armenian Question in the Ottoman Empire 1876 to 1914." In *The Armenian People from Ancient to Modern Times*, edited by Richard Hovannisian, vol. 2, 203–38. New York: St. Martin's Press, 2004.

Hovannisian, Richard, ed. *Remembrance and Denial: The Case of the Armenian Genocide.* Detroit: Wayne State University Press, 1998.

Hovannisian, Richard. *The Republic of Armenia.* 4 vols. Berkeley: University of California Press, 1971–96.

Hovannisian, Richard. "Simon Vratzian and Armenian Nationalism." *Middle Eastern Studies 5*, no. 3 (1969): 192–220.

Hroch, Miroslav. *Social Preconditions of National Revival in Europe: A Comparative Analysis of the Social Composition of Patriotic Groups among the Smaller European Nations.* Translated by Ben Fowkes. New York: Columbia University Press, 2000.

"Iron Ladle by Khrimyan Hayrig." Translated by William Bairamian. *The Armenite,* 4 March 2014. http://thearmenite.com/2014/03/iron-ladle-khrimyan-hayrig/.

Ismail-Zade, D. I. *Graf I. I. Vorontsov-Dashkov: Namestnik kavkazskii.* Moscow: Tsentrpoligraf, 2005.

Ismail-Zade, D. I. *Naselenie gorodov Zakavkazskogo kraia v XIX–nachale XX v.: Istoriko-demograficheskii analiz.* Moscow: Nauka, 1991.

Istoricheskie sviazi i druzhba ukrainskogo i armianskogo narodov. 3 vols. Yerevan: Izdatel'stvo Akademii nauk Armianskoi SSR, 1961; Kiev: Naukova dumka, 1965; Yerevan: Izdatel'stvo Akademii nauk Armianskoi SSR, 1971.

Jahn, Hubertus. "The Bronze Viceroy: Mikhail Vorontsov's Statue and Russian Imperial Representation in the South Caucasus in the Mid-Nineteenth Century." *Russian History 41,* no. 2 (2014): 163–80.

Jedlicki, Jerzy. *A Suburb of Europe: Nineteenth-Century Polish Approaches to Western Civilization.* Budapest: Central European University Press, 1999.

Jersild, Austin. *Orientalism and Empire: North Caucasus Mountain People and the Georgian Frontier, 1845–1917.* Montreal: McGill-Queen's University Press, 2002.

Jones, Stephen F. *Socialism in Georgian Colors: The European Road to Social Democracy, 1883–1917.* Cambridge, MA: Harvard University Press, 2005.

Judge, Edward H. *Plehve: Repression and Reform in Imperial Russia, 1902–1904.* Syracuse, NY: Syracuse University Press, 1983.

Kalishevskii, Mikhail. "Lazarevskii institut—pervoe spetsializirovannoe diplomaticheskoe uchilishche." Moscow State Institute of International Relations (MGIMO) website. Accessed 6 June 2016. http://www.mgimo.ru/study/dean/docs/6420/6624/document145668.phtml.

Kane, Eileen. *Russian Hajj: Empire and the Pilgrimage to Mecca.* Ithaca, NY: Cornell University Press, 2015.

Kappeler, Andreas. *The Russian Empire: A Multiethnic History.* Translated by Alfred Clayton. Harlow, UK: Pearson Education, 2001.

Kappeler, Andreas. "Spaces of Entanglement." *Kritika: Explorations in Russian and Eurasian History 12,* no. 2 (2011): 477–87.

Karny, Yo'av. *Highlanders: A Journey to the Caucasus in Quest of Memory.* New York: Macmillan, 2001.

Karpat, Kemal H. *Ottoman Population, 1830–1914: Demographic and Social Characteristics.* Madison: University of Wisconsin Press, 1985.

Kashani-Sabet, Firoozeh. *Frontier Fictions: Shaping the Iranian Nation, 1804–1946.* Princeton, NJ: Princeton University Press, 2014.

Kazarian, G. M., ed. *Prisoedinenie Vostochnoi Armenii k Rossii i ego istoricheskoe znachenie: Sbornik statei.* Yerevan: Erevanskii gosudarstvennyi universitet, 1978.

Kefeli, Agnès Nilüfer. *Becoming Muslim in Imperial Russia: Conversion, Apostasy, and Literacy.* Ithaca, NY: Cornell University Press, 2014.

Khachaturian, Lisa. *Cultivating Nationhood in Imperial Russia: The Periodical Press and the Formation of a Modern Armenian Identity.* New Brunswick, NJ: Transaction, 2009.

Khodarkovsky, Michael. "Between Europe and Asia: Russia's State Colonialism in Comparative Perspective, 1550s–1900s." *Canadian-American Slavic Studies* 52, no. 1 (2018): 1–29.

Khodarkovsky, Michael. *Bitter Choices: Loyalty and Betrayal in the Russian Conquest of the North Caucasus.* Ithaca, NY: Cornell University Press, 2011.

Khodarkovsky, Michael. *Russia's Steppe Frontier: The Making of a Colonial Empire, 1500–1800.* Bloomington: Indiana University Press, 2002.

King, Charles. *The Ghost of Freedom: A History of the Caucasus.* New York: Oxford University Press, 2008.

Kivelson, Valerie A., and Ronald G. Suny. *Russia's Empires.* New York: Oxford University Press, 2017.

Klein, Janet. *The Margins of Empire: Kurdish Militias in the Ottoman Tribal Zone.* Stanford, CA: Stanford University Press, 2011.

Klier, John. *Russians, Jews, and the Pogroms of 1881–1882.* Cambridge: Cambridge University Press, 2011.

Klier, John. "State Policies and the Conversion of Jews in Imperial Russia." In *Of Religion and Empire: Missions, Conversion, and Tolerance in Tsarist Russia,* edited by Robert Geraci and Michael Khodarkovsky, 92–112. Ithaca, NY: Cornell University Press, 2001.

Kliuchevskii, Vasilii. *Skazaniia inostrantsev o moskovskom gosudarstve.* Petrograd: Pervaia gosudarstvennaia tipografiia, 1918.

Knight, Nathaniel. "Grigor'ev in Orenburg, 1851–1862: Russian Orientalism in the Service of Empire?" *Slavic Review* 59, no. 1 (2000): 74–100.

Kollmann, Nancy Shields. *The Russian Empire, 1450–1801.* New York: Oxford University Press, 2017.

Kotsonis, Yanni. *States of Obligation: Taxes and Citizenship in the Russian Empire and Early Soviet Republic.* Toronto: University of Toronto Press, 2014.

Krbekian, V. G. *Uchastie armian v russko-turetskoi voine 1877–1878 godov.* Yerevan: Antares, 2004.

Lang, David Marshall. *Armenia: Cradle of Civilization.* London: Allen and Unwin, 1970.

Lang, David Marshall. *The Last Years of the Georgian Monarchy, 1658–1832.* New York: Columbia University Press, 1957.

Lang, David Marshall. *A Modern History of Soviet Georgia.* New York: Grove Press, 1962.

Laycock, Jo. *Imagining Armenia: Orientalism, Ambiguity and Intervention.* Manchester: Manchester University Press, 2009.

Layton, Susan. *Russian Literature and Empire: Conquest of the Caucasus from Pushkin to Tolstoy.* Cambridge: Cambridge University Press, 1994.

LeDonne, John. "Frontier Governors General 1772–1825." Pt. 2, "The Southern Frontier." *Jahrbücher für Geschichte Osteuropas* 48, no. 2 (2000): 161–83.

LeDonne, John. *The Russian Empire and the World, 1700–1917: The Geopolitics of Expansion and Containment*. New York: Oxford University Press, 1997.

Lewy, Guenter. *The Armenian Massacres in Ottoman Turkey: A Disputed Genocide*. Salt Lake City: University of Utah Press, 2005.

Libaridian, Gerard. *Modern Armenia: People, Nation, State*. New Brunswick, NJ: Transaction, 2011.

Lieven, Dominic. *Empire: The Russian Empire and Its Rivals*. New Haven, CT: Yale University Press, 2002.

Lieven, Dominic. *The End of Tsarist Russia: The March to World War I and Revolution*. New York: Penguin, 2016.

Lieven, Dominic. *Russia against Napoleon: The Battle for Europe, 1807 to 1814*. New York: Penguin, 2009.

Lindemann, Albert S. *The Jew Accused: Three Anti-Semitic Affairs, 1894–1914*. New York: Cambridge University Press, 1991.

Lohr, Eric. *Russian Citizenship: From Empire to Soviet Union*. Cambridge, MA: Harvard University Press, 2012.

Macfie, A. L. *The Eastern Question, 1774–1923*. London: Longman, 1996.

Marashlian, Levon. *Politics and Demography: Armenians, Turks, and Kurds in the Ottoman Empire*. Cambridge, MA: Zoryan Institute, 1991.

Marshall, Alex. *The Caucasus under Soviet Rule*. New York: Routledge, 2010.

Martin, Alexander. *Enlightened Metropolis: Constructing Imperial Moscow, 1762–1855*. New York: Oxford University Press, 2013.

Martin, Terry. *The Affirmative Action Empire: Nations and Nationalism in the Soviet Union, 1923–1939*. Ithaca, NY: Cornell University Press, 2001.

Massie, Robert K. *Nicholas and Alexandra: The Fall of the Romanov Dynasty*. New York: Modern Library, 2012.

Matsuzato, Kimitaka. "General-gubernatorstva v Rossiiskoi imperii: Ot etnicheskogo k prostranstvennomu podkhodu." In *Novaia imperskaia istoriia postsovetskogo prostranstva*, edited by Ilya Gerasimov, Sergey Glebov, Alexander Kaplunovskii, Marina Mogilner, and Alexander Semyonov, 427–58. Kazan: Tsentr issledovanii natsionalizma i imperii, 2004.

Matsuzato, Kimitaka, ed. *Imperiology: From Empirical Knowledge to Discussing the Russian Empire*. Sapporo: Slavic Research Center, Hokkaido University, 2007.

McDonald, David. *United Government and Foreign Policy in Russia, 1900–1914*. Cambridge, MA: Harvard University Press, 1992.

McReynolds, Louise. *Murder Most Russian: True Crime and Punishment in Late Imperial Russia*. Ithaca, NY: Cornell University Press, 2013.

McReynolds, Louise. *The News under Russia's Old Regime: The Development of a Mass-Circulation Press*. Princeton, NJ: Princeton University Press, 1991.

Miller, Alexei. *The Romanov Empire and Nationalism: Essays in the Methodology of Historical Research*. Budapest: Central European University Press, 2008.

Miller, Alexei. *The Ukrainian Question: The Russian Empire and Nationalism in the Nineteenth Century*. Budapest: Central European University Press, 2003.

Miller, Alexei, and Alfred Rieber, eds. *Imperial Rule*. Budapest: Central European University Press, 2004.

Miller, Alexei, and Erik R. Scott. "Nation and Empire: Reflections in the Margins of Geoffrey Hosking's Book." *Kritika: Explorations in Russian and Eurasian History* 13, no. 2 (2012): 419–28.

Mogilner, Marina. "New Imperial History: Post-Soviet Historiography in Search of a New Paradigm for the History of Empire and Nationalism." *Revue d'études comparatives Est-Ouest* 45, no. 2 (2014): 25–67.

Morrison, Alexander. "Metropole, Colony, and Imperial Citizenship in the Russian Empire." *Kritika: Explorations in Russian and Eurasian History* 13, no. 2 (2012): 327–64.

Morrison, Alexander. "Review Essay: Muslims and Modernity in the Russian Empire." *Slavonic and East European Review* 94, no. 4 (2016): 715–24.

Morrison, Alexander. "Russian Settler Colonialism." In *The Routledge Handbook of the History of Settler Colonialism*, edited by Edward Cavanagh and Lorenzo Veracini, 313–26. Abingdon, UK: Routledge, 2017.

Mostashari, Firouzeh. "Colonial Dilemmas: Russian Policies in the Muslim Caucasus." In *Of Religion and Empire: Missions, Conversion, and Tolerance in Tsarist Russia*, edited by Robert Geraci and Michael Khodarkovsky, 229–49. Ithaca, NY: Cornell University Press, 2001.

Mostashari, Firouzeh. *On the Religious Frontier: Tsarist Russia and Islam in the Caucasus*. London: I. B. Tauris, 2006.

Motrevich, V. P. "Ministr finansov E. F. Kankrin i denezhnaia reforma 1839–1843 gg. v Rossiiskoi imperii." *Biznes, menedzhment i pravo: Nauchno-prakticheskii ekonomiko-pravovoi zhurnal*. http://bmpravo.ru/show_stat.php?stat=243. Accessed 9 October 2019.

Nalbandian, Louise. *The Armenian Revolutionary Movement: The Development of Armenian Political Parties through the Nineteenth Century*. Berkeley: University of California Press, 1963.

Nathans, Benjamin. *Beyond the Pale: The Jewish Encounter with Late Imperial Russia*. Berkeley: University of California Press, 2004.

Nathans, Benjamin. "The Jews." In *The Cambridge History of Russia*, vol. 2, edited by Dominic Lieven, 184–201. Cambridge: Cambridge University Press, 2006.

Nersisian, M. G., ed. *Iz istorii vekovoi druzhby*. Yerevan: Izdatel'stvo Akademii nauk Armianskoi SSR, 1983.

Neuberger, Joan. *Hooliganism: Crime, Culture, and Power in St. Petersburg, 1900–1914*. Berkeley: University of California Press, 1993.

Norris, Stephen M., and Willard Sunderland, eds. *Russia's People of Empire: Life Stories from Eurasia, 1500 to the Present*. Bloomington: Indiana University Press, 2012.

Oganesian, A. Zh. *Rossiia i armiane: Uroki istorii i realii*. Yerevan: Erevanskii gosudarstvennyi universitet, 2015.

Önol, Onur. *The Tsar's Armenians: A Minority in Late Imperial Russia*. London: I. B. Tauris, 2017.

Ovanesov, B. T. "Rol' armianskoi tserkvi v obrazovatel'nom protsesse i sblizhenii ee s russkim pravitel'stvom, XIX–nachalo XX v." *Izvestiia Altaiskogo gosudarstvennogo universiteta* 4, no. 4 (2009): 204–7.

Ovanesov, B. T., and N. D. Sudavtsov. *Voenno-administrativnaia deiatel'nost' armian v Rossiiskoi imperii na Kavkaze.* Stavropol: Nairi, 2008.

Panossian, Razmik. *The Armenians: From Kings and Priests to Merchants and Commissars.* New York: Columbia University Press, 2006.

Petrovsky-Shtern, Yohanan. *Jews in the Russian Army, 1827–1917: Drafted into Modernity.* Cambridge: Cambridge University Press, 2009.

Platonov, Sergei. *Moscow and the West.* Translated by J. L. Wieczynski. Hattiesburg, MS: Academic International Press, 1972.

Plokhy, Serhii. *Lost Kingdom: The Quest for Empire and the Making of the Russian Nation.* New York: Basic Books, 2017.

Pogosian, A. M. *Karsskaia oblast' v sostave Rossii.* Yerevan: Hayastan, 1983.

Polyakova, Lyubov. "Social Policy in the Caucasus on the Eve of the First World War, 1905–1914." *History and Historians in the Context of the Time* 15, no. 2 (2015): 100–105.

Potto, V. A. *Kavkazskaia voina v otdel'nykh ocherkakh, epizodakh, legendakh i biografiiakh.* 4 vols. St. Petersburg: Izdatel'stvo V. A. Berezovskogo, 1887–89.

Pravilova, Ekaterina. *Finansy imperii: Den'gi i vlast' v politike Rossii na natsional'nykh okrainakh, 1801–1917.* Moscow: Novoe izdatel'stvo, 2006.

Preston, Andrew. *Sword of the Spirit, Shield of Faith: Religion in American War and Diplomacy.* New York: Alfred A. Knopf, 2012.

Raeff, Marc. *Michael Speransky: Statesman of Imperial Russia.* The Hague: Martinus Nijhoff, 1969.

Raeff, Marc. "Patterns of Russian Imperial Policy Toward the Nationalities." In *Soviet Nationality Problems,* edited by Edward Allworth, 21–42. New York: Columbia University Press, 1971.

Raeff, Marc. *Understanding Imperial Russia: State and Society in the Old Regime.* New York: Columbia University Press, 1984.

Remnev, Anatolyi. "Siberia and the Russian Far East in the Imperial Geography of Power." In *Russian Empire: Space, People, Power, 1700–1930,* edited by Jane Burbank, Mark von Hagen, and Anatolyi Remnev, 425–54. Bloomington: Indiana University Press, 2007.

Reynolds, Michael. *Shattering Empires: The Clash and Collapse of the Ottoman and Russian Empires, 1908–1918.* Cambridge: Cambridge University Press, 2011.

Rhinelander, Anthony. *Prince Michael Vorontsov: Viceroy to the Tsar.* Montreal: McGill-Queen's University Press, 1990.

Rhinelander, Anthony. "Viceroy Vorontsov's Administration of the Caucasus." In *Transcaucasia, Nationalism, and Social Change,* edited by Ronald G. Suny, 87–104. Ann Arbor: University of Michigan Press, 1996.

Richmond, Walter. *The Northwest Caucasus: Past, Present, Future.* New York: Routledge, 2008.

Rieber, Alfred. *Merchants and Entrepreneurs in Imperial Russia.* Chapel Hill: University of North Carolina Press, 1982.

Sanborn, Joshua. *Imperial Apocalypse: The Great War and the Destruction of the Russian Empire.* New York: Oxford University Press, 2014.

Sarafian, Vahe A. "Turkish Armenia and Expatriate Population Statistics." *Armenian Review* 9, no. 3 (1956): 118–28.

Sargent, Leslie. "The 'Armeno-Tatar War' in the South Caucasus, 1905–1906: Multiple Causes, Interpreted Meanings." *Ab Imperio*, no. 4 (2010): 143–69.

Sarkisyanz, Manuel. *A Modern History of Transcaucasian Armenia: Social, Cultural, and Political.* Leiden: Brill, 1975.

Saul, Norman E. *Distant Friends: The United States and Russia, 1763–1867.* Lawrence: University Press of Kansas, 1991.

Savory, R. M. "British and French Diplomacy in Persia, 1800–1810." *Iran* 10 (1972): 31–44.

Schimmelpenninck van der Oye, David. *Russian Orientalism: Asia in the Russian Mind from Peter the Great to the Emigration.* New Haven, CT: Yale University Press, 2010.

Schimmelpenninck van der Oye, David. *Toward the Rising Sun: Russian Ideologies of Empire and the Path to War with Japan.* DeKalb: Northern Illinois University Press, 2006.

Seredonin, S. M. *Sochinenie Dzhil'sa Fletchera "Of the Russe Common Wealth" kak istoricheskii istochnik.* St. Petersburg: Tipografiia N. I. Skorokhodova, 1891.

Service, Robert. *A History of Modern Russia from Nicholas II to Vladimir Putin.* 2nd ed. Cambridge, MA: Harvard University Press, 2003.

Slocum, John. "Who, and When, Were the Inorodtsy? The Evolution of the Category of 'Aliens' in Imperial Russia." *Russian Review* 57, no. 2 (1998): 173–90.

Snyder, Timothy. *The Reconstruction of Nations: Poland, Ukraine, Lithuania, Belarus, 1569–1999.* New Haven, CT: Yale University Press, 2003.

Somakian, Manoug. *Empires in Conflict: Armenia and the Great Powers, 1895–1920.* London: I. B. Tauris, 1995.

Steinwedel, Charles. *Threads of Empire: Loyalty and Tsarist Authority in Bashkiria, 1552–1917.* Bloomington: Indiana University Press, 2016.

Stoler, Ann Laura. "Intimidations of Empire: Predicaments of the Tactile and Unseen." In *Haunted by Empire: Geographies of Intimacy in North American History,* edited by Ann Laura Stoler, 1–22. Durham, NC: Duke University Press, 2006.

Stoler, Ann Laura. "On Degrees of Imperial Sovereignty." *Public Culture* 18, no. 1 (2006): 125–46.

Stoler, Ann Laura, and Carole McGranahan. "Introduction: Refiguring Imperial Terrains." In *Imperial Formations,* edited by Ann Laura Stoler, Carole Mc-Granahan, and Peter C. Perdue, 3–42. Santa Fe, NM: School for Advanced Research Press, 2007.

Sunderland, Willard. "The 'Colonization Question': Visions of Colonization in Late Imperial Russia." *Jahrbücher für Geschichte Osteuropas* 48, no. 2 (2000): 210–32.

Suny, Ronald G. "Eastern Armenians under Tsarist Rule." In *The Armenian People from Ancient to Modern Times,* edited by Richard Hovannisian, vol. 2, 109–37. New York: St. Martin's Press, 2004.

Suny, Ronald G. *Looking toward Ararat: Armenia in Modern History.* Bloomington: Indiana University Press, 1993.

Suny, Ronald G. *The Making of the Georgian Nation*. Bloomington: Indiana University Press, 1994.

Suny, Ronald G. *"They Can Live in the Desert but Nowhere Else": A History of the Armenian Genocide*. Princeton, NJ: Princeton University Press, 2015.

Taki, Victor. *Tsar and Sultan: Russian Encounters with the Ottoman Empire*. London: I. B. Tauris, 2016.

Ter-Avakimova, S. A. *Armiano-russkie otnosheniia v period podgotovki persidskogo pokhoda*. Yerevan: Izdatel'stvo Akademii nauk Armianskoi SSR, 1980.

Ter Minassian, Anahide. *Nationalism and Socialism in the Armenian Revolutionary Movement (1887–1912)*. Translated by A. M. Berrett. Cambridge, MA: Zoryan Institute, 1984.

Thaden, Edward C. *Russia's Western Borderlands, 1710–1870*. Princeton, NJ: Princeton University Press, 1985.

Thaden, Edward C., ed. *Russification in the Baltic Provinces and Finland, 1855–1914*. Princeton, NJ: Princeton University Press, 1981.

Thomson, Ewa. *Imperial Knowledge: Russian Literature and Colonialism*. Westport, CT: Greenwood Press, 2000.

Tölölyan, Khachig. "Elites and Institutions in the Armenian Transnation." *Diaspora: A Journal of Transnational Studies* 9, no. 1 (2000): 107–35.

Tolz, Vera. "Orientalism, Nationalism, and Ethnic Diversity in Late Imperial Russia." *Historical Journal* 48, no. 1 (2005): 127–50.

Tolz, Vera. *Russia's Own Orient: The Politics of Identity and Oriental Studies in the Late Imperial and Early Soviet Periods*. Oxford: Oxford University Press, 2011.

Tuna, Mustafa. *Imperial Russia's Muslims: Islam, Empire, and European Modernity, 1788–1914*. Cambridge: Cambridge University Press, 2015.

Tunian, V. G. *Echmiadzinskii vopros v politike Rossii, 1873–1903 gg.* Yerevan: Erevanskii gosudarstvennyi universitet, 2002.

Tunian, V. G. *Politika samoderzhaviia Rossii v Zakavkaz'e XIX–nach. XX vv.* 6 Vols. Yerevan: Chartaraget, 2006–2008, 2010.

Tunian, V. G. *Vostochnaia Armeniia v sostave Rossii, 1828–1853 gg.* Yerevan: Hayastan, 1989.

Urushadze, Amiran. "Kavkaz v kontse XIX–nachale XX v.: Problemy upravleniia i modernizatsii na iuzhnoi okraine Rossiiskoi imperii." *Quaestio Rossica* 2 (2015): 144–57.

Vernadsky, George. *Russia at the Dawn of the Modern Age*. New Haven, CT: Yale University Press, 1959.

Vernadsky, George. *The Tsardom of Moscow, 1547–1682*. Pt. 2. New Haven, CT: Yale University Press, 1969.

Volga: Obshchestvenno-politicheskaia gazeta Astrakhanskoi oblasti. "400 let armianskoi diaspore v Astrakhani." Accessed 10 November 2015. http://www.volgaru.ru/index.php?retro&article=1317.

Volkhonskii, Mikhail. "K 100-letiiu revoliutsii 1905–1907 gg. v Rossii: Natsional'nyi vopros vo vnutrennei politike pravitel'stva v gody pervoi russkoi revoliutsii." *Otechestvennaia istoriia* 5 (2005): 48–62.

Voskanian, Vazgen. "Drevniaia Rus' i Armeniia." *Lraber hasarakakan gitowt'yownneri*, no. 1 (1983): 51–60.

Vysheslavtsov, P. "Vzgliad na Zakavkaz'e v khoziaistvennom i torgovom otnoshenii ego k Rossii." *Syn otechestva* 66 (1834): 39.

Walker, Christopher. *Armenia: The Survival of a Nation*. 2nd ed. New York: Routledge, 1990.

Weeks, Theodore. "Between Rome and Tsargrad: The Uniate Church in Imperial Russia." In *Of Religion and Empire: Missions, Conversion, and Tolerance in Tsarist Russia*, edited by Robert Geraci and Michael Khodarkovsky, 70–91. Ithaca, NY: Cornell University Press, 2001.

Weeks, Theodore. *Nation and State in Late Imperial Russia: Nationalism and Russification on the Western Frontier, 1863–1914*. DeKalb: Northern Illinois University Press, 2008.

Weeks, Theodore. "Russification and Lithuanians, 1863–1905." *Slavic Review* 60, no. 1 (2001): 96–114.

Weeks, Theodore. "Russification: Word and Practice, 1863–1914." *Proceedings of the American Philosophical Society* 148, no. 4 (2004): 471–89.

Weeks, Theodore. *Vilnius between Nations, 1795–2000*. DeKalb: Northern Illinois University Press, 2015.

Werth, Paul. *At the Margins of Orthodoxy: Mission, Governance, and Confessional Politics in Russia's Volga-Kama Region, 1827–1905*. Ithaca, NY: Cornell University Press, 2002.

Werth, Paul. "From Resistance to Subversion: Imperial Power, Indigenous Opposition, and Their Entanglement." *Kritika: Explorations in Russian and Eurasian History* 1, no. 1 (2000): 21–43.

Werth, Paul. "Imperial Russia and the Armenian Catholicos at Home and Abroad." In *Reconstruction and Interaction of Slavic Eurasia and Its Neighboring Worlds*, edited by Osamu Ieda and Tomohiko Uyama, 203–36. Sapporo: Slavic Research Center, 2006.

Werth, Paul. "One Eastern Church or Two? Armenians, Orthodoxy, and Ecclesiastical Union in Nineteenth-Century Russia." *Journal of Orthodox Christian Studies* 1, no. 2 (2018): 189–208.

Werth, Paul. *The Tsar's Foreign Faiths: Toleration and the Fate of Religious Freedom in Imperial Russia*. New York: Oxford University Press, 2014.

Whelan, Heide. *Alexander III and the State Council: Bureaucracy and Counter-Reform in Late Imperial Russia*. New Brunswick, NJ: Rutgers University Press, 1982.

Whittaker, Cynthia H. *The Origins of Modern Russian Education: An Intellectual Biography of Count Sergei Uvarov, 1786–1855*. DeKalb: Northern Illinois University Press, 1984.

Whittock, Michael. "Ermolov—Proconsul of the Caucasus." *Russian Review* 18, no. 1 (1959): 53–60.

Wortman, Richard. *The Development of a Russian Legal Consciousness*. Chicago: University of Chicago Press, 1976.

Wortman, Richard. *Scenarios of Power: Myth and Ceremony in Russian Monarchy*. Vol. 2, *From Alexander II to the Abdication of Nicholas II*. Princeton, NJ: Princeton University Press, 2000.

Wortman, Richard. *Scenarios of Power: Myth and Ceremony in Russian Monarchy from Peter the Great to the Abdication of Nicholas II*. Princeton, NJ: Princeton University Press, 2006.

Zakharova, Larisa. "Emperor Alexander II, 1855–1881." In *The Emperors and Empresses of Russia: Rediscovering the Romanovs*, edited by Donald J. Raleigh, 294–333. Armonk, NY: M. E. Sharpe, 1996.

INDEX

Page numbers in *italics* indicate illustrations.

9 781501 750113